Y0-CLC-187

ASTROLOGY AND ALCHEMY

TWO FOSSIL SCIENCES

FOSSIL SCIENCES

ASTROLOGY AND ALCHEMY

TWO

MARK ^Aaron^ GRAUBARD
UNIVERSITY OF MINNESOTA

PHILOSOPHICAL LIBRARY • NEW YORK

Copyright, 1953, by Philosophical Library, Inc.,
15 East 40th Street, New York 16, N.Y.

All rights reserved

Printed in the United States of America

CONTENTS

Introduction — vii

BOOK ONE

THE QUEST AMONG THE STARS

CHAPTER ONE. The Lure of the Skies — 3
1. Primitive Beginnings — 3
2. Astronomy and Astrology in Babylonia — 6
3. Their Diffusion into Greece — 13

CHAPTER TWO. The Celestial Orbs: The Struggle for a Theory — 20
1. The Sacred Circle — 20
2. The Cosmology of Ptolemy — 40

CHAPTER THREE. The Ancient Science of Astrology — 48
1. Ptolemy's Defense — 48
2. Initial Opposition — 64
3. Christian Rejection — 72

CHAPTER FOUR. Restoration After Defeat — 81
1. Christian Opposition Wavers — 81
2. The New Adjustment — 90

CHAPTER FIVE. The Succeeding Centuries — 102
1. The Theological Opposition Persists — 102
2. Two Sceptical Authors — 113
3. The Fear of Comets — 121
4. The Problem Attacked and Solved — 130

CHAPTER SIX. Astrology on the Defensive — 143
1. A Weak Beginning — 143
2. The Attacks Persist — 150
3. A Famous Coup de Grace — 159

v

CONTENTS

CHAPTER SEVEN. The Founders of Modern Astronomy and Astrology's Demise ... 167
  1. The Pre-Copernican Forerunners ... 167
  2. The Giants of Modern Astronomy ... 175
    A. Copernicus ... 175
    B. Kepler ... 183
    C. Galileo Galilei ... 190
    D. Newton, Bacon, Descartes and Others ... 192

CHAPTER EIGHT. The Process Called Change ... 195
  1. The So-Called Copernican Revolution ... 195
  2. Copernicus and His Orbs ... 200
  3. Respect for Mathematics ... 209
  4. The Fate That Was Galileo's ... 216

BOOK TWO
THE QUEST FOR THE NATURE OF MATTER

CHAPTER NINE. The Grand Romance of Alchemy ... 237
  1. A Dreamland of Science ... 237
  2. Early Chemistry and the Beginnings of Alchemy ... 239
  3. Alchemical Principles and Aims ... 249

CHAPTER TEN. The Literature of Alchemy ... 258
  1. The Hermetic Museum ... 258
  2. The New Pearl of Great Price ... 273
  3. A Golden and Blessed Casket ... 274

CHAPTER ELEVEN. The Alchemists in Pursuit of Wisdom ... 279
  1. The Earlier Apostles ... 279
  2. Typical Alchemists of Later Years ... 287
  3. The International Propagandists ... 306
  4. Truth and Martyrdom ... 314
  5. Alchemical Contributions to the Science of Chemistry ... 319

CHAPTER TWELVE. Iatro-chemistry and Phlogiston ... 321
  1. Paracelsus—Portrait of a Rebel ... 321
  2. The Fate of a Movement ... 339
  3. New Trends, New Troubles ... 343

INDEX ... 369

INTRODUCTION

What Is a Fossil Science?

IT has been customary to treat as folly and superstition many of man's past attempts at knowledge of nature or at understanding her phases and processes. It is not uncommon to casually stumble upon some excellent text in the physical sciences or even some erudite modern treatise in the philosophy of science, and read there that science began with Galileo, that the Greek or medieval scholars did not know the meaning of an experiment or of evidence, that people did not know how to count the teeth of a horse but argued for days over their precise number by citing authorities—and many more such foibles. Similar stereotyped notions extend to other areas such as the relation of religion to science. It is more often than not held that the Church fought science because it was jealous of its power or because it wished to keep the minds of men in utter darkness, the better to rule them. That there were conflicts between new ideas and old ones or between new ideas and established institutions, goes without saying. Yet, unless we know accurately the nature of such conflicts, how can we possibly learn from the past to meet our own difficulties in the present or future? Surely clashes and conflicts have not vanished from the life of man, especially since modern psychoanalytic theory postulates them within the mind of even a single individual, to say nothing of the ego in casual or clashing contact with others.

Nor is it fair to assert, as many do, that until the coming of modern science man was loaded down with superstition and did not know how to ask questions and seek for answers. It is far too easy and immature for an Englishman or Frenchman to come to an African or Australian tribe and dismiss native modes of life as savage, or infantile, because native customs seem so different and crude. Only knowledge and experience can serve to tame this superficial drive toward comparisons and judgments, a drive which stifles learning and poisons all understanding. What the science of anthropology has revealed is that culture is a complex series of adjustments in the fulfillment of some basic and some not so basic human needs and desires, which in turn tend to fashion the very man who brought them into being.

INTRODUCTION

Many are the forces which lead a given culture to choose one particular form of an institution in preference to another, and many are the forces which generate disaffection and conflict, change and resistance, or which render one culture rapidly variable, and another stolid and immutable for many centuries. Only study and analysis can teach us the nature of this process, the role of man in these adjustments, his strengths and weaknesses, his tools and handicaps.

To the student of culture one human society is as valuable or as interesting as another. Each one is an experiment set up by nature to bring out new data, nuances and relationships. All enrich his knowledge, raise many problems and answer some questions. They are all different ways of observing Homo sapiens in action, hence all contribute to our knowledge of man.

The same reasoning applies to the history of science. Where, for example, would medicine be if a physician, called to a patient's bedside, correctly diagnosed the ailment and then reprimanded his patient severely for having misbehaved and contracted syphilis, and after completing his sermon stalked angrily out of the room? There were many diseases which were wrapped in shame and disrepute, and medicine would get exactly nowhere with them, had it persisted in this kind of moral haughtiness. The same would apply to the zoologist. How objective would zoology be as a science if it had cast out and denounced all animals it regarded as impure or geologically declining, and concentrated only upon, or gave its blessings to, the modern ones or those that it regarded as up-and-coming? Moreover, would the knowledge of biologic life which the science of evolution so potently stimulated, have had any meaning at all, if fossils were looked upon with contempt because they failed to survive and had therefore to be written off as bad animals or plants? Fossils, indeed, have a lot to teach us about the nature of mutations, the meanings of survival, of fitness, adaptation, as well as the nature of the environment at a given time.

No different is the case with the history of science. Man has always wanted to know and understand the world about him. That world affected him in many ways and invariably left strong, emotional and indelible imprints on his mind, for a variety of reasons. Some because they determined his fate or well-being, such as fire, flood, defeat, crop failure, disease, misfortune, etc. Others because they simply impressed him and he believed they were most vital to his life and welfare, as for example, comets, eclipses or planetary positions. All these aspects of nature he set out to observe and study, and if clever enough, to devise theories for the coordination and interpretation of his data. This he did as best he knew how.

Such are fossil theories. They failed to survive when times, ideas, values, approaches, tools, interpretations and assumptions changed. New ones, more acceptable and suitable, came to take their places, to be modified, expanded or abandoned in their turn. The old theories were not acts of idiocy, or childishness, or concoctions of priests who sought power and found it advantageous to befog or drug the minds of their dependents. They were genuine attainments of a searching mind, operating not in a vacuum but within the web of a culture, tied to a vast network of related beliefs and hypotheses, limited by the store of his data and the scope of his view, and fashioned by the values and beliefs of the time. Within this matrix of data, hypotheses and mental attitudes, he forged his scientific theories in appropriate style. Ornithorhynchus, Mastodon, Trilobite or Tyrannosaurus were not intrinsically crude, vulgar, clumsy or bad animals deserving the wrath of God or physical extermination. They were good and successful animals that endured for many eons, multiplied successfully and inhabited vast areas. They replaced other animals and prospered. True, they ultimately vanished, but only because they were unsuited to meet a changing world about them, or a changing organic environment, which unbalanced their comfortable niche and ultimately drove them to extinction.

Is this not equally true of scientific theories? The astrological outlook came to light as a set of attractive hypotheses displacing whatever beliefs preceded them, or filling a vacancy in the mind. They endured between three and two millennia, though repeatedly challenged. They outlasted many irrelevant, purely emotional and prejudiced beliefs that conflicted with their materialistic and fatalistic tenets, and found their supporters among the learned and the great, and of course the common people as well. Within the womb of astrology, astronomy was bred and nourished, and there never was any competition or conflict between them. Yet, in time, astrology weakened as a scientific theory and failed and faded away. New times, new environments, new values and points of view achieved that which the hostile sceptics, cynics, moralists and all the world's religions failed to accomplish. Astrology was neither stupidity nor superstition. It is merely a fossil of a theory suitable to an environment long since vanished, surviving well for a while, prospering and advancing in its old matrix, but rejected and mocked with the coming of new modes, new interests, new attractions and new fashions. It proved no longer suitable to the needs of the new times and it simply died away, unfought, uncursed and mostly even unchallenged. No hero of astronomy fought it as a scientific St. George, no movement of pioneers of progress speeded its death. Astrology became just a plain, ordinary, common run of the mill fossil idea.

INTRODUCTION

This mode of attack upon outmoded beliefs in science raises many questions. How did the astrological principles come into being? Who were its proponents? Upon what kind of data and postulates were they based? Was there anyone wise or bold enough to challenge them? On what grounds? Was astrology an obstacle to progress or was it the reverse? Who were its friends and who its enemies? Why did one or the other win out and under what conditions? Was it a false theory in science like Lamarckism, or was it sheer nonsense and superstition much as is modern astrology or phrenology? Under what conditions did it perish? And finally what does all this tell us about man, his mode of advancing theories in science, his way of clinging to them, his manner of challenging, defending or abandoning them, his approach to truth, his scepticism or credulity? What about the great scientists, alive at the time; how do they fit into this picture? Are they always on the side of the angels and when does one know which side the angels are or should be on?

These and many other questions can only be answered by cautious and meticulous analyses of the data. We have far too many treatises on The Method of Science and The New Philosophy of Science, The Coming of Science and The Battle for Science. They are, generally speaking, about as useful to the understanding of man's search for scientific truth as were the elegant and eloquent Aristotelian treatises on physics or on generation in the decades before Galileo. The historian or philosopher of science must deal with data and data alone. The sweeping and often fantastic generalizations about the church, the middle ages, the Greeks, the charlatans in alchemy and similar name-calling, must cease once for all or be stated in terms of facts, data and references rather than in terms of general philosophic wisdom or insight.

This volume is an attempt to treat astrology and alchemy in this scientific manner. It does not treat them with contempt, with the superiority of smug or chauvinistic a posteriori, that is, with happy hindsight, or with generalities. It seeks to understand the times, the men involved, the culture or sub-culture in which they lived, their emotional matrix; in other words, it views science as an aspect of human behavior, as a quest for verifiable and communicable knowledge pursued by man as he was at the time. Related to such conduct is probably even the science of today, except that our outlook, values, attitudes, data, tools, skills, self-criticism and standards are different and no doubt better, safer and more efficient. But we are still human, we still have a cultural matrix about us and we therefore still have considerable to learn from our antecedents or cousins. This is not an easy task, and the success of the effort lies with the reader.

INTRODUCTION

This book is essentially an overextended essay which aims at presenting to the beginning student in the history of science a bird's eye view of two dead sciences, seldom considered in detail in one's normal course of studies. It merely collates authoritative researches on many phases of these sciences, and cites easily accessible works for the sake of presenting a unifying interpretation that should be generally helpful to the student of man, of history, or of science.

Book I

THE QUEST AMONG THE STARS

Chapter 1

THE LURE OF THE SKIES

1. Primitive Beginnings

PRIMITIVE man everywhere was always conscious of the burning lure of the heavenly bodies for the sheer reason that they meant so much to his emotional being. He had no pleasant home in which to spend his evenings, no warm bed in which to while away the long hours when celestial doings are at their best. Moreover, he felt himself intimately linked to these mysterious objects or spirits and regarded them as part and parcel of his world, as vital factors in his fate. And no sooner had primitive man gathered in some observations about the impressive world that engulfed him, than he sought to congeal them into a theory, an explanation, a philosophy. That was done by man everywhere, though such interpretations failed to blossom forth into a primitive science. On the contrary. More often than not, a primitive tribe was wholly pleased with the soothing opiate of an explanation, glamorous, imaginative, in full harmony with the prevailing matrix of his philosophy, his faith and folklore. Augmented with a few legends and local embellishments, such speculations seemed fully adequate and gratifying.

Occasionally, however, a given culture would suddenly make a spurt in a scientific direction, develop a curiosity for further details, improve observational tools and instruments, and while retaining all the emotional and fanciful imagery and the unchallengeable values and beliefs of the time, proceed to erect a body of facts and harvest a crop of deductions which seem to us amazingly fanciful only because we have placed ourselves in a position to be amazed. Our times have spun a set of beliefs concerning the nature of man which is as fictitious as the weird folklore of the middle ages. Man was ignorant, it declares, and his mind was infantile until the crucial year one, which to a physicist may be the age of Galileo or Newton, to a biologist the year of Harvey or Vesalius or Darwin, to a chemist that of Lavoisier, etc. Subsequent to those turning points all was light, and prior to them man's mind was shrouded in darkness.

Yet it seems more reasonable to assume that there always were creative innovators and that man did not progress quite so jerkily, changing his mode of thought with one mutation or mental saltation. The mind of man is too intricate to be so rapidly changed. New ideas, inventions or discoveries certainly modify his thoughts and actions, some more radically than others, but human he was before some specific crucial event or idea, and human he remains afterward. The quest for scientific truth is a human activity, pursued by a human being with attributes of the species Homo sapiens, who does not radically alter his conduct by a new theory, any more than a perusal of the Sermon on the Mount makes one a saint ever after.

The fact is, primitive man, like his modern cousin, also observed and respected reality and sought to comprehend it. But he did it within the matrix of his beliefs or hopes, his fears and values, so that the final expression of his quest seems as strange to us as do the customs and beliefs of an alien culture. The common human being behind them is lost in the strangeness of the cultural forms. As in our times, some cultures were visited by an outburst of activity in one field or another, accomplished great results and then watched that activity subside and vanish, more often than not, never to return again. Such visitations crowned the cultures of Chaldea and Egypt, Judea and Greece and Rome and India, though the surviving remnants of their people may at present be walking in foreign cultural paths, in mediocrity, or even in hopeless senility.

To Babylonia we owe man's first attempt at an organized science of astronomy. The Babylonians paid full homage to the prevailing beliefs of the time but simultaneously developed some science as well, though against full-blown religious and astrological backgrounds.

There does not seem to be adequate evidence for the oft-encountered assertion that ancient astronomy originated in the farmer's need for knowledge of the precise time for plowing or sowing. Even today farmers do not really watch the calendar to tell them the time for initiating these activities, but rather go by the season generally, that is, by warmth and thaws, time of sunrise, length of day, the succession of blooming plants, or the appearance of migrating birds which are as accurate chronometers as any which nature could devise. Besides, virtually all Mohammedan countries employ a year of twelve lunar months so that a given month is not always in the same season of the year but traverses them all in its swing through time; and yet agricultural labors do not seem to be handicapped by such a peregrinating arrangement. Moreover, considerable agriculture has been going on in many other lands and cultures without a stable solar clock. In Egypt where agricultural needs were supposed, we are told, to have obliged man to look heavenward for a calendar, the very floods of the Nile were an excellent time indicator by themselves. What could the Egyptian farmer have required celestial reminders for, anyway? If the helical rising of Sirius came together with the floods, could not the latter have reminded him of all he needed to think about, just as efficiently as the former?

The fact is that astronomy was man's first organized science. He devoted to it much energy because all celestial events made a deep imprint upon his consciousness and called attention to themselves in a variety of ways. Man wanted to understand those things which impinged upon his desire to know. If those salient points happened to be practical ones, then he went about investigating them; if they were of imaginary urgency, then he went about investigating them with the same earnestness and determination. Besides, who is to decide what is practical and what is not? If I believe that security lies in wealth and savings, I will go after the attainment of material goods that suit such a goal. If my beliefs tell me that security lies in a better government I may concentrate on that exclusively or in combination with the former. If, on the other hand, I am a product of a culture like that of a Mexican farm worker, I may act like the heroes of Tortilla Flat by John Steinbeck, and not be concerned at all with the future. Or I may become a mendicant friar and put my faith in the love of the Lord rather than earthly goods. There is no apparent reason in the world why the smug and provincial notion of nineteenth century society, that human happiness lies only in the unlimited aggrandizement of material goods, must be an objective truth or law of the nature of man.

Be that as it may, the sciences of the heavens, astrology and astronomy were man's first sciences and the science of medicine one of his very last ones, and to date the science of man has not matured to the status of a recognized science. His own self, his suffering and afflictions, he took readily for granted, calmly submitting to what he called fate, neglecting or rejecting their observation or analysis. To the heavens he was not so casual. The steady stars that circled overhead nightly from east to west and changed with time and the seasons, never deviating from their relative positions; the wandering planets among them that shone so brightly and even varied their luminosities; the sun and the seasons, the everchanging moon so beautifully related to changing conditions on earth, to say nothing of the ominous eclipses, comets and other unusual, hence most meaningful events—all these concerned the observers and thinkers of the time most intimately and acutely, and so they responded to them by inquiry and speculation. Rocks and stones, floods, earthquakes, storms and tides, growth and decay, man often noted and wondered about, yet failed to build a science around them. Not so the events of the heavens. Them he followed with avidity and suspense.

2. *Astronomy and Astrology in Babylonia*

There seems to be a general agreement among scholars that astronomy and astrology sprouted first in Chaldea and Babylonia, where they seemed firmly established, during the third millennium B.C. Such evidence is not as easy to establish as one thinks, but the conclusion seems legitimate enough. It is also agreed that what we call today the scientific aspects of astronomy did not flourish until about the eighth century B.C., in the opinion of one scholar, Cumont, for lack of a reliable or exact system of chronology. The calendar of the third millennium B.C. was a strictly lunar one, consisting, like the Mohammedan calendar of today, of twelve lunar months of 29½ days each, yielding a year of 354 days. To harmonize festivals and ritual with the seasons, no other needs or stimuli seem to be cited, a thirteenth month was added every now and then, which served the purpose well enough. It was not however until the significance of heliacal risings of stars were observed, a solar calendar introduced, and regular observations recorded in relation to a better time scale than a lunar month, that great strides forward could be made. These more advanced steps were not taken until the eighth century B.C.

Let us then survey what the Babylonians did astronomically prior to that time. To begin with, it should be remembered that the culture of Babylonia concentrated all attention upon divination, especially the forecasting of earthly events from the sizes and shapes of livers of sacrificial animals. The intrinsic mystery and lure of the stars found a welcome response in Babylonian observers. This response was whipped into unbounded enthusiasm by the discovery that the everchanging celestial occurrences could be utilized for both day-to-day and long range prognostication. Awareness of stirring events in the skies were practically universal among primitive tribes, as universal as the notions of magic or the need for religion. The uniqueness of the Babylonian contribution lay in its development of a system of organized observation and systematized interpretation and prediction, which necessitated the assignment of meanings and symbols to various juxtapositions and motions of planets and stars. That the planets be given the status of gods was inevitable at a time in man's history when the con-

THE LURE OF THE SKIES

cept of a god was his symbol for an abstracted or isolated force or aspect of nature.

Hence it is no wonder that the Babylonians rested on their laurels after they had laid an adequate foundation for the art and science of astrology. Subsequent to the initial observations and correlations of the ancients, little progress was made until the middle of the first millennium B.C. when astronomy blossomed forth most spectacularly among the Greeks who lent to it trigonometry and ingenious mathematical attempts at constructing systems of planetary motions.

Greatest attention was given to the moon, and the god which represented the moon was accorded highest honors. The month was a lunar one and the appearance of the new moon was not the product of prediction but had to be observed each month. The time of full moon was equally guessed at and a premature full moon, say on the thirteenth of the month instead of the fourteenth, prognosticated evil tidings such as bad crops or pestilence. Eclipses were noted with terror and dismay, their dates carefully recorded, yet their periodicity in a cycle of 18½ years, approximately, was not known until about the third century B.C. Neither was it known until about that late date that they could only take place at certain times of the month and year. Obscurations of the sun were also observed, mock suns, lunar halos and similar events.

The planets too had been identified and associated with divinities. The dual role of Venus as evening and morning star was early recognized and she was associated with the goddess Ishtar who was mistress of vegetation in the season of growth, while during the rainy months of winter she was believed imprisoned in the bowels of the earth. Jupiter had been singled out for special honors early in the rise of astrological thought and the planets Mercury, Mars and Saturn, originally lumped together into a junior trio, graduated in time toward individual differentiation and divine rank.

From the third millennium B.C. on, different months were assigned to represent the different neighboring states and the presence or absence of planets in them variously interpreted. Observations were made continuously but not with great care or accuracy. "The observations were defective . . . and the lists being composite productions of various periods, embody the errors of earlier ages, incorporated in the more accurate records of later periods, though even these too, were based upon merely empirical knowledge. But whatever be the explanation, the ignorance of the Babylonian and Assyrian astrologers is patent; and the infantile fancies which frequently crop out in these astrological texts keep pace with the ignorance." (The Religion of Babylonia and Assyria by Morris Jastrow, New York 1911, p. 221).

Each of the planets was either favorable or ominous. Several prominent stars were included in the list of symbols but they had meaning only insofar as they stood in a certain relationship to the planets. Clearly, to make any predictions at all, the positions of the planets had to be carefully and persistently followed. In this manner their orbits got to be known in a general way. The course of the ecliptic or "pathway of the sun" was mapped out among the stars and its circle was divided into three regions, each devoted to a divinity as well as to a country, necessarily identified with the closest neighbors or rivals. This crude division was apparently found inadequate. Perhaps with increasing familiarity, the band which presumably contained the path of the sun within its confines gained greater prominence. In either case the stars lying near the sun's path soon came to occupy exceptional positions of fancy splendor in the heavenly host. The creative imagination of man, unhampered by other outlets or needs, responded to the mystery of the solar belt with great gusto, so that in the course of several centuries the twelve further subdivisions of the zodiac were discerned and romanticised. The designation zodiac was given to them because eleven of them, all but Libra, the scales, represented animals. Around these twelve constellations man spun fanciful legends which enchant us to this day. These twelve stellar groups helped the purpose of specifying the exact positions of a planet at any particular time, and thus broadened the scope of astrological divination. Only later, and at the hands of the Greeks, were these constellations placed within equal arcs of thirty degrees each, and made to serve an astronomical purpose.

The motive of divination worked similarly in the sphere of awareness to weather. "The character and ever-changing shapes of clouds were observed, whether massed together or floating in thin fleecy strips. Their color was noted, whether dark, yellow, green or white. The number of thunderclaps, the place in the heavens whence the sound proceeded, the month or day or special circumstances when heard, were all carefully noted, as was also the quarter whence the lightning came, and the direction it took, the course of winds and rain, and so on, without rain." (ibid. p. 233) Thus knowledge is usually acquired whenever one sets out to acquire knowledge. He may do it for the purpose of conquest, for the glory of God, for the sake of knowledge per se, for financial gain or for divination. In each case learn he will if he is motivated at all, and in each case the observations and conclusions gathered will be classified, ordered and interpreted in the light of his assumptions and values.

The idea that events in the sky reflect and foretell events on earth was as deeprooted and as implicitly accepted as was the notion of God in the middle ages, or as is the identification of material goods with man's well-being in modern society. Events in the sky represented natural law and constituted the products of the doings and interventions of the gods.

Things did not happen just so, but had definite causes and consequences. The celestial events were at least in part results of the actions of gods and their earthly repercussions were mere consequences. If one only studied the events in the sky and related them to events on earth, one could be sure of the casual bonds between the two. Yet astrological predictions were not all mere empirical observations and correlations. Once general assumptions and beliefs had been postulated, the mind could readily seek out seemingly convincing verifications, and brush aside or explain away discordant results. Given an emotional urge which draws its vigor from man's apparently innate responses, or fancy, or cultural values, and given the reasoning constructed upon such responses, man will, as he did in the case of astrology, continue on his course, expand knowledge and yet persist in his original beliefs and delude himself with faith in their soundness and utility.

The Babylonians did not advance far enough in astrology to elaborate a system of detailed correspondence between celestial and earthly events so as to assign meanings to specific events or places. This evolved in time and was contributed by Greek astrology. But the Babylonian and Assyrian observers did map out the heavens so that its constituents came to symbolize occurrences, dangers and omens which expressed the thoughts, interests, fears and curiosities of the times. Constellations, planets, zodiacal signs and stars were allotted to particular countries on the one hand, and to specific gods on the other. The events to which they referred were of limited stock, namely, invasion, crop failure or luxuriant harvests, plagues, revolts, intrigues in the royal household, or court quarrels, and any catastrophe befalling the royal personage or those near him. In a way this concentration on the national good, and the well-being of the king was part of what contributed toward containment of the astrological pursuit. We shall see later that the more democratic outlook which the Greeks brought with them, actually served to orient astrology toward broader horizons and services by catering to individual fates and wants; its more democratic approach, served from our point of view, to deepen the astrological morass. The Babylonians found royal and national interests, and the two were identical in their mind, quite adequate, and astrology therefore never blossomed forth to the stature it later attained in Greece or Rome, where the individual as citizen had dignity and status.

As was only to be expected, the lore of astrology rested in the hands of the priests. The king received daily reports of the state of the sky and often sent special questions to his chief astrologer for study and elucidation. During the last decade of Babylonian rule, 639–630 B.C., which saw the end of the second Babylonian empire and its surrender to the expanding power of Persia, the royal records show a great decline in astrological references. There is, however, a rise in astrological interest in the period of Persian domination at which time there appeared elaborate calculations of the movements of the sun and moon and the complex orbits of the planets, their heliacal risings and settings, the exact times of their culminations, direct and retrograde movements, and stations. The calendar too was undergoing gradual improvement.

Nevertheless it is difficult to accept Jastrow's interpretation of these events as indicating the beginnings of the conflict between astronomy and astrology, an episode in the supposed long-range struggle between science and religion. The acceptance of scientific laws, argues Jastrow, precludes astrological belief. There is no evidence that such rule of exclusion was ever in evidence. Surely there were no greater respecters of law than the Greek astronomers, and no greater scholar among them than Claudius Ptolemy. Yet it is this same Claudius Ptolemy who is the author of the great astronomical text The Almagest and the equally exhaustive work on ancient astrology reduced to a science, The Tetrabiblos or Quadripartitem. Hence respect for law no more spells the doom of astrology than it spells the doom of religion or ethics. The human mind, as we shall see again and again, makes room for any unbelievable or unpredictable adaptation in belief or practice, and rests contented in its efforts.

It was only natural that persistent observation of the sky lead to its exploitation for the regulation of time. It had been noticed that the sun moved regularly eastward along the belt of the zodiac. This meant that if a certain star or constellation was seen evenings in the west directly after sunset, then in a month or so it would not be seen at all because the sun will have moved into it thus rendering it invisible. Similarly if a certain star is a morning star, which means that it rises early in the morning just before dawn, then in a month or so it will be seen just before dawn about thirty degrees higher in the sky, that is nearer the zenith. Again, the sun had moved away from the star, eastward. Incidentally, the morning that a star is first seen in the east just before the rising of the sun, is called the time of its heliacal rising. In other words, it is the first time the star is seen at all after a long absence brought on by its having been blotted out by the sun which entered its neighborhood as it vanished in the twilight after having appeared nearer and nearer to the western horizon evening after evening. Obviously a year elapses from one day of a star's heliacal rising to the next. Hence a calendar by the stars is in reality not too hard to come by.

Once the path of the sun in the zodiac was mapped out, it was only logical that four points attract the attention of any discerning observer, namely, the two equinoxes and the winter and summer solstices. The equinoxes, or the days of equal day and night, March 21 and September

21, are the days when the sun at noon is directly on the celestial equator, which is always ninety degrees from the polar star. On the day of the summer solstice the sun at noon is highest in the sky, that is, nearest the zenith, and on the day of winter solstice, lowest in the sky. Hence the plane of the ecliptic or sun's path cuts the plane of the celestial equator at an angle, which happens to be 23.5°, and is known as its obliquity. Here was another means of dividing time into years, each year extending from one spring equinox to another. In addition, the year was readily divided into four seasons each marked by the sun's distinctive position in the ecliptic. "A text marks the spring season as beginning on the fifteenth of Nisan, the summer solstice as occurring on the fifteenth of Duzu, the autumnal equinox on the fifteenth of Tashritu and the winter solstice on the fifteenth of Tehetu." (Babylonian Astrology and Its Relation to the Old Testament by Ch. V. McLean, Toronto 1929 p. 18) The biblical feast of Passover also occurs on the fifteenth of Nisan which raises the possibility that an ancient spring festival might have been given new meaning by assigning to it the commemoration of the Exodus from Egypt.

Then there was the lunar month, in all likelihood the oldest timepiece of the skies, and the most obvious. The phases of the moon cannot be easily missed and the period from crescent to crescent constitutes a most natural time unit. The unit of the week came much later and originated apparently from the custom of assigning each of the seven planets to the hours of the day. In time, the planet of the first hour imposed its name on the entire day and thus the seven-day cycle of the week came into being. The last day, the day of Saturn, was one of evil and bad luck and was subsequently converted into a holy day of rest by the people of the Bible. While the Jews referred to it exclusively as the day of the Sabbath, outsiders termed it consistently "Saturn's day." Thus, Dion Cassius, writing in the third century A.D. states that in 63 B.C. Pompey captured Jerusalem because of the Jews' reverence for Saturn's day. "Not only as this came round did they allow the Romans to continue their siege operations unhindered, but the final assault was also made on a 'Saturn's day' and met with no resistance. He then proceeds to give some account of the Jews and in particular how 'they have consecrated the so-called day of Saturn and while performing on it many observances peculiar to themselves, lay their hands to no serious work." (The Week, F. H. Colson, Cambridge 1926 p. 21)

The system of the week diffused very rapidly through the Graeco-Roman world. It is even likely that the Jewish week of the Sabbath originated independently, though it is certain that planetary symbols and influences assigned to the days of the week subsequently became merged or identified with the Jewish or Sabbatical week. It is as the combination of both, the planetary and Sabbatical week, that this unit of time spread to the rest of the world.

The final calendar of Babylonia was a combination of both a solar and lunar year. The normal year was made to consist of twelve lunations or moon cycles, hence six months of twenty-nine days and six of thirty, one of each alternating and each month presided over by a different deity. Since the solar year of 365¼ days exceeds by several days the number which is twelve times twenty-nine and a half, or 354 days composing the lunar year, an additional or an intercolated month was inserted every second or third year. "An attempt was also made to correlate the movements of the planets by means of a six-hundred-year period, since it marked an accordance between the civil and the tropical year, 365¼ days, and also represented the end of the twentieth revolution of Saturn, the fiftieth of Jupiter, the three-hundredth of Mars, and was almost the equivalent of 7421 lunations." (McLean p. 20)

One must not conclude that no reliable measurement of the year was available before the somewhat sophisticated lunisolar year was established. As Nilsson points out: "The time indications from the stars are therefore much older in Greece than the lunisolar calendar, and always existed alongside of the latter—which was of a religious and civil character—as the calendar of peasants and seamen, who must hold to the natural year and its seasons." (Primitive Time-Reckoning by M. P. Nilsson, Oxford Univ. Press, 1920 p. 113). The star-year is very ancient indeed and its discovery was attributed to Prometheus to whom the Greeks gave credit for all science and progress. According to Aeschylus people were ignorant of seasons and the year until Prometheus brought them the hidden lore of the rising and setting stars.

Before the beginning of the first millennium, Babylonian astrology was still emerging from immaturity. The zodiac had been known for a long time and so was the ecliptic, and the periods of planetary revolutions had been fairly accurately noted, which meant that morning and evening stars were identified. Yet rapid progress began to take place, mostly after the early centuries of the first millennium B.C. The equinoxes and solstices, eclipses, planetary positions and heliacal risings of many stars were observed and recorded. "Before 600 B.C. they knew of two kinds of star distances, the one in space, the other in time, i.e., the time lapsing between the heliacal rising of two stars. From 200 onward, eclipses are predicted; the year, day and hour of their appearance is stated; also it is noted whether the shadow covers one-third, one-half or two-thirds of the eclipsed body. . . . The Library of Assurbanipal, which contains tablets from the earliest times to about 626 B.C. shows the knowledge of the heavens to be in the following position:

"1. The Babylonians had traced the ecliptic and divided it into four parts, corresponding to the seasons.

"2. They had tried with partial success to draw up a list of constellations whose heliacal rising corresponded to the twelve months of the year.

"3. They had determined the synodical revolutions of the planets (i.e., as determined with respect to the sun).

"4. They knew that eclipses occurred regularly and tried to foretell them.

"5. They knew that a lunation is nearly twenty-nine and one-half days." (McLean pp. 25-26) The calendar too should be cited here although many modifications were subsequently introduced into it, such as an eight-year cycle (534 B.C.) and then a twenty-seven year period.

While all observation of the sky was sacerdotal, motivated by religion, and part and parcel of it, the knowledge gained was a mixture of what we would call today astronomy and astrology. The Babylonian observer was a priest, the deities were stars, and temples served as observatories. The priest was no more conscious of a distinction between "natural" and "supernatural" components of his thinking, than was J. S. Bach, for example, aware of a similar distinction between religious and secular sentiments in any of his compositions. They observed and thus accumulated data but also maintained certain ideas and cherished certain postulates and interpretations. Similarly, they manipulated numbers, which they regarded as sacred and employed them in divination.

Among the Babylonian contributions must also be counted the scheme of subdividing the day into hours, minutes and seconds. At first the full day from sunrise to sunrise was divided into six watches, three of the day and three of the night. Subsequently both came to be subdivided in Egypt into 12 hours each, and each hour into minutes and seconds. At first the hours were not of the same duration but merely one-twelfth of the day and one-twelfth of the night. Only at a relatively late date were they made uniform throughout the year.

3. *Their Diffusion Into Greece*

While astrology declined in Babylonia during the middle of the first millennium B.C. it took root and flourished in Greece at about that time. Greece had developed some astronomical science toward the beginning of the first millennium B.C. from what we would call purely scientific motivation rather than divination, as had been the case with the Babylonians. By the middle of the millennium, about 500-400 B.C. the Greeks had made considerable progress which began exerting its impact toward the Orient in medicine, geometry, and above all in astronomy. Nevertheless, admits Jastrow, "Whereas in Babylonia and Assyria we have astrology first and astronomy afterwards, in Greece we have the sequence reversed—astronomy first and astrology afterwards." In other words, recognition of inexorable law and mathematical determinism was no safeguard against the advent of astrology, and astronomy continued to flourish in its usual, uneven course for centuries after the astrological intrusion. Jastrow explains the incongruity on the basis of Greek respect for fate and the individual, which obliged them to modify the astrological newcomer to suit their concepts. That is inevitable; yet the new ideas were astrology pure and simple. Since Babylonian astrology centered about the king and his affairs, it was doomed to attenuation or extinction with the fall of the Babylonian empire. Greek science by adopting it presented it with a fertile field in which it grew and prospered, though necessarily in Greek fashion.

The initial Babylonian influence upon Greek learning constituted what we would now call astronomy, rather than the applied phase of it, or astrology. The Greeks also offered hospitality to oriental star-worship and came to assimilate it into their religion, presenting signs of resistance to astrology, which however, was short-lived. It is true that the great astronomer, Eudoxus, and Aristotle's successor, Theophrastus, spoke disparagingly of divination and of the science of horoscopes known as genethlialogy. According to Cumont, "The insatiable curiosity of the Greeks, then, did not ignore astrology, but their sober genius rejected its hazardous doctrines, and their keen critical sense was able to distinguish the scientific data observed by the Babylonians from the erroneous conclusions which they derived from them. It is to their everlasting honor that, amid the tangle of precise observations and superstitious fancies which made up the priestly lore of the East, they discovered and utilized the serious elements, while neglecting the rubbish." (Astrology and Religion Among the Greeks and Romans by Franz Cumont, New York 1912 p. 53)

One would have to employ delicate judgment indeed, to decide intelligently which superstitions may be accepted without loss of national glory and which betray a low national mentality. Certain it is, however, that in time Greece came to accept the entire astrological heritage of the east and, what is more, did not do so at the expense of astronomical progress. Religions do not diffuse as easily from culture to culture as do tools or instruments, or aspects of science, or isolated customs or manners. In Babylonia and Assyria divination was not only deeply embedded in local religious belief and ritual, but stood almost exclusively at the service of the king and his family. Greece had its own elaborate religion and had no intentions of giving it up. It had no king or a symbolic surrogate and was therefore obliged to make subtle adjustments to accommodate the new concepts to its own culture. It did incorporate into its own religion, and without delay, the worship of the planets. Plato refers to them as "the great visible gods." They are considered divine beings moved by an ethereal soul by the famous mathematician Pythagoras, for example, and by others. Plato even goes so far as to accuse Anaxagoras of atheism because the latter regards the sun as fiery matter and the moon as an earth. Hence not only was astronomical science taken over in all its purity, but the theological aspects of star-worship as well. In fact, the science of astronomy was regarded as a gift of the gods even as was mathematics, the outer expression of divine conduct. Man responds to the beauty of the heavenly harmonies by a desire to comprehend them. "He rises to a fervent contemplation of the wondrous spectacle of harmonious movements which surpasses all choruses in majesty and magnificence." (Cumont p. 51) Such contemplation is wisdom and virtue to be compensated or supplemented in future life by "free contemplation of celestial splendors and supreme felicity," according to Plato.

But astrology did fuse with the cultural web of Greece, and quickly at that. "How came the Greeks by astrology, these possessors of exceptional powers of reason, this people to whom all science owes its origin, the first among nations to grasp the concept of knowledge and put it to the service of Truth? How and when did this of all people come by astrology?" ask two scholarly authors. (Sternglaube and Sterndeutung by Franz Boll and Carl Bezold, Berlin 1931 p. 15) The answer seems to lie in the weakening of the traditional religion of the semi-human divinities of Greece under the attack of the stoic worship of reason and law in nature, and the onrush of new and enticing notions streaming out of the Orient. Contact with Babylonian culture was quite intimate and many-sided immediately after the campaigns of Alexander the Great, and the ensuing respect was mutual. Chaldean astronomers, such as Berosus or Kidenas established schools in Greece after the Alexandrian conquest and brought with them all the tables of observations and the accumulated knowledge of Babylonia as well as all the astrological theories and divinational practices. The philosophy of stoicism fell right in line with the glamor of the Orient and its legitimate impact. To the stoics the universe was a vast organism, cemented into a coherent unity by forces of sympathy with Fire as the universal principle, and the celestial bodies as its purest expression. Their religion was pantheism and its fusion with law and causality brought forth their famous tenet of Destiny or determinism in which the regularity of sidereal movements found a receptive niche. Hence the notions of stellar determinism preached by astrology, as well as star-worship, were enthusiastically received, and merged readily with indigenous Greek thought. Even Hipparchus, probably the greatest Greek astronomer, fell victim to the astral religion. Says Pliny: "Hipparchus before-mentioned, who can never be sufficiently praised, no one having done more to prove that man is related to the stars and that our souls are a part of heaven, detected a new star that came into existence during his lifetime . . ." etc. (Natural History of Pliny, Harvard Univ. Press, vol. 1, p. 239) And no wonder. Astrology, if by that we mean all the lore about the skies, the motions of the planets as well as their effects upon man, was a well-knit mixture of science, the rule of fate and pure religion, and brought with it in addition the promise of gratifying that desire in man which had urged him for millennia to peek anxiously into the future by as many methods as he could devise. Such a fortuitous combination is rare indeed, hence its appeal was exceptionally potent, far-reaching and enduring.

During the sixth century B.C. astrology reached Egypt where it is claimed, it had been unknown before. The haughtiest and most exclusive people of the world which had enjoyed uninterrupted domination culturally and militarily for thousands of years thus succumbed as meekly as Greece. Egypt, with her conservative priesthood was obliged to surrender to "the calculators of hours and makers of horoscopes, devoted to the study of Chaldean science." Temples came to be decorated with zodiacs and the Egyptian god Thoth became the deity of astrological wisdom.

In Rome too, the provincial or sectarian traditional religion gave way. Two prominent writers and teachers who lived around the beginning of the first century B.C. Posidonius and Manilius, who were highly influential with the aristocracy of Rome, the royal families and the leading intellectual circles, welcomed a religion based on a philosophy which was scientific and universal. Augustus and Tiberius were enthusiastic adherents of astrology and the sidereal religion was popular with the public generally. The spread of star-worship was aided by a movement, gaining many adherents at the time, under the name of Neo-Pythagoreanism. It expounded the eternity of the universe, the rule of the stars over the sublunary world, the vigilance of airy demons who threaten mankind, and finally a complex symbolism of numbers full of magic powers and meanings thus inviting prognostication. The people who knew this science of magic numbers and their hidden symbolism were known as mathematici and were duly respected and feared. Finally, it should be noted that plain, old-fashioned magic and occult lore stealthily succeeded in staging a pompous comeback in a respectable and learned guise on the crest of this wave of orientalism. This was quite natural. After all, it was the period between the Old and New Testaments, of the tales of Circe and Medea, and magic was still part and parcel of all folklores of the time.

One of the peculiarities of the spread of these new ideas in Rome was their enthusiastic reception by the intellectuals, though in practically no time at all the astrological wave had seeped through to all sections of the population. This was an era of peace and unity in the Roman Empire, where religions and lores mingled freely among the merchants, farmers, slaves and soldiers of subjugated nations. Oddly enough, science, nature-worship and astrology caught the fancy of all races and spread far and wide among intellectuals as well as the masses. All native religions adopted these notions, and virtually all native priests made the new ritual their own. The intellectuals chose as their preferred delicacy the technical and mathematical phases; the common people the glamorous, magical and religious aspects. The traditional Greek or Roman religions had been considerably weakened by time and trends, witness Pliny's unemotional and utterly untrammeled discussion of these religions or even of God. (Natural History Bk 2) Hence the new romantic wisdom of the Orient strengthened by the appeal of science and the magic of numbers could very easily fill the vacuum left behind. That polytheism generally was falling upon evil ways and that monotheism was winning the favor of the thoughtful brave everywhere is as apparent in the third century B.C. in Greece as in later times in Rome. Science was held then in great esteem, probably because of Greek influence, invigorated by the conquests of Alexander and the prestige of Greek learning and culture, generally. Abstract mathematics or numerology was also held in high esteem as was technology. With all these trends astrology was as harmonious as is television or new model cars with the mores of our society. The stellar determinism pleased a cultured people more than the tyranny of a blindfolded fate, inexorable and inscrutable and requiring no wisdom or knowledge to be comprehended. And so Greece had her Berosus, a Babylonian priest who founded a school of astrology on the island of Cos at about 280 B.C. who translated for Greek consumption Babylonian works on the subject and dedicated them to King Antiochus I of Syria. In Egypt the new science was set forth in a work appearing some decades later and attributed to a King Nechepso and a priest Petosiris. Both in Greece and in Egypt, the two powerful centers of learning and prowess, the former newly arisen with Alexander as a world power, the latter a nation reckoned with for many thousands of years past, astrology swept across the breadth and depth of their cultures to become part and parcel of the learning, faith and folklore of poor and rich alike.

It was with the coming of this great combination of science and religion, the great unity of knowledge and augury, of reason and worship, that adoration of the sun became a central feature of the reformed pagan faiths of old. The sun occupied a central position long before the Copernican theory was elaborated.

That the courses of the planets were somehow linked with the sun had already been known to the Chaldean observers of the skies. They knew that Mercury and Venus never got very far from the sun hence their motions were regulated by the sun. They knew that the three superior planets Mars, Jupiter and Saturn were also dependent upon the sun. Their advances, stoppages and regressions were linked with the sun's completion of an annual cycle, or as we would say with a revolution of the earth. They thus realized that the sun was unique among the planets and that he in fact, governed the movements of all, including to some extent even the moon. The sun's relation toward the other planets, or his aspects, determined their motion, which means, impelled them forward, arrested, or pulled them backwards. Even the fixed stars were believed to depend upon the sun whose mass was imbued with the twin powers of both repulsion and attraction, or sympathy or antipathy, according to distance and position. And since the planets and their motions governed earthly events, the sun which was the arbiter of their fates, was necessarily the ultimate ruler of the universe and its denizens. He was "the heart of the world," "the conductor of cosmic harmony," "the master of the four elements and the four seasons, the heavenly power which, by the invariable changes of its annual course, produces, nourishes, and destroys animals and plants, and by the alternation of day and night warms and cools, dries or moistens the earth and the atmosphere." (Cumont p. 131) The sun is thus the governor and the reason of the world. Its energy and radiance animated all living organisms on earth by sending particles of life and fire into them. When these die their vital flame returns to its original abode. Its light is reason, life and intelligence, just as it is illumination and warmth. Hence the sun-worship of ancient Rome where the astral philosophy reached its peak. In 274 A.D. the emperor Aurelian, on returning from Syria where he absorbed the principles of astral knowledge centering around the "invincible sun," bestowed upon it imperial recognition and made sun-worship the religion of the empire. A sun-god was postulated who was an abstract image of the sun, and who resided outside the planetary universe and ruled over it. The visible sun was merely its material expression.

In discussing the actual or imaginary attainments of stellar knowledge, one may tend to overlook the most powerful component in man's attitude toward the stars, namely, the sense of wonder and adoration at the sight of the jewel-studded sky of the Orient, the unfathomable magic and allure of the vast and intimate mystery of nature. It is difficult for modern man to comprehend this sense of awe and religious ecstasy which made men humble before the silent depth of the heavens. Modern man has different taste and numerous outlets for his sense of wonder at nature's majesty and beauty. The only stars we know today are the stars of Hollywood, and even darkness itself is a thing of the past as much as smallpox or migrations. People who take television and rockets for granted cannot get emotionally aroused over blurred dots in the city sky known in literature as stars.

But not so the men of antiquity. "Mortal as I am," writes Ptolemy, "I know that I am born for a day, but when I follow the serried multitude of the stars in their circular course, my feet no longer touch the earth; I ascend to Zeus himself to feast me on ambrosia, the food of the gods." (Quoted by Cumont) And Cumont rightly comments, no wonder the astrologer enjoyed the highest prestige, and quotes Arellius Fuscus, a rhetorician of the Augustan age: "He to whom the gods themselves reveal the future, who imposes their will even on kings and peoples, cannot be fashioned by the same womb which bore us ignorant men. He is of superhuman rank. Confident of the gods, he is himself divine. . . . If the pretensions of astrology are genuine, why do not men of every age devote themselves to this study? Why from our infancy do we not fix our eyes on nature and on the gods, seeing that the stars unveil themselves for us, and that we can live in the midst of the gods? Why exhaust ourselves to the profession of arms? Rather let us lift up our minds by means of the science which reveals to us the future, and before the appointed hour of death let us taste the pleasures of the Blest." (Cumont p. 148–149).

And the astrologers of Rome did seek to be divine, hence ascetic and holy. They were known as mathematici because they were numerologists and they prided themselves on their "chastity, sobriety, integrity, and self-renunciation." Just as science and mystery were inseparable in the search, so were wisdom and sanctity held inseparable in the seeker. "Science is a revelation promised to virtue . . . and true knowledge is the reward of piety." Material goods and earthly glory are vain delusions of little appeal to those who commune with the stars and who find ecstasy in their contemplation and study. With man's usual indifference to inconsistency, the astrologers welcomed scientific determinism, still one of the fundamental concepts of our own culture of science and technology, and enthroned fate as inexorably dictated by the laws of motion and nature. Yet at the same time they strove to be pure of heart and faith, and even prayed for propitious turns of events in accordance with the emotional needs and urges that moved them then, even as they move many great scientists of today.

Chapter II

THE CELESTIAL ORBS: THE STRUGGLE FOR A THEORY

1. The Sacred Circle

NO sooner did the Greeks become aware of the regularity and mystery of the celestial phenomena, than they began to speculate on their origin, the laws which governed their relationships, and the forces which caused their motions. The most primitive conceptions of the nature of the earth and its position in the cosmos find their natural and unpretentious outlet in the writings of Homer. The earth is a circular plate-like affair, covered by the vault of the sky, as indeed it seems to be, encircled by a vast river Okeanos. The outlying zones of this saucer are inhabited by queer beings such as pygmies, and beyond the river Okeanos are the homes of mysterious creatures such as the Kimmerians, the happy land of Elysium and other strange regions. Ultimately one reaches the borders of Hades, the land of the dead which stretches into the far beyond but also into the dark recesses under the earth's surface. The dome of the sky contains the ether and within it the celestial bodies follow their assigned courses. For example, the sun rises in the morning out of the water of Okeanos in the east, travels through the sky on a stipulated route, much like the limited air routes of our air companies of today, and returns to the hollows of that river's deep in the west for the night, to reappear again next morning.

Generally speaking, the early Greek cosmogonies were sophisticated attempts at devising schematized and unified generalizations to account for the direct observations of the human eye. Clearly the earth is flat, and there is a vault above it. That vault is made of solid crystalline material and the stars are attached to it "like nails." The celestial bodies are exhaled fiery clouds "ignited by their motions," and located far away from us somewhere in the infinity of space. It had been suggested from early times that the moon shone with light reflected from the sun, and Leucippus had declared that the moon's markings were caused by the hills and valleys casting shadows on its surface. The milky way, taught

Democritus, consisted of myriads of minute stars, while according to Anaximander it marked the former path of the sun. It had also been known from the tales of travelers that one could see the southern star Canopus barely on the horizon from the island of Rhodes and higher in the sky further south, though that star was never seen in Greece. Empedocles had speculated that solar eclipses were caused by the moon's passage between the earth and sun. It was generally believed that the region around the earth, extending as far as the moon, teemed with evil spirits and exhalations, while the regions beyond the moon were pure and ethereal. The earth was held in position by the rapid spinning of the rotating heavens "as the water remains in a goblet which is swung quickly around in a circle"—explains Aristotle in presenting the views of Empedocles. Initial pressure and compaction gave rise to the air. The North Pole of the heavens had originally been directly overhead but later became depressed downward to the position it now occupies. According to Leucippus, the axis of the heavens inclined to the horizon because the earth was loaded with ice in the north and was therefore weighted downward, while the south end being hotter, was lighter. Others offered the explanation that the tilting occurred spontaneously subsequent to the appearance of life on earth to produce differences in climate. Some philosophers taught that the sun and moon were nearer to the earth than the planets and others proclaimed the reverse.

It would seem as if throughout Greek history there had been forebodings or outcroppings of the notion that the earth was really round. Certain it is that the concept of the sphericity of the earth has been attributed to several philosophers, though the credit generally falls to Pythagoras. Through an error the rumor was also set abroad that Pythagoras or his pupils were as well the founders of the theory that the sun was situated at the center of the cosmos with the earth and planets revolving around it. In reality the Pythagorean scheme of the universe was of another cut.

It had become clear to the Greek philosophers, most of whom were also shrewd observers and mathematicians, that the stars and planets inscribed circular orbits in the sky, completing their diurnal circles in twenty-four hours. This was not easy to accept. Motion was not a suitable quality for a master but rather for a servant. Similarly, motion did not fit an ethereal celestial body but rather did it properly belong to the crudest of all bodies, namely the earth.

The followers of Pythagoras, especially Philolaus, therefore postulated that the earth was carried at the end of a spoke or radius and turned around a center once in twenty-four hours, thus showing one side to the center and the other to the outside world, much like the motion of the moon, or a horse in a merry-go-round. This motion was from west to east, thus making it appear as if all objects in the sky moved round from east to west in twenty-four hours. (Figure 1)

At the center of this merry-go-round was a "central fire," described as the hearth of the universe, the watch-tower of Zeus. Round it moved not only the earth but all the celestial bodies as well. That fire remained invisible because Greece was on that part of the earth situated on the side away from the fire. Beyond India, or other such outlying regions, the fire could probably be seen. Besides, even there, it might be obscured by some other planet, the counter-earth which was postulated for bal-

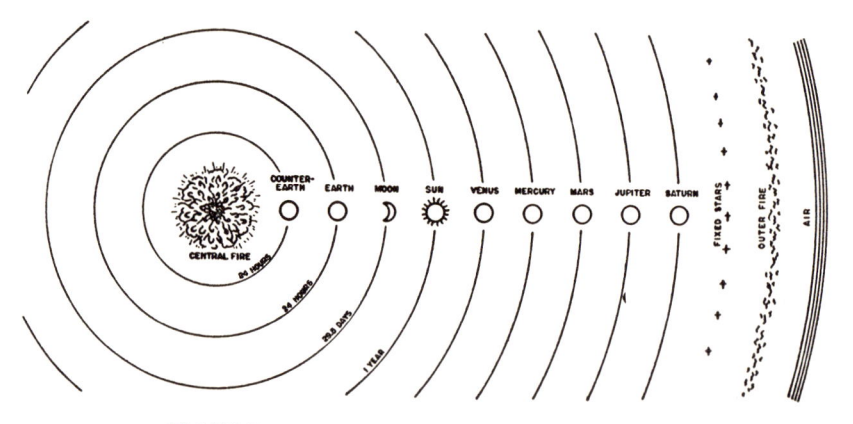

FIGURE 1. THE SCHEME OF PHILOLAUS

ance, or to bring up to ten the number of revolving bodies. Aristotle disapproved strongly of such free and irresponsible multiplication of hypotheses. "They further construct another earth in apposition to ours to which they give the name counter-earth. In all this they are not seeking for theories and causes to account for observed facts, but rather forcing their observations and trying to accommodate them to certain theories and opinions of their own. But there are many others who would agree that it is wrong to give the earth the central position, looking for confirmation rather to theory than to the facts of observation. Their view is that the most precious place befits the most precious thing: but fire, they say, is more precious than earth." (The Basic Works of Aristotle, edited by Richard McKeon. On the Heavens, Bk 2 ch. 13 p. 428)

Clearly then the Pythagoreans had ten moving bodies: the seven planets, the earth, the fixed stars and the invisible counter-earth. In addition, they also postulated an outer fire beyond the fixed stars and infinite space filled with inexhaustible air outside of that. The nearest body to the central fire, disregarding the counterearth, was the spherical earth and outside its orbit was the moon travelling round the central

THE CELESTIAL ORBS

fire at a speed of twenty-nine and a half days per revolution. Outside the moon revolved the sun about the same common center, completing its circuit in one year. Then came the five planets; reports on the sequence assigned to them vary, but they all circled around the central fire in concentric circular orbits.

This scheme accounted for all the observed celestial phenomena with amazing simplicity. The revolution of the earth about the central fire was fully equivalent to the earth's daily rotation. Day prevails when the earth is on the side facing the sun and it is night when the earth is on the opposite side. The sun moved round the central fire in an oblique circle thus giving rise to the plane of the ecliptic. The planets also revolved in planes inclined to the earth's plane of revolution in accordance with observed planetary motions. The irregularities of planetary motions were wholly neglected, while the absence of the expected variations in distance between earth and moon, or earth and sun, were explained away on the ground that the earth was very close to the central fire, while the sun and moon were so far away that the slight differences in distance to the sun or moon were not effectual in changing their apparent diameters.

The followers of Pythagoras also assumed that the moon was a body very much like the earth, though because of its slower rotation it had a day which is 29½ times as long as our day. It had plants and animals which were 15 times larger than the terrestrial ones. The lunar markings were reflections of the earth's seas. There were more lunar than solar eclipses because not only the earth but the counter-earth as well came ever so often between the central fire and the moon. The fixed stars also moved "because all divine things move like the sun, moon, stars, and the whole heavens, as Alkmaeon had said." (J. L. E. Dreyer, History of the Planetary Systems from Thales to Kepler, Cambridge 1906, p. 47).

Another Pythagorean apparently simplified the scheme considerably. Dreyer cites the following quotation from Cicero: "Hicetas of Syracuse, according to Theophrastus, believes that the heavens, the sun, moon, stars and all heavenly bodies are standing still, and that nothing in the universe is moving except the earth, which, while it turns and twists itself with the greatest velocity round its axis produces all the same phenomena as if the heavens were moved and the earth were standing still." (ibid p. 50). Apparently good use was made in Greece of freedom to speculate and lucky strikes were not as rare as modern pride would make one believe.

More ingenious even were the speculations of Eudoxus (408–355 B.C.), a pupil of Plato and one of the great mathematicians of Greece to whom is attributed the authorship of the fifth book of Euclid, "as well as the method of exhaustion, by means of which the Greeks were able to solve many problems of mensuration without infinitesimals." (ibid p. 88) Clearly, these originators of theories which many modern scientists regard contemptuously as childish or primitive fancy, were not "mere speculators." Plutarch recounts that when Plato's opinion was sought on the problem of the duplication of the cube he replied that only Eudoxus and one other mathematician (Helikon) could grapple with that problem. Eudoxus was also the author of the proposal that the calendar be made to consist of three solar years of 365 days and a fourth of 366, the system later adopted by Julius Caesar and known as the Julian calendar.

Eudoxus developed the theory of concentric or homocentric spheres. His own work on Velocities is lost but a summary of it is left to us in Simplicius' commentary. The planets moved in circular orbits round a stationary and centrally situated earth and were attached to spheres, wholly postulated entities and never endowed by him with physical properties. Every heavenly body was located on the equator of such a sphere which by its motion carried it in its course. The poles of a given sphere extended outward and were attached to or embedded in another large sphere, concentric with it. The axes of two such spheres did not coincide, but were at an angle to each other. The outer sphere rotated with a different speed and in a different direction from the inner one and about its own axis. If necessary, a third sphere was postulated with its axis at the proper angle to that of the inner one, and rotating at its peculiar speed and in the desired direction, the two inner spheres would necessarily be carried along by the rotation of the outer one. In this manner the direct motion, the stations, and the retrograde motion of each planet could be accounted for, as well as its motion in latitude. Obviously, only one sphere carried the planet. The others merely contributed to the planet's component motions and were called starless.

The motions of the sun and moon could in this manner be fully described by postulating three spheres for each. The five planets required four apiece, since their motions of stations and retrogressions were more intricate. With the lone sphere for the fixed stars the total was twenty-seven. Unlike previous schemes in which the sphere of the fixed stars dragged the planetary spheres along in its trail, the scheme of Eudoxus assumed each planetary complex to be independent of the stars and of any other planet. No causes for the motions were offered and the mechanism was apparently of a purely mathematical nature.

Thus the lunar orbit was brought about first of all by an innermost sphere which carried the moon on its equator and which revolved from west to east in 27.3 days. The next outer sphere which held the axis of the inner one in its grip revolved along the zodiac in 18½ years. The axis of the inner sphere was inclined to that of the outer one by the angle which the orbit of the moon makes with the ecliptic. Essentially the second outer sphere accounted for the fact that the points of intersection of the orbit of the moon with the ecliptic, the nodes, or the periods in which eclipses can occur, move westward regularly and complete a cycle in 18½ years. The third sphere enveloping the two inner ones revolved with the speed and in the direction of the sphere of the fixed stars, completing its rotation in 24 hours. Similarly, the three spheres of the sun were representations of its triple motion. One had the same motion as the stars to account for the daily path from sunrise to sunset; the third revolved along the zodiac or ecliptic, thus accounting for the year. The second revolved at an angle inclined to the zodiac in order to explain presumably the sun's motion in latitude or the deviation from the line of the ecliptic defined as the middle of the zodiac, as determined by the motions of the remaining planets. This was an erroneous notion but the sphere was used later to account for the cycle of precession.

In the case of the planets, the explanation had to be somewhat more difficult since their stationary periods had to be accounted for, as well as their motion both eastward and westward among the stars. The latter motion occurred periodically as interruptions in the regular or direct motion eastward among the constellations, as the sun did to complete a cycle once a year. Thus, one sphere, the outermost, brought about the daily rotation of the planet from east to west. The second one within it carried the planet in its motion along the circle of the ecliptic. The third and fourth spheres accounted for the planet's change in latitude above and below the plane of the ecliptic and the inequality in its velocity in various segments of its orbit. That the elaboration of a suitable scheme for each planet requires exceptional mathematical skill goes without saying, especially since the Greeks had only geometry to rely upon. From the values employed by Eudoxus for the synodic and zodiacal periods of each planet (that is, the time taken for a revolution from one particular conjunction to the next, and the completion of a revolution along the zodiac, respectively) it is obvious that amazingly careful observations of planetary motions were available to him. (Figure 2. The Scheme of Eudoxus)

To obtain some idea of the magnitude of the task let us consider only one aspect of the problem. Sphere two (AQBR) revolves around its axis AB. On it point P represents the place where one pole of the axis of the first inner sphere is attached. It is this first inner sphere that carries the planet on its equator. (Figure 3.) Clearly the axis of the first sphere is inclined to that of the second and the angle is constant. Now as the outer sphere revolves, it will carry the axis of the inner one with it, and its pole P will inscribe a small circle QPR. The planet on the equator of the first inner sphere is at M. If the first sphere turns in a direction opposite to that of the second, the path described by M, projected on the plane of the circle AQBR is not an easy matter to trace without the aid of modern mathematics. But a mathematician of the caliber of Eudoxus successfully met the challenge. He found that projected path to re-

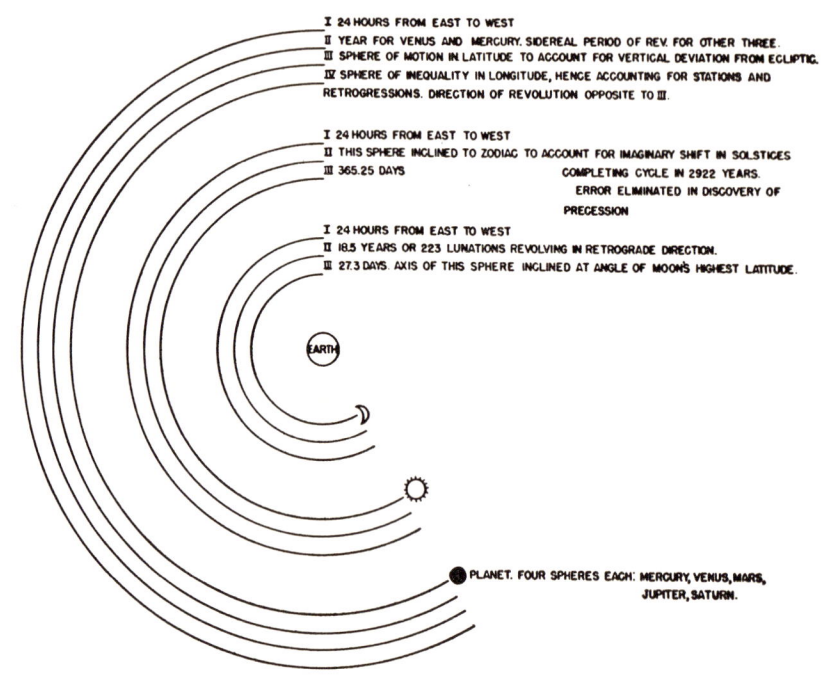

```
I  24 HOURS FROM EAST TO WEST
II  YEAR FOR VENUS AND MERCURY. SIDEREAL PERIOD OF REV. FOR OTHER THREE.
III  SPHERE OF MOTION IN LATITUDE TO ACCOUNT FOR VERTICAL DEVIATION FROM ECLIPTIC.
IV  SPHERE OF INEQUALITY IN LONGITUDE, HENCE ACCOUNTING FOR STATIONS AND
    RETROGRESSIONS. DIRECTION OF REVOLUTION OPPOSITE TO III.

I  24 HOURS FROM EAST TO WEST
II  THIS SPHERE INCLINED TO ZODIAC TO ACCOUNT FOR IMAGINARY SHIFT IN SOLSTICES
III  365.25 DAYS                    COMPLETING CYCLE IN 2922 YEARS.
                                    ERROR ELIMINATED IN DISCOVERY OF
                                    PRECESSION

I  24 HOURS FROM EAST TO WEST
II  18.5 YEARS OR 223 LUNATIONS REVOLVING IN RETROGRADE DIRECTION.
III  27.3 DAYS. AXIS OF THIS SPHERE INCLINED AT ANGLE OF MOON'S HIGHEST LATITUDE.
```

PLANET. FOUR SPHERES EACH: MERCURY, VENUS, MARS, JUPITER, SATURN.

FIGURE 2. THE SCHEME OF EUDOXUS

semble the figure 8 lying on its side, as represented. This figure was called hippopede by the Greeks because it was customary to train horses to describe that figure in cantering. (Figure 4) The planet thus passes the arcs 1–2, 2–3, 3–4, 4–5, etc. in equal times. The length and width of this figure can be obtained from proper ratios and inclinations of the axes of the corresponding spheres, with the long axis lying along the zodiac. Knowing the arcs of retrogression, the stations, and the periods of revolution, all one requires is a little ingenuity and the motion of the planets can be quite well represented.

That many facets of planetary motions were omitted or misconstrued by the theory of homocentric spheres goes without saying. Its inadequacies were both due to incomplete observations and the price of theory. Nevertheless it fitted the case of Saturn and Jupiter very well, was satisfactory for Mercury, poor for Venus and out of step entirely

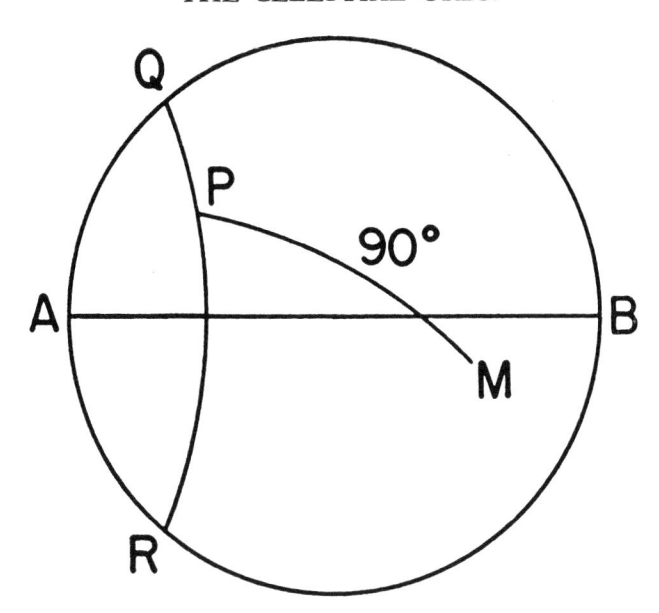

FIGURE 3. "P" IS POINT OF ATTACHMENT OF AXIS OF INNER SPHERE

for Mars, the troublesome planet whose orbit remained a snag and a challenge until subdued by the genius of Kepler. The system failed particularly with regard to motion in latitude which is the deviation above and below the ecliptic exhibited by the path of a planet.

A pupil of Eudoxus named Calippus sought however to fill these gaps. Though his book is lost the core of his reforms is known to us. To correct Eudoxus' serious deficiencies in the instance of Mars, he added another sphere which, as is pointed out by modern scholars, could fairly well account for many of them. Calippus also augmented by one each the number of spheres allotted to Mars, Venus and Mercury, thus

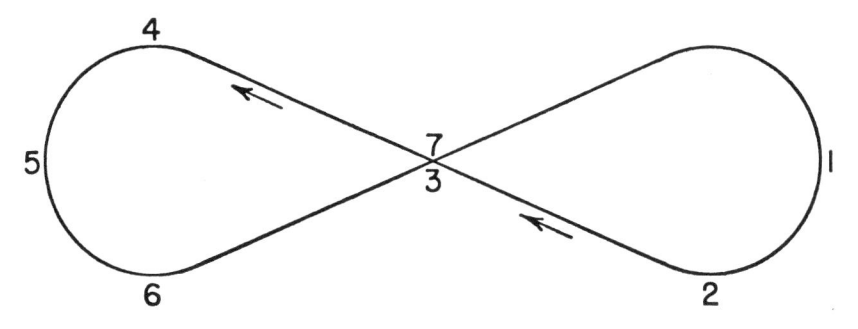

FIGURE 4. THE HIPPOPEDE

eliminating other kinks in his master's theory, though failing of course to bring it to perfection. He added two spheres to the system of the sun which accounted for the sun's inequality in motion in longitude, since it had been established by this time that the velocity of the sun was not uniform in every segment of its orbit. Similarly, to account for the inequality of the moon's orbit, re the ecliptic, two more spheres were added to that body's motion, making a total of thirty-three. Aristotle made an interesting addition. Concerned over the effect which one revolving sphere might have on its neighbor, he interposed additional spheres between any concentric set of two and endowed them with motion equal to but opposite in direction to the exterior one, thus neutralizing its movement and clearing the field for the next enclosed sphere and its motion. In this fashion he obtained fifty-five spheres and apparently regarded them as having physical reality which Eudoxus and Callipus did not.

Since Aristotle has become the arch-demon of nineteenth century rationalism, it is worth noting that in his works On the Heavens and Meteorology, he discusses in considerable detail both the facts and theories of the astronomical knowledge of his days. After considering the Pythagorean scheme already referred to, he examines the question of the earth's rest or motion and concludes that "there is no general agreement." There are the Pythagoreans and those who believe in the stationary earth. "Others, again, say that the earth, which lies at the center, is 'rolled,' and thus in motion about the axis of the whole heaven. So, he states, it stands written in the Timaeus," Plato's famous dialogue on cosmogony. (Aristotle p. 429) Aristotle writes further that there are some "who, setting it (the earth) at the centre, suppose it to be 'rolled' and in motion about the pole as axis." Such an hypothesis, he decides, is untenable since any part of the earth must move "in a straight line to the centre," by virtue of the observed fact that all terrestrial bodies fall downward. Furthermore, if the earth were to have a circular motion, or revolution, it should pass other bodies as do the planets attached to the spheres. Hence "there would have to be passings and turnings of the fixed stars. Yet no such thing is observed. The same stars always rise and set in the same parts of the earth." (Aristotle p. 434) The earth is spherical in shape for many reasons. "Every portion of earth has weight until it reaches the centre, and the jostling of parts greater and smaller would bring about not a waved surface but rather compression and convergence of part and part until the centre is reached. . . . But, the spherical shape, necessitated by this argument, follows also from the fact that the motions of heavy bodies always make equal angles, and are not parallel. . . . The evidence of the senses further corroborates this. How else would eclipses of the moon show segments shaped as we see them? . . . In eclipses the outline is always curved; and since it is the interposition of the earth that makes the eclipse, the form of this line will be caused by the form of the earth's surface which is therefore spherical. Again, our observations of the stars made it evident, not only that the earth is circular, but also that it is a circle of no great size. For quite a small change of positions to south or north causes a manifest alteration of the horizon. There is much change, I mean, in the stars which are overhead, and the stars seen are different, as one moves northward or southward. Indeed there are some stars seen in Egypt and in the neighborhood of Cyprus which are not seen in the northerly regions; and stars which in the north are never beyond the range of observation, in those regions rise and set. All of which goes to show not only that the earth is circular in shape but also that it is a sphere of no great size: for otherwise the effect of so slight a change of place would not be so quickly apparent. Hence one should not be too sure of the incredibility of the view of those who conceive that there is continuity between the parts about the pillars of Hercules (that is, Gibraltar) and the parts about India, (i.e. west and east by circumnavigation of the earth) and that in this way the ocean is one. As further evidence in favor of this they quote the case of elephants, a species occurring in each of these extreme regions, suggesting that the common characteristic of these extremes is explained by their continuity. Also these mathematicians who try to calculate the size of the earth's circumference arrive at the figure 400,000 stades. (9987 geographical miles, the oldest recorded estimate of the size of the earth; present day figure—5400). This indicates not only that the earth's mass is spherical in shape, but also that as compared with the stars it is not of great size." (Aristotle p. 437)

Novel theories of planetary motion come into their own with the speculations of two Greek philosophers Heraclides of Pontus (388–315 B.C.) and Aristarchus of Samos (ca 281 B.C.). According to the famous commentator on Aristotle, Simplicius, Heraclides definitely taught that "the heavens and the stars were immovable and the earth moved round the poles of the equator from the west each day one revolution as near as possible." Later on he states that "Heraclides of Pontus assumes the earth to be in the middle and to move in a circle, but the heavens to be at rest." (Dreyer, p. 126) Heraclides also postulated that Venus moved round the sun and not round the earth. Similar theories of the earth's rotation were in fact attributed to other Greek philosophers throughout the Greek period and references to them occur in several texts. (Dreyer, 127–8)

According to Macrobius, an author of the fourth century A.D. who wrote a commentary on a work by Cicero, there had been advanced what came to be known as the Egyptian theory. This hypothesis presupposes the earth to be stationary and the sun to circle around it and to complete a revolution once a year. The two inferior planets Mercury and Venus in turn revolved around the sun and consequently followed it on its annual course. According to Macrobius "the circle by which the sun moves round is surrounded by the circle of Mercury, but the circle of Venus encloses that again being above it." (Figure 5. The Egyptian System)

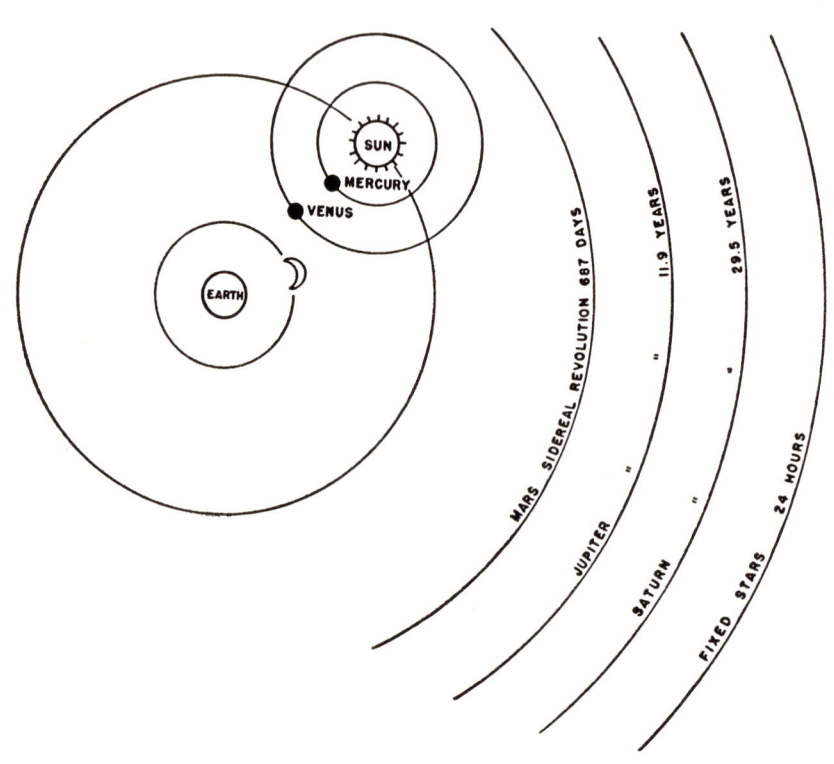

FIGURE 5. THE "EGYPTIAN SYSTEM"

The above cited Simplicius, in discussing a commentary on a work entitled Meteorology by Posidonius (first century B.C.) expostulates on the differences between physics and astronomy. The physicist, he explains, is interested in causes, motion and forces, while the astronomer is concerned more immediately with the need "to investigate in how many ways the phenomena can be represented," so as best to explain the observed events. "Therefore also a certain Herakleides of Pontus stood up and said that also when the earth moved in some way and the sun stood still in some way, could the irregularity observed relatively to the sun be accounted for. In general it is not the astronomer's business to see what by its nature is immovable and of what kind the moved things are, but framing hypotheses as to some things being in motion and others being fixed, he considers which hypotheses are in conformity with the phenomena in the heavens." Here we see the true spirit of science in operation. What is required, the author seems to say, is courage, mathematical ingenuity and respect for the observed facts. A mathematical explanation is good and worthy if it explains or coordinates the facts, regardless of its own physical reality or credibility.

Like Eudoxus before him, Aristarchus of Samos (c. 310–230 B.C.) was no mere speculator. He was a practicing astronomer, the author of a work, still extant, entitled "On the dimensions and distances of the sun and moon." The method he adopted to obtain these measurements was bold and sound. He determined the angular distance between the sun and the moon at a time when the moon is half illuminated, which occurs when the moon is west of the meridian while the sun is setting on horizon. At such a time the angle at the moon or angle m, in the triangle EMS must be a right angle, hence 90°. Aristarchus determined angle e and found it to be 87°, while modern measurement gives it as 89° 50'. From his calculations he deduced the distance between the earth and sun to be about 20 times the distance to the moon. No less an authority than the famous Archimedes (287–212 B.C.) has left us the following: "You know that according to most astronomers the world is the sphere, of which the centre is the centre of the earth, and whose radius is a line from the centre of the earth to the centre of the sun. But Aristarchus of Samos has published in outline certain hypotheses from which it follows that the world is many times larger than that. For he supposes that the fixed stars and the sun are immovable but that the earth is carried in a circle round the sun which is in the middle of the orbit; but the sphere of the fixed stars situated about the same centre as the sun, is so great," that the earth's orbit "bears the same proportion to the distance of the fixed stars as the centre of the sphere bears to its surface. But this is evidently impossible for as the centre of the sphere has no magnitude, it follows that it has no ratio to the surface. It is therefore to be supposed that Aristarchus meant that as we consider the earth as the centre of the world, then the earth has the same ratio to that which we call the world, as the sphere in which is the circle described by the earth according to him, has to the sphere of the fixed stars." (Dreyer 136–7) In other words, Aristarchus assumed that the earth circled about the sun but that the area of that circle was like a point by comparison with the distance to the stars or the surface of the sphere of the stars, since no stellar displacements are observed. Archimedes merely dislikes the unsound mathematics Aristarchus employs, because by definition a point has no magnitude and cannot stand in a specific ratio to anything measurable. Although the work in which Aristarchus developed this idea is not extant, sufficient references abound in ancient literature to establish the essence of his theory of diurnal rotation and annual revolution of the earth. A similar theory was even expounded by Seleucus, as cited by the geographer Strabo, so that the heliocentric theory was quite familiar to antiquity.

Yet the Greek scholars knew that all these theories fell short of satisfying the facts. They had observed that a disc held at the same distance from the eye did not always require the same diameter to hide the moon completely and that the solar eclipses were sometimes total and at other times annular, thus betraying different distances to the moon. The noted variations in the brightness of the planets also gave them concern.

One may therefore be critical of such opinions as the following:

"By abandoning the usual Greek methods of speculation and reliance on supposed general principles, Aristarchus had obtained, almost at one bound, to an accurate understanding of the arrangement of the solar system; he had gained true ideas as to the relatively minute size of the earth. . . . In this way astronomy was started on the right road and we might expect that the rest of the story would be one of rapid progress on scientific lines. Actually it was to be very different." (The Growth of Physical Science, Sir James Jeans, Cambridge University Press 1948, p. 89) This attitude of many brilliant British writers on science and its philosophy, is in every way like the attitude of a drama critic who invariably praises the actor who plays the hero and condemns the one who plays the villain. Why is one to assert that Aristarchus was a greater mathematician or astronomer than, say, Hipparchus, who was the inventor of plane trigonometry, the discoverer of the precession of the equinoxes, reputedly also of Ptolemy's theorem, $\sin (A+B) = \sin A \cdot \cos B + \cos A \cdot \sin B$, spherical trigonometry etc. etc. merely on the grounds that the former enunciated a theory without evidence, providing no new tools or directives, on a blind guess? Such an attitude may be compared to small-nation patriotism. If he is Bulgarian he is great, but if Rumanian, he is second rate. In Balkan affairs this is a tragic guide, in science history it is suicidal.

It had also been known that Mars was always brightest when it crossed the celestial North-South meridian, i.e. when it culminated, at midnight. Under these conditions it had to be in opposition to the sun. As it goes nearer the sun, its light decreased. Clearly then, one was inevitably led to the conclusion that Mars was sometimes nearer the earth, when in opposition, and at other times further from it. Hence Mars moved in an eccentric circle round the earth, with its center on a line joining the earth and sun, since Mars was brightest, therefore nearest the earth when seen directly opposite the sun. To complicate matters still more, Mars was observed not to be in opposition at the same point

THE CELESTIAL ORBS 33

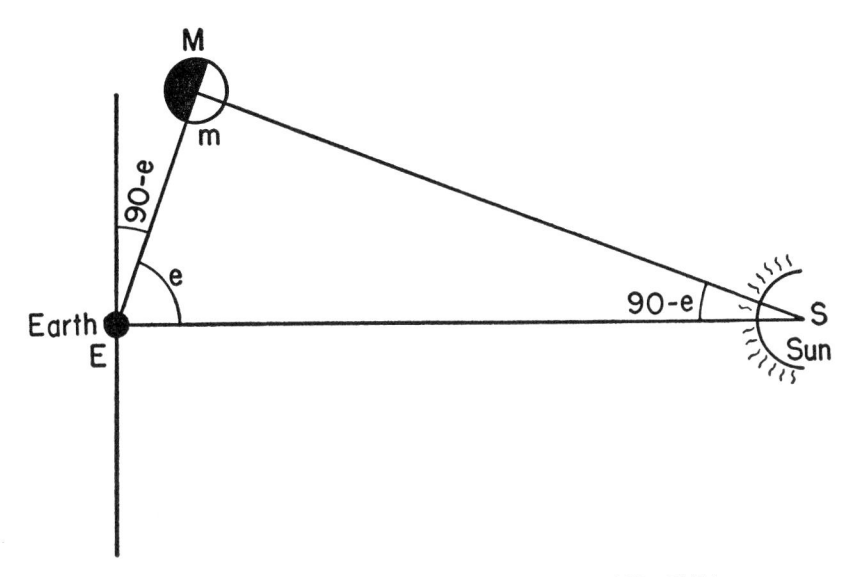

FIGURE 6. DISTANCES TO MOON AND SUN

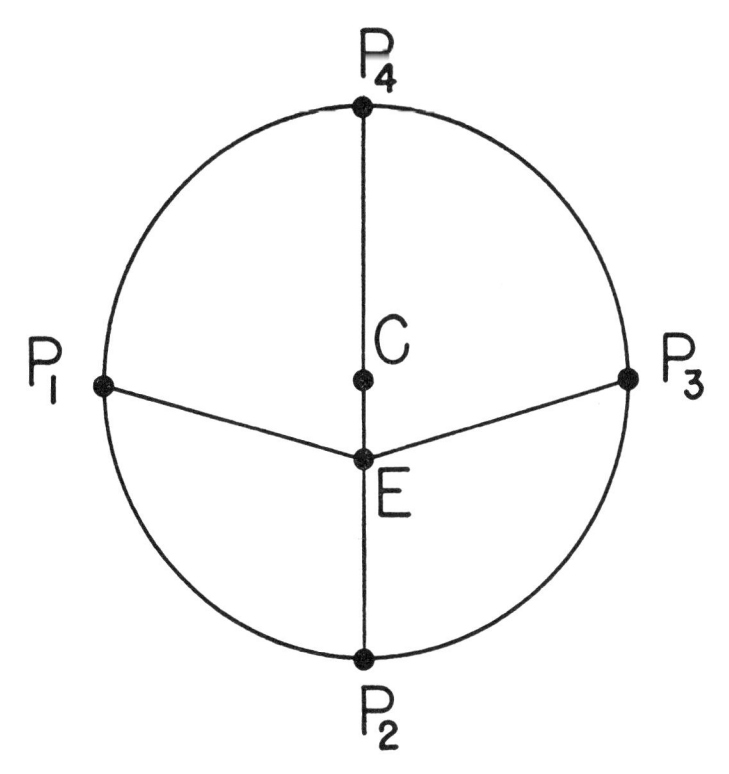

FIGURE 7. THE EARTH "E" IS ECCENTRIC

of the zodiac each year. This meant that the line joining Mars, the earth and the sun, with Mars in opposition, moved in such a manner that the center of the orbit of Mars, described a small circle about the earth in a year. Since Mars took an interval of two years and fifty days between two successive oppositions it was assumed that it took it that long to complete its orbit in an eccentric circle, round the earth.

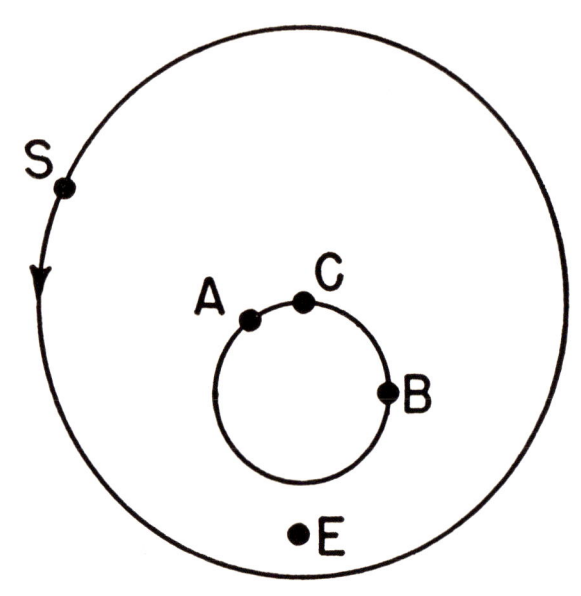

FIGURE 8. A MOVABLE CENTER "C"

According to the eccentric circle theory, the earth was at the center of the Universe. The moon circled round it in 27 days, the sun in a year, "probably in concentric circles. Mercury and Venus moved on circles, the centers of which were always on the straight line from the earth to the sun, so that the earth was always outside these circles, for which reason the two planets are always within a certain limited angular distance of the sun, from which the ratio of the radius of the eccentric to the distance of its centre from the earth could easily be determined for either planet. Similarly, the three outer planets moved on eccentric circles, the centres of which lay somewhere on the line from the earth to the sun, but these circles were so large as always to surround both the sun and earth." (ibid. p. 145)

To gain a clear notion of eccentrics let us consider the following. Suppose the earth not to be at the center of the circle inscribed around it by a planet. This will happen when the earth E is situated within the circle described by planet P with C as center. (Figure 7) This device

THE CELESTIAL ORBS

is sufficient to account for the planet's variable distance from the earth. But observation soon proved that this arrangement failed to explain all planetary irregularities. The scheme was therefore pushed one step further by assuming a movable instead of stationary center C. This is shown in the next diagram. (Figure 8) Here P revolves upon an eccentric circle with its center at C, while this center is also revolving along a smaller circle CAB. The point S will not, under these conditions, describe a circle, but "will trace a nearly circular path determined by a) the relative velocities of the outer and inner circles; b) the relative lengths of the radii of the two circles; and c) the direction of their motions, for they may turn in the same direction or in opposite directions. If ABC is itself an eccentric circle, we have the case of an eccentric on an eccentric." (Three Copernican Treatises by Edward Rosen, Columbia University Press 1939 p. 35) In this manner movable eccentrics could be employed with considerable accuracy to account for a planet's orbital deviation from a circle, though they could be used only for superior planets that make numerous apparent loops.

The following scheme of presenting the concept of a movable eccentric may prove of additional aid. In this diagram (Figure 9) the planet P moves on a path ABM while the center of that circle moves in the

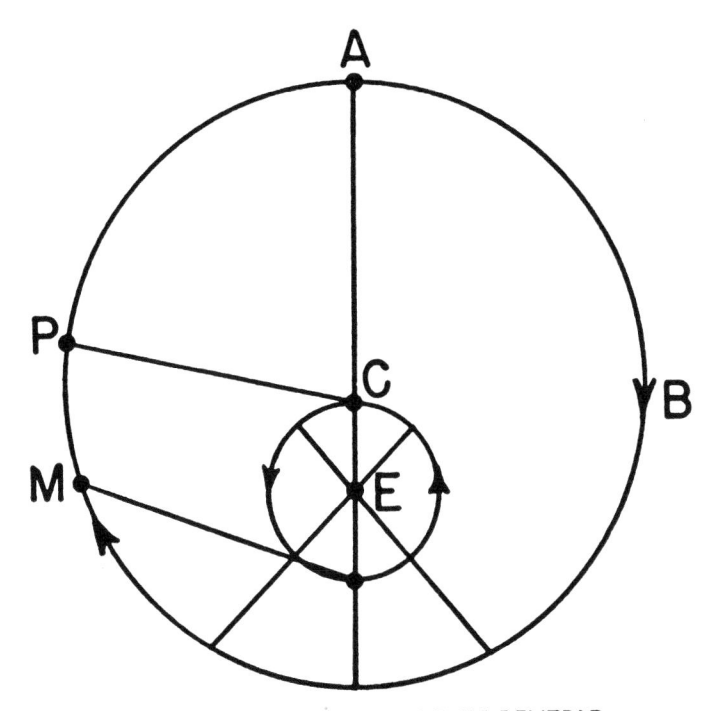

FIGURE 9. THE MOVABLE ECCENTRIC

opposite direction along the small inner circle which has the earth E as its center. Originally the movable eccentric idea was employed to account fully for the orbits of the superior planets Mars, Jupiter and Saturn while epicycles were employed for the two inferior ones. In the course of time, however, the movable eccentric was abandoned.

The other scheme, which presented itself in the course of time could accomplish the same objectives by means of epicycles. (Figure 10) Consider a point C moving along the circle C_1 C_2 C_3 with its center at O. Let C in turn be the center of a small circle of radius CP, with point P moving in the opposite direction at such a velocity as to allow P to describe the circle CP at the same time as it takes OC to complete its own circle. The point P will then describe the circle P_1 P_2 P_3 P_4. P is a planet and O represents an imaginary center of its apparent path. In this scheme the small circle carrying P around C is called the epicycle, while circle C_1 C_2 C_3 upon which moves the center C is called the deferent. It is quite clear that the path of the planet is P_1 P_2 P_3 P_4. It should be noted that the same results are obtained, that is, the same path of P results, if an eccentric circle is described about E, a point within the circle and off center, but on the line joining points E, O, P_2 P_4. P_2 is termed the apogee because it is the point at which the planet is most distant from E, and P_4 is the perigee, or the point at which the planet comes nearest E.

As can be seen from Figure 11, the course of a planet can be represented by an epicycle as well as by an eccentric circle. On the same figure it can also be seen that by postulating an epicycle the Greek astronomers very cleverly accounted for the periodic halts apparent in a planet's eastward motion among the stars, the so-called stations, which are followed by brief retrogressions, that is, the planets' motion westward among the stars and their subsequent resumption of their eastward path. The planet thus describes a loop, an event which perplexed the ancients no end, since it defied the beauty of a circular orbit. On the Copernican theory the cause of those loops is easily explained. The earth's motion is more rapid than that of an outside or superior planet, hence in passing it the line of sight from the earth will yield an illusory picture of the outer planet's motion first in a forward, then in a backward direction. This can be seen in Figure 12. How skilfully the epicycle accounts for these loops can be seen in Figure 11.

According to Ptolemy, it was the mathematician Appolonius of Perga who employed the notion of an epicycle to account for the stationary and for the retrograde motion of the superior planets. All that was required was to assume the planet to move upon an epicycle in the same direction as the deferent. By properly adjusting the radii of the epicycle and the deferent as well as the velocities of rotation of the planet and

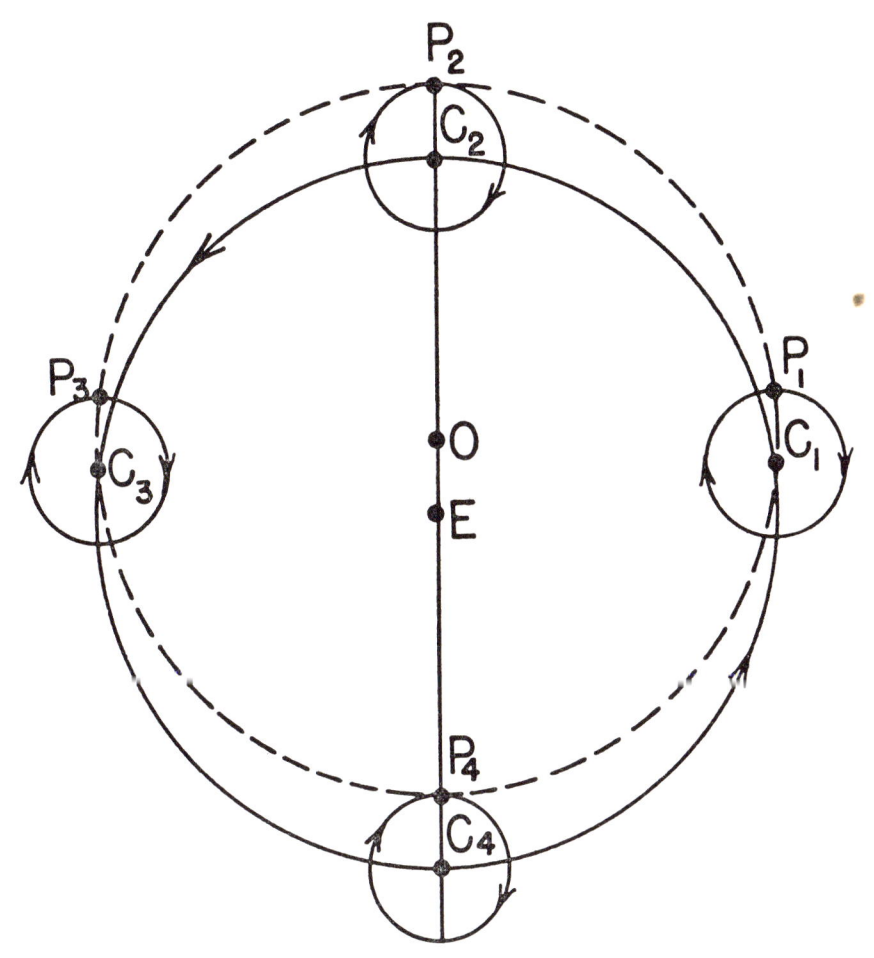

FIGURE 10. EPICYCLES AND ECCENTRICS

the center of its epicycle it is possible to obtain seemingly stationary and retrograde motions. One can also make the proper adjustments for the planet's conjunction and opposition. The cases of the inferior planets, Mercury and Venus can similarly be accounted for. The centers of their epicycles lie on a line joining the planets with the sun and earth. This takes care of the faithful proximity of these planets to the sun. Their centers on the deferent therefore make a complete circle around the earth in the same period as the sun, that is, in one year. However, the planets also move on an epicycle which accounts for their "irregularity," that is, their increasing and decreasing distance from the earth, or the sun. Generally speaking, the deferent took care of the inequality of motion in longitude, that is, unequal rate of motion along the zodiac,

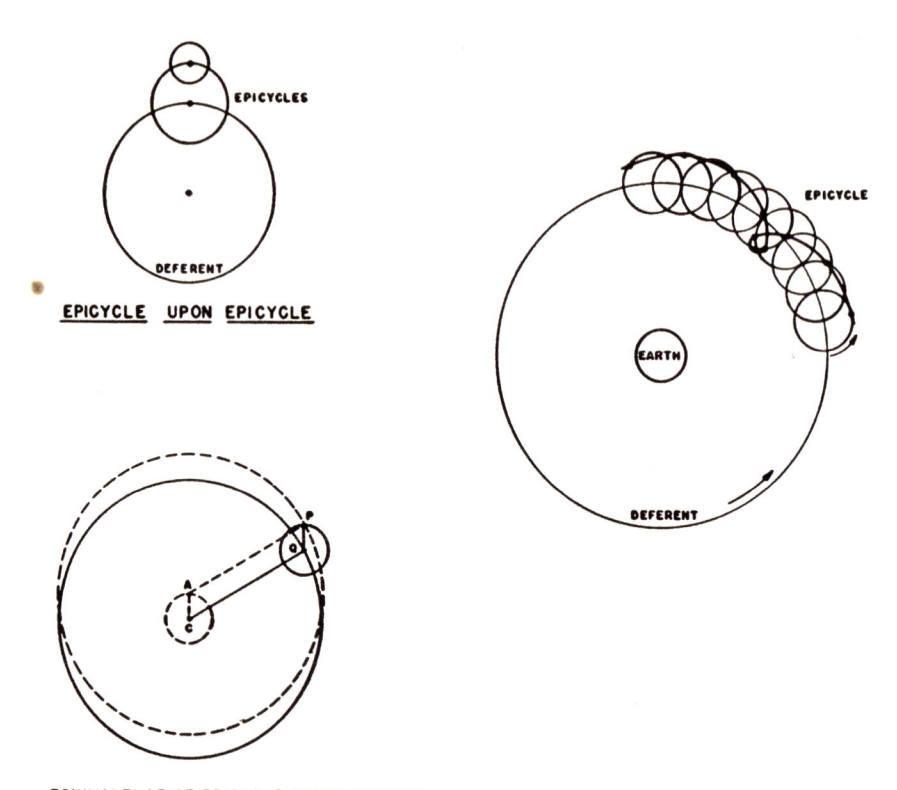

FIGURE 11. THE INGENIOUS IDEA OF THE EPICYCLE

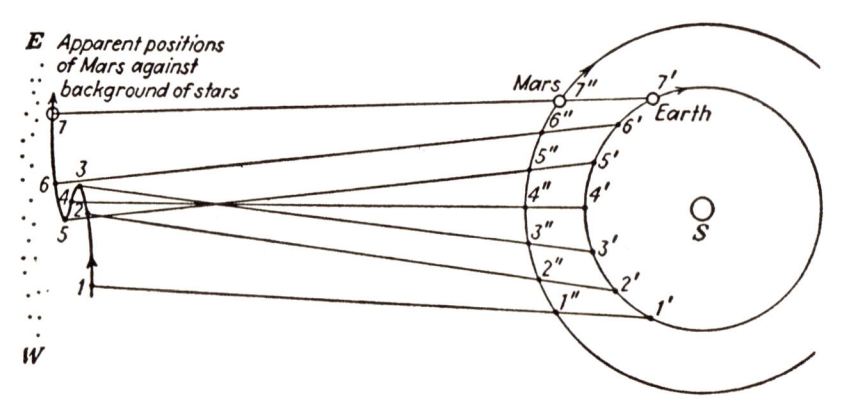

FIGURE 12. REAL AND APPARENT MOTIONS OF MARS, ACCORDING TO THE COPERNICAN SYSTEM

and the epicycle took care of the unequal motion in latitude or vertical deviations from the ecliptic. For the epicycle motion about the sun Mercury requires 88 days and Venus 225. Incidentally, epicycles can also serve to represent the motions of the sun and moon, which bodies do not display stationary and retrograde motions but are involved instead in variable velocities. (Figure 13)

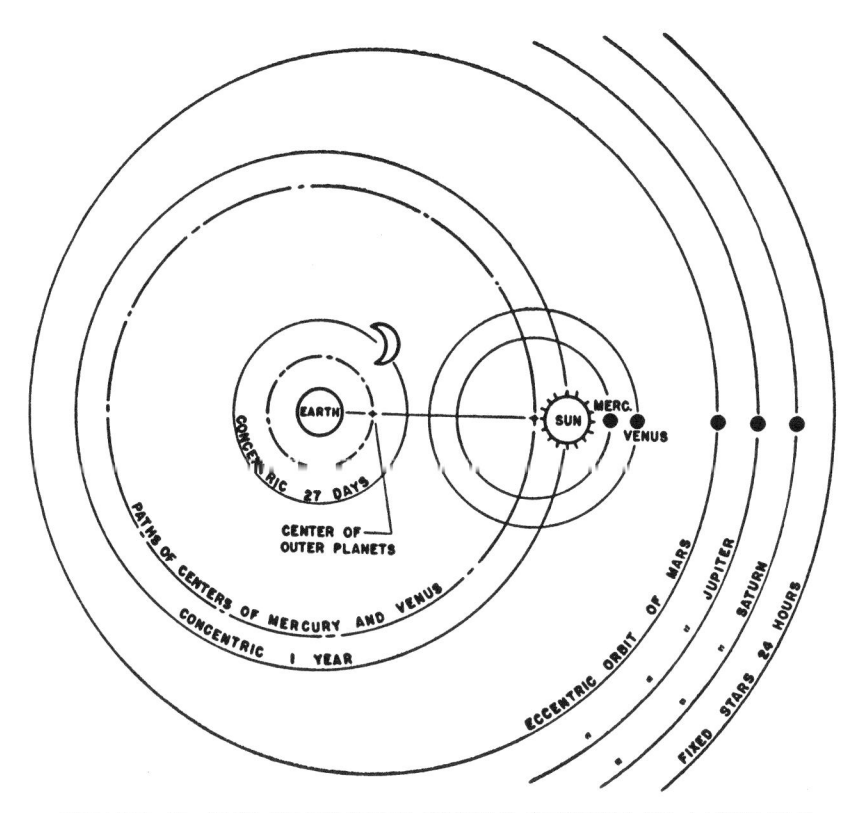

FIGURE 13. THE ECCENTRIC CIRCLE THEORY OR MOVABLE ECCENTRICS (Of Apollonius and others)

Hipparchus (ca 190–120 B.C.) "who in this (the motions of the moon) as well as in other departments of astronomy advanced science more than any other ancient astronomer before him had done" (Dreyer p. 160) made use of both eccentrics and epicycles. It was Hipparchus who discovered the precession of the equinoxes and developed plane spherical trigonometry to aid him in his calculations. He was a great and original observer and collated and organized much of the accumulated observations of Babylonia and Alexandria passed on by preceding generations. Out of these data he elaborated the theories of the sun and moon by the use of epicycles. In the case of the sun, one epicycle of proper radius, direction, and velocity with respect to the deferent, accounted for the inequality of its different rates of motion in the solar orbit, which we observe as the unequal lengths of the four seasons. The motions of the moon offered some hardships but Hipparchus successfully employed epicycles here as well, though he was aware that some lacunae persisted. The five remaining planets presented truly serious difficulties and Hipparchus failed in harmonizing their observed motions. He did however combine eccentrics and epicycles in whatever explanation he was emboldened to advance.

2. *The Cosmology of Ptolemy*

Claudius Ptolemy, the last of the constellation of brilliant and ingenious Greek cosmologists, and one whose works have come down to us in greater measure than those of other astronomers, built largely upon the teachings of Hipparchus. He prospered in Alexandria and made observations between 127 and 150 A.D. and his great work, Syntaxis which is commonly known by the Arabian term, the Almagest, remained until only about 400 years ago the sole and basic authoritative text on ancient astronomy. This work is a masterpiece in logical coordination of data and their theoretical harmonization. Like most of his predecessors, Ptolemy was not primarily concerned with a true picture of the physical mechanism of celestial operations. He and his brilliant predecessors were primarily concerned with "saving the phenomena" or in our language, explaining the facts. But theirs was an age of geometry and of abstract reasoning, and so like Heracleides, the Pythagoreans, and other schools, Ptolemy used spheres and epicycles merely to account for the perplexing facts and unite them neatly by a mathematical, i.e. geometrical device. Thus we find, for example, the great commentator on Aristotle, Simplicius, remark, as previously cited, that by assuming rotation, Heracleides "considered the phenomena accounted for." Again, another great commentator on Plato, Proclus, states: "History teaches us that by the Pythagoreans have the eccentrics and epicycles been invented as a sufficient means and the simplest of all." His comment on the schemes of Heracleides and Aristarchus is that these philosophers thus "supposed that the phenomena can be saved." (Aristarchus of Samos, Sir Thomas Heath, Oxford Press 1913, p. 254) In the same spirit Ptolemy too, invariably begins his every argument by saying, "Let us imagine a circle." In one place he explains, "I do not profess to be able thus to account for all the motions at the same time; but I shall show that each by itself is well explained by its proper hypothesis." It seems to have been generally taken for granted by the mathematical and astronomical originators, as well as teachers and commentators, that the goal is to "save the phenomena" and that all suggestions are mathematical schemes and not mechanical models.

The following summary of Ptolemy's approach is given by Dreyer: "In the beginning of his first book Ptolemy shortly recapitulates the fundamental assumptions of astronomy. The heavens is a sphere, turning round a fixed axis, as may be proved by the circular motion of the circumpolar stars and by the fact that other stars always rise and set at the same points on the horizon. The earth is a sphere, situated in the centre of the heavens; if it were not, one side of the heavens would appear nearer to us than the other and the stars would be larger there; if it were on the celestial axis but nearer to one pole, the horizon would not bisect the equator but one of its parallel circles; if the earth were outside the axis, the ecliptic would be divided unequally by the horizon. *The earth is but as a point in comparison to the heavens*, because the stars appear of the same magnitude and at the same distances inter se, no matter where the observer goes on earth. It has no motion of translation, first, because there must be some fixed point to which the motions of the others may be referred, secondly, because heavy bodies descend to the centre of the heavens, which is the centre of the earth. And if there was a motion, it would be proportionate to the great mass of earth and would leave behind animals and objects thrown into the air. This also disproves the suggestion made by some, that the earth, while immovable in space, turns around its own axis, which Ptolemy acknowledges would simplify matters very much." (Dreyer p. 192)

One of Ptolemy's main contributions lay in his improving upon Hipparchus' oversimplified representation of the complex phenomena of the moon's orbital motions. He finally reduced that body to an epicycle upon an eccentric deferent, which considerably bettered the fit to the observed data. In other respects he further complicated the scheme by introducing an equant or the distance between the earth and the imaginary center of the eccentric circle, laid off on the axis joining the points of opposition and conjunction (the line of apsides) out on the other side of the earth. Thus if the center is C and the earth is at E, then the equant $CQ = CE$.

Ptolemy postulated this new concept because he observed that there was a difference between the mean place of a planet and its observed position, and that the difference varied on different loci of the epicycle. To account for these differences on the unassailable basis of uniform motion, he assumed a varying radius "so that the centre of distances must be nearer to the earth than the centre of uniform motion." In other words, there was a center of equal motion and a center of equal distances and the two did not necessarily coincide.

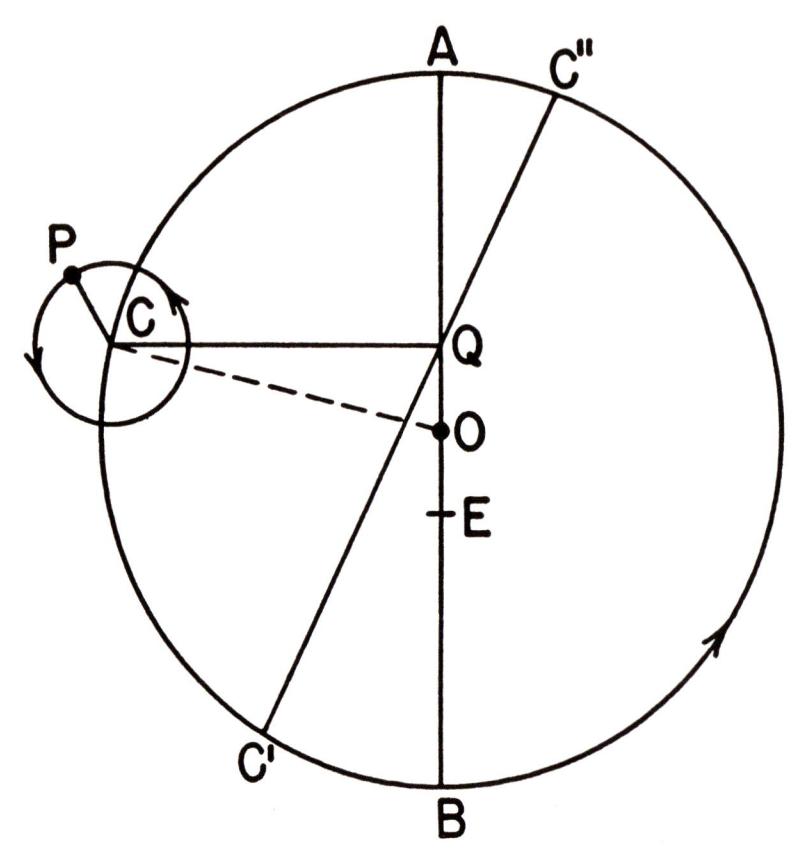

FIGURE 14. PTOLEMY'S EQUANT

Ptolemy's concept of the equant was a revolutionary departure from the firmly rooted, orthodox tenet of uniform circular motion and is well worth examining. (Figure 14) Let O be the center of the deferent on which the planet P moves on an epicycle, with its own center at C. Both C and P move in the same direction, here counterclockwise. On the diameter of the deferent, E represents the earth lying with points Q and O so that QO = OE. The equant functions much like a simple, fixed eccentric circle with O as the center and the earth at E. In the case of such an eccentric the radius OC turns through equal angles in equal times. With the equant this is not so. The point C revolves so that seen from the earth it appears to be moving in terms of angular displacement more slowly at apogee A and more rapidly at perigee B. That, in fact, was the main reason for introducing the equant. It is a scheme to account for unequal angular motion. The center of the epicycle C thus moves uniformly on the deferent, hence has the angle CQA increase uniformly.

THE CELESTIAL ORBS

This was a rather tricky and ingenious device. The simple eccentric can also be made to account for the apparent non-uniform angular motion of planets as measured from the earth, though not so well. To obtain a good fit with the observed data it was merely necessary to properly adjust the points Q, O and E, determine the desired ratio of the radii of deferent and epicycle, and choose the proper directions, velocities and inclinations of the various circles. The equant is of special interest because curiously enough it was its bold unorthodoxy that Copernicus resented and rejected. To him the sanity of the circle meant uniform circular motion, hence uniform revolution about the circle's very own center and not about foreign or artificial ones. In Ptolemy's equant the angular velocity about Q is always the same but from E it will be faster at B than at A. Ptolemy thought he did well by accounting for observed inequalities in orbital velocities of planets by this scheme which saved the notion of uniform circular motion. Not so Copernicus. He wanted uniform circular motion about the true center and not an eccentric point.

When it came to the planet Mercury, Ptolemy was even more radical. He made the point Q revolve in a small circle and even found it necessary to place it halfway between O and E, thus doing considerable juggling. But then Mercury was a difficult planet to handle and Ptolemy felt that any mathematical device which could account for the facts is welcome. Thus there were now three reference points for the circles of deferent and epicycle, the earth E, the center to one side and the equant to the other. All that to save the phenomena, explain the inequalities, such as, unequal speeds in longitude, latitude or stations and retrogressions. No one dreamed of changing the circle into an ellipse, for example, or to some other derivative form.

It must be made clear that the sanctity of the circle or sphere did not come to the ancients as a sudden bolt of inspiration. The evidence which conspired to force them into that position was overwhelming. The dome of stars overhead revolved night after night in perfect circles which anyone could observe and measure. That dome revolved about an axis, and giving due consideration to the southern constellations which began to be noted as one moved southward, the conclusion was inevitable that the stars were attached to a sphere. Says Ptolemy: "It is reasonable to assume that the first ideas on these matters came to the ancients from observations such as the following. They saw the sun, the moon and the other stars moving from east to west in circles always parallel to each other; they saw the bodies begin to rise from below, as if from the earth itself, and gradually to rise to their highest point, and then with a correspondingly gradual decline, to trace a downward course until they finally disappeared, apparently sinking into the earth. And then they saw these stars, once more, after remaining invisible for a time, make a fresh start and in rising and setting repeat the same periods of time and the same places of rising and setting with regularity and virtual similarity.

"They were, however, led to the view of a spherical heaven chiefly by the observed circular motion described about one and the same center by those stars that are always above the horizon. For this point was, necessarily, the pole of the heavenly sphere, since the stars that are nearer this pole revolve in smaller circles, whereas those further away make larger circles, proportionately to their distance, until the distance reaches that of the stars not always visible. And of these latter they observed that those stars nearer the stars that are always visible remained invisible for a shorter time while those further away remained invisible for a correspondingly longer time." (Ptolemy, Almagest, A Source Book in Greek Science by M. R. Cohen and I. E. Drabkin, N.Y. 1948. p. 122–123)

Ptolemy then considers in all fairness and objectivity the possibility of linear motion by the stars, rejecting it as unsound and unreasonable. He does the same with "the suggestion that the stars are kindled when they rise from the earth and again are snuffed out when they return to the earth." He then concludes: "In a word, if one should suppose any other form of motion of the heavens save the spherical, the distances from the earth to the heavenly bodies would necessarily be unequal, however and wherever the earth itself might be supposed to lie situate. Consequently the sizes of the stars and their distances from one another would have to appear unequal to the same observers at each return, since the distances from the observers would sometimes be greater and at other times smaller. But this is not seen to be the case. For what makes the apparent size of a heavenly body greater when it is near the horizon is not its smaller distance but the vaporous moisture surrounding the earth between our eye and the heavenly body. It is the same as when objects immersed in water appear larger and in fact the more deeply immersed the larger." (ibid p. 124) Ptolemy then continues with the argument that if there were no spherical motion "it is impossible that the instruments for measuring hours should be correct." Moreover, "just as the motion of the heavenly bodies is completely without hindrance and the smoothest of all motions, and the most easily moved of all shapes is the circular for figures and the spherical for solids, so also since the polygon with the greater number of sides is the larger of regular polygons having equal perimeters, it follows that in the case of plane figures the circle is greater than any polygon of equal perimeter, and in the case of solid figures the sphere is greater. And the heaven is greater than all other bodies."

Ptolemy has one more argument. "Various physical considerations, too, lead to the same conclusion. Thus the aether consists of finer and more homogeneous parts than does any other body. Now surfaces of bodies of homogeneous parts are themselves of homogeneous parts, and the circular surface in the case of plane figures are the only surfaces that consist of homogeneous parts. The aether not being a plane surface but a solid may therefore be inferred to be of spherical form. A similar inference may be made from the fact that nature has constructed all earthly and destructible bodies entirely of circular forms but forms not having homogeneous parts, while she has constructed the divine bodies in the aether of spherical form having homogeneous parts. For if these bodies were flat or quoit-shaped their form would not appear circular to all observers at the same time from different places of the earth. Hence it is reasonable to infer that the aether which encloses the heavenly bodies, being of the same nature, is of spherical form, and, because of its composition out of homogeneous parts, moves with uniform circular motion." (ibid, p. 125)

This kind of reasoning, so cautious, so logical, and so respectful of facts gathered by the "ancients" and critically sifted by Ptolemy and his contemporaries, and reinforced by their own observations and deductions, explains the long-enduring appeal and power of that hypothesis. One may take it almost as a generalization that when a theory maintains itself for as long a period of time as the circular hypothesis did, dominating the minds and thoughts of the scholars of seventeen centuries from Hipparchus to Copernicus, then the data and logic it rested upon must have been quite firm and sound. And the same applies to the problem of the absolute immobility of the earth, treated in the Almagest in an identical manner as the problems of the circularity of celestial orbits and the sphericity of heavenly bodies.

Consider further, to give a final example, the logic of the first paragraph of the fourth chapter of the Almagest, entitled, That also the Earth taken as a Whole is Sensibly Spherical. "Now," says Ptolemy, "that also the earth taken as a whole is sensibly spherical, we would most likely think out in this way. For again it is possible to see the sun and moon and the other stars do not rise and set at the same time for every observer on the earth, but always earlier to those who live towards the rising, and later to those living towards the setting. For we find that the phenomena of eclipses taking place at the same time especially those of the moon are not recorded at the same hours for everyone, that is relatively to equal intervals of time from noon, but we always find later hours recorded for observers towards the orient than for those towards the occident. And since the difference of the hours is found to be proportional to the distance of the places, one would reasonably suppose the surface of the earth spherical with the result that the uniformity of curvature taken as a whole always assures every part covering those following in the same way. But if the figure were any other, this would not happen as can be seen from the following considerations . . ."(Ptolemy, Mathematical Composition, [Almagest] The Classics of St. John's Program, R. Catesby Taliafero, 1938, p. 8) One can safely say that the entire Almagest is filled with this kind of lucid, scientific reasoning except for the mathematical part which, to one who likes geometry, is simply paradise. Little wonder then that after reading what scientific textbooks have to say about Ptolemy, as a rule, one loses faith in the historical fairness of modern scientists and in the hope that at least among the wise and the learned justice must prevail.

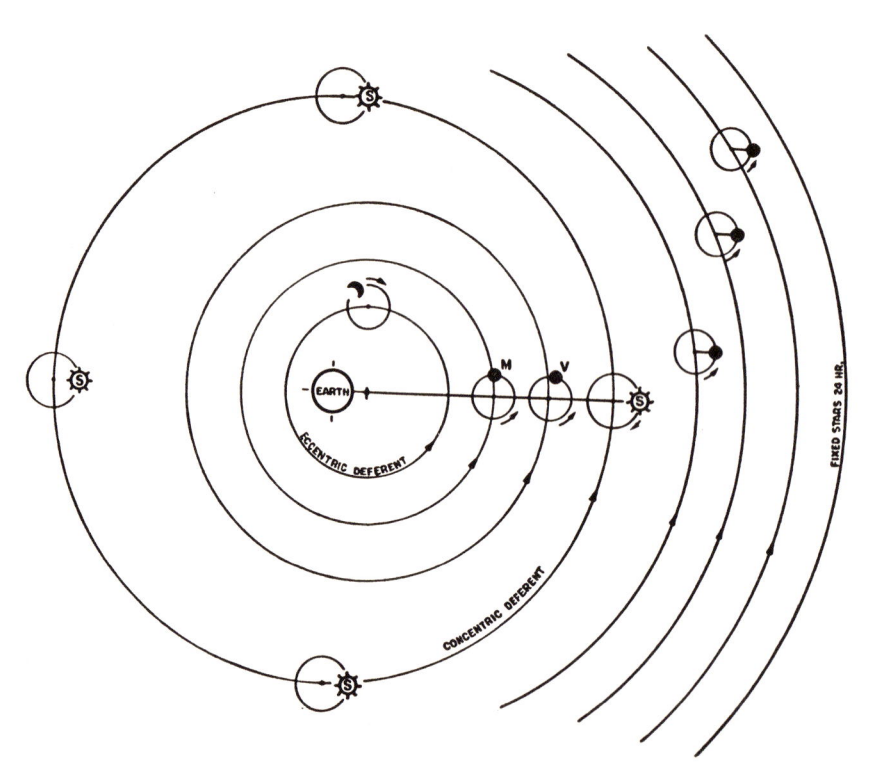

FIGURE 15. THE SCHEME OF PTOLEMY
(Modification of Hipparchus)

Thus the fundamental concept that none but circular paths suited the motions of heavenly bodies acted as a belief trap from which the brilliant genius of Greek thought sought in vain to escape. Observations were gathered with faithful perseverence, difficulties were noted and the need for taking them into account frankly declared, yet all effort was directed toward retention of the circle, with as many modifications as

THE CELESTIAL ORBS

the mind could invent—but retain it they did nonetheless. They never saw a sacred circle in the sky or on the earth. Its sanctity was a purely mental or spiritual figment. All the factual deviations and negations encountered could neither cause its overthrow nor suggest another form. The more "inequalities" or deviations from uniform, circular motion were observed, the more they fell back upon mathematical ingenuity to introduce further complexity and save the circle.

Yet Menaechmus (375–325 B.C.) described conic sections by examining cross-sections of a cone and by demonstrating that they could be either circles, ellipses, parabolas or hyperbolas. Later, Apollonius (260–200 B.C.) continued the study of this subject by working out the equations for these curves just as thoroughly as Euclid before him had elaborated the equations and properties of the circle. It is Apollonius who gave them their modern names and to students of mathematics the ellipse should have been as well known as the circle or the triangle. But it was universally accepted that only a circle was suitable to celestial bodies and the minds of all brilliant men of those days dared not, it seems, see beyond it.

Not so with the earth's position as center of the universe. Mathematical freedom of speculation dared on several occasions to advance rotation of the earth and even revolution in an orbit with the sun and the heavens stationary. Though such motions went strongly against the grain, they cropped up several times as plausible possibilities. But the concept was rejected not so much because the thought pattern of Greece was opposed to it, but as Ptolemy makes clear, the evidence of the senses, the facts and common observation, proved such a hypothesis utterly untenable. Here the enslaving force was not an invisible value, such as a circle, but observation and facts, as then seen and comprehended. It was for this reason that Ptolemy rejected diurnal motion. Orbital revolution seemed equally fantastic. Thus, he postulated epicycles for the superior planets, and was obliged to make the arms joining their centers with the planets be ever parallel to the line joining the earth and the sun. Nevertheless, he refrained from binding those planets in any way to the sun. He was similarly obliged to put the center of the epicycles of Mercury and Venus on the line joining the earth and sun, so as to force those planets to be always on one side of the sun or the other, and thus revolve with it, yet was unable to take the step which had been taken by others, Heraclides, for instance. In this manner virtually all the phenomena were most cleverly accounted for and yet within the assumption of circular motion, however complex. (Figure 15)

Chapter III

THE ANCIENT SCIENCE OF ASTROLOGY

1. *Ptolemy's Defense*

THE first authoritative statement of the Greek system of astrology in its scientific maturity has also come down to us from the pen of Claudius Ptolemy. Ptolemy was a great astronomer by all standards and the author, as we have seen, of the Almagest, that rich storehouse of all astronomical knowledge of antiquity. It was Ptolemy's genius that organized and coordinated this vast knowledge into the Ptolemaic System, a coherent and orderly scheme for integrating the known facts into a theoretical structure that served mankind quite adequately for thirteen centuries and constituted the pinnacle of the mathematical and astronomical learning of the middle ages. The same Ptolemy also wrote the Tetrabiblos or The Quadripartite Mathematical Treatise, A Mathematical Treatise in Four Books, and dealing exclusively with what the author considered as social or applied astronomy, hence what we term today astrology. "The book is a systematic treatise on astrology," says its translator, "but it should be remembered that in Ptolemy's time the two words astrologia and astronomia meant much the same thing, 'astronomy' and that he called what we mean by astrology, 'prognostication through astronomy' which indeed it was, in his estimation." Ptolemy, Tetrabiblos, F. E. Robbins, Heineman 1940 p. IX.)

From the very first sentence of the Introduction one is impressed with the evidence for this statement. "Of the means of prediction through astronomy," says Ptolemy, "O Syrus, two are the most important and valid. One, which is first, both in order and effectiveness, is that whereby we apprehend the aspects of the movements of the sun, moon and stars in relation to each other and to the earth, as they occur from time to time; the second is that in which by means of the natural character of these aspects themselves we investigate the changes which

THE ANCIENT SCIENCE OF ASTROLOGY

they bring about in that which they surround. The first of these, which has its own science, desirable in itself even though it does not attain the result given by its combination with the second, has been expounded to you as best we could in its own treatise (i.e., The Almagest) by the method of demonstration. We shall now give an account of the second and less self-sufficient method in a properly philosophical way, so that one whose aim is the truth might never compare its preceptions with the sureness of the first, unvarying science, for he ascribes to it the weakness and unpredictability of material qualities found in individual things, nor yet refrain from such investigation as is within the bounds of possibility, when it is so evident that most events of a general nature draw their causes from the enveloping heavens. But since everything that is hard to attain is easily assailed by the generality of men, and in the case of the two before-mentioned disciplines the allegations against the first could be made only by the blind, while there are specious grounds for those levelled at the second—for its difficulty in parts has made them think it completely incomprehensible, or the difficulty of escaping what is known has disparaged even its object as useless—we shall try to examine briefly the measure of both the possibility and the usefulness of such prognostication before offering detailed instruction on the subject." (ibid p. 3–5)

Here we have the frankest confession and the most perspicacious insight into the problem of the modern dichotomy of natural versus social science. The first, says Ptolemy, referring to astronomy proper, i.e., the motions of the heavenly bodies in relation to each other, is science in its simplest form. However, as such it is not so useful to man, nor so complex as the second, astrology. Like a true scientist, he admits the latter is subject to a "less self-sufficient method in a properly philosophical way" and does not yield results as clear-cut as the first, which deals with regular and unchangeable motions of celestial bodies. The second deals with material things, part and parcel of the sublunar, hence imperfect, or crude world of ours, where individuality is rampant and divergence from Plato's perfect forms, practically the rule. True, the former is surer and purer. But "one whose aim is truth," hence the lover of science, need not abandon a difficult field merely because it is difficult. He must struggle with it and bear in mind that it can never be as glamorous as the former; but it must be subjected to pioneering labors because it is part of reality, nonetheless. The common herd will find it easy to ridicule as they found it easy to ridicule modern art, psychoanalysis or relativity, or as many physicists and chemists get childish pleasures out of snubbing the social sciences. With rare tolerance, Ptolemy admits that these mockers have a show of reason on their side, and to do them justice their arguments must be met.

Only "a very few considerations would make it apparent to all, that a certain power emanating from the eternal ethereal substance is dispersed through and permeates the whole region about the earth which throughout is subject to change." This is comparable to the introductory statement of the Declaration of Independence that "we hold these truths to be self-evident, etc." This ethereal substance or as we say it, ether, changes the elements fire and air by virtue of its own motions, and these sublunar elements in turn exert an effect which changes not only fire and air but also such bodies as "earth and water and the plants and animals therein." Ptolemy then makes a few further assumptions which he obviously does not attempt to justify for the sheer reason that he assumes them to be so blatantly self-evident, since no serious student of science or nature at the time ever thought of challenging them. Among these fundamental assumptions Ptolemy enumerates the effect of the sun upon "everything on the earth, not only by the changes that accompany the seasons of the year to bring about the generation of animals, the productiveness of plants, the flowing of waters and the changes of bodies, but also by its daily revolution furnishing heat, moisture, dryness and cold in regular order and in correspondence with its position relative to the zenith." The moon, he continues, affects all things mundane "for most of them animate and inanimate, are sympathetic to her and change in company with her; the rivers increase and diminish their streams with her light, the seas turn their own tides with her rising and setting and plants and animals in whole or in some part wax and wane with her." As stars and planets signify hot, windy or snowy conditions of the air by their various positions, their effects are felt accordingly on earth. Furthermore the stars and planets are in certain relationships or aspects to each other. That situation too leads to corresponding mundane changes. Though the sun's action is constant, it is diversely modified by a waning or growing moon or by the planets in their heliacal risings or settings, thus presenting the earth with a variety of effective forces. Moreover, just as finished objects or organisms are celestially affected, the more so are things in the process of being compounded, such as growing fruit, seeds or the impregnation of animals. These facts are discerned easily enough "even by those who inquire, not by scientific means, but only by observation." Even dumb animals are aware of the causal relationships between heavenly configurations and earthly consequences. More refined observations however are often made by sailors who rely on special phases of nature to deduce predictions of importance to their trade. Not being trained observers they often err. But if it is true that knowledge is power, it is equally obvious that accurate study of celestial movements and configurations, will reveal the essential qualities of the various bodies, "and if one is capable of determining in view of all these, both scientifically and by successful conjecture, the distinctive mark of quality resulting from the combination of all the factors, what is to prevent him from being able to tell on each given occasion the characteristics of the air from the relations of the phenomena at the time, for instance, that it will be warmer or wetter? Why can he not too, with respect to an individual man, perceive the general quality of his temperament from the ambient at the time of his birth, as for instance that he is such and such in body and such and such in soul, and predict occasional events, by use of the fact that such and such an ambient is attuned to such and such a temperament and is favorable to prosperity, while another is not so attuned and conduces to injury?" Ptolemy therefore concludes that opposition to this science "on the score of impossibility has been specious but undeserved."

There have been sound reasons behind the arguments of the doubters or detractors. Many practitioners have been poorly trained or have made frequent mistakes, which is only to be expected in so difficult or "many-sided an art." This is a human frailty, not the fault of the science. Besides, many of its practitioners are in it for gain rather than truth or wisdom, and pretend to know more than the facts permit. But then the same is true for philosophy generally. Must that study be abolished because some rascals or pretenders exploit it? Ptolemy leans backwards even further and says: "Nevertheless it is clear that even though one approach astrology in the most inquiring and legitimate spirit possible, he may frequently err, not for any of the reasons stated, but because of the very nature of the thing and his own weakness in comparison with the magnitude of his profession." Science has to be in part conjectural and never absolute. Here, he says, we are dealing with conclusions of events on earth which were caused or foreshadowed by celestial configurations. From numerous such correlations the ancients deduced the science of astrology as we know it today. But circumstances in the causative set of events cannot be quite identical, nor can the earthly consequences be fully so either. Too many variables are involved and anyone who thinks he can take them all into account is deluding himself. Hence predictions cannot always be accurate. And when nativities are at stake, i.e., foretelling fates and characters of individuals from conditions at birth, then clearly the task is made most complex at best. The nature of the seed enters as a factor, and if ambient and horizon are the same, the heredity alone determines the genus of offspring, whether it be man or horse, etc. The place of birth is equally important. In different countries, hence under different cultures and races, the individual will be different "in body and soul," even if the conditions of the ambient are the same. Besides, "all the aforesaid conditions being equal, rearing and customs contribute to influence the particular way in which a life is lived." Of course, the moon is the primary factor underlying all else, since all other conditions emanate from it. Nevertheless, he is a bold man who would claim that he can master the whole picture, at this time, "from the motions of the heavenly bodies alone." Hence the science of prognostication, i.e., astrology, cannot be dismissed "for we do not discredit the art of the pilot for its many errors." On the contrary, we should "welcome what is possible" and be grateful we have advanced that far. Nor must we expect or demand too much "but rather join in the appreciation of its beauty, even in instances wherein it could not provide the full answer; and as we do not find fault with the physicians, when they examine a person, for speaking both about the sickness itself and about the patient's idiosyncrasy, so too in this case we should not object to astrologers using as a basis for calculation nationality, country, and rearing, or any other already existing accidental qualities."

Where would one find such humility and logic in the defenders of modern sciences which are in similar straits? Do the proponents of Marxist theories of value, exploitation, class struggle, revolution, dialectical materialism etc., plead with such gentleness and patience for the difficulties of their art and the complexities of their field? Proud of the era of science and progress that distinguishes us from the barbarians of old, we forget that today detractors do not survive in lands where such believers are in power and where the gentlest of dissenters are ruthlessly exterminated. Does Ptolemy anywhere employ invectives of the kind that fill the pages of Marx or Lenin or the speeches of their followers, or sympathisers?

There is one more point which Ptolemy examines in his orderly manner. Granted that "prognostication by astronomical means is possible," is astrology in any way useful or beneficial? True, astrology can go no farther than the effects of the ambient which embrace "the original endowments of faculties and activities of soul and body, occasional diseases, endurance for a long or short time, and besides, all external circumstances that have a directive and natural connection with the original gifts of nature, such as property and marriage in the case of the body and honor and dignities in that of the soul, and finally what befalls them from time to time." Many had attacked astrology on the grounds that even if all this were so, was astrology of any real value? Positively, says Ptolemy. It is good for the human spirit to know things, especially of the kind which forecast events both human and divine. It has practical value in that it helps perceive "what is fitting and expedient for the capabilities of each temperament" hence something akin to our vocational guidance. True it may not lead to "riches, fame and the like" but then, neither does philosophy, and yet we do not condemn that noble study for such foolish reasons.

Besides, is it really useless? Events which might normally "cause excessive panic and delirious joy" would have their sting allayed by "foreknowledge which accustoms and calms the soul by experience of distant events as though they were present, and prepares one to greet with calm and steadiness whatever comes. A second reason is that we should not believe that separate events attend mankind as the result of the heavenly cause as if they had been originally ordained for each person by some irrevocable divine command and destined to take place by necessity without the possibility of any other cause whatever interfering. Rather is it true that the movement of the heavenly bodies, to be sure, is eternally performed in accordance with divine, unchangeable destiny, while the change of earthly things is subject to a natural and mutable fate, and in drawing its first causes from above it is governed by chance and natural sequence." Hence knowledge of the future may, if it is uncontrollable, prepare the person psychologically for the blow. But not all events are inexorable. Some permit human interference which foresight may help parry or modify effectively. There is divine destiny but there is also mutable fate.

In addition, things happen to human beings which have nothing to do with the individual's temperament and propensities, "for example, when men perish in multitudes by conflagrations or pestilence or cataclysms, through monstrous and inescapable changes in the ambient, for the lesser cause (the particular) always yields to the greater and stronger (the general or universal); other occurrences, however, accord with the individual's own natural temperament through minor and fortuitous antipathies of the ambient." Having made the outcome of a complex situation devolve upon a scientific basis in which the stronger prevails over the weaker, Ptolemy then remarks that certain events are inescapable in so far as they are determined by the first cause. Others however can be averted or annulled by human intervention, so long as that is tempered with knowledge. There are instances in which nothing can be done, "but this is due to ignorance and not to the necessity of almighty power." This in fact is the case throughout nature. Some diseases, mishaps, inorganic events and the like can be brought under control where knowledge is available, others cannot, "for certain things, because their effective causes are numerous and powerful, are inevitable, but others for the opposite reason may be averted." A good physician has the power to avert fatal results by curing an illness or injury if his science has made adequate headway so that he can diagnose the damage and duly master it. "We must believe the physician, when he says that the sore will spread or cause putrefaction, and the miner, when he as-

ASTROLOGY AND ALCHEMY

serts that the lodestone attracts iron; just as each of these, if left to itself through ignorance of the opposing forces, will inevitably develop as its original nature compels, but neither will the sore cause spreading or putrefaction if it receives preventive treatment, nor will the lodestone attract the iron if it is rubbed with garlic (a false belief of the time); and these very deterrent measures also have their resisting power naturally and by fate; so also in the other cases, if future happenings to men are not known, or if they are known and the remedies are not applied, they will by all means follow the course of primary nature; but if they are recognized ahead of time and remedies are provided, again quite in accord with nature and fate, they either do not occur at all or are rendered less severe." Hence it is only reasonable that some people employ their foreknowledge of the seasons, "the significance of the constellations and the phases of the moon" and take proper precautions to guard against their consequences, "always contriving cooling agents against summer and the means of warmth against winter"; they also watch the fixed stars for proper breeding and sowing times, since seasons can be identified as well by the stars as the sun. Yet when it comes to extension of these very same principles to particular instances of men, their temperaments and fates, they hesitate and desist. Ptolemy regards celestial control of temperament, its ebb and flow, in the same light as he views heat and cold and their rise and fall with the seasons.

We can do something about the weather, why not about temperament? "Since it is obvious that, if we happen to have cooled ourselves against heat in general, we shall suffer less from it, similar measures can prove effective against particular forces which increase this particular temperament to a disproportionate amount of heat." True, in many instances, there is mighty little that can be done because primary causes are at work which man is not as yet in a position to control. "But I think just as with prognostication, even if it be not entirely infallible, at least its possibilities have appeared worthy of the highest regard, so too in the case of defensive practice, even though it does not furnish a remedy for everything, its authority in some instances at least, however few or unimportant, should be welcomed and prized and regarded as profitable in no ordinary sense."

Observe the Egyptians who were renowned through antiquity for their skill in medicine. They reached their high level of attainment by "uniting medicine with astronomical prediction," which they never could have attained had they accepted as axiomatic the unmodifiability of the rule of heavenly bodies. In reality, they studied the motions of the stars and planets in the sky and the ways and means of intervening in their causative process. They thus developed their "iatromathematical system or medical astrology, in order that by means of astronomy they may succeed in learning the qualities of the underlying temperatures, the events that will occur in the future because of the ambient, and their special causes, on the ground that without this knowledge any measure of aid ought for the most part to fail . . . and by means of medicine, through their knowledge of what is properly sympathetic or antipathetic in each case they proceed, as far as possible, to take precautionary measures against impending illness and to prescribe infallible treatment for existing disease."

Here then we have an intimate view of Ptolemy as teacher and scientist, struggling to defend a field of study and a mode of approach in full awareness that it required justification against weighty attacks. Astrology was his cherished science, and he was about to propound its lore and logic to the world. Yet observe his guarded manner of speech, his sound scientific reasoning. No obloquy, no invectives, no mention even of opponents' names. Instead one is confronted with a recitation of their arguments, accompanied by lucid and fair considerations, and replies in a most laudable and considered manner.

His mode of thought deserves special examination. We know how facile moderns are with such terms as far-sighted, superstitious, truly scientific, or supernatural when evaluating the work of an ancient writer or investigator. Like inveterate moralists reviewing the life story of some historical character, or like youngsters watching a movie in rapt excitement, our moderns, too, feel called upon to classify each event as good or evil, each feature as righteous or sinful. If a view agrees with current scientific theory, it is obviously scientific. If it differs, then, needless to say, it is superstitious, or permeated with supernatural rubbish.

When is Ptolemy supernatural and when is he strictly materialistic? The answer is that the question is sterile from its very inception. Ptolemy observed, thought and studied as a member of Alexandrian culture with all its beliefs and values. He regards himself as a practical and conscientious scientist who, after producing his classic in observational and mathematical astronomy is now ready to continue his task in the field of applied astronomy. He knows it is beset with difficulties but he never dreams of permitting enthusiasm for his subject in any way to fog his vision. On the contrary, he seeks out weaknesses and shortcomings and lays them on the table as an honest scientist should. He is concerned with facts and deductions, causes and generalizations, all examined in the light of reason, duly equipped with scientific humility and caution. How can we declare him to be scientific when he talks about the effect of the sun upon seasons and some human activities, and unscientific when he weighs the effect of the sun upon others? The generalization concerning the effect of the sun on earth and man was sound enough, as was also the generalization concerning the influence of the moon on tides, procreation of animals (some) and other events. That it affected as well human moods seemed obvious enough. Hence why question that both influenced or even determined human temperaments and fates? When we devise a generalization today, do we check upon each item covered by its sweep? That is precisely what a generalization aims at obviating. Hence it takes time and the advent of many new facts, ideas and interests before it is revealed that generalizations have limitations, and what these limitations are.

After acquitting himself of his initial task of meeting all current criticism of astrology in the first three brief chapters, Ptolemy sets out to outline the essence of the science of prediction through astronomy, beginning with the power of the planets. The sun heats and dries, the moon moistens and putrefies, though it has some light and heat too, Mars dries and warms, Jupiter "heats and humidifies . . . and produces fertilizing winds." Venus warms by virtue of her proximity to the sun and humidifies because of proximity to the moon, while Mercury also vacillates rapidly between drying and humidifying. Of course, this way of reproducing Ptolemy's ideas will probably be totally meaningless to those who are unfamiliar with the meanings of the terms and concepts of ancient thought. We shall encounter their notions of matter, its origin and composition in subsequent sections and on several occasions. Suffice it here to say that heat and cold to them were not the same as understood by us. Heat was energy released as well as temperature, fire and the subjective feeling of warmth, while the term moisture embraced water, softness, fluidity and similar qualities. The four basic elements of which all matter was constituted were earth, water, air and fire. These elements possessed four basic qualities namely, heat, cold, wetness and dryness in diverse combinations. Earth referred to mass and solidity, water to moisture, air to the vaporous or gaseous state and fire to heat and energy. Any substance could and usually did possess more than one element and its unique properties were the product of the interaction of the various qualities of the constituent elements. Just as we say today that some stars are in a given state of atomic forms and reactions, deduced from spectroscopic analyses, as in the case of white dwarfs or red giants, so the ancients designated the planets on a similar scale, presupposing a material condition behind their classification or description.

Planets were either beneficent or maleficent; some ruled the day and were regarded as masculine, others the night which made them feminine. Depending upon their positions with regard to the sun, hence their aspects, planets showed increasing or decreasing powers. A waxing moon was productive of moisture at first and later of heat, while upon waning she radiated dryness in her initial stages and subsequently cold.

THE ANCIENT SCIENCE OF ASTROLOGY

The fixed stars too have special powers, especially those located within the constellations of the ecliptic, the zodiac. Within each constellation the powers vary. For example, "the stars in the head of Aries (the ram) have an effect like the power of Mars and Saturn, mingled; those in the mouth like Mercury's power and moderately like Saturn's; those in the hind foot like that of Mars, and those in the tail like that of Venus." (ibid p. 47) This is not only true of all the stars in the other zodiacal constellations but also of those north and south of the ecliptic.

The seasons too are described in terms of the four qualities; spring is moist, summer hot, autumn dry and winter cold. The same is true of the four regions; east "excels in dryness because when the sun is in that region whatever has been moistened by the night then first begins to be dried"; and dry winds originate there. The southern region is hot, the west is moist "because when the sun is therein the things dried out during the day then first begin to become moistened" while the north is cold "because through our inhabited world's inclination it is too far removed from the causes of heat arising from the sun's culmination." Clearly "the knowledge of these facts is useful to enable one to form a complete judgement of temperature in individual instances." The potency of any set of stars necessarily changes with the regions in which it is situated, the directions of motion and the seasons. One must bear in mind that the zodiacal signs have properties of their own, which "arise from their kinship to the sun, moon and planets . . . absolutely and relatively to one another." Like the planets these twelve signs contain six masculine and diurnal ones while the other six are feminine and nocturnal in alternating order.

Of great significance were the aspects or the spatial relationships of the planets and signs to each other. When two bodies are from each other an angular distance of 180°, they are in opposition, and will, of course, have six signs or zodiacal constellations between them; when they are 120° apart they are said to be in trine position, when 90° apart they are in quartile and finally when 60° apart they are in sextile position. Signs which are removed equal distances from any of the two equinoctial points are either commanding or obeying. Those in which the sun abides in summer, and the days are thereby made longer, are the "commanding." Conversely, those below the equinox are the "obeying." Signs which are removed equal distances from either of the two solstices are "equal" because such signs will have days of equal length, hence also nights of equal length. They are also said to "behold" each other. In addition there are signs which can share none of the above relationships and are termed "disjunct" or "alien."

The planets also stand in some specific relationship or other and show familiarity with the various signs of the zodiac through what is called their houses. Leo, which because of its position in the ecliptic comes closest to the zenith is assigned to the sun. It is masculine. Cancer is feminine, is proximately situated and is assigned to the moon. As a result, one zodiacal semicircle was classified as solar and the other as lunar. Within each semicircle a constellation was assigned to each of the five planets as its own and placed in agreement with their position in relation to the earth. Thus each planet had two signs 180° apart and of appropriate qualities.

The zodiac can be divided into three latitudinal circles. In its center we would have the equinoctial line joining both equinoxes. North of it would be a line parallel to it and passing through the northernmost point, i.e., the summer solstice, the zone between this circle and the equinoctial forming the tropic of Cancer. The zone between the equinoctial and the southernmost point of the ecliptic, namely the winter solstice, forms the tropic of capricorn.

Since early antiquity the sequence of the signs, i.e. the constellations of the zodiac, was held to be as follows: Aries the ram, Taurus the bull, Gemini or twins, referring to the conspicuous stars Castor and Pollux, Cancer the crab, Leo the lion, Virgo the virgin, Libra the scales, Scorpio the scorpion, Sagittarius the archer, Capricornus the goat, Aquarius, the water carrier, and Pisces the fishes. They formed a circle within which were inscribed four equilateral triangles joining three signs spaced equal distances from each other, as for example, Aries, Leo, and Sagittarius or Taurus, Virgo and Capricorn. Needless to say each triangle was packed with symbols and meanings, was presided over by a planet, with a second one assisting, etc. In addition the twelve signs were arranged into three groups of four in which the first of each group or the second etc., began a triplicity which constituted another bundle of significances and intertwined meanings.

Now, when the sun passes up with the southern semicircle of the ecliptic and reaches Aries, the sign of the vernal equinox, it is making its transition to the northern semicircle. Aries is thus called his exaltation, "since there the length of the day and the heating power of his nature begin to increase." Conversely Libra, the sign of the autumnal equinox is called his depression. Saturn which is opposite to the sun has these signs reversed. "And since the moon, coming to conjunction in the exaltation of the sun, in Aries, shows her first phase and begins to increase her light, and as it were her height, in the first sign of her own triangle, Taurus, this was called her exaltation, and the diametrically opposite sign, Scorpio, her depression." Similar reasoning assigned respective exaltations and depressions to the other planets. In addition, each sign of the zodiac was divided into regions ruled by the five planets. These were the terms, and they were expressed in degrees. Had all the

THE ANCIENT SCIENCE OF ASTROLOGY

planets played equally important roles in each sign, each would have a term of 6°, since the span of each sign is 30°. They ranged however from 3° to 8° and varied in different constellations. The method of determining the term to be occupied by any planet in any of the signs was quite elaborate and gave rise to much controversy. Further units of subdivision of signs were places, equivalent to 2½° each, and degrees.

When a planet is similarly situated with respect to the sun and the moon, it is said to be in "proper face." Planets may be in their own "chariots" or "thrones" when in other positions or aspects, or may be said to "rejoice." A planet that precedes another is said to "apply" to it, while the one that follows is said to be "separated."

Book II of the Tetrabiblos deals with "procedures for dealing in detail with those matters which lie within the limits of possibility of this kind of prognostication by astronomical means, holding everywhere to the natural method of exposition." Such prediction may be of two kinds; general, relating to entire races, countries and cities, and specific, bearing on individuals. The former is "swayed by greater and more powerful causes than are particular events" and are therefore stronger, hence more easily determined than individual fates. They deal with "wars, famines, pestilences, earthquakes, deluges and the like," or meteorological events such as storms, drouths, crop failures etc.

Celestial latitude and longitude account for national characteristics. People of the southern hemisphere "have black skins and thick, wooly hair, are contracted in form and shrunken in stature, are sanguine in nature and in habits are for the most part savage because their homes are continually oppressed by heat." These are called Ethiopians. Northern peoples "who have the Bears over their heads, since they are far removed from the zodiac and the heat of the sun, are therefore cooled; but because they have a richer share of moisture, which is most nourishing and is not there exhausted by heat, they are white in complexion, straight-haired, tall and well-nourished, and somewhat cold by nature; these too are savage in their habits because their dwelling places are continually cold." These are the Scythians. Intermediate zones produce intermediate types, easterners are masculine and mathematical while the western intermediates are "feminine, softer of soul and secretive, because this region, again, is lunar for it is always in the west that the moon emerges and makes its appearance after conjunction." The customs of a country are equally determined. Just as people living near the sea become good sailors, those on plains good horsemen, so are their natures and temperaments similarly determined. The four quarters of the inhabited world have their respective governances and the study of the celestial rulers of each region and country constitute a weird combination of geography and anthropology. In so far as the triangles and triplicities of the zodiac with their ties to the planets compose quite a complex celestial map, it is easy to see how they could readily be made to account for the diversities of the earthly regions, climates and cultures. Ptolemy warms up to this subject since he is also the greatest geographer of antiquity and the author of a geography which was a classic text like his Syntaxis for nigh a thousand years.

Speaking of the eastern part of North Africa he discusses the various countries there situated such as Cyrenaica, Marmarica, Egypt, Thebes, the Oasis, Arabia and Middle Ethiopia. He discusses the celestial causes which determine why "those who live in these countries . . . are worshippers of the gods, superstitious, given to religious ceremony and fond of lamentation; they bury their dead in the earth, putting them out of sight, on account of the occidental aspect of the planets. . . . Under command they are humble, timid, penurious and long suffering, in leadership courageous and magnanimous; but they are polygamous and polyandrous and lecherous, marrying even their own sisters, (a custom among the royal families of Egypt) and the men are potent in begetting, the women in conceiving, even as the land is fertile. Furthermore many of the males are unsound and effeminate of soul and some even hold in contempt the organs of generation through the influence of the aspect of the maleficent planets in combination with Venus occidental. Of these peoples the inhabitants of Cyrenaica and Marmarica, and particularly of Lower Egypt are more closely familiar to Gemini and Mercury; on this account they are thoughtful and intelligent and facile in all things, especially in the search for wisdom and religion; they are magicians and performers of secret mysteries and in general skilled in mathematics (i.e., astrology and magic). Those who live in Thebais, the Oasis and Traglodytica are familiar to Libra and Venus; hence they are most ardent and lively of nature and live in plenty. The people of Arabia, Azania, and Middle Ethiopia are familiar to Aquarius and Saturn, for which reason they are flesh-eaters, fish-eaters and nomads, living a rough, bestial life." To complicate things further, each sign ruled over nations scattered widely over the inhabited world. This scheme was most helpful in the interpretation of eclipses where not only the sign in which it occurred mattered, but also those above the horizon at the time. Moreover the duration or time of termination of the eclipse was different for different signs, and Ptolemy devotes much time and several chapters to this topic. There is first the region affected, the period, the kind of effect, its nature and quality, all of which depend upon the disposition of the planets at the time. The colors of eclipses and comets were of course most significant.

There are next the new and full moons within the signs which mark the four crucial points of the ecliptic—Aries which then contained the vernal equinox, Cancer the summer solstice, Libra the autumn equinox and Capricorn the winter solstice. Each season of the year could thus have its weather and general fate easily forecast. Here the signs alone are of importance in that they add their share to the general prognostication. No mean task is "the investigation of weather in detail," for which beside some acute interpretation one is also obliged to observe the sun in all its phases, the moon "in its course three days before or three days after new moon, full moon and the quarters," whether it is clear, has halos, what are their colors and the clouds about them. Comets, shooting stars and rainbows also have their portents.

Book III deals with the science of individual prognostications. Here the crucial point is the starting point, which in human fate is the moment of conception. That point is not easy to determine except under ideal circumstances. In most cases one has to be satisfied with the moment of birth instead. To know the stars at conception means to "determine the special nature of body and soul, to examine the effective power of the configuration of the stars at that time. For to the seed is given once and for all at the beginning such and such qualities by the endowment of the ambient; and even though it may change as the body subsequently grows, since by natural process it mingles with itself in the process of growth only matter which is akin to itself, thus it resembles even more closely the type of its initial quality." Curiously enough after declaring how important that moment of conception is, Ptolemy proceeds to tell us how to get all the information needed from the stellar configuration at the moment of birth since that is the next best. By comparison with conception, birth is "equal or rather even more perfect in potentiality, and with reasonable propriety would the former be called the genesis of human seed and the latter the genesis of a man. . . . Accordingly one may with good reason believe that the position of the stars at the time of birth is significant of things of this sort, not however for the reason that it is causative in the full sense, but that of necessity and by nature it has potentially very similar causative power."

The fraction of the hour of birth presents great difficulties. Sun-dials are not accurate enough for the purpose, nor are clepsydrae or water clocks, operating on the same principle as hour-glasses. Only a horoscopic astrolabe, an instrument consisting of one or more graduated circles with a movable arm attached at the center, are refined enough. The significant events to ascertain are the ascension or the sign of the zodiac which rises at the moment, and the syzygy or the positions of the moon in opposition, i.e., the full moon in conjunction or the new moon preceding birth. One can then know what planets rule the sky. This analysis is referred to as the Science of Nativities or genethlialogical science. This science has several subdivisions, which deal with the fates of the parents, "with events both before and after the birth, such as the account of brothers and sisters," with happenings at birth and finally with post-natal matters. The latter embraces the entire fortune of the subject, his lot and his future. "We shall sketch each of these subjects briefly, explaining as we said before, together with the effective powers by themselves, the actual procedure of investigation; as for the nonsense on which many waste their labor and of which not even a plausible account can be given, this we shall dismiss in favor of the primary natural causes. What, however, admits of prediction we shall investigate, not by means of lots and numbers of which no reasonable explanation can be given, but merely through the science of the aspects of the stars to the places to which they have familiarity, in general terms, however, which are applicable to absolutely all cases, that we may avoid the repetition involved in the discussion of particular cases."

Ptolemy then proceeds to enumerate the relevant factors to examine and analyze, such as the mid-heaven concerning possible action, the location of the sun in order to know all about one's parents, the ruling planets in their positions, powers and aspects, whether ascendant i.e. rising at the moment or culminating, which means crossing the meridian, whether their motion is direct, that is, moving eastward slowly among the stars as does the sun once around in a year, or retrograde which is in the opposite direction as the planets do briefly every now and then. Details of these tasks occupy the rest of Book III under such headings as Of Parents, Of Brothers and Sisters, Male and Female, Twins, Length of Life, Bodily Form and Temperament, Injuries and Diseases and finally the Quality of the Soul. The fates of parents are ascertained by declaring the sun and Saturn to represent the father, and the moon and Venus the mother. Once that is done further symbolizations become relatively easy and all possible contingencies bearing on the fate of parents and the fates of other members of the family can then be deduced. Needless to say the bulk of guidance and instruction is reserved for prognostication bearing on length of life, a most lengthy and complex account, worthy of so vital a subject. The appearance and build of the "native," as the individual under examination is called, get due attention and bodily injuries and diseases come in for their respectable share, and so do the problems of the spirit, soul, mind and reason of the native. Few mental or psychic features are neglected. All are fully and meticulously accounted for through detailed and intricate divination. Abnormal psychology, including epilepsy and insanity, comes in for its share. Signs can even be read which foretell when mental ailments can be cured "by medical treatments, a diet or drugs" or not at all. The configurations of the planets foretell or rather determine sexual excesses. When "Mars or Venus are made masculine the males

THE ANCIENT SCIENCE OF ASTROLOGY 63

become addicted to natural sexual intercourse and are adulterous, insatiate, and ready on every occasion for base and lawless acts of sexual passion, while the females are lustful for unnatural congresses, cast inviting glances of the eye . . . and perform the functions of males."

Book IV is concerned with material fortune, riches and honor. "Saturn brings riches through building, or agriculture, or shipping ventures, Jupiter through fiduciary relationships, guardianships or priesthoods, Mars through military operations and command, Venus through gifts from friends or women, and Mercury through eloquence and trade." Not to be overlooked is getting rich by inheritance, when Saturn is in aspect with Jupiter which is then "in a bicorporeal sign or holds the application of the moon." Next are the omens for dignity and happiness or dependency or insecurity. Mercury "makes his subjects scribes, men of business, calculators, teachers, merchants, bankers, soothsayers, astrologers, sacrifices, and in general those who perform their functions by means of documents, interpretation and giving and taking." Each planet governs or indicates a similar bundle of occupations and callings. Saturn produces a sorry lot of professions such as "murderers, sneak-thieves, burglars, pirates, cattle-thieves, villains. If Jupiter testifies they produce men-at-arms, duellists, energetic, clever persons, busybodies, who meddle in others' affairs and thereby gain their living." All the details are cited on events leading to marriage, and are not to be outdone by any of the other elaborate discussions. Children, friends and enemies are fully looked into and so are the native's chances for foreign travel which is deemed sufficiently important to earn a special section. The work terminates with the manner of prognosticating the native's mode of death.

By way of conclusion the author warns that general destinies take precedence over special cases which principle must be carefully borne in mind when particular fates are investigated. Cultural, racial and natural features are not to be overlooked or confused since they are essential backdrops for individual horoscopes.

The age of the native is most revelant to any predicted event. At this point Ptolemy develops the theory that the ages of men are seven in number and are ruled by the seven planets. Also one must not permit evil connotations in one corner of the sky or one aspect of it, influence the other. "One may, for example, lose a relative and receive an inheritance, or at once be prostrated by illness and gain some dignity and promotion" etc. All in all, the rules laid down must be used wisely and with skill on the part of the astrologer.

Ptolemy's work is not only the culmination of organized astrological thought in Greece but marks the completion of the battle against the initial opposition to astrology. There had been strong opponents of astrology in Greece, centuries before Ptolemy, as well as in later Rome. Yet, as Lynn Thorndike was the first to demonstrate, "we somehow do not find their assault upon astrology especially impressive or satisfactory." (Thorndike, Lynn. The Place of Magic in the Intellectual History of Europe. Columbia Univ. Press 1905 p. 89)

2. Initial Opposition

From its very moment of birth astrology met with opposition. The pioneering sourcebook of Greek astrology was a work by two probably mythological authorities, Nechepso, a king of Egypt and Petosiris, a priest. The style of the book is prophetic and revelational. Its authorities are Hermes and Asclepios, the patron saints of alchemy, wisdom and medicine. It originated not later than the second century B.C. and constitutes the foundation of Greek astrology, superseded only by Ptolemy's Tetrabiblos. And it was in the same century that the first attacks upon astrology were recorded. "The brilliant representative of the new academy, Carneades, employed all the tricks of his feared dialectics as ardently against the evidence for the existence of God as against the possibility of astrology." (Sternglaube und Sterndeutung, by F. Boll and C. Bezold. Berlin 1931 p. 24) His arguments were as sound and sensible and as rational as any of the later attacks. Yet, astrology managed not only to parry all their darts but vanquish them decisively and emerge with flying colors. Arguments involving the extent of sympathy (i.e. interaction) between celestial bodies and earthly events, arguments bearing on fate, chance and free will were quite relevant and did not rightly deserve blanket dismissal. The argument that determinism, which is implicit in the absolute rule of the stars, necessarily involves the inexorable rule of fate and therefore renders useless virtue, responsibility and ethical goals, was a potent reproach against astrology and was avidly brandished by moralists, politicians and honest critics. But astrologers readily countered this challenge by saying that fate may have its decrees but free will may become master nonetheless, and overpower it. "The wise man rules the stars" was already the slogan of these early defenders of astrology, and was piously reiterated later by Ptolemy and his successors. To believers in the astrological faith the fates decreed by the stars were a product of natural relationships and natural law. Any man falling into deep water should surely drown in consequence of the relative densities of flesh and water. But man may learn to swim and thus defy or modify this law of nature. Knowledge is power and a natural course may thus be altered and controlled. Besides, as we have seen in Ptolemy, foreknowledge prepares the mind for the inevitable, even when control is impossible. That in itself is of great value.

But other arguments were not so easily dismissed, though dismissed they were in the end and with a fair display of logic. The spheres of the heavens are vast and extremely remote. Hence their motion is most rapid to be completed in twenty-four hours. How can one nowadays, ran the argument of the opposition, with the clumsy timepieces available, namely water clocks, determine the exact moment of rise of the ecliptic at birth, since conception is so inaccurate? Besides how is one to decide upon the exact moment of the birth of a foetus? Also, three creatures born at the same instant in the same community may have widely divergent fates; one may become a proud king, the second a miserable beggar and the third a plain beast of burden, say a donkey. Conversely individuals of diverse times of birth may meet the same fates in battle or on sinking ships. As Carneades put it, can one assert that all the heroes of Thermopylae or Salamis were born at the same moment, under the same stars? How can astrologers have reliable evidence for their statements when it takes the constellations thousands of years to return to identical positions? Reference is here made to the precession of the equinoxes which completes its period in about 26000 years. But then the Chaldeans were credited to have pursued their science for anywhere between 490,000 and 720,000 years.

For a while Carneades held the field and the stoic standard-bearer Panaitios gave ground and rejected both divination and astrology which were at first so dear to the stoic philosophy. But this defection was short-lived. Posidonius and others reverted to type and astrology gained strength year after year. Against a few skeptics it could muster many authorities and at the time of the founding of the Empire with Julius and Augustus Caesar, the belief in astrology was well nigh universal, among the ignorant as well as among the learned. Figulus, Varro, Tacitus and a host of other writers mirror its great strength. It permeates religion and philosophy, the decorative arts as well as science, and governs the individual's fears and hopes. In a word, it became part and parcel of the beliefs of the time, overcoming differences in language, climate and politics, as much as did the theories of evolution, psychoanalysis, electricity and movies act similarly in our times.

That the world of antiquity accepted the fundamental principles of astrology goes without saying. Galen, the father of experimental physiology and the highest authority on experimental biology and medicine during the middle ages, is the author of a treatise entitled Prognostication of Disease by Astrology. This advances the widespread notions of astrological medicine. A physician ought to know and make use of astrology. The moon's stay in each sign of the zodiac and its relation to the other planets has definite significance for the health and disease of the individual and can serve for prognosticating the nature of illnesses and afflictions besetting man, their courses and effects. In another treatise entitled Critical Days, Galen continues to expound his astrological beliefs not "by reason or dogma, lest sophists befog the plain facts, but solely, we are told, upon the basis of clear experience." (Lynn Thorndike, History of Magic and Experimental Science, Columbia Univ. Press vol. 1 p. 179). He gives the same argument as Ptolemy that the moon surpasses other planets in governing the earth because of its proximity. The phases are, of course, of salient potency. They produce changes in the air, thus governing conceptions and birth and "all beginnings of action." Galen runs through the whole gamut of astrological lore in the usual technical detail. But Galen strongly condemns the Pythagorean theory that critical days are significant in medicine by virtue of their ordinal positions. He ridicules the prevailing idea that odd numbers are masculine and even ones feminine, or the significance of the number seven occurring as it does in the Pleiades, the Bears, the gates of Thebes or deltas of the Nile, all of which number seven. To combat the superstitions about the number seven he strains his astronomical knowledge to prove that the periods of the moon's quarters are not quite seven days each.

Pliny makes short shrift of astrology at the very beginning of his Natural History which is an illuminating and admirable account of the science of Rome during the first century A.D. as reported by a great scholar, a keen observer and a rich personality. The stars, he says, "are attached to the firmament, not assigned to each of us in the way in which the vulgar believe, and dealt out to mortals with a degree of radiance proportionate to the lot of each, the brightest stars to the rich, the smaller ones to the poor, the dim to those who are worn out; they do not each rise with their own human being, nor indicate by their fall that someone's life is being extinguished. There is no such close alliance between us and the sky that the radiance of the stars there also shares our fate of mortality. When the stars are believed to fall, what happens is that owing to their being overfed with a draught of liquid they give back the surplus with a fiery flash, just as with us also we see this occur with a stream of oil when lamps are lit. But the heavenly bodies have a nature that is eternal—they interweave the world and are blended with its weft; yet their potency has a powerful influence in the earth." (Pliny —Natural History, Loeb Classical Library 1946, Bk II ch. VI p. 189) Elsewhere Pliny also shows his freedom from tradition by ridiculing "belief in gods without number" and their anthropomorphic characterizations. He rejects the "warnings drawn from lightning, the forecasts made by oracles, the prophecies of augurs, and even inconsiderable trifles—a sneeze, a stumble—counted as omens."

On the other hand Pliny's attitude to knowledge is deepfelt and earnest. Consider what he has to say about the moon. "But the wonder of everyone is vanquished by the last star, the one most familiar to the earth, and devised by nature to serve as a remedy for the shadows of darkness—the moon. By the riddle of her transformations she has reached the wits of observers, who are ashamed that the star which is nearest should be the one about which we know least—always waxing or waning, and now curved into the horns of a sickle, now just halved in size, now rounded into a circle; spotted and then suddenly shining clear; vast and full-orbed, and then all of a sudden not there at all; at one time shining all night and at another rising late and for a part of the day augmenting the light of the sun, eclipsed and nevertheless visible during the eclipse, invisible at the end of the month when she is not believed to be in trouble; again at one time low down and at another up aloft, and not even this in a uniform way, but sometimes raised to the sky and sometimes touching the mountain-tops, now borne up to the North and now carried to the South. The first human being to observe these facts about her was Endymion—which accounts for the traditional story of his love for her. We forsooth feel no gratitude toward those whose assiduous toil has given us illumination on the subject of this luminary, while owing to a curious disease of the human mind we are pleased to enshrine in history records of bloodshed and slaughter, so that persons ignorant of the facts of the world may be acquainted with the crimes of mankind." The concluding comments are of special interest, coming as they do from a Roman general and dignitary. The entire passage indicates, however, Pliny's regard for facts and science.

Yet Pliny declares that "Saturn is of a cold and frozen nature," eclipses are "the most marvellous and indeed portentous occurrence in the whole of our observation of nature," Jupiter "is rendered healthy," Venus exerts "an influence which is the cause of the birth of all things upon earth; at both of its risings it scatters a genital dew with which it not only fills the conceptive organs of the earth but also stimulates those of all animals." The stars or planets are signs of weather to come and influence events on earth. Democritus used his knowledge of astronomy to corner the olive market and put to shame business people who had no use for natural philosophy. But Pliny condemns belief in horoscopes or predictions by the stars of social events. He is critical also of astrological medicine and generally adheres to these beliefs except for occasional backsliding into the astrological mores of the times.

Regarding astrology Pliny is probably the most cautious of the writers of antiquity. Intermediate between Pliny and Ptolemy stands Seneca, author of Natural Questions or Problems of Nature. He is critical of many notions and customs of the time, such as incantations, instances of what we would today call supernatural beliefs, which he terms the vice and luxury of the Romans, prevailing lack of interest in science, and many practices he labels superstitions. Yet he accepts divination in "well-nigh all its branches."

Seneca's work, Quaestiones Naturales, deals almost exclusively with problems of the physical world namely "astrology, meteorology and geography," unlike Pliny's work which is more in the nature of an encyclopedia. Seneca, who styles himself a stoic, ridicules many superstitions of his time. The belief that "this frame of things is but a fortuitous concourse of atoms, the sport of chance . . . tossed about at random in the confusion of thunder, cloud and storm, and the other forces by which the earth and its purlieus are haunted" is labeled by him "the madness of vulgar error; even the philosophers are tainted by it." (Seneca, Physical Science, edited by John Clarke, Macmillan 1910 p. 7) He labels the theories of the origin of "torch and beam meteors" as proposed by Epigenes, "a tissue of falsehoods" and disagrees with Aristotle on numerous occasions. "To suppose either that actual stars fall or leap across the sky, or that some portion of them is taken away or pared off, is sheer folly" is his way of refuting beliefs. He loves evidence, and he tests as many claims and assumptions as he thinks require testing. His solemn warning runs in these words: "Better examine the cause of the phenomenon itself than form surmises as to why Aristotle has applied the name She-Goat to a ball of fire." (p. 9)

Yet Seneca accepts omens as if he were unaware of the fact that they had ever been challenged. That very same ball of fire named She-Goat by Aristotle "appeared when Paulus was engaged in the war against Perseus. . . . We saw a similar portent about the time of the death of the late Emperor Augustus. We again saw one when Sejanus was executed. A warning of the same kind preceded the death of Germanicus." He raises the question whether man should be conceited enough to believe "that the gods send out previous intimation of the death of great men? Do you imagine that anything on earth is so great that the Universe should perceive its loss?" He asserts however it is the current belief "that fires of the class referred to are produced by violent friction of the atmosphere." Shooting stars are signs of storms and so are stars which occasionally settle on the sails of ships. "History has put on record that on the day of the late Emperor Augustus' entrance into Rome on his return from Appolonia, a parti-colored circle, such as is wont to be seen in a rainbow, appeared round the sun. The Greeks call it a halo."

Seneca was an avowed believer in omens. In discussing the causes and nature of lightning he comments that "Lightning portends the future too. Nor do the signs it gives refer to only one or two events. Often a complete series of fate's succeeding decrees is intimated, with proof too

THE ANCIENT SCIENCE OF ASTROLOGY

plain to demonstration far more distinct than if it were recorded in writing." (p. 79) Lightning is something special in the world of omens. "Anything threatened by unfavorable entrails or inauspicious birds will be cancelled by favorable lightning." He argues against the belief of the Tuscans that these things happen for the sole purpose of conveying tidings to man. "Just in the same way as birds give favorable omens, though they are not moved on their flight for the express purpose of meeting us God moves them too, it is urged. You imagine He has so little to do that He can attend to trifles of this sort, if you will have Him arrange visions for one, entrails of victims for another." These things, he admits are directed by divine agency but not with such simple directness. On the contrary. "Everything that happens is a sign of something that is going to happen. . . . An event that belongs to a series thereby becomes capable of being predicted." Only our ignorance prevents us from deciphering the meanings of most events. He views the world as a vast organism in which one event is a sign of others functionally interlinked with it, just as a headache is a sign of illness or a smile of gratification or happiness.

The stars are divine and worthy of worship. "The Chaldeans confined their observation to the five planets. But do you suppose that the influence of so many thousands of other bright stars is nought? The essential error of those who pretend to skill in casting the horoscope lies in limiting our destinies to the influence of a few of the stars, while all that float above us in the heavens claim some share in us. Perchance the lower stars exert their force on us more directly, and the same may be true of the stars that by reason of their more frequent movements turn their view upon man in a different way from that in which it is turned upon other living creatures." (p. 81) And lest in our age of ignorance and prejudice we take the trodden path of our culture and conclude that Seneca no doubt knew no science or was just the usual old fogey of antiquity, one should only read his discussion of the rainbow or floods and clouds to realize one's error. But such a possibility is far off since his books are read even less avidly than were Galileo's by the Aristotelians in his day.

There were a few attacks upon astrology even after Carneades. Cicero, just prior to the formation of the empire, in his De Divinatione conducts a debate between himself and his brother on the merits or futility of divination. It is all right to make predictions on the basis of scientifically attained knowledge, and such foreknowledge is not divination. "For those things which can be perceived beforehand either by art or reason or experience or conjecture you regard as not the affair of diviners but of scientists." The usual methods of divination, claims Cicero, are neither reasonable nor scientific. Experts and their methods disagree; the sympathies or connections between events which they postulate are imaginary; dreams signify nothing; some divinations require unnatural occurrences. "In your effort to prove soothsaying true you utterly pervert physiology," as in believing that a heart can vanish from the victim. "For there will be something which either springs from nothing or suddenly vanishes into nothingness. What scientist ever said that? The soothsayers say so? Are they then, do you think, to be trusted rather than scientists?" Besides, it does one no good to know the inevitable. (Cicero, ed. H. M. Poteat Univ. of Chicago Press 1950. pp 338–462.)

Cicero's attack on divination generally was based on appeal to common sense. How can the shape of a fat bull's liver or heart have any connection with divine power which ultimately is the cause of all things? Daily experience and observation speak against such a causal connection. Divination simply does not make sense in the light of science.

Cicero also attacks in the same vein the pretensions of astrology. The influence of stars upon human fates cannot be real because the spaces separating the earth from the heavens are so vast. Some claim the stars only determine aptitude and vocation but Cicero doubts even that, to say nothing of horoscopes. Astrologers claim, mocks Cicero, that all men born at the same moment are of the same character regardless of diverse aspects of the sky in different regions. That, as we know, cannot be regarded as a valid argument since most astrological authorities took care of this point by postulating regional constellations and powers. In fact it was from such evidence as the cold, hard and cruel character of the Northern races and the hot tempered South that astrologers deduced their notions concerning the effect of regional constellations on races or nations.

Cicero reiterates old arguments when he asks whether all the men who perished at Cannae could have been born under the same stars, or when he states that there must have been other men born simultaneously with Homer and yet remained unknown and ungifted. He cites the oft-repeated argument about twins. Some had identical fates and temperaments though born hours apart, others had different characters and futures though born as close to each other as possible.

To the above cited arguments the astrologers had stock answers. In the case of identical twins born apart it was clear, they said, that a time interval was inevitable, and the ensuing similarity was conditioned by the fact that their fates were stamped on the foetus or egg at the moment of conception, which obviously took place simultaneously. If their fates were different, then catastrophic events intervened, which were under the influence of some specially superimposed star or celestial event. This was also the stock answer to the argument of the dead at Thermopylae and Cannae. The fates of men are stamped by the stars at conception or birth, not by magic but by the natural reaction between the earth and the heavens. Those fates can be averted or modified by planned action, or by accidents, themselves effected by special causes issuing from some appropriate corner of the heavens. For instance, argued the astrologers, a sick individual goes to a doctor to be treated. After due treatment and some visits to the office the physician declares him cured. Should this sound individual then fall or throw himself under a chariot and die, he will not thereby contradict or mock the doctor's prognosis. That remains right, if so it was when uttered, though an accident intervened. Similarly, the stars' prognosis is right and unalterable, though an accident may occur. And these are due to other stars.

Now, in the case of twins who were different or had diverse fates, clearly their natures could have been stamped upon them at birth. The stars revolve 15° an hour which is 15 minutes of arc in one minute, a significant angular distance which the astrologers' instruments are too crude to notice. With time and progress this deficiency will be overcome.

The astrologers had also met the Homer argument as well. They insisted that no supernatural aid need be invoked here. If parents are different, and it is they who contribute seed, surely the product must be different. The stars can only act on the given seed. Though born at the very same moment different individuals must have evolved from different eggs. The astrologers also suggested that if man's fate is fashioned by the stars, the fates of animals and the natures of inanimate things are also determined by the heavens. Such a conclusion seemed to Cicero too foolish to debate. Yet there is evidence in his other writings, that sceptic though he was toward horoscopes and prognostications, Cicero never really challenged the basic influence of stars and planets upon man, and even accepted the mystic power of numbers, though his attack upon divination and astrology was reasonable and bold.

Favorinus was another challenger. To him all prognostication was the invention of charlatans and marvel-mongers. Extrapolation from the effect of the moon on tides to that of other planets on man was unsound and unjustified. The data of the Chaldean astrologers are not extensive enough and are applicable besides to their own limited region. Favorinus, like Cicero, seems unaware of the fact that the astrologers had made allowances for regional and national constellations. There are many invisible stars, continues Favorinus, acting on the world and these cannot be taken into account. Hence astrological conclusions are unreliable. He, too, cites the famous argument from twins and points out that the stars at conception are not the same as those at birth. If time at birth is a factor then, he claims, the measurements are not exact enough, considering the instruments available. To which, of course, Ptolemy replied—Is the science to be condemned because it is in its embryonic stages? Man, contends Favorinus, should not meddle with the future. It is unnatural that the stars determine external events, and intolerable that they determine acts of people, which stem from the will and spirit. Astrologers predict big things but are incapable of foreseeing small events. And do the stars also control the fates of little animals? Anyway, why be limited to the detailed events of the lives of puny, insignificant human beings, worthless creatures in the vastness of nature?

Another writer against astrology was Sextus Empiricus. Many of his arguments had been cited before, such as that many men born under any stars may die at one and the same moment (the heroes of Thermopylae and Salamis again), or vice versa, many men born at the same time have different fates, namely the argument of Homer, the halfwit and the ass we have already encountered. This, as we also saw, has been parried with the wholly logical argument that the constant effect of the stars fashions different matter in diverse yet predetermined ways. His main point seems to be that even if one grants that the stars exert an influence upon human fates, such influences cannot be accurately measured since not only are the moments of conception and birth hard to determine, which indeed they are, but also the precise moment when a planet leaves one zodiacal sign and enters another. Dials and water-clocks are not sufficiently exact or reliable. Observers stationed at different latitudes and longitudes would arrive at wholly different conclusions. Even the moment of sunset cannot be accurately determined due to reflection and refraction acting on luminaries near the horizon.

So much for the opposition. The fact that there was such a questioning attitude, such a rational challenge in an atmosphere thick with acceptance and faith in magic and astrology, is in itself of interest. It shows that the human mind never really submits fully, and the questioning attitude is never dormant. On the contrary, from the very defenders of astrology or magic we learn that basic acceptance of a principle or a belief pattern does not preclude violent criticism of aspects of it which to us seem inseparable from the whole, or that belief in one form of superstition necessarily forebodes lack of sound criticism of another.

3. *Christian Rejection*

The real attack upon astrology, directed also against magic or science in general, was launched by Christianity after its victory over paganism in Rome. The reasons are quite understandable. Christianity brought

THE ANCIENT SCIENCE OF ASTROLOGY

with it new possessions and a new faith, namely that of social justice, the nobility of love of man, kindness, self-effacement, love of God, the insignificance of earthly life and the imminent return of Christ. Science, or rather, awareness and knowledge of the material world which spelled power over nature, the only kind known hence magical power, lost the attraction it had held for the Greeks and Romans and sank into oblivion. Only one thing mattered, love of God and man, the millennium, the kingdom of heaven. Why worry about puny things in this vale of tears when there was glory and eternity in the offing after death?

Christian opposition to science, magic and astrology was, however, slow in developing. Early patristic writers still betray the heritage of the impact of science on Greek thought and speak with utter respect of magic and astrology. For example, in his analysis of the patristic literature such as the Recognitions, Lynn Thorndike points out that "astrology is respectfully described as the science of mathesis" and astrologers as mathematici i.e. magicians and numerologists. Astrology is not viewed as contrary to religion but an aid in its attainment. The patriarch Abraham "being an astrologer, was able from the rational system of the stars to recognize the Creator, while all other men were in error, and understood that all things are regulated by His Providence." (L. Thorndike, Hist. of Magic & Exp. Sci. vol. 1, p. 411) The twelve apostles were called the twelve months of Christ, and astrological symbolism and creeds inject themselves everywhere, while complete freedom of will is repeatedly conceded. Sufferance of astrology draws the line at the claim attributed to some astrologers that the world is run by fortuitous chance, and one's particular fate by the horoscope. Genethlialogy, or the belief in complete stellar determinism is rejected, and free will as well as divine providence are defended. The hero of famous myths and legends of that era is Simon Magus, a great scholar, sage and master of magic. As usual with stories of magicians, Simon is pictured as learned in astrology, but he also comes close every now and then to deceit and even murder. Learning is wonderful and even awesome, but much to be feared on occasion, since it wields vast power and can be exploited for selfish and evil purposes.

In another patristic work, The Confessions of Cyprian, we note, as it were, a second phase in the beliefs of the time. Simon Magus dies an unrepentant magician. Cyprian was a great scholar of nature, divination, astrology and magic and a pagan sage who studied in Greece, Egypt and Chaldea, thus acquiring all the learning of the time. He was a great priest, healer and magician famed all over the world. But one day a young man asked his assistance as practitioner in magic in winning a maiden who had rebuffed him. The young lady happened to be a Christian who was determined to offer her virginity to Christ. All Cyprian's magic and learning proved futile against her. She defied Cyprian's plagues and marvels with the mere sign of the cross. Cyprian's devil was balked and defeated at each turn by superior tricks just as the magic of the Egyptians was beaten by Moses, and Cyprian burned his books of magic and became a Christian.

Strange that while Galen speaks so disparagingly of Moses and Christ because they were believers or even practitioners of magic, the early Christian writers had by the third century A.D. been launched well on their way in a bitter fight against magic in all its forms. This soon came to include astrology as well. Origen attacks magic but is easy on astrology. Tertullian, on the other hand, definitely classifies astrology with magic. "Astrology," he says, "nowadays, forsooth, treats of Christ; it is the science of the stars of Christ, not of Saturn and Mars." Astrology was a legitimate science until Christ was born. After that great event all curiosities about nativities or interest in them must cease. "For since the gospel you will never find sophist or Chaldean or enchanter or diviner or magician who has not been manifestly punished." It is a good thing, says Tertullian, that "mathematici" or astrologers "are forbidden to enter Rome or Italy," because they used to be consulted in regard to the life of the Emperor. In this attitude toward astrology he is joined by Lactantius of Gaul who lived a hundred years later and who also lumped astrology with magic and condemned them both alike. Astrology is also discredited by Hippolytus, though, according to Thorndike, he merely employs the arguments of Sextus Empiricus, the sceptic. A treatise written in 382 A.D. in Constantinople by Gregory of Nyssa entitled Against Fate, marks a serious and lengthy attack on astrology which is presented as a pagan belief. St. John Chrysostom labors hard and devoutly to explain away the story of the three magi who saw Christ's horoscope in the sky and came to Bethlehem as a result. This passage in the gospel according to Matthew is no admission of astrological principles. The three Magi referred to Christ as king of the Jews, which proves their ignorance anyhow, and in addition the star of Bethlehem was no real star. "Some invisible virtue put on the form of a star." Besides, God desired to show the Jews that while they rejected prophet after prophet, the noble scholars of the east were impressed merely by the sign of a star and thus followed God's command. The story of the star proved a sore point with the Christian writers of the period and could not, in fact, be successfully brushed aside.

There were, on the other hand, patristic writers like Basil (329–379 A.D.) author of Hexaemeron, which is a series of sermons preached apparently during early morning hours to artisans on their way to work and evenings while his audience was on its way home. Basil knew Greek science, but he ardently defends the Bible. When he discusses the biblical account of creation and admits the contradictory views on the subject by Greek philosophy and science, he is somewhat bewildered. He finally declares that the Scriptures cannot be wrong, evidence or no evidence. "Upon the essence of the heavens we are contented with what Isaiah says. . . . In the same way, as concerns the earth, let us resolve not to torment ourselves by trying to find out its essence. . . . At all events let us prefer the simplicity of faith to the demonstrations of reason." Yet Basil knows Greek science quite well and follows it dutifully when he sees no conflict. Otherwise the literal acceptance of all major or casual references in the Bible constitutes his immutable faith. Belief in magical marvels, spontaneous generation, the myths of birds or cures, all are calmly accepted as part and parcel of the science of the time, except when some concept here or there or some detail happens to clash with his faith. Astrology he condemns, particularly horoscopes. Free will, he declares, must not be endangered by any belief, since it is essential to the Christian faith. He admits, however, that "the variations of the moon do not take place without exerting great influence upon the organization of animals and of all living things." The moon, he declares, makes "all nature participate in her changes."

It is in the writings of St. Augustine (354–430 A.D.) that Christian opposition to astrology and incidentally also magic, appears at its best. He devotes ten chapters of the Fifth Book of the City of God to a refutation of astrology but entirely on religious grounds. "But those that hold that the stars do manage our action, or our passions, good or ill, without God's appointment, are to be silenced and not to be heard, be they of the true religion or be they bondslaves to idolatry of what sort soever; for what does this opinion do but flatly exclude all deity. . . . And what part has God left him in thus disposing of human affairs, if they be swayed by a necessity from the stars, whereas He is Lord of stars and men?" (St. Augustine, The City of God, Everyman's Library vol. 1, p. 143–4, 1945) It would be understandable or tolerable if astrologers only claimed that the stars were "signs, not causes of such effects." But, to begin with, many astrologers talk as if the stars were really causes. Besides, how about twins? And here St. Augustine starts reiterating all the arguments which had been cited again and again in the preceding eight or nine centuries. Many sets of twins born only a brief time interval apart, must have been conceived at the same moment, yet have more diverse fates than two strangers. On the other hand, according to Cicero, Hippocrates, "that excellent physician, wrote that two children that were brethren, falling sick, and the sickness waxing and waning in both alike, were hereupon suspected to be twins." This was attributed by the Stoic writer Posidonius, a friend of astrology, to be due to the stars. But his reasoning is unsound. The similarity of their fates is better explained by the similarity of their temperaments which are due to their common heredity and physical and social environments. On the other hand, twins that show diverse fates and characters are wisely and well explained by Hippocrates to have enjoyed "diversity of nourishment and exercise . . . effected by their will and inclination and not by their bodily constitution." Both, the observed similarity and dissimilarity of twins argue against the horoscope shaping their characters. St. Augustine seems to think that "diversity of will, act and manners" is more significant in accounting for diversity of character than even common heredity.

To prove that even though twins may be born only a short interval apart, the action of the sky is determinant nonetheless, the astrologer Nigidius turned a potter's wheel as fast as he could and threw ink on what seemed one place on the wheel's edge, and when the wheel was stopped several stains were seen far apart. "Even so, said he, is the swift course of heaven, though one child be born after another in as short a time as I gave these two marks, yet in the heavens will be passed a great space." But this argument, says Augustine, is "far more brittle than the pots that were made by that wheel." If the skies are so laden with portent even to twins born a short time apart, how can astrologers predict fates of non-twins when they do not even know or comprehend the shorter distances? And if they say that large celestial intervals determine big things and smaller intervals only minor features, then surely they are wrong since many twins show great differences in wits, will and fate.

Jacob and Esau were twins born so close together that Jacob held Esau by the heel. Yet look at the disparity in "their lives, manners and actions" which was so great that they were bitter enemies. The mere reference to this hallowed event leads our author into a lengthy and involved argument. Is it the moment of conception that determines character, or fate, or only petty events? If twins' being born apart changes their horoscopes, are some phases only changed and not others? And how can two individuals conceived at the same moment and under the same constellation be born at different times? And if two women give birth at the very same moment to babies who should share the same fate, how can the stamp of their moment of conception be wiped out or cancelled, since the astrologers themselves admit that the two events are not identical? And if all twins are conceived at the same moment why should some twins have dissimilar fortunes at all?

St. Augustine then argues that conception must occur at the same moment because it is common knowledge that once a woman conceives she cannot conceive again until after her pregnancy is terminated. And "if the destinies of twins be changed by their several (i.e. different) times of birth, why may we not rather conceive that before their birth they were appointed by destiny to several births? Shall not then the will of the living man change the fate of his conception?"

He is loath to leave the subject and belabors the point with a story of a set of twins of his acquaintance one of which is female, the other male. They also differ widely in their temperament, habits and fates. "Were their diverse horoscopes (think you) the cause that in their birth he became a man-child and she a woman? Wherefore though it is no such absurdity to say that there are some planetary influences that have effect only upon diversity of forms in bodies, as we see the alteration of the year by the sun's access and departure and diverse things to increase and decrease, just as the moon does (Crabs for example and all shell-fish; besides the wonderful course of the sea): yet it is absurd to say that the mind of man is subject unto any of these powers of the stars. Those who strive to make us connect our actions with the stars do but urge us to inquire whether the differences that exist even in bodies themselves can be attributed to that source. For what is so pertinent unto the body as the sex thereof? And yet we see that two twins of diverse sexes may be conceived both under one constellation."

Elections of days for particular activities about which man perforce shows signs of anxiety, such as marriage, planting or sowing, St. Augustine regards as too foolish to deserve refutation. "Can a man change what his fate has appointed, by choosing this day or that?" he asks. The astrologers, to whom St. Augustine refers as mathematici, are living a life of vanity and delusion. He first proves that the stars should affect or mold the fates of plants and beasts, as well as men, and then proceeds to ridicule these "most skilled mathematicians" for tolerating such droll ideas. God has given free and unconstrained wills to human beings and that is all there is to it. "These being considered, it is no evil belief to think, that the astrologers do presage many things wonderfully and truly, but that is by a secret instinct of evil spirits (whose care it is to infect, deceive and confirm men's minds in this false and dangerous opinion of fate in the stars) and not by any art of discerning the horoscope, for such is there none."

Since St. Augustine relies largely upon Cicero's De Divinatione, he feels called upon to make clear his stand on Cicero's other views. The hero Tully feels obliged to renounce divination by denying all prescience and foreknowledge whether of God or fate. That does not suit Augustine's taste and he declares that "their opinion is more tolerable, that ascribe a fate unto the stars than his that rejects all foreknowledge of things to come. For to acknowledge a God and yet to deny that, is monstrous madness." In other words, free will has to be saved but not at any price. Man must have free will and God full foreknowledge of things to come.

One can thus hardly claim that St. Augustine disbelieved in astrology. He merely defended the Christian beliefs in man's freedom of will to choose the path of God who holds him accountable for evil. All else mattered little. It is likely that St. Augustine never read Ptolemy and thus lived in ignorance of his having met all the old arguments, only a small fraction of which St. Augustine cites and refutes as though they seemed new and weighty to him. We are confronted here with conflicting ideologies where the friends of science and of law and order in nature, are definitely to be found among the mathematici or astrologers. Like his brethren in faith, St. Augustine has little use for science generally. The glory of God and the message of his only son, Jesus Christ, who died to bring love on earth, were too new and inspiring to permit other distracting interests.

The views of St. Augustine marked the culmination of the Christian opposition to astrology. It is in essence inconsistent and unclear except on two issues, man's will, and the power and prescience of Almighty God. The basic assumptions of astrology remain unchallenged, its works and theories unread and unstudied. The general Christian unfriendliness to science leads St. Augustine to counsel his readers to shun all of astronomy, since it may lead to the error of astrology and its nativities. Knowledge of the course of the moon is useful in setting the date of Easter but knowledge of the stars makes no contribution toward a better understanding of the Scriptures. When he discusses elsewhere the belief of some astronomers that many stars are as big or bigger than the sun but appear small because they are far away, he merely points out that it contradicts the statement in Genesis that the sun and moon were created by God as "two great lights." He then comments further that this point hardly merits critical analysis, since "Christians have many better and more serious matters to occupy their time than such subtle investigations concerning the relative magnitude of the stars and the intervals of space between them." (L. Thorndike, Hist. of Magic & Exp. Sci. vol 1 p 521) It is wholly fair to say that this religious partisanship in judging or rather battling the scientific views of antiquity, this lack of interest in all other intellectual pursuits, characterizes the Christian attitude to science for the next five or six centuries.

As if to prove that unity seldom prevails, there has come down a work entitled Mathesis written by Julius Firmicus Maternus who thrived when St. Augustine was born, hence in the midst of the Christian attack upon astrology. (A Roman Astrologer as a Historical Source, Julius Firmicus Maternus, by L. Thorndike, Classical Philology vol. 8, pp 415–35, 1913; and Hist. of Magic & Exp. Sci. vol. 1 p 525) As the title indicates it is a book on astrology written by a learned Christian who is also the author of another work On the Error of Profane Religions, ad-

THE ANCIENT SCIENCE OF ASTROLOGY

dressed to the first Christian emperor Constantine the Great and his son Constans.

The Mathesis is a spirited and suppliant defense of astrology in the name of logic and piety. Of course God created the universe and man. Prayer is good for the soul and free will is its salient attribute. But the stars nonetheless decree and control man's fate. Morals and free choice are essential for the good life, and the human soul is indeed immortal. Yet the stars are part of God's creation and serve as signs in his heaven. The astrologer must be learned but he must also be upright, unselfish and pious to shine as a model to the rest of mankind. He also considers in detail the arguments often cited against astrology and refutes them one by one. Astrology is misunderstood and misrepresented. Its defamers do not study it or experiment in it. Admittedly, many astrologers are inexpert and even deceitful. Astrology has been repeatedly tested and proved legitimate. The human spirit which conceives religion and other sciences can unravel astrology too. Horoscopes are as nothing by comparison with the really difficult task of mapping the courses of planets, which the mathematici have attempted and with such amazing success. All about us we see fate at work. Otherwise how can one explain the fact that good and noble men like Socrates, Plato, or Pythagoras met with ill fate, while such men as Alcibiades and Sulla prospered.

Firmicus then devotes the second half of his book to the science of casting horoscopes. Thorndike has made an excellent quantitative analysis of references to institutions and values in Firmicus in order to reconstruct a cross-section of the period. He finds frequent references to many current religions and their practices, to temples, priests and divination. Magic and religion are often linked to holy exorcists who "stay in temples in an unkempt state and always walk abroad thus" frightening demons and wicked spirits out of their human abodes. There are references to religious games and contests, and to individuals who grow rich through religion. Mathematici, that is, astrologers, were not the only fortune-tellers at the time, since Firmicus mentions all kinds of diviners, augurs, readers of dreams, and seers. Magic is clearly recognized as a valid art or science, and is usually referred to in conjunction with medicine, philosophy, astronomy or religion. Its secret practices are not favorably regarded, however. The indications are that in the fourth century Rome still had a cultural life, and the text cites many diseases and contains references to medical practitioners and specialists. This book of Firmicus seems to stand alone in that period and the author points out the scarcity of astrological books in Latin. While he refers to few authorities, he does claim to have based most of his knowledge on the authority of three astrological heroes of mythical origin, Hermes, Nechepso and Petosiris, mentioning also Ptolemy and Hipparchus. "An

Abram or Abraham is also cited several times." He also refers to two previous astrological works of his own. It would seem that unlike modern times even Christianity when wielding full power in Rome, did not execute all deviationists, but permitted books on a forbidden science which it strongly and unreservedly condemned. This is all the more remarkable when we bear in mind that it was a time of high emotional tension and a period of ebullient, adolescent passion about a new faith, fed by the fire and vitality of a new faith.

Chapter IV

RESTORATION AFTER DEFEAT

1. *Christian Opposition Wavers*

ALTHOUGH the onrush of Christianity definitely put all science in the doghouse, the basic astrological folklore which dominated the minds of the lay and the learned, never wavered or weakened. It was merely not in evidence for a while. But wherever learning did put in an appearance in the centuries known as the Dark Ages, astrology was sure to be there, though at first somewhat shy and immature. Hence it is that references to astrological or celestial divination are found in few manuscripts of the pre-tenth century era.

It is with the translations from the Arabic which sprouted like mushrooms in the twelfth century, that astrology begins to show signs of a genuine comeback. This wave was preceded, "in the eleventh and even tenth century by numerous signs of Arabic influence in the works of astronomy and astrology and also by translations of Arabic authors." (Thorndike vol. 1, p. 697) Among these early works one encounters a manuscript like the Mathemetic of Alhandreus, Supreme Astrologer (eleventh century), which already bears signs of fairly mature treatment. A twelfth century work entitled Natural Questions by Adelard of Bath discusses these topics with the scientific zest and breadth worthy of Pliny, Galen or Seneca.

Adelard was an Englishman who, like most scholars of the time, had travelled widely and reflected the current fashion by displaying greater regard for the learning and wisdom of the infidel Mohammedans than for that of the Latin West. In his work he treats problems in alchemy, mathematics, animal behavior, and of course astrology. The four elements are still safely enthroned and so is the notion that the stars are "those superior and divine animals" which function as "the causes and principles of inferior nature." In the words of Thorndike, Adelard proclaims that "One who masters the science of astronomy can comprehend not only the present state of inferior things but also the past and the future." The stars are imbued with life and are also referred to as

81

"those superior animals" whose fire is gentle and harmless, hence "obedient to and in harmony with sense and reason." The planets have specific meanings and influences. Each nation is under the aegis of a particular planet which accounts for national fates and characteristics. Similar respect for astronomy and astrology is shown by the influential teacher and writer of the same period, William of Conches, an Englishman like Adelard and a lover of philosophy and science. He speaks of the study of celestial events by the methods of fable or the methods of astronomy and astrology. By astrology he implies the actual study of observable phenomena and by astronomy their theoretical interpretation. The qualities and virtues of each planet were arrived at by prolonged observations carried on by the ancients. "As the tides follow the phases of the moon, so, William believes, a universal flood conflagration may be produced by the simultaneous elevation or depression of all the planets." Thunder and lightning are regarded as natural phenomena not related to divination, but comets are special signs of events to come.

"Throughout the twelfth century," says Thorndike, "from its first years to its close may be traced the transit of learning from the Arabic world, and more particularly from the Spanish peninsula, to northwestern Europe. Three points may be made concerning this transmission: it involves Latin translation from the Arabic; the matter translated is largely mathematical, or more especially astronomical and astrological in character; finally, it is often experimental." Manuscript after manuscript of that period bears witness to the fact that a strong interest in science prevailed among the learned, as well as the realization that the available or familiar Latin works were inadequate for that purpose. Complete knowledge could only be attained through mastery of the Arabian translations. It was also felt that experience and experiment were the very foundation of astrological tenets. A MS by one, Pedro Alfonso, states: "It has been proved therefore by experimental argument that we can truly affirm that the sun and moon and other planets exert their influences in earthly affairs. . . . And indeed many other innumerable things happen on earth in accordance with the courses of the stars, and pass unnoticed by the senses of most men, but are discovered and understood by the subtle acumen of learned men skilled in this art." Even medical astrology makes its appearance in the literature of the day. This was the age of the great translators such as Robert of Chester, Hermann of Dalmatia, Gerard of Cremona, William of Conches, John of Spain, Plato of Tivoli and a host of others. The list of translations included Ptolemy, Euclid, Archimedes, Galen, Aristotle, and a number of the outstanding Arabian authorities in medicine, mathematics, astronomy and astrology, namely, Alkindi, Alfarabi, Messahala, Geber the alchemist, Isaac, Rasis, Avicenna, and many others.

The ambivalent attitude toward astrology which became apparent at the time is virtually discernible in all the writings of the period. On the one side we have such writers as Bernard Sylvester, Daniel of Morley and Roger of Hereford, who accepted astrology as modern and scientific, with the feeling that they were ahead of the times and free from the superstitious shackles which restrained many scholars from its fascinating truths on purely religious grounds. Among the latter were such authors as Hildegard of Bingen and John of Salisbury, both of whom fully accepted the astrological assumptions but denounced or questioned one phase of astrology or another on the old grounds of free will and the uncontestable providence of the Lord, as opposed to scientific determinism implied in the rule of stellar orbits. John of Salisbury's opposition may be summarized in these words of his: "Would, that the error of the mathematici could be as readily removed from enlightened minds as the works of the demons fade before true faith and a sane consciousness of their delusions. But in it men go astray with the greater peril in that they seem to base their error upon nature's firm foundation and reason's strength." (Thorndike v. 2, 164) Hildegard too, castigates mathematici as "deadly instructors and followers of the Gentiles in unbelief." God alone guides and rules the world in His own fashion and the stars are of no matter.

But these views were probably in the minority. Several authors writing on scientific subjects pointed out that nature follows regular laws and patterns even though God rules the world. The sphericity of the earth is generally accepted. The Augustinian friar Alexander Neckam goes even so far as to criticize sharply many of the biblical statements concerning nature. He declares, for example, that the scriptural assertion that "God made two great lights" cannot be taken seriously because "The historical narrative follows the judgment of the eye and the popular notion," while science tells us that the moon is certainly not one of the largest planets. And he is all for science. "Science," he says, "is acquired at great expense, by frequent vigils, by great expenditure of time, by sedulous diligence of labor, by vehement application of mind." But it repays dividends in the practical needs of peace and war. "What craftiness of the foe is there that does not yield to the precise knowledge of those who have tracked down the elusive subtleties of things hidden in the very bosom of nature?" (ibid. v 2, 196) He admits that some mysteries of nature have not yet been solved because nature is reluctant to have them unveiled and zealously guards them as if saying, "This is my secret, this is my secret!" And Neckam's attitude is far from being unique or even in the minority. It is the opinion of the opposite school of thought that is conspicuously out of step.

During the thirteenth century it is no longer permissible to speak of the acceptance of astrological thought as a trend. Rather is it the scientific folklore of the time, much as are mesons and neutrons today. The thirteenth century, referred to as the century of greatness, (J. J. Walsh, The Thirteenth, Greatest of Centuries, New York, 1929) is indeed remarkable for the rapid culmination of medieval science, the thin beginnings of which were hardly discernible in the tenth century. Among the centuries preceding the seventeenth it is most conspicuous for the large number of outstanding names and the virtual complete recapture of the science of antiquity. If no additions whatever were made to the learning of Pliny, Galen, Hippocrates, Euclid, Aristotle, Plato, Lucretius and others, at least the hiatus left by their temporary eclipse was completely eliminated and further development thus made possible.

Among the writers of that period so masterfully analyzed and summarized by Thorndike in his complete survey of medieval MSS, century by century, only one author is to be found who still has not managed to reconcile his Christian faith with the new science. William of Auvergne was "a Christian theologian whose works present an unexpectedly detailed picture of the magic and superstition of the time." He was bishop of Paris from 1228 to his death in 1249 and a master of theology in its university. He was well versed in "both the occult literature and the natural philosophy of the day, and has much to say of magic, demons, occult virtue, divination and astrology." He is the author of a voluminous work on natural philosophy entitled The Universe, in which he displays the greatest regard for scientific investigations and naturalistic explanations of phenomena. Too many people, he complains, find it easier to have recourse to the Creator's omnipotence as the cause of anything they observe, than to study assiduously the immediate and natural causes. It is an egregious error thus to overlook the beauty and value of science. He even apologizes for his superficial treatment of astronomy which by right deserves separate and detailed treatment. He does it, he explains, merely to offer the average man a view of the depth and truth of this subject which can be garnered even without pompous documentation and flowery rhetoric. In spite of all this, and in spite of his frequent references to "innumerable experiences" and "books of experiments," it goes without saying that William's writings are full of the spiritual, the religious, the miraculous and the magical. Marvels of magic are performed with the aids of demons. "Superstitious observance of the stars, the elements, images, figures, words and names, times and seasons, beginnings of actions and finding objects" are equivalent to the worship of idols and demons. Other impressive operations are apparitions or skillful deceptions. There is however a "part of natural science which is called magic." Works or marvels performed by virtue of such powers or such knowledge are legitimate, and are never performed with the aid of demons. But they must not be done for evil purposes. Moreover the employment of images, incantations and charms make no sense and should be discredited. Mere words cannot effect the deadly or fantastic deeds that sorcerers claim. Angels occupy physical space in their own regions, just as do the stars in their respective celestial zones.

William also goes into the philosophy of magic and witchcraft. There were incubi and succubi, he asserts, though he expresses doubt that they are capable of sexual intercourse, as many claim. They may merely give that impression. Occult virtues are real and marvelous, and "spiritual substances can overcome weight which holds bodies at rest and produces lightness which makes motion easy." Transformations of men into werewolves are not to be credited, however. Many natural objects have the power of driving away demons. His views on astrology are quite unsettled in some respects but specific in others. The heavenly bodies are apparently endowed with animated souls but not by a single world soul as some philosophers state, because "it is manifest that human souls are nobler than those they put in heavenly bodies." But evil and misfortune of the kind astrologers so avidly predict, cannot be ascribed to celestial bodies but to "human perversity or the imperfections inherent in the matter of our inferior world." The latter may spring from the fact that inferior matter may not always be properly attuned to the harmonious reception of the stellar impact. The occult virtues lodged in the stars are indeed great, far greater even than those lodged in precious stones. The very effect of the sun on earthly events and human life, alone would prove that the planets and the stars, which in spite of their apparent closeness are separated by enormous spaces, exert similarly telling influences. It is wrong and sinful for Christians to believe that the motions and positions of the stars in their celestial courses determine the fates of men and nations. And, he remarks with almost modern passion, "Against that error, one ought not so much to dispute with arguments as fight with fire and sword." Admittedly, the stars were created before God brought forth vegetation, animal life and human beings; and granted also that the stars aid considerably in the generation of living things and their conservation. Just the same they are no causes of events on earth, not even signs. The only things they govern in our sublunar world are the four elements and the four humors, and these only of beings that are not endowed with free will. Sidereal control over moral and intellectual phases of man's life is irreligious and out of the question, either one or both. Of course the multitude of men lead, it is sorrowful to say, neither moral nor intellectual lives, but rather are their dispositions vile and emotional in the manner of brutes. Hence astrologers may predict with a fair degree of accuracy anything pertaining to mob action and second, to individual fates involving emotional vices, since these do not spring from man's moral sense or his soul but from his physical constitution. Besides, even such causality may be modified by prayer. Ptolemy's horoscopes and nativities are stigmatized as insanity and William bemoans the fact that such writers enjoy mighty reputations among the "simple and stupid multitude."

All the other writers of the thirteenth century follow a different tune. Let us consider first the outstanding encyclopedists of the time such as Thomas of Cantimpré, Bartholomew of England and Vincent of Beauvais, though, as we shall see, many other contemporary writers virtually scanned the entire field of human learning. Thomas was a Dominican monk whose De natura rerum was intended by him to include all knowledge available at the time, so that in his own words "there will scarcely be found among the Latins so much and so varied material compressed into a single volume." It treats of the human body, each member rating a full chapter, its ailments and cures. After devoting a volume to the soul, it proceeds to a discussion of the races of man, stressing of course the strange, the monstrous and the unusual, for example, hermaphroditism. These are followed by volumes on the quadrupeds, birds, marine monsters, fish, serpents and worms, which topics fill more pages than the subjects on man. The succeeding books deal with the vegetable kingdom; two of them are devoted to herbs, aromatic and medicinal trees, while the subsequent ones treat of fountains and waters, precious stones, the seven metals, the seven regions of the air, the sphere, the seven planets and meteorology, finishing with a final volume on the universe and the four elements. His authorities are both the ancient Greeks, above all Aristotle and Pliny, as well as the patristic writers, the more modern Arabs, and many Latin authors of the preceding decades. "Thomas of Cantimpré must be reckoned as one of the most credulous of our authors," says Thorndike. His attitudes to authorities is generally unquestioning and almost reverent. One encounters in his writings all the animal myths and fables that lured the fancy of ancient and medieval minds. The marvelous in animal powers and passions, their anthropomorphic wiles and whims, kindnesses and hates, instinctive insights and ethics, to say nothing of the occult virtues and idiosyncratic habits of each species. That his works contain many valuable comments of factual validity goes without saying, and has been recognized by modern historians of science.

Particularly noteworthy is his account of the mariner's compass, already alluded to by Neckam in the preceding century, though without as much detail. According to Thomas a variety of the rock adamant can attract iron, even to the extent of tearing it away from a magnet. "When sailors cannot direct their course to port amid obscure mists, they take a needle and, after rubbing its points on adamant, fasten it transversely on a small stick or straw and place it in a vessel full of water. Then by carrying some adamant around the vessel they start the needle rotating. Then the stone is suddenly withdrawn and presently the point of the needle comes to rest pointing towards the star in question." (ibid. v 2, p. 387–8) Although it is true that both the adamant and the magnet were generally associated with magic, it seems quite clear that as early as the twelfth and thirteenth centuries the magnetic needle was actually employed in the mariner's compass, and as our general authority on the subject of this chapter points out, there seems to be little, if any, evidence that sailors anywhere displayed any fear of using it because of its reputed connection with magic.

With regard to astrology Thomas' attitude bears the stamp of the pattern of the times well in the making. The planets are inanimate, their movements are determined, and each one of them, particularly when in the ascendant, has a sharply delimited function. Venus affects generation, Mars makes men bellicose and choleric, while Jupiter guards their safety and health, though it is false to hold with Martianus that if Jupiter were the sole planet all men would be immortal. Free will and God's special instances of intervention are the only natural manifestations exempt from stellar action. The argument for planetary influence is the usual one. Since the effects of the sun and moon are obvious, "why should we not with entire reason believe the same of the other planets?"

No different is the situation in the writings of Bartholomew, a Franciscan friar of vast learning who wrote his encyclopedic opus On the Properties of Things to serve, in his words, as "a simple and rude" compilation of available knowledge for the average reader or for people who, like himself, are not too erudite. His avowed object is to elucidate many things and natural properties obscurely referred to in the Holy Scriptures; but he manages nonetheless to introduce a considerable number of contemporary ideas and customs as well as some original observations. His nineteen books treat successively with the topics of God, the properties of angels and the nature of demons, the mind and soul of man, the human body, and its parts and their functions; volume six entitled "Of Ages" deals with domestic life and its amenities, seven with diseases and their cures (in seventy chapters), and among other things prescribes cures and restraints for mental illnesses and describes numerous animal poisons and marvels; the eighth book discusses the universe and celestial bodies, the ninth deals with time and its subdivisions, the tenth with fire and the other elements, the eleventh with air and its "passions" by which is meant winds, snow, rain, dew, thunder etc., the twelfth with animals that are creatures of the air, the thirteenth with waters and fish, including whales, the fourteenth with the earth, its mountains, caves and deserts; the fifteenth book deals with contemporary rather than biblical geography, the sixteenth with gems, metal and minerals, the seventeenth with trees and herbs, the eighteenth with animals, real and imaginary served as the middle ages loved them, and finally the nineteenth treats the subjects of "color, odor, savor and liquor." Thus the work truly encompasses the entire storehouse of medieval knowledge and thought, and in the medieval manner. This means that side by side with much fanciful material there is some shrewd observation, wide coverage of literature both of antiquity and contemporary sources, a modicum of scepticism, gentle criticism of authoritarian interpretation of biblical meanings, here and there impassioned arguments against one view and for a contrary or a contradictory one, neither of which we can help smiling upon today, and finally love for the occult and the marvelous, mingled with respect for evidence and experimentation as then understood.

Bartholomew's astrological notions are quite simple. Since his starting point is meant to be the Bible, he devotes much space and thought to the waters above the firmament and the empyrean heaven. After paying his respects to the early saints who insisted on the belief in manifold heavens, Bartholomew proceeds to render the position of the "philosophers" i.e. Aristotle, Ptolemy and the others who believed in a single heaven, containing many orbs and spheres, which conflict with the greater aggregation of light in the stars, thus accounting for their contrary effects on sublunary events as expressed in generation and corruption. According to the author and following Aristotle, "the Creator established the heaven as the cause and origin of generation and corruption, and therefore it was necessary that it should not be subject to generation and corruption." Hence the universe is divided into two parts: Above the circle of the moon outward there extends the noble, superior and incorruptible portion, while below it earthward there is contained the inferior, passive and corruptible earth which is wholly subject to the action of the superior regions. The rays emanating therefrom converge "as toward a center upon the earth's surface and exert a concentrated impression there; and the science of perspective also illustrates this. The three less stable elements, air, fire, and water, obey the firmament even to the extent of local motion, as is illustrated by the tides. The element earth is not influenced in this way, but produces diverse species from itself in obedience to the celestial impressions which it receives." The latter statement thus refers to the very foundation of alchemical philosophy.

The constellations of the zodiac are named after animals because they possess their respective properties. They are in addition either hot or cold, masculine or feminine, nocturnal or diurnal. They harmonize with the elements in sets of three, and also with the cardinal points, and interact in specific ways with the planets. Each sign governs a particular bodily organ or region. The Ram, for example, "dominates the head and face, and produces a hairy body, a crooked frame, an oblique face, heavy eyes, short ears, a long neck." The signs do other things as well. Virgo, for example, is "the house of sickness, of serfs and handmaids and the domestic animals. It signifies inconstancy and changing from place to place" to say nothing of the occult properties possessed by each sign. The planets have their usual effects. Mars "disposes men to mobility and levity of mind, to wrath and animosity and other choleric passions; it also fits men for arts employing fire such as those of smiths and bakers. Just as Saturn produces agriculturists and porters of heavy weights, and Jupiter on the contrary turns out men adapted to lighter pursuits such as orators and money changers." The fixed stars help prognosticate the weather and, according to the mathematici, bear good and bad tidings.

The third encyclopedist cited, Vincent de Beauvais, is, in the opinion of most historians the leading figure among his peers. His voluminous Mirror of Nature is part of a vast work of which the others are The Mirror of Doctrine and The Mirror of History. Vincent was a Dominican sub-prior and tutor to the children of Louis IX or St. Louis of France. As in the case of William and Bartholomew the very matrix of his thoughts and outlook was theological. As in the previous cases his primary authorities and guides were ostensibly the saints and patristic writers, but these become rapidly and hopelessly overshadowed by the more cogent authorities such as Pliny and Aristotle from the world of antiquity and Rasis, Avicenna, Albumasar, Averroes and others from the moderns. Essentially their subject matter is very much the same, and needless to say so is the mode of approach.

Vincent begins with an elaborate discussion of the nature of dreams. He quotes many authorities to the effect that dreams are to be accounted for by the state of health of the dreamer, his digestion, his thoughts, his hidden wishes or dispositions of which he may not even be aware in his wakeful hours. Dreams merely serve as signs not as causes of future events and are vague for that very reason, hence requiring interpretation in which art the configurations of the sky play a major role. With these preparatory comments he proceeds to a full discussion of astronomy and astrology. Incidentally these two terms are used interchangeably almost throughout the century. Vincent's treatment of the subject is typical of the intricate, psychological processes of laborious harmonization which were hard in the making in his day. He supports the church fathers in their condemnations of diviners and mathematici, but quotes approvingly all the ancient and modern authorities in their assertion that the stars dominate the fates of the inferior world and man. He disagrees with those commentators who interpret Aristotle to have implied that the stars were alive but claims they are composed of a heavenly and incorruptible nature. True, they do not have souls, but "there are intelligences in the spheres of the heavens who serve the First Cause or Mover and that, although the saints abhor giving these the name of souls, yet they concede that intelligence or angels move the heavens and the stars at the nod of God."

The influence of the stars is powerful and universal affecting all. Each plant, each animal, each natural process, has its controlling star. Only man's reason, his free will and the acts caused by them are exempt. The full scope and techniques of astrology are examined in meticulous detail, including the action of the planets upon the development of the foetus in the womb. As Augustine points out, however, the stars do not control man's sexual behavior. Comets signify, of course, war, pestilence and famine. He even accepts the virtues and powers of astrological images which he compares in effectiveness to the well-known potency of gems. Since Vincent's three Mirrors became the most popular reference work of the middle ages, they in a way are symbolic of the new ideological adjustment which had quietly been synthesized between the relatively naive Hebrew-Christian cosmogony and the scientifically sophisticated Greek astronomy and astrology. The original enthusiasm for Christian ethics and social values which the patristic writers bequeathed upon a newly converted world, had apparently worn off by the tenth century. Resistance to secular learning was greatly weakened and with the coming of the new knowledge, a new world view replaced the old. During the thirteenth century this new view attained maturity. In regard to the phenomena of the sky the new philosophy involved the compromise of saving free will and accepting astrology, a complete victory for Ptolemy and his Tetrabiblos. No astrologer, in fact, ever questioned or dreamed of denying free will. His slogan had always been "The wise man rules the stars."

2. *The New Adjustment*

The same attitude pervades the writings of the other great teachers and scholars of the period. Michael Scot was astrologer to the Emperor Frederick II whom George Sarton styles "one of the most romantic figures of European history." (George Sarton, Introduction to the History of Science vol. II part II p. 497). In Sarton's words: "He was not simply a patron; the genuineness of his philosophical and scientific curiosity is sufficiently proved by the questions he submitted to Michael Scot and Ibn Sab'in, by his contempt of superstition, and above all by his own scientific activity." Michael Scot was a prominent enough clergyman to be pushed by Pope Honorius III in 1224 for the archbishopric of Cashel in Ireland, which he rejected because he was unfamiliar with the language. He was to be recommended three years later by Pope Gregory IX to the archbishop of Canterbury for a high position as a great theologian and scholar, versed "not only in Latin but also in the Hebrew and Arabic languages." Michael lived early enough in the thirteenth century to have done valuable translations from the Greek and Arabic. He translated Aristotle's History of Animals, as well as numerous other works on animals from the Arabic, Avicenna's commentary on such works, Aristotle's De caelo et mundo, the De anima with a commentary by Averroes, and the Metaphysics. He was also the author of an Introduction to Astrology, a Commentary upon the Sphere of Sacrobosco, the great astronomical text of the middle ages, and finally of three large works entitled Liber Introductorius, Liber Particularis, and Physiognomy.

Since Michael was a practicing astrologer it is apparent that already in the thirteenth century the church not only refrained from persecuting astrologers, as many historians claim it did, but tolerated the practice among its highest dignitaries. And Michael's views on astrology were of the full grown, reestablished variety. Astrology is a difficult and noble study. The signs and planets are not causes; by their motions they merely indicate "something of the truth concerning every body produced in this corruptible world." The stars do not work by magic; rather should their action be compared to that of a magnet's upon iron. It goes without saying that he discusses the star of the Magi, every writer on the subject did that, uses the terms astronomy and astrology interchangeably, condemns nigromancy, magic and superstition, some "superstitious" astrology, and is opposed to sorcerers and tricksters. Various forms of divination such as "augury by songs of birds, interpretation of dreams, observance of days, or divination by holocausts of blood and corpses," are true but forbidden to good Christians as evil and sinful. But all the doctrines of astrology are fully expounded and accepted, the effects of moon and stars, the detailed action of planetary aspects, exaltations, conjunctions, friendships and enmities. Nativities, horoscopes and elections, as well as the importance of astrology in the practice of medicine are given their full credit. Free will, reason and divine intervention are in no way imposed upon or interfered with by the stars. He goes into lengthy discussions on the matter of the influence of the moon on conception, development of foetus, the effect of the moon on menstruation, the role of the stars in the determination of the child's sex, and similar problems.

Exactly the same situation prevails in the case of the other influential figures of the century, namely, Robert Grosseteste, Albertus Magnus,

Thomas Aquinas and Roger Bacon. Grosseteste was a clergyman, bishop of London, a prominent statesman and renowned and respected scholar. His books are filled with the spirit of science and conscious reliance upon reason and experience, referring to many authors as experimenters. His books deal with vision and perspective, lenses and light, astronomy, geometry and mathematics. He is the author of a treatise on time reckoning and of a vast philosophic work, Summa philosophiae, in nineteen volumes. His discussion of mathematics includes of course astronomy and that involves astrology. All events and activities in the inferior world are motivated and guided by the motions of the superior bodies. The seven planets are identified with the seven metals; earthly disharmony can be corrected by the application of knowledge of celestial harmony. Astrology cannot only serve to guide activities and predict the future but also to cure diseases and curb passions. The four elements and the qualities are subject to the signs and planets and so are the animal and vegetable kingdoms. Needless to say, man's free will and his rational soul are exempt from stellar influence.

No different is the attitude of the two great Dominicans Albertus Magnus, who was beatified, and Thomas Aquinas, who was canonized, and the famous Franciscan, Roger Bacon. Albert is the author of eight books on physics, six on psychology, eight on celestial bodies, a volume on geography, twenty-six books on zoological topics and five on minerals, to say nothing of books on general topics and his classical works on philosophy. Albert is regarded by many modern historians as the father of the method of science in the middle ages, a second naturalist of the stature of Aristotle, the father of modern botany, etc. He had no doubt great scientific curiosity and scholarship, and was an original and acute observer. Wherever possible, even in religious incidents, he stressed the importance of natural causes and their investigation, since they are the instruments of God's will. "It is not enough," he says, "to know in terms of universals, but we seek to know each subject's own peculiar characteristics, for this is the best and perfect kind of science." Elsewhere he says, "For experience is the best teacher in all matters of this sort." Frequent in his writings are such phrases as, "I have tested this," or "I and my associates have experienced," or "I have proved that this is not true." Albert displays more than his share of scepticism. He often accuses authors of merely repeating rumors rather than citing facts they observed or experienced, and often belittles or contradicts stories by popular authorities as unacceptable, as "not based upon experience," or as "read in story-books rather than proved philosophically by experience," etc. But that in more than a thousand and one cases he is as credulous as any of his contemporaries, need hardly be stressed.

The heavens and the stars are intermediaries between the First Mover, or the Supreme Intelligence, and earthly matter. Hence the stars are God's instruments. The planets produce the usual effects and their conjunctions are full of weighty import. So, of course, are the zodiacal signs. Comets forbode wars and the death of kings. The well established Christian caveat is fully respected; man's free will and his rational soul are not under the power of the stars. Here Albert is a little more courageous than others. He declares: "There is in man a double spring of action, namely nature and the will; and nature for its part is ruled by the stars, while the will is free; but unless it resists, it is swept along by nature and becomes mechanical." This is clearly a great concession to astrological universalism. Albert is at great pains to prove that astrology never defended all-out fatalism to the exclusion of free will, and hence was never really incompatible with Christianity. He repeatedly cites Ptolemy to prove his point and quotes his famous admonition that knowledge of astrology gives the wise man power to modify or annul the effects of the stars. Like many another defender of astrology, Albert has few kind words to say about the practitioners of the art. It is they who brought the art or science of divination into disrepute, because "almost all men of this class delight in deception and, being poorly educated, they think that what is merely contingent is necessary, and they predict that some event will certainly occur, and when it does not, those sciences are cheapened in the sight of unskilled men although the defect is not in the science, but in those who abuse it. For this reason wise Ptolemy says that no judgment should be made except in general terms and with the cautious reservation that the stars act per aliud et accidens (subject to other forces and to accidents) and that their significations meet many impediments. Moreover, the pursuit of sciences dealing with the future would be idle, if one could not avoid what one foresaw." (ibid. v. 2 p. 585)

Albert musters an interesting argument as evidence for stellar influence, although he ascribes it to Plato, Ptolemy and Galen, three good authorities at any time. Young boys, he says, who as yet do not wield free will already show the imprint of the heavens upon their constitution, as for example when they display special aptitudes. Environment is often helpless to undo that celestial determinism. When, for instance, such children are forced by parents, who show disregard for the dictates of nature, to enter into different trades, it is found that they never attain any remarkable proficiency in them, clearly because they are destined for something else. Little wonder then that in addition to horoscopes Albert fully accepts elections, that is the choice of favorable hours for certain actions. He also believes in the power of astrological images engraved on precious stones at favorable times. He reiterates the views of Augustine but is at great pains to prove that they are completely reconcilable with the views of all the authorities he had employed to prove the very notions Augustine condemned. All of which just about summarizes the philosophic revolution of the time.

Aquinas too insists that "Reason and experience, saints and philosophers," have proved over and over again that celestial bodies rule all inferior matter. Like Albert he finds no compunction in perverting the truly impassioned attacks upon astrology by the patristic writers into veritable defenses of it. Like all the other authoritative theologians of the time, he does not bat an eyelash in doing that because he feels apparently that once he exempted the human soul and intellect from celestial rule, not too difficult a task if it is agreed that they are not material in nature, the road is open for being honest and scientific about the whole matter, without any danger of heresy. Strangely enough, though Albert is the great scientist and not Aquinas, it is the latter who denies that gems with astrological engravings are in any way more effective medicinally than ordinary gems.

Roger Bacon has been credited with numerous discoveries and inventions, and is supposed to have endured intense persecution as a result of his advocating the experimental method. As Thorndike points out, neither assertion has a shred of evidence behind it. In a masterly chapter he concludes that Bacon was a typical product of medieval thought. "In other words, Bacon continues the Christian attitude of patristic literature to a certain extent; and his book is written by a clergyman for clergymen, and in order to promote the welfare of the Church and Christianity. There is no denying that, hail him as one may as a herald of modern science. Secondly, he is frequently scholastic and metaphysical; yet thirdly, is critical in numerous respects; and fourthly, insists on practical utility as a standard by which science and philosophy must be judged. Finally he is an exponent of the aims and methods of what we have called 'the natural magic and experimental school,' and as such he sometimes comes near to being scientific. So there is no other book quite like the Opus Maius in the Middle Ages, nor has there been one like it since; yet it is true to its age and is still readable today. It will therefore always remain one of the most remarkable books of the remarkable thirteenth century." (ibid. v. 2. p. 678)

Surely, Bacon was a man of impassioned enthusiasm and possessed of a none-too-common sense of the practical and experimental. The following passage quoted by Thorndike amply attests to that, as well as to the fact "that an interest existed in mechanical devices, and that men were already beginning to struggle with the problems which have recently been solved." Writes Bacon: "Machines for navigation can be made without rowers so that the largest ships on rivers or seas will be moved by a single man in charge with greater velocity than if they were full of men. Also cars can be made so that without animals they will move with unbelievable rapidity; such we opine were the scythe-bearing chariots with which the men of old fought. Also flying machines can be constructed so that a man sits in the midst of the machine revolving some engine by which artificial wings are made to beat the air like a flying bird. Also a machine small in size for raising or lowering enormous weights, than which nothing is more useful in emergencies. For by a machine three fingers high and wide and of less size a man could free himself and his friends from all danger of prison and rise and descend. Also a machine can easily be made by which one man can draw a thousand to himself by violence against their wills, and attract other things in like manner. Also machines can be made for walking in the sea and rivers, even to the bottom without danger. For Alexander the Great employed such, that he might see the secrets of the deep, as Ethicus the astronomer tells us. These machines were made in antiquity and they have certainly been made in our times, except possibly a flying machine which I have not seen nor do I know anyone who has, but I know an expert who has thought out the way to make one. And such things can be made almost without limit, for instance, bridges across rivers without piers or other supports, and mechanisms, and unheard of engines." (Quoted by Thorndike v. 2, p. 654. See also Roger Bacon, Opus Majus tr. by Robert Belle Burke U. of Pennsylvania Press, 1928 vol. 1, pp. 27–52.)

On the matter of astrology Bacon's attitude is entirely in conformity with the new spirit. "It is manifest to everybody that the celestial bodies are the causes of generation and corruption in all inferior things." The stars were regulated by angelic intelligences. The nature or "complexion" i.e. character of an individual is determined by the sky at conception and at birth. The functions of the body in health and disease are under the influence of the stars; hence medical treatment should hinge upon astronomical configurations, and the physician should be cognizant of the fact that hour by hour the bodily states vary with the changing positions of the planets. For these purposes the zodiac and the moon must also be taken into account with proper care and caution. Evil and good conduct in men is accounted for by the stars, as well as the possibility of resurrection. A strong personality may by the power of his will stem or change the force of the stars, though groups cannot ever be strong enough for that. Different regions of the earth are inhabited by different races and nations because the latter are under the influence of different constellations. Planetary conjunctions are of particular efficacy in religion, Christianity being associated with Mercury which is most impelling when in Virgo, while Venus denoting sensuality represents Mohammedanism. From such beginnings Bacon lunges into a series of prognostications concerning the fates of historical figures, nations and religions that are of ominous import. Even the birth of Christ is brought under the rule of the stars. Elections, horoscopes, images and favorable hours, in a word, the entire astrological arsenal is elaborately and devoutly expounded. He even goes so far as to declare that "the astronomer can form words in elect times which will possess unspeakable power" over matter and over men. Needless to say that the numerous stories to the effect that Bacon was persecuted by the Church for his astrology are no more factual than the fables that he was persecuted for his advocating reliance upon experimental evidence.

Three supporters of astrology have gained special fame and deserve consideration. They are Guido Bonatti, Peter of Abano, and Cecco D'Ascoli. Bonatti was the author of an astrological work entitled Liber astronomicus in which he expounds the complete astrological folklore of the period, using the words astronomy and astrology interchangeably. As an exponent of the science he is bold and outspoken and quite militant in his defiance of some clerical detractors of the subject whom he treats with utter contempt. He refers to "some fools among those wearing the tunic" who deny fortune as determined by the stars and leave room only for the will of God. Fortunately, he says, there are many among them who know better even if they are ashamed to admit it in public. If fortune did not exist, then anyone with the slightest intelligence would go after the acquisition of wealth. Yet we know there are many wise and learned men "who do not have enough to eat." If there were no fortune it would be necessary to believe that God is mad or unjust, which means that these rejecters of astrology are guilty of heresy. There was apparently some opposition to astrology on the part of Churchmen and Bonatti is far from taking it lying down but, on the contrary, is consistently on the offensive. Yet his appeal is mainly to theologians. The author defends astrological images, elections and interrogations, to say nothing of the orthodox phases of the subject. His book was regarded as an authoritative work for centuries after its appearance.

Even more famous as scholar and astrologer was Peter of Abano, author of The Conciliator, and many treatises on medicine, philosophy and astronomy. He was a great traveler and translator, and apparently enjoyed a vast reputation in his lifetime, being considered a second Aristotle. Unfortunately he owes his fame in modern times to his difficulties with the Inquisition which presumably burned his bones after his death. As Thorndike points out, the circumstances of Peter's conflict with the Inquisition are far from clear or certain, though there is evidence that such a conflict existed. Yet the fight was not over science or astrology as some historians have claimed. The sole authority for Peter's posthumous punishment, Thomas of Strassburg, Prior-General of the Augustinian order from 1345 to 1357, regarded Peter as a heretic because of his doubting such miracles as raising the dead. Peter's reason had been that some sick people can fall into a trance for three days. He denied that Lazarus was in the tomb four days "since the first and fourth days were incomplete," hence he might have been afflicted with that particular disease. And, adds Thomas, who admired Peter as a great physician, "in this his iniquity he was deceived and received the reward of his error. For I was present when in the city of Padua his bones were burned for these and his other errors." The reports are so contradictory that it is difficult to ascertain the fate of Peter's bones after their possessor in life gave up his soul. It is certain that Peter had some trouble with the Dominicans, that his confessors were two Franciscans and that his will directs that he be buried in the Church of St. Anthony the Confessor in Padua which belonged to the Franciscan order. Moreover, it seems that his property was not confiscated, as it certainly would have been had he been condemned by the Inquisition. His books appeared in print soon after the invention of movable type; he was lauded by Michael Savonarola, the grandfather of the famous monk of Florence, himself a great physician and medical writer, and by Regiomontanus, the well known mathematician of the fifteenth century and one of the widely renowned medieval, pre-Copernican astronomers. If his teachings were under ban by the church, then surely many churchmen defied that injunction in favor of his learning.

The Conciliator consists of two hundred questions or topics which Peter and his associates have been discussing for many years, many of a purely medical nature, others dealing with general science. Here are some of the questions: "Does the marrow nourish the bone? Is manhood hotter than childhood or youth? Is life possible below the equator? Is a small head a better sign than a larger one? Are the arteries dilated when the heart is and constricted also when it is? Is musical consonance found in the pulse? Can a worm be generated in the belly? Is death more likely to occur by day or by night? Are eggs beneficial in fevers? Should one take exercise before or after meals?" Etc. Since Peter was most famous as physician and enjoyed a highly lucrative practice, it was not unnatural that he also acquire a reputation as magician. His attitude toward magic was, however, no different from that of his contemporaries while it is for astrology that he reserved his true penchant. And here too his views are of the current type though flavored with some more than average enthusiasm.

Astrology, he claims, is a science which makes extremely high demands upon its disciples. They must possess "a thorough acquaintance with all the infinite detail of nature and the powers of mind and body."

It is a wonderful science even though it is plagued by many impostors and deceivers. In its pure state it "speaks the truth in most cases and very rarely fails of correct prognostication except in certain particulars." He meets honestly all the diverse objections that had ever been advanced against astrology and cites the opinions of all the established authorities in science, philosophy and religion. He harps upon the fact that though the science is difficult and complex, it is honorable and noble. Those who attack it in the name of religion are "hypocrites."

Precious stones and herbs cannot owe their marvelous virtues to the elements that constitute them, but must derive from the stars. Only experience can tell us what these virtues are, since they can in no way be deduced from a priori reasoning. As medical authority he advises that "those who pursue medicine as they should and who industriously study the writings of their predecessors, these grant that this science of astronomy is not only useful but absolutely essential to medicine." Besides, astronomy can also foretell changes in weather so relevant to the cure. The medical practitioner should also look up the patient's horoscope for proper and complete diagnosis. No surgery should be performed when the stars or planets are unfavorable. The eighth sphere of the stars is of special importance in determination of historic events, though planetary conjunctions, of greatest significance in individual fates, can modify history as well. All of these hypotheses are applied to biblical events. Believing that knowledge is power, Peter explains that by further study of the sky and the occult virtues of the heavenly bodies, the astrologer will ultimately find himself in a position to even influence future events and transform threatening misfortune into anything desirable. Credence is given to astrological images and amulets.

In no sense different is the outlook of Cecco D'Ascoli who was actually condemned by the Inquisition and burned in Florence in the year 1327, and his works, the poem l'Acerba, thought to be a parody of Dante's Divine Comedy, and a Latin treatise on astrology were burned with him, and all people retaining copies of these books were declared excommunicated. Two fairly contemporary manuscript accounts of Cecco's fate are contradictory. One claims that in 1324 Cecco was found guilty of uttering malicious or blasphemous words against the Catholic faith and was condemned for it by the Inquisition of Bologna and sentenced to semimonthly confessions, numerous daily recitals of prayer, occasional fastings, listening to a weekly sermon, loss of all his astrological books, his right to teach astrology, loss of his professorial chair, his doctor's degree, and a fine of seventy pounds Bolognese. Three years later the Inquisitor of Florence apparently decided that he had relapsed, summoned Cecco before his tribunal and declared him a heretic and handed him over to the secular powers to burn him at the stake, since the Church can spill no blood.

In another account, a contemporary, Villani, charges specifically that Cecco was condemned for his book The Commentary on the Sphere, a typical astrological work. He was warned to abstain from the pursuit of astrology and violated the prohibition. Cecco denied he had broken the pledge but attributed his persecution to special hostility of a Franciscan friar who was both bishop and chancellor to the duke of Florence. Cecco was a court colleague of his, serving as astrologer to the duke. The writer, Villani, accuses Cecco of having been too bold in his prognostications and of maintaining that the stars spelled absolute necessity and had priority over free will and divine predestination or prescience. But Villani also reports that Cecco made many amazing predictions but was unfortunately a very vain man and worldly in his tastes. Villani also accuses Cecco of teaching that the sky gives forth evil spirits which when subjected to incantations can work wonders if they also happen to be properly adjusted to their constellations.

Yet, an examination of Cecco's writings fails to reveal anything in them that is different from what had been generally advocated by contemporary writers on astrological subjects. The stars control fates and characters as well as the rise and fall of cities and nations. Romans are corrupt because they are under the influence of the signs, hence the importance of astrology in medicine. The mind of man is as much under the influence of the heavens as his body. The moon in different signs has a diversity of effects, good and evil, material and spiritual. It is the stars that explain why an apparently intelligent man will often choose as his wife a silly woman of low birth rather than a "beautiful, noble and intelligent one." Man simply carries out what the juxtaposition of the constellations have declared. Dreams also come under stellar rule. Astrological images can even work as love charms, provided of course they are composed at the proper time.

Nevertheless Cecco, like everybody else, expressly states that he believes in the freedom of the will. He tells his students that according to "our and the true Faith," the all-powerful circle of the zodiac, "though it may be the cause of life, yet is not the cause of our will or intellect except as a tendency, and so I hold and truly believe, although other astrologers hold the contrary, saying that all things which are generated and corrupted and renovated in the inferior world of generation and corruption have efficient causes in the superior world which is ungenerated and incorruptible. . . . That argument I will overthrow. . . ." He also goes out of his way to condemn the notion that founders of new religions including Moses, Merlin and Christ are born of the spirits called incubi and succubi as will also be the future Antichrist. This is contrary to the Christian faith, he declares. "Whence that beast Zoroaster and some following him say that Christ was born under the dominion of those quarter-revolutions (of the eighth sphere) from the virtue of incubi and succubi, of whom I have spoken to you above, but it seems horrible to me even to write such words." Christ our Lord, he says, was the true son of God, born of the glorious Virgin, and is not the product of celestial factors. Rather is He the maker of celestial bodies. The exceptional events that occurred at his birth were miracles effected by divine intervention. To finish off his manifestation of devotion, Cecco concludes his book with the statement that if any of his words are offensive to the spirit of his faith he will gladly submit his work for correction by the very holy church of Rome. Needless to say, Cecco condemns magic, like everybody else, but supports its basic assumptions, also like everybody else. Magic and necromancy are contrary, he insists, to the Christian faith. Demons are wicked things. Beware of them; their aim is to deceive good Christians to the discredit of our Lord Jesus Christ.

It would therefore not seem reasonable to suppose that Cecco's condemnation by the Inquisition and his subsequent execution were due to his views on astrology, which were in no way divergent from those generally maintained at the time by the very pillars of the Church and of philosophic orthodoxy. More relevant to the understanding of his fate is the fact that he was a practicing court astrologer. Such people invariably incur the hostility of many, all of whom are powerful at one time or another. And if such hostility reaches adequate vindictiveness and heat, as well it may with people in this line of activity, then execution on trumped up charges is readily achieved, witness the deaths of Thomas More, Francis Bacon and others in England where other rationalizations than heresy or astrology were used, and without benefit of Inquisition. Moreover, Cecco was a man of high temper and vituperative language and even in his lectures and writings indulged in violent controversy and personal abuse. It was a small matter for him to insist, for example, that the stars at the head and tail of the dragon are in reality points of intersection of circles and not serving the sole purpose of delineating the shape of the zodiacal sign "as a certain physician of ours of Ascoli argued together with his mother who was as big a fool as himself." He also seems almost to specialize in berating physicians, and one of the victims of Cecco's vitriolic attacks, the physician Gualfridinus, a learned scholar of high repute, is cited by Villani to have been "a great cause of Cecco's death."

In the witchcraft trials of later times and in the kind of victims that were caught in the net of the craze, the student of man has ample opportunity to realize the importance of these circumstantial factors in the building up of a situation which leads to inevitable tragedy, like the chain of events in a Dostoyevsky novel. The excuses and arguments cited are merely natural and facile rationalizations. Besides, if the arguments for the persecutions were to be taken seriously, the number of people who qualify for the same punishment is usually quite large. Yet, a single personality is usually chosen for persecution, and that one gets there for many reasons, most of them determined by the character of the victim, or by the conditions which might have tragically crowded in upon him.

Chapter V

THE SUCCEEDING CENTURIES

1. The Theological Opposition Persists

FOR three and a half centuries the astrological assumptions held firm sway over the minds of the great majority of naturalists, physicians, alchemists, astronomers, philosophers and teachers of the times. The only professional group which showed occasional hesitation or even opposition consisted of the theologians who seemed to have suffered from a blind spot afflicting them more as an occupational hazard than a creed. Every now and then some fanatical zealot would rub his eyes as if after a sudden awakening and declare, as if he had hit upon some novel discovery, that astrology went counter to God's preordained will and to man's freedom of choice and was therefore antagonistic to Christianity. As we shall see, these outbursts were taken in their stride, and by the gentle controversy they generated, probably kept interest in astrology alive.

Astronomical books made their appearance in steady succession, so as to supply the basic information required "for perfect knowledge of judgments of the art of astrology which arise by regulation of nature by the effects of the planets." (ibid. III p. 125) And though the range of such basic information was quite considerable, in most texts it was avowedly presented as preparatory for what was to follow, namely application to astrology. Thorndike's summary of the content of the Exafrenon, an early fourteenth century astronomical work would illustrate the point. "For various reasons, but especially to predict the revolution of the year, one should know the time of the entry of the sun into the first minute of the sign Aries. It is also important to know the entry of the sun into every degree of the zodiac. Second, one should know how to determine the degree of the ascendant in the east at the time of one's judgment since from it the time of the twelve houses are measured. Third, one should know the natures and substantial powers of the planets and their dignities, which last are five in number: the house, exaltation, triplicitas, terminus and facies. Fourth, one must know their accidental powers derived from the diversities of their movements in epicycle, station, progress, and retrograde, their distance from the sun, their rising and setting, their motion of access and recess, and the effect of their deferents and eccentrics. For all this one must find the true places of the planets and employ canons, tables, and almanac. The planets further have certain accidental properties from their own natures, such as being masculine or feminine, diurnal or nocturnal, bright or dark, fortunate or unlucky. The fifth requirement is to place the planets in their houses and signs and determine their relationships to one another. One is then prepared to prognosticate future happenings 'naturally contingent' but if any of these preliminaries has been overlooked or slighted, one must be prepared for error or failure. Our author tries, as we have already seen, to allow for the error in the Julian calendar and the retrocession of the solstices and equinoxes." (ibid. III p. 125-6)

The attitude of astronomers to their subject was universally of this nature. In fact it was very much like the attitude of the contemporary mechanical engineer to the laws of mechanics in which he studies theoretical principles and their applications. No more than the author quoted above did any other writer of the times have the slightest suspicion that on one page he was being scientific and on the other he was harboring supernatural delusions and magical nonsense.

During the fourteenth century astrological treatises continued to appear at a steady pace. What may be surprising is that "only three years after the astrologer, Cecco d'Ascoli, perished at the stake, another Italian who was a Dominican friar completed a work of medical astrology 'to the praise and glory of the supreme and ineffable Trinity, the utility and advantage of medical men, and the health of the infirm.'" (ibid III p. 213) Nor was Niccolo di Paganica, the author referred to, the only priest, friar or theologian who wrote openly and enthusiastically on astrology. There was Ugo de Castello, another Italian Dominican who wrote a commentary on the Sphere of Sacrobosco and a treatise on critical days, hence on the subject of medical astrology. Similar works of the same period are extant by renowned theologians such as Robert Holkot, the Franciscan John of Paris, the Augustinian Dionysius de Rubertis de Burgo Sancti Sepulchri, or Augustine of Trent, who is the author of a pest tractate before the occurrence of the Black Death. In it he complains that the physicians of his time "prescribed one medicine for all humors, not knowing the roots of the infirmities. And this pestiferous error happened to many physicians because of their ignorance of astronomy." To rectify this evil he expatiates on the nature of sickness as determined by the constellations, what kind of persons are susceptible at given periods, what regions or cities, and the particular effects of the several planets.

From time to time writers appeared who felt the need for justifying the study of astrology in general. John of Saxony was one such. In his commentary on the Isagogicus of Alcabitius, the standard, authoritative, Arabic text on astrology, he improves upon the original data by materials of his own, acquired by means of the newer instruments which he had developed. The celestial movements can only be studied by employing either instruments or tables. In addition, the profession of astronomer requires certain qualifications of which the great Ptolemy cited three: "Stability of intention, humility of disposition, and abdication of earthly possessions." With exceptional frankness he comments that the last requirement "is displeasing to many and to me." He adds a fourth one however, namely a natural ability, or disposition toward the subject. "For I have seen good scholars in logic and general philosophy who could make no headway in astronomy and arithmetic."

Opposition to astrology he states, comes from ten types of objectors. Some deny the planets any power over sub-lunar beings. Others claim that their effect lies in universal relations, not in particulars, while still others believe they determine only the necessary, not the possible. Then there are those who want to limit their power to the weather. Some object to astrology on the ground that it cannot be considered experimentally founded since thousands of years would have been required for the accumulation of reliable data. Others point to the lack of agreement among the astronomers as to the paths and positions of the planets. Numerous objections come from those who tried to be practicing astrologers but failed. Among the defamers are physicians who think they can heal successfully without knowledge of the stars. Some are objectors because they follow the road of the vulgar crowd and oppose anything that demands learning and thought. Finally there are those who oppose the science because it is beset with so many pretenders and incompetents who care more for gold than honest labor.

To these divisions of astrological opposition originally identified and classified by Albumasar, John adds his own group which consists of those who object to astrology on religious grounds. He considers their hostility groundless since, "many astrologers have affirmed the creation of the world, 'which is the first fundamental of the Faith.'" But John is apparently aware of the advisability of keeping a safe distance in such matters and throughout his writings he scrupulously avoids theological involvements of any kind. In discussing, for example, the effect of the great conjunctions upon the rise of religions, he is cautious enough to state: "But it is not expedient to speak much of this matter, for it is a thing which does not agree with our faith. But if anyone de-

THE SUCCEEDING CENTURIES

lights in these things and wishes to reduce the changes that take place in religions to the motion of the superior bodies, let him read the work of Albumasar on great conjunctions."

And there can be little doubt that Christianity did serve as the only persistent source of opposition to astrology, as indeed we have already seen in the case of the tragic end of Cecco d'Ascoli. From that date until 1492 when the Parlement of Paris was preparing the condemnation of the astrologer Simon de Phares there was skirmishing of a sporadic nature between astrology and some Christian doubters of its orthodoxy. The main cause for the lack of a coherent and concerted campaign was the ambivalence of the churchly attitude. The skeletal structure of the astrological credo was universally accepted but its possible intrusion upon theological dogma was feared. And the attitude of the Churchmen was like the attitude of contemporary preachers and moralists to the expanding social freedoms of young women in our times. Some view it with trepidation and growing alarm while others, equally moral and devoted, take it in their stride as the trend of the times and make peace with it on their own terms, some with more protest and pain, others with less.

Simon de Phares was a man of wide learning and considerable stature as a man of success. He had studied medicine at Montpellier and attended the Universities of Paris and Orleans. He was astrologer and physician to John, the duke of Bourbon and was implored by Louis XI to change posts in his favor. He was apparently reluctant to do that and spent four years in search of medicinal herbs in the Alps, until the king died, in 1483. Five years later the duke of Bourbon died and Simon settled in Lyons to practice astrology. He attained sufficient fame there to attract the young king of France, Charles VIII, who visited him in his study and watched him in the process of predicting. Either the royal visit or his spreading fame or possibly both, brought him into conflict with the archbishop of Lyons who seized his library and sent its volumes for examination to the faculty of theology of the University of Paris. Simon was enjoined from practicing his art in the interim. He consequently took his case for the return of his books and license to practice to the Parlement of Paris in 1491, where it lingered on the records for several years even though, or perhaps because, Charles VIII urged that body in writing to act speedily and favorably on the case of "our dear and well-beloved astrologer, Simon de Phares," who is being unjustly persecuted by the bishop of Lyons. Parlement did nothing of the kind but about two years or so after the king's entreaty, voted to submit Simon's books for examination to the faculty of theology of the university. That august body announced in February 1494 that after considering the case before them for a period of ten months which time was needed for the examination of the confiscated books, they had reached the conclusion that the ars mathematica or the divinatory arts are to be condemned. These arts involved horoscopes, nativities, interrogations and elections, but apparently excluded the annual predictions so popular at the time. Eleven of Simon's books, out of a total of two hundred confiscated, were ordered burned. These included treatises by Albumasar and Abraham Judaeus, the Isagogue of John of Spain, a work by William of England explaining how to diagnose a patient's illness by reference to the stars and without resorting to an examination of the urine, a Latin translation by Pietro d'Abano of a pseudo-Hippocrates on astrological prognostication from the moon, and finally a work by Firminus de Bellavalle on weather prediction. As is often the case with book burning, it is done sloppily and without consistency. Says Thorndike: "The volumes condemned included some of the most used books of medieval astrology and medicine. It does not seem that censure of them even by so high and learned a body as the faculty of theology of Paris would have effect in restricting their circulation or influence. Nor does the faculty seem consistent in what it condemns and approves. While one treatise on weather prediction is condemned, another by Alkindi on the same subject and with the same title, De mutatione aeris, is approved." (ibid. IV, p. 549) Be that as it may, the Parlement rejected Simon's appeal and condemned him in costs. Taking cognizance of the fact that Simon had confessed to revealing thefts, secret thoughts and hidden treasures, the Parlement disregarded his admission of guilt and penitence and ordered that he and his books be handed over to the bishop and inquisitor of Paris for further questioning. All this apparently happened while the king was away on his Italian campaign, and might well have been a move in the game of cat and dog between king and parliament.

Contrary to the claim of some historians, Simon does not seem to have met his death at the hands of the Inquisition. Four years after his condemnation, his calumniator, the Chancellor Rochefort, died "confounded and put to shame," and Simon expresses the rather immodest plea that he hoped to see the members of the Parlement skinned alive. All this he records in a work entitled A Collection of the Most Celebrated Astrologers which is dedicated to Charles VIII. Astrology, he writes, was founded way back in antiquity by the sages of old and was pursued assiduously by the Hebrew patriarchs, the heroes of Greek mythology and the mighty kings of ancient Assyria and Babylonia. After this introduction he continues with a recital of the names of ancient and early medieval scholars expatiating particularly on the scholars in the subject whose labors prospered during his own time i.e. the fourteenth and fifteenth centuries. Thus we learn from his pen that in 1430 a Master Jehan de Guignecourt, a renowned doctor of Paris, was obliged to defend before the entire University Ptolemy's Almagest, "which some fool theologians had wished to condemn." Then there was a Spanish physician and astrologer named Louis de Langle who was an expert healer and prognosticator and aroused the envy and anger of some local ignoramuses who brought him up on charges of superstition before Charles VII. The king however listened to his case without bias and realized that Louis made authentic astrological forecasts which were highly accurate to boot, and freed him and blessed his return to Lyons to continue his practice there. As usual, the book contains the expected mixture of scientific items in intimate association with the crassest superstition.

In spite of this continuous, running fire from many theologians, and unrelenting distrust on the part of orthodox theology, astrological publications never slackened their flow. Moreover, at the very time that Simon de Phares was having his troublesome encounter with the inquisitor and Parlement, a well-known astrologer and physician, Paul of Middelburg in Zeeland, professor of astronomy at the university of Padua in 1479 and a year later the personal physician to the duke of Urbino, and in addition the author of regular annual predictions, was made bishop of Fossombrone in 1494, and remained in that post till 1533 when he was called to Rome by Pope Paul III for the purpose of being invested a cardinal. During the Lateran council of 1512–1517 he was most prominent in connection with the ever-increasing concern over calendar reform.

Another religious who wrote voluminously and outspokenly on astrology at that very time was Marsilio Ficino who describes himself as priest and physician. He is aware that some may find it incongruous that he as a priest should be preoccupied with astrology or medicine. But, he argues, Christ himself was healer, and the ancient priests of Persia, Chaldea and Babylonia required thorough knowledge of astrology. Besides, God who guides dumb animals to suitable medicines through the influence of the stars, will surely want priests to practice astrological medicine. He similarly claims that natural magic is to be distinguished from diabolical and is as entitled to fair study as is medicine or agriculture. It is folly to assume that astrologers ascribe literal meaning to such notions as the animosity between Venus and Saturn, since all celestial bodies are in reality moved by love. What is meant is that these planets have divergent effects.

Celestial determinism in human events is beyond question. "To live and act successfully one should learn what one's horoscope and astrological endowments are, and where they may be most favorably exercised, and then follow one's natural bent. Astronomy should be our guide in procreation of offspring, in preparation of banquets, in building and clothing." (ibid. IV, p. 565) It goes without saying that he is most cautious not to impinge upon religious tenets. He points out that so long as astrologers admit divine providence and human freedom, and what astrologer failed to do that, they are within their rights and liberties, to practice freely their science. Astrologers know that religion is not determined by the stars, that the birth of Christ and the origin of Christianity were not caused by the stars, but were merely foreseen through their serving as signs. Nevertheless Ficino is also the author of a treatise against astrology, which would seem to indicate that an attack upon astrology did not signify an attack upon its foundation.

Astrological medicine of the period under consideration received considerable attention. There is a prominent treatise on this subject by Andalo di Negro of Florence in which he "sets forth how to tell from the stars whether the patient will die or live, whether he will refuse to see or speak to anyone, what the cause of the infirmity is, whether the physician in attendance is honest and capable, bad or fraudulent, whether the patient will be delirious, and so on. He even assumes to discover such delicate distinctions from the planets and houses as that the doctor will be 'evil in his own nature, but good by accident.' Or he instructs how to select the best time for bleeding, cauterizing, operating, administrating laxatives, and so forth." (ibid. III, p. 194) Boccaccio, writing in 1359 says of Andalo: "And you have known, best of kings, how great was his circumspection, how grave his deportment, how vast his knowledge of the stars. Not only by the rules of the ancients did he know the movements of the stars, as we have many a time made proof, but since he had traversed nearly the whole world, and had profited by experience under every clime and every horizon, he knew as an eyewitness what we learn from hearsay." (ibid., p. 195)

Another outstanding writer along these lines was Geoffrey of Meaux, author of A Compendium of All Judicial Astronomy dealing with medical astrology, and of a large work on the comets of 1315 and 1337, respectively and of a tract on the plague. The latter was a favorite topic with astrologers of the time. The Black Death, which occurred in 1348, could not be caused by the conjunction of Jupiter and Mars, as many claimed, since such conjunctions occur every three and a half years. On the other hand, the conjunction of Saturn and Jupiter was a minor one and could not alone have caused it. Each could, however, have been sufficiently effective in combination with an eclipse of the sun which took place close enough to present a possibility.

Having thus introduced the celestial cause, he proceeds with a treatment of the corresponding remedies. People of certain horoscopes are naturally more susceptible than others, and those born under Saturn, had better avoid cold, eat and drink in moderation, sweat several times a week, rub their chests with a sponge dipped in wine which had been cooked with two ounces of linseed and three of camomilla, sweat in a warm bed and drink spiced brandy. A somewhat different treatment is prescribed for those whose horoscopes place them under different planetary influences. His painstaking diagnosis in the above spirit terminates, however, with this bit of advice: "Let everyone avoid standing long or communicating with anyone having that pestilential illness, since it is contagious in that it is poisonous and deadly in every respect." Needless to say, in his exposition of the principles and practice of astrological medicine, Geoffrey has ideas of his own, criticizing others for hasty conclusions and inaccuracies and advancing his own pet system of tenets and interpretations.

The study of conjunctions and their interpretations seemed to play an important role in the astronomy of the times. Special significance was ascribed to the conjunction of the three superior planets, Mars, Jupiter and Saturn which took place in 1345, antedating the Black Death by three years. Among those who grappled with that ominous event we find an astronomer of the caliber of John de Murs. John was a rather remarkable scholar since still as a student at the university of Paris in 1318 he employed a kardaja, or a sextant with a radius of fifteen feet for purposes of observation, which compares quite favorably with the mural quadrant employed by Tycho Brahe two hundred and fifty years later and possessing a radius of less than seven feet. The kardaja of John de Murs had an arc of one twenty-fourth of a circle, hence a sixth of a quadrant, and was placed "on an immobile stone" and "as absolutely straight as possible."

He was the author of several mathematical works such as Canons of a Table of Proportions, Speculative Music, an attempt at a solution of the problem of squaring the circle, a work on reform of the calendar, a commentary on the Alfonsine Tables, a disquisition on eclipses and a tract entitled The Geneology of Astronomy. In addition, he also wrote several mystical and cryptic prognostications based upon the conjunction. In one of them, the least obscure one, "Three chieftains of the celestial militia, born of noblest lineage, are hastening from remote parts o'er many a desert and by tortuous route to a general council in the year of Christ 1345 on the last day of the shortest day of the Latins, that is in the beginning of that in which the creation occurred. Evidently March is meant, when the sun enters Aries. One of them is an old man, dark, and of sombre visage—obviously Saturn. The second is just, pious, handsome, chaste, devout, merciful—meaning Jupiter. The third is ruddy, bellicose, impetuous, no other than Mars." (ibid. vol. III p. 306) The second chieftain will meet the third on the first day of the month after midnight and will bring to the world "wars, slaughter, floods, corruption of the air, epidemics, discords, and unexpected catastrophies from above." On the fourth day at daybreak, the first and third will meet and that event will bring "discords, deceits and frauds, wars, violent winds, and disease." Later in the month the first and second will meet and there will ensue "changes of kingdom, appearance of prophets, sedition of peoples, new rites, and finally a horrible blowing of winds." After accomplishing these their appointed tasks, our three heroes return to their own countries by another route.

There is a more prosaic prediction by John and Firminus. It foretells the time and location of the conjunctions, and points out that the triple events gain special significance from the fact that they occur in March, the month of the vernal equinox when growth is young and gentle and hence more amenable to influence. The fact that the conjunctions will be preceded by an eclipse renders the events even more meaningful in their impact on the world. Saturn is bound to be more influential than Mars but Jupiter will hold his own pretty well. The aggravating action of the preceding eclipse will be felt for a period of three months and three quarters.

The other prophecies and predictions were cut in a similar pattern, though most of them centered around conjunctions and but few can even remotely claim to have foreseen the coming of the Black Death. Among those few may perhaps be named John of Bassigny who foresaw a pestilence afflicting the whole world and carrying off close to two-thirds of the population. The year he gave was 1352, four years late but the details are good enough. Without mentioning 1345 as the year of the awesome conjunctions he does cite that year as the beginning of the woes he foretold. His predictions, he claimed, rested not on the stars alone but on contacts with learned scholars he encountered during his most extensive travels, among whom were a Syrian and a Chaldean in about 1336, and a Jew in 1342. Not knowing their languages he made use of an interpreter but, he adds, he "was with them for practically two years." His prophecies employed the customary allegorical style of such writings, and their contents too was full of scourges, floods, disasters, rebellions, devastations, treason, breach of faith, invasions by infidels, dissension, civil strife, and crushing doom here and yon. "And ere the world reaches the year of our Lord 1382, the church universal and whole world will grieve for the destruction, depopulation, devastation, and spoliation, of the most noble and most famous city which is head and mistress of the entire realm of France." Needless to say, such a tale of gloom could not be conceived without its respectful tithe to the church and the pope. Both will be overcome by evil men and their evil doings and even secular authority will be smothered by engulfing waves of unprecedented iniquity. The pope will change his seat and find no place of refuge and France will be very badly off. The Irish and Scots will invade England and wipe her out. A good pope will arise who will even have a good emperor to help him but their effect will be short-lived. Evil will return stronger than before and things will get so bad that the end of the world will be adumbrated by a host of false prophets and at last, antichrist.

A typical prognostication was that of Trithemius, a learned abbot and master of alchemy. Writing toward the close of the fifteenth century he cites the text of a contemporary astronomer who predicted the coming of the Black Death. "There will be but one lord of the world. The Roman Empire will be exalted. There will be many struggles on earth. The tyrant king of the Gauls will fall with his barons. There will be an unusual and fearful amount of thunder. There will be great effusion of blood. The pope with his cardinals will be dissipated. There will be great famine in the lands. Also pestilence and terrible and incalculable loss of human life through the whole world. There will be great heat in the summer and excessive cold in the winter. The seeds will decay in the ground. The injury of the king will be avenged and the queen of Venus will pass in flight to foreign lands. Fleas, locusts, and venomous animals will abound on the face of the earth, and there will be many signs and wonders in the air." Writing many years after the event, Trithemius points out that many things predicted did indeed come true but not all of them. Also the astronomer might have deduced them from preceding events rather than from stars exclusively. It is, however, of interest to find that Trithemius repeats an account reported as well in the work of Giovanni Villani, author of a history of Florence written at about the time of the plague, to the effect that in 1347 a vast vapor descended from the north and settled over the earth terrifying the population and with justice because that same year it rained innumerable forms of minute animal life in the East and out of their corruption came a great pestilence.

Mention of one more astrological prognosticator may not be amiss here. John of Eschenden was probably the most conspicuous English astrological prognosticator of the fourteenth century, particularly prominent because of his claim to have predicted the Black Death of 1348. And judging from the general style and tone of such pronunciamentos he may well have had good reason for his claim. The year 1345 saw an eclipse of the moon and conjunctions of the three major planets. Eschenden predicted the occurrence of the eclipse "nineteen days, nine hours and forty six minutes" after the beginning of March, and proceeded to foretell the sombre and farflung effects of that event. Needless to say, the circumstances of the eclipse were thoroughly examined and its range and consequences minutely scrutinized. Because the eclipse would start the second hour after sunset its effects will begin to be felt in the second month after its occurrence, and since it will last for three hours and forty two minutes its effects will endure for eight years and six months. "During these eight years and six months," summarizes Thorndike, "men and beasts will suffer long diseases, and there will be death and many wars and flight, cold and much rain and snow in their seasons, and violent winds and damage to navigators, great corruption in the air and great scarcity of crops from excessive cold and rains and worms. This will increase human mortality. The injury to crops and fruits will come especially at harvest time in the autumn." (ibid. III p. 327) The sordid details of this bundle of gloom are then carefully dissected. At one time the sun will temper the malice of Saturn and at another Mercury will prevail and leave his imprint, but apparently in the long run Saturn will become lord over all, bend the fixed stars to his will and make things just about as black as could be.

When Eschenden gets to the discussion of the effects of the conjunctions he has about exhausted the store of evil and is obliged to fall back upon a repetition of the same kind of gloom he had broadcast previously. Conjunctions were in fact his forte. He did not put much stock in interrogations and elections which he regarded as "the more ignoble and less useful parts" of astrology, while the subject of horoscopes he viewed with gentle suspicion. And so his major book on celestial indications deals with first the age of the world, the universe, the planets, the fixed stars, and the signs of the zodiac. From this preliminary discussion he proceeds to weather prediction, and that at great length, then to universal calamities such as pestilences, famine, floods, earthquakes, fires, wars, high prices and concludes with the correlation between the celestial signs and their interpretation for purposes of prognostication. He quotes numerous works and authorities and maintains throughout an erudite and scientific tone.

Apparently Eschenden concluded the volume while the Black Death was in full rage and interestingly enough he had the following to say: "Just as I wrote in the year of Christ 1345. For whatever I have said to you now about the aforesaid effects, that same thing I predicted then in accordance with the opinion of the astronomers. And the aforesaid evils came to pass immediately afterwards and that abundantly. For so great was the mortality in the world in the year of Christ 1347 and 1348 that the whole world was upset and in many lands cities and vills were left deserted, and the few who remained alive in them fled from those places leaving houses and possessions, nor did men dare to visit the sick or bury the dead for fear of infection from them." (ibid. III p. 331) Yet he did not wholly attribute the plague to the stars. He emphatically declares that there is "a great proof that the said mortality was produced by God in the first way, forsooth by the lunar eclipse and aforesaid great conjunctions as by natural instruments. Since that mortality and the other effects mentioned were predicted before any of their effects happened. And that same prognostication was founded on the books of the astronomers."

In a similar, perfectly honest and scientifically reasoned manner Eschenden discusses the nature of pestilence, beginning with an analysis of their generation by the great celestial orbs and their revolutions, and continuing with the effects of the signs and the seasons on corruption of the air and the production of epidemics, and concluding with preventives and cures which medical lore supplies for their defiance. He does take the subject quite seriously since he cites numerous references to all the renowned authorities of the period on the astrological causes of corrupt airs and pestilential winds, which count their numerous victims among men and animals. Needless to say that our author's discussion of the kind of cure medical science had to offer at the time seems about as efficacious in our eyes as his discussion of the initial causes residing in celestial configurations.

Of special interest is his description of the personality and training that go into the making of a good astrologer. He must start with faith in God, a deep sense of humility, eschew praise and the want of glory as well as pride even in his own wisdom or learning. He must be lawful in all his conduct, chaste and sober, abstain from illicit practices such as magic, necromancy and geomancy, and avoid impossible and incredible accounts. A true astrologer must not be over-fatalistic nor must he accept the signs he reads as final and unalterable. "But what Catholic would deny that heat and cold and all the impressions of the air come from the celestial bodies, or that mortality and pestilence, failure of crops and famine, have the same source? Who would deny that certain constellations sometimes dispose men to strife and war?" This need for constant assurance that there was no real discrepancy between the scientific and the religious aspects of their beliefs was of course paramount in all works on astrology.

2. *Two Sceptical Authors*

Two writers of the fourteenth century deserve special attention, Nicolas Oresme and Henry of Hesse. Nicolas was a theologian of Paris, a translator of and commentator on Aristotle, a writer on political and economic topics, author of a treatise on money, and a mathematician of some repute. He had written in addition several essays against astrology. In the first treatise he is rather contradictory in his attack on that sci-

ASTROLOGY AND ALCHEMY

ence in that he starts his work by presenting arguments extolling princes who take an interest in its tenets since the art as a whole is bound to be of great help to them. He finishes the book, however, with a rebuttal of these very arguments. Besides, his main concern seems to be with princes. Thus, the intervening chapters advise princes how to spend their time profitably and the text then proceeds to expose the folly of astrology but follows this with a discussion of which aspects of the subject are to be studied and which to be eschewed.

Nicolas was also the author of further attacks upon astrology as well as other forms of divination. Unlike other opponents of his day, he introduces a novel point, namely, that mathematically it is far from settled whether the orbits of the planets are commensurable or not. In a treatise entitled On the Commensurability or On the Incommensurability of Celestial Motions the two muses Arithmetic and Geometry argue precisely this point. Quite naturally Arithmetic argues that such a beautifully complex and harmonious system as that of the planets, the heavens and the stars would have to have their velocities in numerical proportions, "for if anyone should make a mechanical clock, would he not make all the wheels move as harmoniously as possible?" Since this is stated in 1370 it seems quite obvious that the mechanical clock was already a reality then, as Thorndike points out. In the absence of strict regularity there would be no prediction of aspects or conjunctions or eclipses, no tables and no astrology, and no music of the spheres.

But when Geometry has her say she points out that there can be beauty without regularity, and motion without commensurability since the divinity can do anything. If the movements of the celestial bodies were commensurable, eclipses of sun and moon would occur at regular and constant positions which in fact they do not do because of the motion of the lunar nodes. Nor can one be certain about the music of the spheres. Hence the implication of Nicolas Oresme's arguments is that astrology cannot be regarded with certainty because the regularity which it presupposes is vitiated by the possible incommensurability of the heavenly motions. As a translator of Aristotle, Nicolas exploits that philosopher's lack of enthusiasm on the subject to refute astrological rationalization wherever possible. He even uses Arabian sources, the very fountain springs of the astrological stream to refute their reasoning, citing both Avicenna and Averroes. It goes without saying that in his vast erudition Nicolas could not escape citing Cicero, Vergil, Seneca and of course the old anti-astrological standby, Augustine. He does not neglect to refer to the arguments from religion, free will and the fact that Christ's birth was supernatural and not celestially determined. There is also the old stuff about twins. Besides, the very preoccupation with the future is a bad omen, claims Nicolas, hence no wonder many astrological texts put the science under the reign of the malevolent planets, Saturn and Mercury.

The action of the heavenly bodies can only involve light and heat. These emerge from them in pyramidal form so that as Nicolas puts it "the shorter and more obtuse the pyramid is, so much the stronger is the action and virtue." It was unnecessary to postulate a mysterious effluvium emanating from the stars since all earthly events could well be accounted for by the light and heat from the heavens and the four elements and their qualities on earth. And why should a planet have a different influence when in the ascendant than when in some house or other or when some other planet is in aspect? What scientific meaning can one assign to the notion that the sun has greater power on Sunday than on Monday, or that a given planet exerts greater powers at one hour than another, or that degrees of a sign have sex or colors, or even virtues?

In addition there are, alas, many deceivers among the astrologers everywhere. Sometimes they hit on the truth by sheer luck and at other times they demand credit for false prognoses or for statements arrived at through secret inquiries. Yet it must also be admitted that there are some true ones as well. "I say that the prince and any other person should greatly honor true students in astrology who make tables of observations and critical rules for judgments and those who know how to consider scientifically the nature of things, discriminating the true from the false." (ibid. III p. 416) Weather prediction is possible and desirable but the knowhow has not yet been attained. It must also be admitted that from conjunctions and revolutions and even comets one can safely predict such general events as famine, floods, pestilence and wars but not in sufficient detail, for example, to know the exact country in which the war will break out or in which month. Nicolas has similar reservations concerning nativities. They are all right for predicting the physical constitution and natural inclinations of an individual but are useless for contingent events affected by fortune, free will or matters beyond our control. Interrogations and elections are utterly pointless. He had in fact experimented extensively with elections, having shared in the popular credulity toward them, but had no success. An astrologer subsequently explained to him that his very nativity was opposed to his attaining any skill in that art, yet no astrologer had ever told him that before. In disgust he compares diviners by hydromancy, pyromancy or sortilege to the alchemist. "Just as alchemists are most often deceived and are wretched and unfortunate, so are all who trust in the aforesaid arts (i.e., the divinatory) nor is it to be wondered at, since those fatuously presume to know the secrets of nature, and these the secrets of fortune."

All that scepticism must not be taken to mean, however, that Nicolas was outside the bonds of his epoch and free from superstition. In his *On the Configuration of the Qualities* he develops the customary notion of the times that there are two kinds of magic, the kind wrought with the aid of demons and the kind which makes use of the hidden powers of nature. He fully accepts the existence of demons but believes that natural magic is of the kind "for which some rational reason can be rendered and in which, even if a demon is invoked, absolutely no external effect is produced thereby, although the sin which is committed in such an act sometimes is suggested by the devil." And even magic is not always the work of demons. Incantations and figures employed by magicians are false since different regions employ different invocations, as do different sects in a given region or even different magicians. Besides, some magical wonders are produced naturally as when certain old women, especially of the type having double pupils in their eyes, "often are able to produce wonders by imaginative virtue from the corrupt state of the brain." Hence it is the imagination which is responsible for many of these wonders and not demons, and often sick people find it easy to perceive similar fancies and illusions. "As therefore the said effects can be produced naturally from sickness or some other occasion, so it is possible that the feats of the magicians may be by way of art which imitates nature without other action of a separate spiritual substance." While performing feats of magic the mind of the magician is altered by the ferment of his sensitive spirits, hence little wonder that he may really undergo the experiences of unique fancies and delusions. In addition the semblance of magic may also be achieved by altering the human spirits or senses as is done by drugs, or the colors and shapes of objects may be changed by subjecting them to special treatment with things having particular virtues, and also mathematically by mirrors and optical illusions. It is common knowledge that many stones and herbs have occult virtues, and should be employed judiciously and for beneficial purposes only not as poisoners use them. It is also known that "subterranean spirits or gases, exhalations or fumes," affect the mind and stupefy the senses producing visions as in the case of the Delphic oracle or the purgatory of St. Patrick. Nevertheless Nicolas prefers to attribute the effects of such exhalations to demons. It is true that there are some naturalists who explain all occult phenomena by reducing them to natural causes. Yet Nicolas would not go so far, and cautiously leaves some acts to be explained by demonic action only.

His book *On Fascination* reveals how painful logical thought could be to a philosopher with naturalistic leanings in the fourteenth century. Fascination cannot be exercised by mere will of the mind. Such a view is "remote from philosophy and not consonant with our Faith," which in modern language might read "which is unmaterialistic and unscientific and contrary to Stalinism or Marxism." In our author's view fascination can be explained without resorting to demons. Fascination is defined as "the impression of suffering or infection made on a human being or other animal by the glance of another man or animal." Inanimate objects, herbs and trees do not possess the power while animals do. Hence it emanates from the sensitive soul rather than the rational (pertaining to man) or the vegetative (pertaining to plant and animal), and its channel of operation is the eye, and the medium is the visual spirit. The imagination, the soul, are the loci of initiation of action. Their action may be so intense as to affect and deform or corrupt the body, which in turn will alter and corrupt the surrounding air or any material objects in the vicinity. Thus the basilisk can kill a man by its glance alone, and a wicked old woman, whose brain spreads corruption through the body will be able to infect other people, especially the tender bodies of infants by merely fixing her glance upon them. Similarly a wolf can render a man speechless. The concept of spreading corruption was a real thing to people like Nicolas at the time, as real as is the mechanism of economic determinism to many moderns. Thus Nicolas cites an instance of a man who made a mirror which when held before a criminal would become coated with a black cloud, the product of a guilty conscience acting upon the humors and spirits of the guilty man and resulting in this telltale emanation. Moreover, the visual spirit carrying the vapor of fascination is differently affected by different passions, and differently received by the victim.

In part of his work, which may not be from the pen of Nicolas Oresme, there is an interesting reference to the magnetic needle acting as compass, presumably observed by the author at Venice. "The sailors have a needle mounted on a pivot in the center of a copper table. From this center lines lead to the circumference along which are designated the names of the cities and harbors and their distances apart. They start the needle revolving by moving a magnet rapidly about it. Then the magnet is suddenly withdrawn and plunged into a receptacle full of water. Thereupon the needle, relieved from the necessity of revolving after the magnet, in good time comes to rest pointing toward the pole, and the sailors even on a dark night can shape their course accordingly." Obviously, inventions such as this one could easily be made by people who maintained Nicolas Oresme's views and even far less enlightened ones, since Nicolas must be regarded as one of the most critical and scientific minds of the fourteenth century.

An attitude to natural events wholly similar to that of Nicolas Oresme's is displayed in the writings of Henry of Hesse, a German theologian of Paris, who in a way continues the mode of approach so well propounded by his predecessor. His scepticism toward astrology sprang from his philosophical notion that God or the First Cause initiates terrestrial events by direct action and not, as most philosophers believed, through the intermediation of the celestial bodies. He also postulated a common and universal force which can cause events in contradiction to the natures and inclinations of the objects it acts upon. Hence there was very little room or need for astrology in his scheme of things. He considers the action of the stars purely mechanical and compares it to an experiment first employed by Adelard of Bath in the twelfth century. If one holds one's finger tight over a small opening in the top of a jar containing water and having an outlet tube at the bottom, one prevents the water from falling out until air is let in. The sky acts much the same way and human manipulation can fully control it. Henry is thus enabled to deny the significance of planetary aspects.

Nevertheless the stars are not wholly ineffectual. They are secondary and imperfect causes only in comparison with the First Cause, but in contrast to inferior matter and forces they remain superior and perfect. This type of argument could very easily bring astrology in through the back door but Henry does not do that. He goes so far in fact as to deny all occult virtues or causes as unnecessary. He explains the action of the magnet upon iron by suggesting that the action of the magnet evokes a quality within the iron that causes it to move toward the magnet. Hence the magnet with the iron affixed to it weighs no more than the magnet alone, since the iron raised itself toward the magnet. The virtues of spices need not be claimed to be occult. Their effects upon man, like the action of certain odors or drugs, are fully explained by their heating or chilling action upon the brain. Nor does one require to postulate occult action of healing herbs or various medicaments. While they themselves possess different qualities, so do the different organs or parts of the body, hence the diverse effects obtained.

Henry finds it even unnecessary to grant Aristotle's concept that the heavens are composed of a fifth essence, distinct from and superior to the four inferior elements. He believes that these four elements and their four qualities can well account for such phenomena as spontaneous generation from stellar putrefaction, corruption of the air, pestilence, weather changes and similar events. The four qualities and their derivatives are subject to the conditions of intension and remission, to uniformity and difformity, proportion and configuration, all of which supplies quite a variety of ensuing changes. Henry gets, unfortunately, lost in his new array of modifying conditions and declares they are unmeasurable, which hardly helps matters, since as Thorndike points out, "we dimly pass from the occult to the unmeasurable," which leaves his scepticism quite limited. "He denies occult virtue but accepts all the old occult phenomena: spontaneous generation, the transmutation of metals, the possibility of dead dogs breeding live foxes, dead saints that still grow beards, the marvelous mandragora, and what not. Indeed, while Henry has taken up with a new theory, he has no new facts at his disposal and therefore not unnaturally still accepts the old fictions." (ibid. III, p. 491) However, as we shall see below, the same could rightly have been said of Copernicus, and yet his theory did so much to enrich human thinking and to stimulate extensive experimental research.

Of special interest is Henry's refutation of comets acting as signs of future happenings. Henry accepts the Aristotelian doctrine that comets are exhalations of earthly vapors ascending to the upper spheres of air and fire. Since they form in midair they cannot exert much influence on the earth below. Winds may accompany comets but are not necessarily produced by them. Similarly pestilences often follow the appearances of comets not because they are produced by them but because both are the product of the same set of events. Both stem from the pestilential vapors arising from the putrefying viscera of the earth, which have the power to poison people who dig wells and which produce both plagues and comets. Besides, how can one predict at all from comets if it is uncertain where they first appeared, and in which constellation. His scepticism toward comets is in every way remarkable. So is also his criticism of Ptolemy's Tetrabiblos for insufficient substantiation of his assignments of the planets to their diverse houses.

Henry's attacks on astrology were persistent and relentless, though the run of his arguments is not exceptionally novel. The motion of the planets interferes with and obscures the action of the starry sphere; accurate prediction is impossible because of reflection and refraction of starlight by water, clouds or rainbow; astrologers gain their positions at court because of patronage; they are too close to magicians, necromancers and geomancers in outlook and in their practices; they reason ex post facto; recently they predicted a very cold winter but it turned out to be warm, while the great inundations in France and Germany of the current year, 1373, they failed to foresee in any way; besides, it is doubtful that floods are caused by the stars to begin with, and he proceeds to propound a naturalistic explanation, which of course remains a mere explanation. The previous summer had been very hot and dry, so that the earth became hard and porous. The subsequent heavy rains then filled the earth's caverns and floods ensued.

His tractate against the doctrine of conjunctions consists of three books: the first runs into seventeen chapters and is merely a critical dissection of the doctrine of conjunctions; the second, eight chapters, revolves around the argument that even if the assumptions of the astrologers concerning the power of conjunctions are granted, they are still not in possession of adequate knowledge to make accurate predictions; the third, of four chapters, gives the whole subject a somewhat curious twist by arguing that in any case crop failures and ensuing hunger as well as plagues can just as well be predicted "from the ordinary influence of the stars without recourse to conjunctions, eclipses, and revolutions." The astrological assumptions are after all insecure, observations are difficult, its web of hypotheses often conflicting with both natural philosophy and Christian theology. Many of its categories are arbitrary, e.g. the division of the zodiac into signs, facies and termini; similarly, epicycles and deferents are mere mathematical inventions to "save the phenomena"; the number of spheres is uncertain.

Yet his critical attack does not always have smooth sailing. He argues, for example, that had the conjunction of 1345 been really influential in causing the plagues of 1373, a kind of prolonged action which he is loath to grant in the first place, its effects should have been discerned much sooner, apparently in total ignorance of the Black Death of 1347-1348. Besides, he argues, the conjunction of Saturn and Jupiter in 1365, marked a change from an aerial to an aquatic triplicitas and should, therefore, have annulled the previous action, and the "beneficent influence of Jupiter should have counteracted the pestilential tendency of Saturn." And why, he asks, should the tertiary or quaternary aspect be more benign than the sextile? It is true that the magnet shows different powers in parts of Norway and it is possible that the planets may act more powerfully when they are opposed to each other as in musical consonance, yet mathematical figures cannot possibly concentrate or dilute whatever stellar action there be. Henry, who had elsewhere declared his belief in the existence of critical days in disease as determined by the position of the moon, cannot obviously be taken at his face value when he argues against the power of aspects.

Another difficulty with conjunctions is that they are interpreted by inadequately trained astrologers. They do not realize that inferior conditions and substances are as important as superior, and that proper interpretation of celestial events requires knowledge of geography, climate and above all political and social affairs. The good astrologer should study past conjunctions and subsequent phenomena to establish true cause and effect relationships, carefully note the ascendant of the region concerned, the nativity of the reigning monarch and the alignment of the constellations at his coronation, if he is to interpret political events accurately. Having retreated so far he seems tempted to go further and states that "many combinations of the movements and positions of the stars are 'useless and sophistical,' and that it is consequently difficult to tell which constellations cause natural effects." There undoubtedly are some which are delusory and others conditional; hence

THE SUCCEEDING CENTURIES

the good astrologer must learn how not to be fooled. To strengthen his tottering logic Henry then proceeds to prove that such calamities as pestilence can well be caused by other factors than conjunctions, namely a disturbance in the proportion of humors; he is obliged to concede, however, that the malevolent action of a poisonous plant or venomous animal can be duplicated by an appropriate configuration of the stars. As if to top the merry-go-round, he finishes off with the further concessions that such planets as Saturn or Mars can surely produce pestilence, and that the action of the stars can persist for a variable period of time just as iron after having been acted upon by a magnet remains magnetized for some time. By way of apology for the inconsistencies, it should be pointed out that throughout his works Henry conceives of stellar influence as physical radiation, "which may be shut off by the interposition of other bodies as one excludes the moist effect of the moon by closing the window," or rather the shutters. Even the intervention of thick clouds would either intercept the rays or permit very little to filter through. Hence the influence of stars on man is much like the action of the sun or moon.

It is in all probability correct to assert that practically all science showed a significant decline in the fourteenth and particularly in the fifteenth centuries as compared with the thirteenth. (Glenn E. Tyler, A Study of the Factors Involved in the Decline of European Science in the 14th and 15th Centuries. M.A. Thesis, The University of Minnesota, 1947) It is certainly true that the astrological writings of the 15th Century seem more standardized than those of the thirteenth and that the science of interpretation of the heavenly doings has become fairly settled, and even the struggle against astrology has considerably subsided. A plateau in the curve seems to have been reached in which there is no pioneering, no search to speak of, no specific lacunae to grapple with, no specific doubts to strengthen. There is only the art to practice.

3. *The Fear of Comets*

The Fifteenth Century also sees the continuation of cometary discussions and predictions and seems to have been blessed with enough comets to be concerned about, most conspicuous of all being the comet of 1456, known to us as Halley's comet. That same year Rome saw two comets and naturally a number of judgments, all of which were dire. Since life too had its full share of calamities, the expected correlation between prediction and ensuing events maintained its good record of the past. That year Rome experienced an attack of the plague and Naples several earthquakes. Interpreting that comet for Alfonso V, king of Aragon, the humanist, Giannozzo Manetti points out that poets, theologians and historians ascribe earthquakes to divine judgment, while natural scientists, astrologers and philosophers attribute them to natural causes. He records and discusses 210 past earthquakes and reaches the conclusion that the one at issue was a natural, not a miraculous one.

The real contemporary issue lay elsewhere, however. Aristotle's notion that comets resulted from earthly emanations was generally accepted. Since we have already seen Ptolemy's approach to astrology, we might take a fleeting glimpse at Aristotle's idea, particularly since it is often remarked that the Stagyrite was no supporter of the astrological art. (A. Bouché-Leclercq, L'Astrologie Grecque. Paris 1899) There can be little doubt, however, that, as Wedel points out, the Aristotelian philosophy supplied orthodox astrology with "a rational explanation of the universe which captivated the best scientific minds down to the time of Kepler and Tycho Brahe." (T. O. Wedel, The Medieval Attitude Toward Astrology. New Haven, Conn. 1920, p. 4) Aristotle discusses coming-to-be and passing-away, that is, birth and death, generation and corruption, and growth and decay of bodies on earth, and concludes that their causes lie in the motions of the heavens. Now, the sphere of the stars, or the eighth sphere, revolves uniformly and uninterruptedly about the earth and must therefore be eliminated as a possible causative mechanism of matters mundane. For a celestial body to be effective its "movements must . . . be more than one, and they must be contrasted with one another either by the sense of their motion or by its regularity." (On Generation and Corruption, Bk 2, Ch. 10. Basic Works of Aristotle R. McKeon, editor. p. 526) It is the movement of the sun in the ecliptic that fulfills these requirements. "And there are facts of observation in manifest agreement with our theories. Thus we see that coming-to-be occurs as the sun approaches and decay as it retreats; and we see that the two processes occupy equal times. For the durations of the natural processes of passing-away and coming-to-be are equal. Nevertheless it often happens that things pass-away in too short a time. This is due to the 'intermingling' by which the things that come-to-be and pass-away are implicated with one another. For their matter is 'irregular,' i.e. is not everywhere the same: hence the processes by which they come-to-be must be 'irregular' too, i.e. some too quick and others too slow. Consequently the phenomenon in question occurs because the 'irregular' coming-to-be of these things is the passing-away of other things." (ibid. p. 527) The motion has to be circular "for that is the only motion which is continuous." All natural transformations are circular and that which initiates all movement "must be single, unmoved, ungenerated, and incapable of 'alteration.'" Heavenly bodies have the capacity to "return upon themselves" while men and animals do not. It was this kind of reasoning which was further extended to the planets as well, since it

THE SUCCEEDING CENTURIES   123

would be not only pointless but impossible in an orderly, teleological universe to have so many celestial planetary bodies revolve in the zodiac, in beautiful circles, without moving, i.e. affecting corruptible things below.

It would seem to us now that one of Aristotle's major sources of error was his unshaken logical belief in causation. So potent was his faith in causes that he postulated four of them: the material cause, "that out of which a thing comes to be and which persists"; the formal cause, "the form or the archetype"; the efficient cause or "the primary source of the change or coming to rest, e.g. the man who gave advice is a cause, the father is cause of the child"; and the final cause, "in the sense of end or 'that for the sake of which' a thing is done." (Aristotle, Physics Bk II Ch. 3, p. 240–241) By setting the eighth sphere in motion God could not but let loose a cause which initiated great doing. "For he needs no contrivance or the service of others, as our earthly rulers, owing to their feebleness, need many hands to do their work; but it is most characteristic of the divine to be able to accomplish diverse kinds of work with ease and by simple movement, even as past masters of a craft by one turn of a machine accomplish many different operations. And just as the puppet-showmen by pulling a single string make the neck and hand and shoulder and eye and sometimes all the parts of the figure move with a certain harmony; so too the divine nature by simple movement of that which is nearest to it imparts its power to which next succeeds, and thence further and further until it extends over all things. For one thing, moved by another, itself in due order moves something else each acting according to its own constitution, and not all following the same course but different and various and sometimes even contrary courses; . . . So it is with the universe; by a single revolution of the whole within the bounds of day and night, the different orbits of all the heavenly bodies are produced, though all are enclosed in a single sphere, some moving more quickly, others more slowly, according to the distances between them and the individual composition of each. For the moon accomplishes her circuit in a month, waxing and waning and disappearing; the sun and the heavenly bodies whose course is of equal length, namely those called the 'Lightbearer' and Hermes, perform their revolution in a year; the Fiery star in double that period; the star of Zeus in six years; and lastly the so-called star of Cronos in a period two and a half times as long as the heavenly body next below it. The single harmony produced by all the heavenly bodies singing and dancing together springs from one source and ends by achieving one purpose and has rightly bestowed the name not of disordered but of ordered universe upon the whole." (Works of Aristotle. Edited J. A. Smith and W. D. Ross. Vol 3 De Mundo p. 399a. 1923) Though stemming from a spurious work of

Aristotle, this passage faithfully represents the philosopher's attitude.

It is in his Meteorology that the full conception of the origin of comets is developed. Together with a faithful summary of the views of his predecessors Aristotle presents his own analysis of available data, based of course on his preceding philosophy of natural relationships. "When the sun warms the earth the evaporation which takes place is necessarily of two kinds, not of one only as some think. One kind is rather of the nature of vapor, the other of the nature of a windy exhalation. That which rises from the moisture contained in the earth itself, which is dry, is like smoke. Of these the windy exhalation being warm, rises above the moister vapor, which is heavy and sinks below the other." (ibid. Meteorologica Bk 1, 4 341b) The external layer of the earth's atmosphere, that nearest the heavens consists of some kind of fiery matter, "so that a little motion often makes it burst into flame just as smoke does; for flame is the ebullition of a dry exhalation. So whenever the circular motion stirs this stuff up in any way, it catches fire at the point at which it is most inflammable. The result differs according to the disposition and quantity of the combustible material. If this is broad and long, we often see a flame burning as in a field of stubble; if it burns lengthwise only, we see what is called 'torches' and 'goats' and shooting-stars. . . . So the material cause of all these phenomena is the exhalation, the efficient cause sometimes the upper motion, sometimes the contraction and condensation of the air. Further, all these things happen below the moon. This is shown by their apparent speed, which is equal to that of things thrown by us; for it is because they are close to us, that these latter seem far to exceed in speed the stars, the sun, and the moon." (ibid. Bk 1, 4, 342a)

Aristotle then discusses "the nature of comets and the 'milky way,'" giving an excellent survey of the views of philosophers who preceded him. One cannot but be impressed with their courage and skill in manipulating crumbs of evidence bearing on a most complex problem and yet hit upon amazing bits of truth. Aristotle's own views are that comets are not planets because they often appear outside the circle of the zodiac and several of them have been seen on rare occasions simultaneously. Nor can their locus of appearance or all else known about them be harmonized with this hypothesis. Besides, some comets have tails, and all of them have been seen to vanish above the horizon, without setting. His own theory he expounds as follows. Motion produces heat, "indeed, moving bodies are often actually found to melt." The sun heats by virtue of its rapid motion just as shooting stars catch fire when they encounter potent friction in the earth's atmosphere. The earth's driest exhalations reach the outermost layer of the earth's air layers, where "a comet is formed when the upper motion introduces into a

THE SUCCEEDING CENTURIES

gathering of this kind a fiery principle not of such excessive strength as to burn up much of the material quickly, nor so weak as soon to be extinguished, but stronger and capable of burning up much material, and when exhalation of the right consistency rises from below and meets it. The kind of comet varies according to the shape which the exhalation happens to take." If the exhalation is like "a heap or mass of chaff into which a torch is thrust, or a spark thrown" then it will burn rapidly to yield a shooting star; but if the "fire were to persist instead of running through the fuel and perishing away, its course through the fuel would stop at a point where the latter was densest, and then the whole might begin to move. Such is a comet." It may form thus anywhere in space or in the immediate proximity of a given star and under its special action. In the former case, which is the far more common, the comet "falls behind the motion of the universe, like the rest of the terrestrial world." In the latter case it moves like a halo in harmony with its star or planet.

That comets "foreshadow wind and cloud" is perfectly logical to Aristotle since their very "origin is plainly due to the plentiful supply" of dry exhalations. All the evidence of past appearances of comets points to events corroborating that correlation, and he cites many dates and records.

Another learned and thoroughly naturalistic writer on the subject of comets in antiquity was Seneca whose views are expounded in his Natural Questions. Since he lived at the time of Nero, whose tutor he was, his summary of the intervening four centuries between his times and those of Aristotle are of special interest. Outstanding among these are the views of Apollonius of Myndus who claimed that there were many comets in the universe, that they were not optic illusions, as was maintained by others, that they were planetary bodies, that "there is no reason to suppose that the same comet reappears," that their orbits are very remote, that they are seen only when they come close to the earth in the lower part of their course, and that they vary considerably in size and particularly in color. The colors of comets seem to have impressed themselves on everyone regardless of attitude toward their meaning as omens.

Seneca's exhaustive and enlightened discussion bears evidence of the intellectual vitality of a period in which so much attention was paid to basic meteorological phenomena from a sound point of view. There are many philosophers whose ideas about comets Seneca reviews, and well they are worth recording, considering the times and the knowledge available. There was, for example, Epigenes, who postulated a kind of comet that appears low down because it derives from "the earth's exhalations, both dry and moist," and another type which derives from exclusively dry materials, appears in higher celestial regions, "has a more definite resemblance to stars, traversing an orbit and passing through the zodiacal signs." The ascent of dry matter causes whirlwinds which are abetted by the discord of the merging moist and dry elements, and the commotion produced leads to fires which form the comets. Seneca, incidentally, does not like this theory and opposes it with arguments which are as physico-chemical in nature, and as irrelevant as those presented in its defense by Epigenes.

Then there was Artemidorus of Parium, who suggested that there were numerous planets and not all of them need be seen or known, hence it is quite likely that comets are really planets whose orbits are such as to bring them close to earth only at times. At other times their orbits take them so far from the earth as to make them invisible. But Seneca did not like that kind of reasoning on the ground that one is obliged to assume that "either all stars (i.e. planets) move, or none of them does." There was another philosopher, Zeno of Citium, whose none-too-popular theory was that comets were an illusion created by the convergence of rays from different stars to a focus, yielding diversely shaped spots of light.

The degree to which the search of the time touched upon experimental procedures can best be seen from the following excerpt from Seneca's work: "Aristotle has finely said that we should never be more reverent than when we are treating of the gods. We enter a temple with all due gravity, we lower our eyes, draw up our toga, and assume every token of modesty when we approach the sacrifice. How much more is all this due when we discuss the heavenly bodies, the stars, the nature of the gods, lest in ignorance we make any assertion regarding them that is hasty, or disrespectful; or lest we wittingly lie. Let us not be surprised that what is buried so deeply should be unearthed so slowly. Panaetius and others, who will have it that a comet is not an ordinary star but the mere counterfeit of a star, have bestowed careful treatment on the question whether all seasons of the year are equally fitted to produce comets and whether all quarters of the sky are equally suitable for their creation. They have inquired, too, whether they can be formed in all regions through which they can pass and have discussed other points of a like kind. But all these questions are foreclosed by my statement that they are not accidental fires, but inwoven in the texture of the universe, directed by it in secret, but not often revealed. And how many bodies besides revolve in secret, never dawning upon human eyes? Nor is it for man that God has made all things. How small a portion of His mighty work is entrusted to us?" (Seneca, Physical Science, Bk VII, Ch. XXX p. 304) In the same category belongs the observation of Posidonius that during a solar eclipse a comet becomes visible although it had not been visible before because of its proximity to the sun. In fact, one might almost say that it was the ancients' regard for data that was the cause of their persistence in error, but how were they to know that the data they so assiduously gathered and paraded at their erudite and vituperative discussions were to prove utterly irrelevant? It is easy for us to smile when we read their scrupulous classifications of comets, their meticulous descriptions of shapes, colors, and positions in the comfort of our present knowledge. "Different kinds of comets," says Seneca, "are pogoniae (bearded), lampades (torches), and cyparissiae (like cypress trees), and all the rest of them: they have a thin tail of fire." (ibid. p. 40) Similarly the Byzantine author, John Laurentius Lydus, whose death occurred exactly 500 years after the death of Seneca (565 A.D.) "repeated the classification of comets which had grown up since Aristotle's time, naming and describing nine divisions which he said were taught by Aristotle or ten as taught by Apuleius Romanus. His divisions were 'hippias, xiphias, pogonias, docias, pithus, lampadias, cometes, disceus, typhon, cerastes.' Citing Ptolemy as his authority, Lydus gave the name of an additional type of comet, 'salpinx.'" (C. Doris Hellman. The Comet of 1577: Its Place in the History of Astronomy. New York 1944, p. 43) These same writers would meet with our condemnation had they neglected to state those observations, and had these phenomena turned out to be relevant in the light of some future theory. Yet, in the search of scientific truth, precisely how is one to know which observations will prove valuable and which not?

Seneca's own views bear the usual marks of his critical logic. He disagrees with the Aristotelian notion that comets are transitory fires. "It is distinctive of a star (i.e. a planet) that it describes a curve in its orbit. Whether other comets had this circular orbit I cannot say. The two in our own age at any rate had. Again, everything kindled by a temporary cause quickly gives out. . . . A comet has its own settled position. For that reason it is not expelled in haste, but steadily traverses its course; it is not snuffed out, but takes its departure. If it were a wandering star (planet), says someone, it would be in the zodiac. Who, say I, ever thinks of placing a single bound to the stars? Or of cooping up the divine into narrow space? These very stars, which you suppose to be the only ones that move, have, as every one knows, orbits differing from another. Why then should there not be some stars that have a separate distinctive orbit far removed from them?" Assuming, he continues, that the orbit of every planet must somewhere touch the zodiac, "then, I say the comet might have such a wide orbit that at some point it may coincide with the zodiac. This is not necessary, but it is possible."

Then comes some of his typical logic and his grand and classic utterances: "I do not agree with my school here (i.e. the Stoic) for I cannot think a comet is a sudden fire, but I rank it among Nature's permanent creations. First of all, everything that the atmosphere creates is short-lived; such things arise in an element that is fugitive and changeable. How can anything continue the same for long in the air, which itself never remains the same? It is always in a state of flux, and its quiet is short-lived. . . . I said a moment ago that no fire could be lasting which arose from some defect in the atmosphere. I have now to add further that it can by no means be fixed and steady. Both torch and lightning and shooting star and any other kind of fire forced out of the air by pressure, are in flight; none of them is visible save in the course of its fall. But a comet has its own settled position. For that reason it is not expelled in haste, but steadily traverses its course; it is not snuffed out, but takes its departure. . . . Do you suppose that in this great and fair creation among the countless stars that adorn the night with varied beauty, never suffering the atmosphere to become empty and sluggish, there are only five stars that are allowed to move freely, while all the rest stand still a fixed, immovable crowd? Should anyone ask me: Why then, has their course not been observed like that of the five planets, my answer to him shall be: There are many things whose existence we allow but whose character we are still in ignorance of. We shall all admit that we have a mind by whose behest we are urged forward and called back; but what that mind is which directs and rules us no one can explain any more than he can tell where it resides. One will say that it is breath; another, a kind of harmony; another, a divine force and part of God; another, subtlest air; another, disembodied power. Some will even be found to call it blood, or heat. So far is the mind from being clear on all other subjects that it is still in search of itself. . . . Why should we be surprised then that comets so rare a sight in the universe, are not embraced under definite laws, or that their beginning and end are not known, seeing that their return is at long intervals? It is not yet fifteen hundred years since Greece 'Counted the number of the stars and named them every one.' And there are many nations at the present hour who merely know the face of the sky and do not yet understand why the moon is obscured in an eclipse. It is but recently indeed that science brought home to ourselves certain knowledge on the subject. The day will yet come when the progress of research through long ages will reveal to sight the mysteries of nature that are now concealed. A single lifetime, though it were wholly devoted to the study of the sky, does not suffice for the investigation of problems of such complexity. And then we never make a fair division of the few brief years of life as between study and vice. It must, therefore, require long successive ages to unfold all. The day will yet come when posterity will be amazed that we remained ignorant of things that will to them seem so plain. The five planets are constantly thrusting themselves on our notice. . . .

Yet it is but lately we have begun to understand their motions. . . . The heavenly bodies may not stand or turn away. All advance; once the signal is given they start on their race. Their career will end only with their existence. This eternal creation has motions that suffer no recall. . . . Men will some day be able to demonstrate in what regions comets have their paths, why their course is so far removed from the other stars, what is their size and constitution. Let us be satisfied with what we have discovered, and leave a little truth for our descendants to find out. . . . Nature does not turn out her work according to a single pattern; she prides herself upon her power of variation. She has made some things larger, some swifter than others; some stronger, some more limited in power; . . . She does not often display comets; she has assigned them a different place, different periods from the other stars, and motions unlike theirs. . . ." (ibid. p. 298-301) Throughout his work Seneca's style and scientific logic sparkle with similar lucidity and perspicacity.

Yet throughout the period of the development of science in western Europe the views of Aristotle rather than those of Seneca prevailed. The reasons for this strange preference may lie in the fact that Aristotle's theory seemed more coherent, more harmoniously linked with an overall philosophy than did Seneca's explanation. After all, Seneca merely offered a possibility which to his age seemed quite unstimulating. There was nothing any one could do with it except say—well, possibly so. Not so with Aristotle's. Every item of his explanation was part and parcel of the belief web of the times, and when we say belief web we mean the emotions, thoughts and personality pattern of behavior of most of the people of the period. Heaven was different from earth hence heavenly bodies were made of different matter, they were celestial, ethereal, empyreal. Also, they were permanent, immutable and beyond generation and corruption. They revolved in perfect, circular orbits and affected bodies and events below. In no way could comets be made to fit there. If Seneca thought they belonged he had much to upset, much to explain, and much to prove. For his ideas to stick a new belief matrix was necessary, and such was not available nor in the making. And so long as the scientific belief pattern of antiquity dominated the thoughts of men, or as some people have it, so long as Aristotelian authority prevailed, Seneca's speculations could not possibly find any fertile ground to fall upon or even a minority to appeal to.

No wonder then that cometary theories stood still until the sixteenth century. Says C. Doris Hellman in her excellent study The Comet of 1577: "During the twelve centuries which followed the death of Ptolemy little was added to cometary theory. Belief in comets as evil omens was strengthened. Comets were associated with particular planets or constellations, and it became of utmost importance to determine the place in which a comet first made its appearance. However, the fourteenth century witnessed some attacks on astrology. (As we have seen that had been happening all along. M.G.) The previously established classifications of comets were repeated and somewhat elaborated. The chief value of those years to the development of the theory of comets was in the continued observations of those phenomena and the consequent increase of data on the subject, and the repeated efforts to interpret comets." (p. 65)

4. The Problem Attacked and Solved

The initial steps in the coming revolution in cometary thought were taken in the fifteenth century. The number of observers increased as did even the number of general tracts and prognostications. Such men as Peurbach, Regiomontanus, Apian and Cardan, to mention only a few, did much to raise new problems and stimulate the search for more data. The matter of the comet's distance from earth, especially the matter of parallax, became of vital importance. It was not, however, until the appearance of the new star, or nova of 1572, that the search for parallax became serious and led to the new concept of the true role of comets in the solar system. The nova of 1572 probably did as much to shake people's ideas in the nature of the universe as his encounter with new races and cultures, which began at about that time, did for the inception of his new ideas about man and social forces. Significantly enough, it was Tycho Brahe, the greatest observer of the skies before the discovery of the telescope, one of the last defenders of astrology, the most rational and authoritative opponent of the Copernican system, who also published the most accurate and exhaustive study of the nova of 1572, and also happened to be the man who proved that comets had no parallax and were therefore located beyond the sphere of the moon. The latter conclusion brought him in direct conflict with the Aristotelian conception and marked a veritable revolution in human thought.

"On the evening of the 11th November 1572, Tycho Brahe had spent some time in the laboratory, and was returning to the house for supper, when he happened to throw his eyes up to the sky, and was startled by perceiving an exceedingly bright star in the constellation of Cassiopea, near the zenith, and in a place which he was well aware had not before been occupied by any star. Doubtful whether he was to believe his own eyes, he turned round to some servants who accompanied him and asked whether they saw the star; and though they answered in the affirmative he called to some peasants who happened to be driving by, and asked the same question from them. When they also answered that they saw a very bright star in the place he indicated, Tycho could no longer doubt his senses, so he at once prepared to determine the position of the star." (J. L. E. Dreyer, Tycho Brahe Edinburgh 1890, p. 38) To measure the position of the star Tycho made use of a 19 foot quadrant which yielded greater accuracy than anything in existence then. The star was visible for nigh on to eighteen months and Tycho watched it change color, decline in magnitude and finally disappear in March 1574. All measurements indicated it belonged to the eighth sphere, hence was even outside the spheres of the planets. It was not a comet, since these are below the moon as products of the earth's atmosphere. The book on the new star was Tycho's first work and he had not yet begun to question any of the known theories. Tycho also foresaw dire consequences that would follow the appearance of the new star simply because that was the case after the only other of its kind in the past, namely after the new star which had made its appearance about 125 B.C. at the time of Hipparchus. His study concludes with an orthodox astrological interpretation of the new event judging its meanings from its positions and path.

Accurate observations of the nova of 1573 were also made by Michael Maestlin, Kepler's teacher, John Dee and Thomas Digges in England, Munosius in Spain and Hagecius in Bohemia, all of whom concluded that the new star was not in the earth's atmosphere, had no parallax and was located in the sphere of the stars. There were many others who made valuable observations and whose conclusions corroborated the status of a nova as a star, even if they failed to establish it. On the other hand there were quite a few competent observers who considered the star as a comet and thought they detected an angle of parallax in its course. However, the very fact that a considerable number of highly reputable astronomers were obliged to assert that the nova was stationary among the fixed stars was sufficient to shake the security of past conceptions. That effect may not have been immediate or explicit but it was real and potent nonetheless. The act of undermining security in a belief is not as plainly visible as a sunrise, in a group any more than in an individual, but its effect is deepseated, gnawing and discernible in time. The experience of the nova proved valuable to the event which followed it five years hence, namely the first comet which was carefully observed with parallax in mind, the comet of 1577.

Foremost among its observers was Tycho Brahe whose data forced him to the decision that the observed comet was supralunar thus contradicting Aristotle's notion that all comets were earthly exhalations burning in the infra-lunar atmosphere. But there were others who also reached the same conclusion. Maestlin, Roeslin, William IV, the Landgrave of Hesse Cassel, Cornelius Gemma are only some of the illustrious astronomers who not only took numerous measurements but published scholarly treatises leading to the inescapable conclusion that the comet was far out in space beyond the moon's orb. Many placed it among the planets and some among the stars, but the exact location was of secondary importance. What really mattered was whether the comet, as Aristotle had postulated, was a meteorological phenomenon produced in the earth's atmosphere by the celestial aristocracy, or a symptom of novelty coming into being in the superior world. The decision was as significant to the thought pattern of Europe then as was, say, the decision to be weighed in 1919 whether atoms of oxygen and hydrogen were produced from nitrogen and helium or not. In both cases the conclusions reached were of strategic import to a pattern of conceptions. A similar conclusion had to be reached in the days of Lavoisier concerning the nature of phlogiston and combustion.

As we shall see again and again, the demise of the Aristotelian notion of comets was not the product of revolutionary attitudes or rebellious opponents of authority or tradition, unless we bestow such titles upon all scientific workers or seekers after knowledge, which would also place Aristotle high on such a list. Tycho was one of the staunchest astrologers and a respectful opponent of Copernicanism. Maestlin, another rebel in cometary belief, was a follower of Copernicus and even shy of astrology because, as he said, he was too absorbed in the position and motion of the comet to bother about its astrological meanings. Yet, "Maestlin realized that he was breaking with the Aristotelian tradition which placed comets in the air, so he said that Aristotle wrote about comets in his own time and that then parallax was unknown. Maestlin repeated the Aristotelian theory of comet generation, which he said could be applied only to comets in the elementary, not in the aethereal regions. He thought that Aristotle would have changed it had he known of heavenly bodies found by parallaxes. Maestlin seemed to think that some comets were elementary, others aethereal. He rejected Aristotle's theory and concluded that the generation of comets was a mystery, the key to which was held by God." (p. 152) Aristotle, however, was not wholly ignorant of parallax, as can be seen from his statement that if the earth were to rotate and revolve, as some postulate, "there would have to be passings and turnings of the fixed stars. Yet no such thing is observed." (De Caelo Bk. II Ch. 14) Be that as it may, Maestlin is not the heroic "Fighter Against Aristotle." Rather is he the simple, honest human being struggling with a new concept which is part of his thoughts, against another concept which is also part of him. Nor is he an opponent of astrology. "He said that he did not care to write about the comet's meaning, concerning which much had been written, but he was interested in its position and motion. He felt that he could not rely on predictions made by men who erred in the comet's position and motion." (p. 153)

The third person mentioned above, Helisaeus Roeslin, was primarily

THE SUCCEEDING CENTURIES

a court physician, an alchemist and a student of the cabala. He also had other scholarly interests and wrote on a number of subjects. He was involved in a controversy with Kepler over the latter's support of the system of Copernicus which he opposed because it defied physical science and scripture. He himself preferred the Tychonic system which he regarded as the most reasonable at the time, and which he claimed to have independently arrived at, though he never sought either to deny or belittle Tycho's role as its recognized sponsor and founder. His book on the comet appeared in 1578 and his data were fairly accurate. Finding that the comet was supra-lunar he suggested that there might be a sphere of comets among the planetary orbs. He even tried to equip the comet's orbit with an epicycle to account for its vertical motion and to fit it into the postulated band of previous comets. Like Maestlin he concluded that apparently not all comets behaved as Aristotle stated and that some of them belonged to the ethereal region. The last chapter of his work deals with significances and prognostications.

And so on down the line. The scholars who helped overthrow the Aristotelian doctrine of comets were not out to revolutionize astronomy. They were concerned with a particular and limited problem of gathering the best data with the best possible tools and of interpreting them in the most reasonable manner. They did not regard Aristotle as an enemy any more than they regarded their own views as imbecilic. Conversely, when their conclusions conflicted with those of any of their favorite authorities, even Aristotle himself, they had no fear in saying so, and thought no more of it than we do today of contradicting an author or a colleague.

It is also true, however, that many observers of the time were so much under the influence of the traditional belief pattern that their observations suffered as a result. Some of these were skillful astronomers, such as Hagecius, Scultetus, Nolthius, Busch and a few others. Hagecius, for example, was a renowned physician and scholar, an astronomer and mathematician of note, a pioneer in geodesy and cartography, and court physician to Rudolph II, the famous patron of the arts and sciences. He was also a great believer in astrology and as physician considered it indispensable to effective medical practice, and even published a work on metoposcopy, or the reading of character from face to forehead. Like other believers in divination he frequently complained "that many pseudo-prophets were misusing human credulity; and he severely criticized those who added false prophecies to calendars." Though the author of many astrological calendars and ephemeridae, he states in the preface to his metoposcopy volume published in 1562, "that with advancing age he was losing interest in all kinds of prophesying," another indication that some forces of disaffection were beginning to undermine the will to seek or practice divination. In the instances cited it would seem to be preoccupation with problems regarded more interesting, or more novel, or more important. His tract on the nova of 1572 was significant and his observations were in close agreement with the findings of Tycho, and elicited from him the admission that the occurrence of something new in the heavens was apparently a possibility. He was an active supporter of the movement for calendar reform. Though he was deeply religious, he "was a true scientist in the sense that he was willing to change his mind when he was shown to be in error." He found at first a parallax of 5 to 6 degrees for the comet and concluded it was below the moon. But when Tycho pointed out to him errors in his calculations he changed his mind and admitted its supra-lunar nature. His work contained a full astrological analysis of the event, a defense of the divine nature of comets and their function as omens.

There were also men like Scultetus, also well known as scholar, astronomer, mathematician, astrologer and jurist. He "was particularly interested in calendar reform. He defended it, although a Protestant, and expressed his regret that some people fought against a good proposal because of hate for its initiators." Like Hagecius, he also was famous as geographer and cartographer. His tract on the comet is highly mathematical, though in spite of a great show of spherical triangulations he concluded that the comet showed parallax and was therefore sublunar. There were in addition many observers who altogether failed to take the problem of parallax into account, regarding the atmospheric nature of comets as established.

It is customary in our age to ascribe all causes of retardation in scientific progress to lack of technological equipment. While this is often the case, there are apparently other causes, such as emotional ones which are also effective in blocking the advent of doubt. There were good quadrants in the fourteenth century, according to Thorndike. "Historians of science have made a great deal of fuss," he states, "about the mural quadrant of Tycho Brahe at the close of the sixteenth century, as if it constituted a remarkable modern advance in the development of astronomical instruments. Tycho's much vaunted device had a radius of about six feet and nine inches, and the aforesaid historians of science have often contrasted this with the small dimensions of medieval portable astrolabes. But three centuries before Tycho our undergraduate employed a Kardaja (instrument resembling quadrant) with a radius of fifteen feet for his astronomical observations. Its arc, it is true, was only one sixth that of a quadrant. And if Tycho's quadrant had the advantage of being affixed to a wall, our medieval undergraduate's kardaja was at least set up by him 'on immobile stone' and as 'absolutely straight as possible.' " (Vol III p. 295) Admitting even that Tycho did have better

THE SUCCEEDING CENTURIES

quadrants than his famous mural one, since Dreyer states he built one for Paul Hainzel with a radius of 19 feet (Tycho Brahe p. 31), it is still a fact that instruments could not have been the main factor in the search for parallax. Rather was the search initiated by the weakening of the emotional bonds to Aristotelianism brought on by the shock of the nova of 1572.

In spite of the fact that the researches just cited performed the invaluable task of bringing to the fore the question of parallax in an impressive manner, the world refused to be much impressed, and the belief in comets went on as before. In a study of the comet of 1680, more than one hundred years later, J. H. Robinson writes: "The credulity of the mass of mankind remained much the same until the end of the (seventeenth) century. But it was during this period as well that the forces of rationalism and science were preparing for the attack that was to prove so effective, following the appearance of the comet of 1680. . . . Undoubtedly the spectacular character of these prodigies (of the seventeenth century) had much to do with the continuance of the superstition in such vividness. Certainly, the literary impulse was fostered to a high degree. . . . The comet of 1557 gave rise to something over forty contemporary treatises. But when we come to the comets of the seventeenth century, we find a very much more abundant literature." (The Great Comet of 1680 by James Howard Robinson, Northfield, Minnesota, 1916. p. 12)

"The works appearing in 1680 refer, almost without exception, to the baneful character of this great portent," he continues. This is particularly significant in the light of the fact that in 1665 there appeared the Dissertation sur la nature des comètes by Pierre Petit in which the author seeks to reestablish the views of Seneca as against those of Aristotle. Petit was the general superintendent of the ports and fortifications of France, and a student of astronomy. He also advocated the view that comets have regular orbits which necessitate their return in due time. He attacked astrology generally and had the backing of no less powerful a ruler than Louis XIV of France who presumably urged him to write his tract so as to fight superstition in the kingdom, although we have been repeatedly propagandized by many historians that kings and priests usually seek to advance superstition among their dependents. Apparently the treatise exerted little influence. In spite of it, and even in spite of the availability of the data on parallax, seventy years of telescopic observations, Galileo, Newton, the observation of the transit of Venus by Horrox in 1639, and the spread of the Copernican conception, the fear of comets remained strong. "Out of about one hundred works resulting from its appearance, but a few can be adduced as evidence of a spirit of thorough scepticism. Only four of the works examined have

136 ASTROLOGY AND ALCHEMY

been found to belong unquestionably in this class." (ibid. p. 58) On the other hand, there were no conspicuous scientists who even wrote on the significance of the comet. Closest to the scientific stamp come Erhard Weigel, Professor of Mathematics at the University of Jena, and the discoverer of the comet, Gottfried Kirch, "the first astronomer who systematically sought for comets with a telescope." Both men wrote scientific pamphlets on the comet, yet both were convinced of its function as omen indicating a variety of things, none of them good. Apparently, the world was to wait two more years for the comet which became famous as Halley's comet and which that famous astronomer studied in 1682.

It is of interest that Robinson devotes the longest chapter in his abovementioned treatise to a discussion of Pierre Bayle's Pensées Diverses sur la Comète, which was published in 1682. This work of Bayle was put out in an English translation in 1707 under the title Miscellaneous Reflections Occasioned by the Comet Which Appeared in December 1680 (London), and was no doubt widely read in France, England and Germany. Diderot claimed that it was Bayle's book that made the comet of 1680 famous, and Voltaire stated in his Century of Louis XIV that were it not for Bayle the march of reason would have been far less lively. There can be no denying that the work hammers away relentlessly at the belief in comets as omens or as causes of dire events on earth. Yet one cannot help feeling that the paeons of praise for Bayle's rationalism are unfair to the workings of the mind of man and misrepresent its enormous task, its wonderful accomplishments as well as its torpid limitations. Praise it surely deserves; but why not a word about the manner in which the challenge to cometary belief is brought forth, on what fulcrum does its balance swing, what gave Bayle the courage to do what others before him could not or dared not do?

Bayle was no scientist. He was Professor of Philosophy at Sedan and wrote the book because he was bothered by his students with all kinds of questions regarding the message or meaning of the comet. He thinks a comet is a comet and that is all there is to it. He is sceptical just as Carneades was sceptical or Diogenes cynical which means on general, philosophical and temperamental grounds, hence for the same reason that Kepler was a mystic or Aquinas and Galileo deeply religious. In many respects it may be claimed that Bayle was far more remarkable than his admirers seem to be aware of. For example, his recognition of the role of personality in conduct and the superficiality of professed belief as compared with the strength of character of some individuals, his view of the importance of sentiment and emotional forces in the will to belief, seem like startling adumbrations of future discoveries. To these psychological pointers should be added his stress of traditional and cultural patterns as agents affecting the responses and thought habits of the individual. These contributions were of no small merit in his day.

Equally striking are Bayle's common sense scepticism, so pleasantly wedded to vast erudition and a lively style, and his utter disregard of science. He seems to think it irrelevant to the argument he is bent upon. He states: "From hence it is easy to show that People are grossly mistaken when they fancy that the exhalations of the Comets may easier descend upon the Earth, than the Exhalations of the Earth rise up towards the Heavens. For whatever System we chuse, we must allow that the motion round any common Center in the World is very considerable: Let it be round the Earth, as the University-men will have it; or round the Sun, as Copernicus and his Followers; or part round the sun, and part round the Earth, as Tycho Brahe suppos'd, 'tis much the same to me: it being a constant truth, that the Comets always appear in a part of the World where there are Bodys which move round a common Center; by consequence these Bodys indeavour with all their might to get at their greatest distance from this Center, and have more force to remove off than all those Bodys which lie between them and the Earth. From whence it follows that the matter round the Comets has no such easy task in descending upon the Earth, and that 'tis altogether as hard for it to get down thither, as for the terrestrial Matter to climb up to Heaven." (above p. 19) His scepticism is best expressed by such statements as: "Allow that the Comets did discharge a great quantity of Exhalations as far as the Earth; does it therefore follow that Mankind must be sensibly affected by 'em? By no means!" Thus we must concede, he frankly admits, that the comet diffuses "through the whole extent of the Vortex of the Sun" particles of its matter, much as a lump of sugar dissolves in water. But since the space is so vast, man cannot be affected by it. Were such reasoning applied to ultra-violet or cosmic rays, it certainly would not be either helpful or sound. He argues with similar logic, proved thoroughly false in the light of future scientific findings, that "the moment the Comet disappears, the malignant Qualitys it had produced from without, are intirely extinguished," as should follow from Aristotle's reasoning.

Why should I assume that comets must forebode only evil, he asks. Why can I not suppose that "this drossy Matter coming once to precipitate, leaves a ferment and fatness, which renders the Soil exceeding fertile, like the Slime which the Nile bestows upon Egypt?" That, of course, is a good question but hardly damaging to the defenders of the belief, since they could always point to enormous amounts of evil in the wake of comets, and little good. But then Bayle went on to attack all of astrology as chimeral, impertinent and "a scandal upon human nature." His stress upon psychology is new and bold. "Men love to be deluded, and therefore are ready to forget all the times the Astrologer fails, and remember those alone when his Predictions were thought to be true." (p. 35)

Bayle challenges many beliefs which we call today superstitions, such as lucky days, omens, unlucky names, etc. He often cites data to prove a given point, as when he refers to the fact that a given medical author has examined the marrow of the bones of many animals on all kinds of days and found no correlation between the phase of the moon and the quantity of marrow. Nor is the temperature or weather in any way related to the conditions on new or full moon days. Learned men, doctors and men of reputations are not to be trusted implicitly since they may not have fully informed themselves on a particular issue. Nor do numbers count since a given belief accepted by millions may be wrong, and that advanced by a single person free from prejudice "and the result of a judicious examination, carry'd on with exactness, and supported with a deep insight into things. And as 'tis rightly observed, That one Eyewitness is better than ten Hearsays; so we're assured, that one Man of good sense, who only advances what he has well considered and found to bear the Test of all his Enquirys, gives more weight to his Opinion than a hundred thousand vulgar Souls, who follow like a Flock of Sheep, and pin their Faith on their Leader's Sleeve. 'Tis doubtless on this account Themistius and Cicero have so frankly declared. The first, that he wou'd sooner believe what Plato only signified with a Nod, than what all the other Philosophers shou'd depose on Oath: And the last, That Plato's single Authority, without further proof, broke the utmost Obstinacy of his Spirit." Which brings up the question precisely what is Bayle arguing here? At the beginning of the chapter he denies the value of reputable authority as against one exact observation, but then proceeds, in his effort to deprecate respect for numbers, to praise the tyranny of authority if it has the glamor or merit of Plato. (p. 94)

Bayle devotes considerable space to the fact that belief in comets stems from pagan notions and fears. Moderns inherited that belief and maintain it because they are superstitious. "You see the Antients and Moderns, the Christians and the Pagans, perfectly agreed about Eclipses presaging great Calamitys. And yet 'tis a notorious Error. 1. Because Eclipses can do no harm; 2. Because they can be no Signs of harm." (p. 102) Having already proved the first point he laboriously takes up the second. Eclipses are not signs but natural events caused by given motions and positions. To be a sign a particular event must be determined by the same cause as that of which it presages. We may use a given event such as the sun's shadow to inform us of a certain obligation, say, to go to church. Hence eclipses are either connected with the chain of events eliciting evil or are sent by God to inform us of its approach. Neither is correct. True, God does send signs of his coming chastisements, but how can he send as a sign something which occurs naturally and several times a year? "That such Signs might make Impression on reasonable Creatures, they ought to be rare and uncommon, and they ought to be destined, not to presage the ordinary Accidents which traverse human Life in every Year and every stage of it, but to denounce those peculiar Plagues with which God visits the World in the greatest Fury of his Wrath." (p. 108) Now the same logic and truth applies to comets. They are frequent; there were twenty six in the last forty three years. And how could they be signs when they are often unseen and must be discovered by astronomers, who may not even be religious? "The Providence of God, infinitely wise, never does things so little to the purpose." Besides, "Comets are the ordinary Works of Nature, which without regard to the Happiness or Misery of Mankind are transported from one part of the Heavens to another, by virtue of the general Laws of Motion and which more or less approach the Sun, and appear at one time more than another, as their meeting with other Bodys to which God lends his Concourse, requires they should." (p. 111) Why on earth, he asks, should God have sent warnings to pagans? To remind them they are not pious and thus induce them to return to the ways of their faith, hence to greater and more devotional idolatry? This is of course preposterous. Moreover, if comets are presages they must be miraculously produced, which means that God "has wrought a great number of signal Miracles to inflame the dying Zeal of Idolaters, and prompt them to offer Sacrifices, and Vows, and Prayers to their false Divinitys with greater Devotion than ordinary." Hence comets are no miracles and were no presages in the days of the pagans and are none today.

Pierre Bayle, the hero of rationalism, then proceeds to speculate or perhaps explain what is really going on in the world re comets. We all know, he says, what happened when Brennus, the chief of the Gauls, invaded Greece and pillaged the temple of Delphos, the seat of the famous oracle. The devil bestirred himself when he saw that customers would no longer be flocking to his den to replenish his coffers with costly gifts. Parenthetically it should be noted that the economic motive rings truly modern and is not often encountered in those days. And so the devil announced to his priestesses that he would never give up. And did he let them have it! "The earth shook, and open'd in a thousand Places to swallow up the Besiegers; the Thunder broke with a Crash so terrible, that all thought the great Machine of the World was flown in shatters; Lightning flashed from all Quarters of the Heavens; Rocks of a prodigious Bigness roll'd down from Mount Parnassus, and in their fall ground numbers of the Gauls to Atoms." (p. 117) The same thing happened when Xerxes pillaged the same temple on a previous occasion. "And why all this? Not that Men might become wiser or better; that they shou'd conceive a Horror of Sin, and a Love for Holiness; the Devil had rather see all the Temples in the World rifled, than do the least thing to forward such a Change. What then was the meaning on't? Why, he wanted more Sacrifice, and wou'd nourish Superstition and Idolatry in the Minds of Men; . . . What tricks has he not played to have Children sacrificed to him?" Why, he brought the most brutal, the most horrendous and bloody misfortunes upon the Pelasgians because they refused to sacrifice to their gods, as they had vowed, a tenth of their fruits. "Ancient History is full of Instances of this kind, which shew as clear as Noon-day, that the most effectual means the Demons us'd to stir up the sacriligious Worship of Idols, and push the superstitious Ceremonys of the Gentiles to the practice of the horriblest Crimes, was by frighting the World with Prodigys, and accustoming Mankind to judge they were so many Denunciations of Evils to come, and Imputations of Negligence in the Service of the Gods." (p. 119) Would God stoop to such folly? Of course not, hence comets cannot be signs or presages. Besides, there probably are no prodigies at all. The demons cause many natural effects to be taken as prodigies to confound man and undermine his reason, which was not difficult to do. "I shall only observe, the Demons had no hard Task to persuade there was Prodigy and Mystery almost in every thing; for we must own, to the Scandal of the Human kind, it has a strong propensity this way; and in all probability the Soil was so kindly for this sort of Fruit, that it had brought forth an abundance without the trouble of cultivating. I can easily conceive how Men sunk in Ignorance and Error, might come to have sad Apprehensions of future Evils on the sight of an Eclipse of the Sun or Moon." (p. 125) And there are terrible things in nature, such as earthquakes, inundations, and hurricanes, tempests and fires which rightly threaten and frighten man. Hence little wonder that he is also awed or terror-stricken by such natural displays as eclipses or comets.

Bayle, as already mentioned, is fully aware of the fact that the belief in cometary omens and fears derives from human weakness and pagan tradition. Nevertheless, he shows true adumbration of the modern spirit, though of questionable accuracy, when he devotes several chapters to the proposition that the spread and sustenance of superstition was purposefully promoted by politicians, priests and poets. Regretfully he admits that there are many Christians who still cling to this pagan vestige of superstition, and he even tries to explain "Why the Fathers don't condemn the Presages of Comets." He insists, however, that comets can have nothing to do with miracles because "when God Almighty will'd the Sun shou'd bear witness by its Darkness at the adorable Mystery of

THE SUCCEEDING CENTURIES

the Passion of Jesus Christ, he pitched on a time at which this Darkness cou'd not possibly be natural." (p. 126) And comets are natural phenomena.

What seems to bother Bayle the most is the argument that comets are signs to restrain pagans and Christians from atheism. What interest would God have in striving to perpetuate paganism by preventing pagans from becoming atheists? "And on this give me leave to tell you my Thought that in all probability the Devil finds his account more in Idolatry than Atheism; . . . Atheists pay him no Homage directly or indirectly, and even deny his existence, whereas he has such an interest in the Adorations rendered to false Gods. . . ." (p. 233) While this argument goes on pointlessly for several chapters, Bayle does display rare tolerance and understanding of other cultures and customs; and imbued as he is with the learning of antiquity he is fully aware of the deep morality of Greece and Rome. Because of his previously mentioned psychological approach he is bold enough to advance the view that even atheists can be decent, noble and moral. But, alas, "Man does not act by his Principles . . . but almost always turns in favor of his inordinate Affections (i.e. Passions)." There is vast diversity of ways and means of serving God but complete uniformity in the reign of passions, "in all Countrys, and in all Ages."

Bayle is a philosopher by profession and a deeply religious yet broadminded person. His book is disjointed and rambles interestingly, learnedly, and with infinite charm, all over the fields of history, philosophy, religion, biblical commentary, and just so 'human interest' comments adorned with moral trimmings. When after numerous digressions of a hundred pages or so he finally returns to the subject of comets he has very little to add. He does summarize ineptly in six sentences or so five theories concerning the nature of comets, beginning with the Aristotelian and ending with the Cartesian, only to declare triumphantly that "Neither of these Hypotheses discovers any natural Connexion between the Comets, and what happens upon Earth after their Appearance."

Bayle is aware of the fact that the prevailing opinion of astronomers in his day seems to be that comets show no parallax, hence are supra-lunar, and that they form part of the solar system, hence tend to return regularly in their orbits round the sun. The basis for this view is stated thus: "All support their Opinions by the Testimony of Diodorus of Sicily who relates, that the Astronomers of Egypt and Chaldea foretold the Return of Comets. Let them do their best, they shall find a hard matter to reconcile their Notions to the Phenomena; and the Authority of Diodorus will stand them in little stead, because we're informed by other hands, that Eudoxus who first taught the Greeks what he had learned in Egypt concerning the Motions of the Stars, made no mention of Comets. Whence we may reasonably conclude, the Egyptians had then made no Observations upon 'em." (p. 430) But then, he goes on to say, supposing it is true that comets do return, "I say, there's no probability that Comets, and the Bodys which, by altering our Elements produce Pestilence, Famines, Tempests, and Earthquakes, shou'd act several times successively by exactly the same Advances; because the Dispositions which must concur to these great Disorders in the Earth, are in a perpetual Change." Cities perish, marshes are drained, mountains disappear and rivers vanish or change their courses; where there was sea there may be dry land and vice versa.

While the author possesses vast knowledge of science, especially of the sciences of antiquity, and no doubt as teacher of philosophy and of recent science, he nowhere uses it as the main prop of his arguments. The central figure of the discussion, one might almost say, is not the comet but God and Bayle's logic, both of which are fine things but hardly our modern guides to scientific truth. The fact that the book exerted such a strong influence, though it came more than a hundred years after the absence of cometary parallax had been established, indicates that apparently facts are not always employed to their full import, and that the kind of reasoning employed by M. Bayle may be of great social importance for progress.

Chapter VI

ASTROLOGY ON THE DEFENSIVE

1. A Weak Beginning

BEGINNING with the second half of the fourteenth century astrology is firm in the saddle of the cultural life of the middle ages. It is so secure that nothing much of interest occurs to challenge it, which may well be the reason for the relative attenuation of scientific labors in that interval. It has chalked up a complete victory over the opposition it encountered from religion, and was wholly safe from persecution so long as it kept away from unequivocally dangerous ground, such as the horoscope of Christ or topics dealing with plainly divine or miraculous occurrences not determined by natural causes. Otherwise prognostications and ephemerides continued on an even keel and the art was studied and practiced everywhere. It was taught at universities, discussed by the intelligentsia, clerical or lay, and held in awe by the masses as well as by the courts of kings and popes.

One noteworthy event did take place in the closing decade of the fifteenth century, namely the publication of *Disputations Against Astrology* by Pico della Mirandola, which was an open attack upon astrological principles and practices by one who had been an enthusiastic student of the art in his youth. In other words, he was much in the position of these modern intellectuals who in their search for salvation had embraced communism or Nazism, and having subsequently found them false and brutal, exposed their faults with candor and some bitterness, but, nevertheless, also with some personal experience of inestimable scientific value. Pico's work consists of twelve books, the first of which, curiously enough, is devoted to the argument that all critical minds of antiquity were hostile to astrology. He includes in his list such men as Albertus Magnus, as well as Roman emperors whose persecutions of astrologers were motivated by fear rather than scepticism. Sound astronomers practice astrology, he claims, because they wish to extract money from gullible princes, a truly modern explanation, which according to Thorndike, appears in the *Disputations* for the first time. Pico declares that many books of high repute extolling astrology are falsely attributed to Plato and Aristotle, and asserts that others ascribed to Albertus Magnus derive in reality from the pen of Roger Bacon.

In the subsequent books Pico proceeds to point out that astrological predictions are uncertain, useless and, contrary to the claims of such men as Roger Bacon and Pierre d'Ailly, harmful to religion. Their opinions are contradictory and often rooted in sheer ignorance. Admitting that nothing happens in the physical world without the influence of the heavens, he insists that secondary (i.e. earthly) causes are of supreme importance in the determination of specific events. Besides, whatever force is exerted by the stars is part of their motion and light. The signs of the zodiac and the astrological houses are artificial divisions and specific signs can in a way be connected with the weather. Equally artificial are all the rules astrologers predict by, and whatever evil prevails on earth derives more from the nature and interactions of the four elements than the movements of the heavenly bodies. Moreover, the effects of the sky are physical in nature and can in no way be claimed to influence the human character, his mentality or fortune.

Most events about which astrologers are consulted are chance occurrences which are not ruled by the sky. Should a person, for example, leave a house a few minutes before it collapses, then obviously he owed his rescue to divine intervention rather than the action of some benign planet. Besides, "The stars are intermediaries only between God and earth, while the angels are intermediaries between God and men." Nor can the fates of people be foretold from their horoscopes at birth, much less the fates of his relatives. Elections and interrogations are utterly silly and groundless. Pico devotes an entire book to a condemnation of conjunctions and upbraids astrologers for applying their lore to the birth of Christ or Noah's flood or the star of Bethlehem. He also condemns the long prevailing belief in the magnus annus or the notion that both planets and constellations will ultimately return to the position of their original starting point, and history will then begin to repeat itself.

He objects strongly to aspects since how can angular distance be so important a determinant in earthly events. He argues that the special proximity of planets is a far greater factor than all the artificial divisions invented by man. Not all the stars and planets are probably seen and even concerning those known to man, there is wide disagreement among the astrologers. The exact moment of birth is difficult to determine. Assigning different stars to rule over different parts of the body is wholly arbitrary and unsubstantiated, so is the business of allotting to planets the reign over different hours. The Chaldeans originated the errors of astrology by exaggerating the roles of the stars and by not

ASTROLOGY ON THE DEFENSIVE

being sufficiently philosophical to control that propensity. They were aided in their false stress by idolatry, demons, and a tendency to be mathematical and speculative.

It must not be overlooked, however, that Pico did believe in lucky days, the virtues of gems, which, incidentally he attributed to the heat of the sun alone and not to the stars; he believed that southerners are colder inside than northerners, breathe warmer air for that reason and are in consequence effeminate; in addition, the excessive solar heat relaxes them, so that their internal heat is diluted and they develop a dark skin as a result. The moon has a moistening effect which waxes and wanes with the corresponding variations in that body. The moon does not affect the tides, as many believe, but does affect the humors of the body. Belief in numbers is rank superstition but the number seven is important, not because it corresponds to the number of the planets, but because of its occult powers.

There is no doubt that Pico's book exerted a strong influence on his generation mostly because of his reputation as a learned nobleman. It also evoked many substantial replies which, judging by the fact that astrology continued on its happy course, one would conclude, were more effective than the attack. Besides, Pico's attack on astrology was, no more than Bayle's attack on comets, rooted in science. As Thorndike puts it: "Pico della Mirandola's leanings were towards magic and the cabala rather than mathematics and natural philosophy, and his attack on astrology was in a sense an attack on science, or at least more in the nature of a religious retreat than of a scientific advance." (vol V, p. 5)

The slight waning in scientific vitality which became noticeable in the second half of the fifteenth century continues into the sixteenth. Humanism laid more stress on eloquence and literary style rather than science, and the development of print expanded the market and thereby stimulated the issuance of compendiums, epitomizations, and popularizations, often at the expense of scholarly but none too popular original works. As if compensating for this evil, the transition to print was gradual and numerous manuscripts were circulated for many years after the printed page had become a commonplace.

The humanist stress on literary and stylistic values coupled with its reverence for the classics led to an attenuation of scientific interest and creativeness. Specialization became much rarer than in the previous two centuries and vituperative controversies more common. "The poise of the medieval schoolmen, who carefully stated the arguments on both sides and dispassionately rebutted these that seemed to militate against their own conclusions without indulgence in personalities or arguments ad hominem, gave way to one-sided advocacy of a certain theory or point-of-view with no attempt to do justice to other ways of thinking but rather a straining of every nerve to discredit them and their holders. This might even take the form of personal insults and detraction." (ibid. vol. V, p. 9)

Pico della Mirandola had had an interesting earlier career. He came to Rome before he was twenty-four, published nine hundred theses and defied challengers to a disputation on any or all of them, offering to defray expenses to candidates who would have to travel to Rome for that purpose. He had come from Paris where thirteen of his nine hundred theses were condemned as "bordering upon heresy." Many of them were favorable to magic as a science or art, and to the cabbala. This was in 1486 and twenty years previously the University of Paris had condemned twenty-seven or twenty-eight volumes on the magic arts belonging to an astronomer, Master Arnold Desmarets, because they "contained many superstitions, many manifest and horrible conjurations and invocations of demons, many concealed heresies and open idolatries." The subject of magic remained, nevertheless, a lively topic and Pico's courage in defending it was noteworthy. There were others at Paris who in spite of official condemnations either debated or published statements in defense of magic and its conformity with the Christian faith. But in Rome Pico did not get very far with his theses. Pope Innocent VIII who was friendly to him at first and permitted him to borrow books from the apostolic library, appointed a commission to examine his theses "lest the minds of the faithful, and especially of simple persons who are wont to flock to public disputations of this sort, be corrupted." Needless to say the commission found plenty wrong; seven were declared heretical and six others pretty bad but not quite that bad.

In his theses Pico is unequivocally for astrology, not merely in principle but in its numerous ramifications and applications. He affirms the existence of demons, approves with everybody else the attitude of the Church toward bad magic but then proceeds to extol the powers and wonders of natural magic, "the practical and most noble part of natural science," which can reach full expression only through the mystic efficacy of the Hebrew language, arcane numbers, figures and characters. The cabbala is of inestimable value to such magic and is in reality a great tower of Christian strength. His approach is wholly theological and saturated with abstractness. Thus, as Thorndike points out, he describes Providence "as statuitively in God, ordinatively in intelligence, executively in the soul, denunciatively in the sky, terminatively in the whole universe." (ibid. vol. IV, p. 495) Mathematics he regarded as most harmful to a true theologian.

Apparently the commission's condemnation was not quite as final as decisions by purging committees of modern times, because Pico published one year later at Naples a reply entitled *An Apology*, in which he defended those propositions of his which had been declared heretical and accused his judges of heresy and barbarism. The pope then responded with a bill condemning all his theses and Pico made his submission to an investigating pair of bishops acting as inquisitors. Pico soon fled, however, and the pope then also condemned his *Apology* and prohibited its being printed. Pico was arrested in France and imprisoned for some time, and the authorities not wishing to bring him to trial in Paris where he probably could muster many followers, he was soon permitted to return to Italy. He settled in Florence where Lorenzo de Medici interceded for him and the succeeding pope Alexander VI absolved him of guilt.

Pico's defense of magic and mysticism had evoked some interesting replies, particularly one by Pedro Garcia, bishop of Ussellus in Sardinia, and later of Barcelona, and a member of the original commission to examine Pico's nine hundred theses. Garcia opposes magic of any kind, as contrary to the Catholic faith and the spirit of science. Natural magic is not part of natural science, and occult virtues are not subject to investigations by man and are employed exclusively by demons. Natural objects are devoid of mystical powers. If flowers and stones were possessed of such powers, should not man have them on a larger scale, which obviously he does not. Aristotle knew of no such occult powers. True, the magnet and the jasper do have marvelous powers, the latter in stemming the flux, but they are beyond human comprehension. Such virtues are not due to the power of matter alone but to the influence of the heavenly bodies. Lest Bishop Garcia be acclaimed a defender of science, the following quotation cited by Thorndike should be noted: "Moreover, to assert that such experimental knowledge is science or a part of natural science is ridiculous, wherefore such magicians are called experimenters rather than scientists. Besides, magic, according to those of that opinion, is practical knowledge, whereas natural science in itself and all its parts is purely speculative knowledge." The heavenly bodies are moved by angels whom God assigned to that task. Knowledge of the sky is useful to workers in agriculture and medicine, though familiarity with the virtues of natural objects may even be more so. But magic is an evil superstition worked by demons which many deluded people seek to imitate.

Similarly, Pico's later work in the opposite vein, also elicited weighty defenses, but this time of astrology. Pico's own position was defended by a nephew of his, Giovanni Francesco Pico della Mirandola, author of *The True Causes of the Calamities of Our Times*, attributing them to chance and fortune rather than the stars. Their astrological opponents were numerous and included scholars, teachers, physicians, defenders of demonology and witchcraft who regarded astrologers as enemies of belief in these notions, theologians as well as critics of the church or of orthodoxy. But these disputatious works contributed little that was new. Noteworthy perhaps is the fact that there did appear in 1508 a work by Johann Essler of Mainz entitled Speculum Astrologicum, with the subtitle "Of the causes of errors in astrology resulting from neglect of the time equation," which was actually a serious criticism of astrology by an astronomer employing professional arguments. Past experience, says Essler, has amply demonstrated, that astrological predictions are off the mark, apparently because they follow false tables. The Alfonsine Tables are better than those of Thebit ben Corat, and the latter's are better than those of Ptolemy. The reason for the progressive improvement is the fact that the obliquity of the ecliptic diminishes with time, hence, the later tables are more in accord with reality. It was a common error of the times to assume that the angle of the ecliptic to the equator was getting more acute. With smug superiority Essler comments that the common herd of astrologers pay no heed to such fine points which invalidate their labors. He fully approves of astrological medicine since it was highly esteemed by Hippocrates and Galen, and a number of later spurious medicinal writers.

That the defenders of astrology fought back boldly and without restriction is apparent throughout. For example, in 1522 there appeared a work by a priest John ab Indagine or von Hagen, on chiromancy and physiognomy, dedicated to Albrecht, Archbishop of Mainz, and containing strong attacks upon scholastic theology. "In his introduction John inveighs equally against 'those dogs who calumniate astrology' upon the one hand, and against 'that most inept theology which they call scholastic, that is, the Thomist or Scotist,' on the other hand." (Thorndike, vol. V, p. 175) That many good scholasts were famous astrologers seems to bother him little. He speaks of the popes as being hostile to astrology, though this is not quite correct, since many of them were friendly, and the papal bulls against its practice came only later. The works of Indagine, it should be added, saw many editions.

Planetary conjunctions were a great subject of concern to astrology through the years. "Four main features may be discerned in the literature connected with the conjunction of 1524: first, the perennial tendency to predict great ills from such conjunctions; second, a more recent tendency to decry the stress laid by Arabic astrologers upon such conjunctions and to revert to the Ptolemaic emphasis upon eclipses; third, the separate question of the possibility of a second deluge or Sindflut, its moral and theological as well as astrological and meteorological interest; fourth, a number of personal controversies and literary duels between persons who were more often rival astrologers than defender and opponent of the art. For although the question of a flood might seem to give theologians or other opponents of astrology an opening for attacks on the art, it was rather disagreement among the astrologers themselves that especially marked the outburst of writings on the subject." (ibid. vol. V, p. 180).

The attack upon or defense of astrology are not the tasks of any specialized group. Agustino Nifo, the famous fighter against demonology, in part defends the prognostication of a flood which seems to have frightened the population at the time, and devotes a work in three volumes to that assignment. He gives all the pros and cons since the rainbow is a steadfast reminder that God will have no more of that stuff and yet astrology cannot be brushed aside. He feels better in predicting universal diseases such as morbus gallicus, i.e. syphilis, or the Black Death as consequences of conjunctions. We also find men like Brother Michael de Petrasancta, a Dominican doctor of sacred theology and the arts, regent of a convent and professor of philosophy at Rome, who defends the validity of astrology in general and prognostications in particular. There is bad astrology and good astrology; he is all for the good kind and against the bad, and against dishonest practitioners. Also the predicted flood does not have to be a universal deluge, the kind the Bible says will not recur; there will be merely local inundations. On the other hand, there were many nonecclesiastical writers who opposed astrology and many scholars, especially the practitioners and physicians, who heatedly defended it. The disagreement among astrologers was endless and unpredictable. Nothing was above a disputation and there was no telling what a fellow would pick on. Yet on the whole, these incessant disagreements must have exerted a most salutary influence because they helped weaken the public's confidence, and figuratively speaking, undercut the foundation upon which the belief rested.

No doubt the astrological physicians, and one encounters few if any healers who belonged to a different category, took the art most seriously. Thus, we find Jacobus Benatius, a physician and professor of medicine and astrology at University of Bologna from 1501 to 1528, who distinguishes three kinds of prognostication: divine or prophetic, medical, and astronomical. "Some would add a fourth variety produced by melancholy, but Benatius doubts if it can be scientifically reduced to natural causes, unless one takes refuge in occult properties." Miracles and supernatural events come from God but natural occurrences are due to the sky and of course to actions stemming from man's exercise of his free will. Another physician and professor at the same university shows his contempt for the skeptics by declaring: "Those who think that the sky, adorned with so many and so great stars, exerts no effect on those things which are included within its circuit, expose themselves and their knavery shamefully." (Iacobus Petramellarius) In a volume on monsters published at Bologna in 1642 and edited by the professor of medicinal simples and prefect of the natural history museum and the botanical garden of the university, we find a similarly sarcastic reference by the author, Bartholomaeus Amotosinus, to "the opinion of those who persuade themselves that a most noble body such as the sky effects nothing in these inferiors but produces merely light and through light heat." There can hardly be any doubt that the defenders of astrology regarded themselves as the abused and misunderstood devotees of scientific truth.

It was only to be expected that the attitude of the popes to astrology was no different from that of the rest of the learned and religious world of the middle ages. Leo X, son of Lorenzo the Magnificent (1513–1521), the much praised patron of the Renaissance, and above all Paul III (1534–1549), the pope to whom is attributed the reform of the Church after the excesses of Leo X and his nephew Clement VII (1523–1534) who as Medicis exploited their office for Italian politics, were surrounded with scientists, particularly astrologers and exponents of divination and magic. Paul III had dozens of astrological prognostications dedicated to him and had numerous horoscopes taken of his own fate and fortune. It should not be overlooked that Adrian VI (1521–1523) and Clement VII had predictions addressed to them as well, though by far not as many, and Leo X was a close second to Paul III. It was to Paul III that Copernicus dedicated his De Revolutionibus and Colombo his book on anatomy. Books on baths, treatment of syphilis, on mathematics and other learned topics composed by the most eminent scholars of the time, were also dedicated to him. His court was teeming with scholars who wrote on demons, Hippocrates, eclipses, conjunctions, geometry, hermaphroditism, arithmetic, alchemy and the spread of pestilences. His private physician is reported to have confirmed the thesis that the unicorn's horn, which the pope had acquired for twelve thousand gold pieces, was as efficacious in the cure of the plague as it was reputed to be. The astrological books dedicated to him cover the entire spectrum of astrological problems of the middle ages, including the risky question of the geniture of Christ or the pope's nativity.

2. *The Attacks Persist*

As matters developed, this happy state of affairs did not continue without serious vicissitudes. We have seen that the basic conflict between religion and astrology could only be temporarily ameliorated or in some way or other slurred over, but it could not apparently be forever successfully resolved. And toward the end of the sixteenth century the irreconcilable discord came into the open with the Bull of Sixtus

V, in 1585, against astrology and magic, and its reinforcement by a Bull of Urban VIII in 1631. But before we consider these drastic measures it will repay us to survey the scene in its totality.

Paris, the greatest center of learning at the time, was not as deep in astrology as were the famous universities of Italy. In spite of its remoteness from Rome, theologians controlled its university, and astrology, though not altogether proscribed, was certainly not encouraged or permitted to prosper. We have already seen what befell Simon de Phares at the end of the fifteenth century, and it might be added that a spirit of insecurity prevailed long afterward. Yet, not many years after the de Phares affair, we find the Spaniard Pedro Cirvelo, born in 1470, and a student of theology at Paris from 1492 to 1502, an editor of the Speculative Arithmetic and Geometry of Thomas Bradwardine published in 1495 and of the Sphere of Sacrobosco in 1498 (in which he alludes to the first voyage of Columbus), challenge in a work of his of 1521, the right or competence of theologians with no training in geometry to sit in judgment upon astrologers. In his opinion he, Cirvelo, is fully qualified to do that, but not the average run-of-the-mill theologian. He is aware that there are many cheap and vulgar astronomers who are prone to illicit astrology and arouse the opposition of the theologians. He is also aware, he remarks, that as theologian he is under oath to solve any question of philosophy with prior consideration to strengthening the Faith, and that is precisely what he has been doing all along. Hence, he is bold enough to offer this handbook of judicial astrology to the public in the belief that it is free from all vanity and divination. The book was not printed at Paris but at the university of Alcala, Spain. It is a conventional exposition and defense of astrology dealing with weather prediction, horoscopes, a condemnation of interrogations and elections as vain and false, faith in conjunctions, and ending with an attack on the unfairness of Pico's rejection of the art. It might be noted in passing that this same Cirvelo published that very year a work against magical superstition such as false astrology, nigromancy, superstitious divination, the occult arts which rely upon the aid of demons, superstitious remedies, curse by words, belief in lucky days or hours and exorcisms.

There was, however, an astrological work published at that time in Paris by a well-known astrological writer, Albert Pigghe, a philosopher, mathematician and theologian, who after an initial condemnation of the excesses of astrologers, chides the theologians for equating religion with ignorance and decries the prevailing lack of knowledge of astronomy and astrology at Paris. He then proceeds to his job of predictions from eclipses and conjunctions, though he views the latter with sceptical forebodings as to their reliability. A year later he published a treatise "on the equinoxes and solstices and celebration of Easter and restitution of the ecclesiastical calendar."

In 1535 there made his appearance at Paris, one Michael Servetus, made famous through his execution by his friend and erstwhile colleague, Calvin. He had by that time published two treatises on the Trinity, a dangerous enterprise for anyone not a recognized authority on theology, and edited Ptolemy's Geography. His young friend, Pierre Paulmier, Archbishop of Vienne, obtained for him a lectureship at the university, and Servetus held forth on geography, mathematics and astronomy. No sooner had his course begun than he was accused of teaching judicial astrology which was forbidden at Paris. Servetus then wrote a defense of his views, entitled *An Apology*, but was not permitted to print it. To top his troubles it appears that he and a surgeon had dissected a human body though Servetus had no medical degree. That heinous crime brought upon him the full ire of the dean of the medical faculties, which was even further inflated by his publishing a treatise on a purely medical subject involving purging, Galen and Hippocrates. In his works Servetus boasts of the scope of his forecasts and their great accuracy, and attacks his adversaries for doubting Galen's faith in astrological medicine. When Servetus proceeded with the publication of the forbidden pamphlet, the dean of the medical faculty went after him in earnest and Servetus soon found himself before the court of the Inquisition which, however, cleared him of the charge of heresy. The Parlement of Paris, however, obliged him to destroy all copies of his book.

But books on astrology were being published nevertheless. They were few in number and they all decried the excesses of the majority of astrologers and condemned bad or illicit astrology, and sought to mollify the antagonism of many theologians. After paying their respects to these niceties, they then proceeded to the business of propounding astrology as they saw it, arguing violently against other astrologers who prefaced their writings in a similar vein. A frequent complaint by Parisian astrologers was that their subject was in disrepute and near oblivion in that learned and mighty metropolis. In that they were probably right because in Germany, the Netherlands, Spain and Italy astrology had no obstacles of the kind they encountered. Mathematical and medical astrologers prospered, as did also the ordinary professionals, as well as the alchemical adepts who invariably did some dabbling in astrology on the side.

There is ample evidence everywhere that astrology was trying to improve its methods and raise its standards. There is hardly a prominent man of the time whose horoscope is not available from the pen or calculations of some prominent astrologer who often might be a man of the stature of Galileo. Physicians never ceased to seek out ways and

ASTROLOGY ON THE DEFENSIVE

means of improving their diagnosis, and the moon and constellations were vital elements in that endeavor. There was widespread feeling that part of the inadequacy of astrology was due to the poor astronomical tables. The hypothesis of the ninth sphere was also blamed. But these same complainers would often publish ephemerides based on the available tables. Some astrologers go so far as to assert that they find Ptolemy's astrology naive and feel the urgent need for its reformation "on the basis of reason, solid principles and experience." (Joannes Francus Offusius) This same author strives hard to measure the influence of the stars quantitatively, since the stars exert their effect "through the four qualities rather than occult influence." Hieronymus Wolf (1516–1580) lists seven uncertainties which in his view are weakening its position and presumably require immediate clarification, "namely, controversy as to the number and motion of the heavens, as to the motion of the planets, the method of constructing the horoscope, disagreement as to the effects of the stars, uncertainty as to the beginnings of kingdoms and cities and great conjunctions and trigoni, the dissimilitude between twins, and the uncertainty as to the instant of birth." (Thorndike, vol. V, p. 114) But astrologer Wolf remained apparently unhampered by his doubts. He read in his horoscope the day of his own death and as that day came and went, and death failed to claim him, Wolf, as a true astrologer, remained undaunted. He had not given the planet Mars its full weight, he concluded, and thus, apparently allowed an error to slip in.

There was little uniformity in the texts and arguments of the astrological authors. Generally speaking, the Arabian extensions of Ptolemaic astrology are discredited as overimaginative and magical. Yet, even within the more down-to-earth Ptolemaic science, with its sound objectivity and materialistic decorum, disagreements raged as steadfastly and germanely as they do to this day among philosophers, where no school of thought retains a master's stamp very long and no two followers the same path. Actual techniques differed with respect to every astrological symbol or meaning, such as drawing up a horoscope, interpreting conjunctions and similar processes. Even if agreement existed on methods, it broke down concerning the tables to be employed and their reliability. In addition, each accuses the other of being superstitious and unscientific. Each condemns the charlatans, practitioners, whose work may tend to endanger religion and free will, subject the mind or miracles to the motions of the sky, infringe upon the contingency of some events by declaring them all to be predetermined, and of similar transgressions. Most conforming were the physicians, perhaps because they knew exactly what they wanted, and generally speaking, had so many

ASTROLOGY AND ALCHEMY

other things to bicker and argue about that they hardly needed the celestial arena.

The essential contradiction between the concept of divine rule combined with miraculous intervention, and the impersonal, materialistic, deterministic and scientific principles of astrology, lay dormant within the very core of the folklore of the time. Like a bomb it could explode any moment. Besides, there were also other factors. The learned man is invariably respected but he is also feared. And when learning may imply magic, then this ambivalent attitude can assume serious proportions and be readily transformed into the pathological. The astrologer was wise and learned in the mysterious and complex fields of stellar wisdom and wisdom in those days went with magic. In addition, the astrologer could foresee or read the future, and therefore wielded inordinate powers. Such men are to be feared, much as was Medea, although she repeatedly saved the lives of the heroes, yet she did it by magical means. Should such people turn against you, they can spell your doom.

This popular fear of magic, as we shall see, lurked behind the witch mania. But the persecution of astrology came mostly as part of this general sentiment and appeared to emanate from church leadership. By the middle of the sixteenth century the church authorities were preoccupied with the pursuit of heresy. The Lutheran reformation was just emerging from its swaddling clothes and the Catholic church was awakening to its menace. From the campaign against the reformers the Inquisition passed on painlessly to the related task of persecuting the devotees of the occult and illicit arts. Essentially the punitive arm of the church was after chiromancy, geomancy, hydromancy, or nigromancy, but sooner or later astrology had to be sucked into the stream, and by the middle of the century the indices of forbidden books carried several titles of astrological works.

The Index of 1559 carried many magical titles and such illicit practices as witchcraft, auguries, incantations, "divinations of judicial astrology, concerning contingent future events or the succession of events or fortuitous happenings, exempting only those natural observations which are written to aid navigation, agriculture and medicine." Among the prohibited authors are several well-known composers of Prognostications and some practicing astrologers. Several opponents of divination are also listed, such as Caspar Peucer and Joachim Camerarius, probably because of their protestant leanings. But one also finds on the list a work on inventions and names which have no connections with magic or science. The Spanish list even carried the title of Ptolemy's Tetrabiblos. Pope after pope beginning with Julius II issued edicts against magic and heretics, which often meant reformers.

Nevertheless, the bulls of the second half of the sixteenth century do

ASTROLOGY ON THE DEFENSIVE

not name astrologers specifically but only fulminate against diviners, with one exception. Even the bull of Sixtus V is thus directed. In the sole exception referred to, astrologers were to be sentenced to do penance and be exiled from the papal states. In 1556 a papal order expelled astrologers from the churchly states and yet, as the commentator observes, Pope Julius II waited for a propitious astrological moment to lay the cornerstone of the castle of Galliera and the erection of his own statue at Bologna. And there were many other decrees after this one, though the church's main concern was heresy, and the occult arts were secondary. But as we have already seen, the clergy were as much involved in magic, its beliefs and practices, as was the rest of the public. Little wonder then that with the advance of the century we note stricter interpretation and enforcement of the antimagical decrees, with the result that many well known books were prohibited and well known authorities persecuted.

The amateurishness with which the persecution appears to us to have been conducted in those days is a genuine tribute to the skill achieved in that art in our own times, and bears witness to the wonders of progress. Cardan, the famous physician and astrologer, lectured at the medical school of the university of Bologna from 1562 to 1570 when he was arrested at the request of the Holy Office, "kept a prisoner for 77 days, and then confined in his house for 86 days more." Subsequently his books were prohibited and he was enjoined to abstain from lecturing and publishing. All this, fourteen years after the printing of the offending volume De rerum varietate, when the superstitious author had reached the ripe age of seventy. What would not a man like Trotsky or Bucharin have given to be thus persecuted. Yet this is not quite all. Having friends and patients in the college of cardinals he went to Rome and lived there in retirement on a papal pension!

Then there is the case of Francesco Barozzi, a Venetian noble who studied and probably lectured in Padua, a world traveler, renowned for his erudition. He is the author of several books on geometry and cosmography, and a translator of Hero and Ptolemy. He was condemned in 1587 for possessing books on magic after he had sharply condemned the inquisitors for entering his library. He subsequently hid his books in defiance. Brought before the Inquisition he confessed to collecting books on magic and necromancy, performing experiments with spirits and employing the skill thus acquired to check a drought in Crete. He was assigned penances, made to pay for silver crosses in churches and sentenced to imprisonment at the discretion of the Inquisition. He seems to have died in his home leaving his great library, his wonderful mirrors and many instruments to a nephew.

His scientific ideas are rather curious. In his Cosmographia he divides astrology or astronomy into cosmography and judicial astrology. The former is further divided into astronomy and geography, and the latter into weather prediction and genitures, or horoscopes. His astronomy is thoroughly Ptolemaic and he refers once to the heliocentric theory as "the false opinion of Aristarchus and Copernicus."

The Neapolitan scholar Giovanni Battista della Porta also encountered on several occasions the accusing finger of the Inquisition. It was at his house that the Academia de Secreti met, an organization which accepted only people who could boast some invention or discovery. Porta was accused by the Inquisition of employing demons but was acquitted. His academy, however, was closed as given to the illicit practice of magic.

The bull of Sixtus V, of January 5, 1586, marked a sharp departure from past attitudes. It aimed specifically at judicial astrology and divination, stating that God alone foresees the future and man is ignorant of that power and the demons impotent in it. Predicting future events which occur because of natural causes is permissible but not of fortuitous or contingent events, which art is claimed by wicked impostors or the deceit of demons, but which actually negates man's free will. The casting of nativities is illegal, the human soul being guarded against the stars by a kind angel. Permitted is only astrological prediction in agriculture, navigation and medicine.

To what extent the bull was effective in Italy is questionable. It certainly was without any influence north of the Alps. Some astrological books continued to be published in Venice, for example, by Gallucius in which one finds all the old topics. Works on physiognomy appeared with ecclesiastical approval, works on nativities, and bordering subjects.

The case of Porta is interesting because it duplicates in some ways the previously discussed conversion of Pico della Mirandola. In his *Celestial Physiognomy*, published in 1603, years after he published works on occult matters which evoked the charge of magic, he expounds his doctrine that a man's future can be readily discerned from his countenance, and he violently condemns astrological predictions. He ought to know, he says, since he had dabbled in it in his childhood until it was declared hostile to the true faith by the holy father. He, then, not only desisted from practicing it but launched upon an examination of its principles and found them inane and groundless. The only solid base for the science of divination is physiognomy, governed by the humors and qualities of the human body. Having condemned astrology, he then proceeds to cite what all the great astrologers of history had to say about their art. Porta's student, Giovanni Battista Longo carries the argument still further by claiming that Porta laid the foundation for the true science of physiognomy by studying human physiognomy,

ASTROLOGY ON THE DEFENSIVE

celestial physiognomy, the signatures of plants, and examined the "hands, feet and foreheads of executed criminals and persons who suffered a violent death or died without confession." Those who interpret physiognomic features according to Aristotle and Polemon are charlatan empirics and ignorant. Other authors retained some astrological beliefs, and claimed that the edict meant only Arabian astrology, which is the superstitious kind and not the kind they were promulgating.

In Spain the bull seems to have been little heeded. The very fact that in 1631, Pope Urban VIII was obliged to reaffirm it is sufficiently telling. The decree of 1631 specifically forbids predictions dealing with ecclesiastical and political matters, the life of the pope and his relatives to the third degree, which reveal some of the motives behind the repressive act. We shall meet Urban VIII again in connection with Galileo and get a deeper insight into the problem of persecution. Suffice it to point out here that just as astrology audaciously continued on its course after St. Augustine and the early opposition in the twelfth or thirteenth centuries, and ultimately established a compromise between its creed of determinism and Christian dependence on God and free will, so too after these two edicts, astrological publication and discussion continued. It lacked the impetus of the previous wave, for understandable reasons. After all, this was happening in the sixteenth century, the century of Copernicus, Tycho Brahe, Kepler or even Galileo. New interests began to undermine the security of the old astrological assumptions or to draw attention away from them.

But astrologers did not fold up shop and move into other fields, which they might well have done. Professionals like Antonio Pedro (1614–1675) start out by declaring that they compose their arguments and treatises "in the true sense of the bull of Sixtus V, which Urban VIII confirmed and strengthened." But, he goes on, there is superstitious, hence illicit astrology and the scientific kind, the kind he is about to expound and in which he has been interested all along. Another writer might even say that in his youth he had been interested in the other kind but not any more, ever since he had read the opinion of the holy father. Or may we even find one like Thomas Campanella who in his *Apologia*, printed in Paris in 1636 with the approval of the Sorbonne, claims that he is opposed to the superstitious astrology of the Arabs and Jews, and then in the name of impartial objective discussion takes to task the papal attitude by defending the truth of stellar determinism, though in such a manner as to protect himself against the lurking danger, especially since he had been repeatedly in trouble with the Inquisition.

It should not, however, be presumed that there was no serious opposition to astrology. As we have indicated repeatedly, there simply was never a time when opposition was absent. Most renowned among the opponents of astrology after Pico della Mirandola was Thomas Liebler, better known as Erastus (1513–1583). He was born in Switzerland, was educated in Italy, and settled in Germany, first as court physician to the Count of Hennesberg, later as professor of medicine at the university of Heidelberg, but finished his career as professor of theology and ethics at Basel. His attack on astrology was contained in a work which was essentially a defense of the strictures against astrology by the famous monk and reformer, Jerome Savanarola, whose work he translated into German. And Savanarola's work was essentially a digest of Pico's. Divination, says Erastus, is the work of demons and astrological divination is unsound and contrary to the Christian faith. It is magic, impious and evil. The heavens do not confer marvelous virtues on earthly things, and to explain spontaneous generation one does not require to postulate heavenly influence since its occurrence is due to a property of matter, inherent in its nature. Erastus also attacked the Paracelsan medical philosophy, and based his arguments against astrology upon the Aristotelian theory of comets. Tycho Brahe, a friend of astrology, who had just disproved that cometary theory upon finding no parallax in the comet's orbit stated quite rightly that if Erastus based his arguments against Paracelsus and astrology upon that kind of evidence, then neither the medical profession nor the astrologers had anything to fear from him.

Nevertheless, Erastus did deny that comets caused dire events on earth. In conformity with his Aristotelian faith he believed that comets betokened heat and drought but could not produce pestilence. They were a divine sign, like the rainbow, but not a cause. He was opposed to the alchemical theory of transmutation, as well as to all forms of magic including characters, amulets, words and figures. The only kind of occult virtue he can tolerate is the one that resembles the action of the magnet. As to witches, he is dead set against them. Witches are known to have vile and lustful relations with demons, and must be mercilessly exterminated.

Even late in the sixteenth century the attacks against astrology are of the same sort. Marcellus Squarcialupus and Andreas Dudith among others cited by Thorndike (vol. VI, chapter 35) basically reproduce the same pattern. While Erastus rested his anti-astrological arguments on Aristotle's materialistic approach to comets or for that matter, upon science in general, others like Squarcialupus, for example, were against the Aristotelian theory of cometary origins. Brahe applauded that stand but commented that it would have been better had the author supported his position by mathematical proof and astronomical observations. Yet, it was Brahe who was the astrologer and Squarcialupus the bitter opponent of the art.

ASTROLOGY ON THE DEFENSIVE 159

The list of astrology's detractors constitutes an interesting array of personalities, motivations, backgrounds and reasoning. They are fascinating material for psychoanalytical studies in logic and personality, and surely serve more than anything else to reveal the fragile skeleton of what we call consistency and the frail claims of those who think they can squeeze the "method of science" into a packaged nutshell and market it in a cellophaned formula. Apparently, one can no more package the method of science than one can patent a formula for the nature of man or the good life.

3. A Famous Coup de Grace

The only criticism of astrology that stems from the pen of a scientist is the work entitled *The Vanity of Judiciary Astrology* or *Divination by the Stars*. Lately written in Latin, by that great scholar and mathematician, the illustrious Petrus Gassendus; mathematical professor to the king of France. The Latin text appeared in 1655 and the English translation in 1659. The author, a Frenchman, Pierre Gassendi (1592–1655) became lecturer in theology at Digne, his birthplace, and became a monk in 1617 and later was lecturer at the University of Aix. He was a prolific writer and initiated his career with a dissertation on the mystical philosophy of Robert Flood and subsequently became famous for his critical writings on the philosophy of Descartes. He was one of the first defenders of the philosophic point of view of Francis Bacon and the experimental method. According to the writer of the article on him in the Encyclopedia Britannica, he "added little to our knowledge of physical science" and was "not a consistent empiricist." He was an enthusiastic atomist, yet accepted the reality of God and of an immaterial and immortal soul. He did perform some original researches in astronomy such as the study of the transit of Mercury. He traveled widely, was provost of the Cathedral of Digne and in 1645 occupied the chair of mathematics at the College Royal of Paris. In other words, he was not what we would today call a pure scientist but rather a philosopher who had the additional virtues of being well versed in theology and in science. "That Gassendi deserves honorable mention in the history of philosophy will hardly be doubted," says the author of *The Philosophy of Gassendi*, G. S. Brett. Hence, even this attack upon astrology was not a contribution of pure science but of philosophy and theology employing science.

Now, as to the book itself. Gassendi's knowledge of antiquity is vast and so is his knowledge of astrology. He devotes the first part of his book to a review of the origins of the art and then to an exposition of its tenets and practices. Already in chapter 4, however, he asserts "that the risings and settings of the stars are not the causes, but only signs of tempests, and mutations happening in the air; contrary to the vulgar opinions." For example, in ancient times the dog star rose about the middle of July which event, because of the precession of the equinoxes now takes place a month later; yet the heat of the season remains unchanged in time. Only the directness of the sun's rays and its stay above the horizon determines summer heat. Also, "the Dog-star (for example) which to us is a significator of Heat, to the Antipodes is a Signe of Cold." Then, two contiguous areas or countries may have different weather no matter what star is overhead. The ancients made up tables for centuries lying in the same parallel. But this is inaccurate since weather conditions differ even with regard to regions east and west, not only north and south. At best weather prediction is most uncertain, and the signs of the stars are not much help. "Hence we may come to understand that those Tables do indeed contain what their Authors observed to have happened in those Years, during which they addicted themselves to make and record their Observations; but cannot be extended to another series of Years." (p. 21)

As to astrology proper, its fundamental principle "is what all men readily confess; viz. that the Stars are not meer Signes, but also natural Causes of very many effects." We all know what the sun does to inferior life and processes or the action of the moon. And sublunary bodies no doubt feel the impact of the stars as well. "For since the Stars ought not to be conceived idle and ineffectual; and that there are some certain Effects, which cannot be referred to any other Causes but them, as the Critical mutations of diseases, and the inequality of seasons, etc." Yet scholars soon fall into the error of assigning to the stars all kinds of meanings which are "meer childish toys and old wives' dreams." All reason rests on experience and what one should say about the effects of the luminaries is that whatever these effects may be, they are derived exclusively from those properties that stem from their light and heat. Furthermore, the stars are general causes acting here below and particular events should be ascribed to particular causes in the immediate environment. Different flowers have different odors which are due to their essential oils. Oil is the general cause, their distinguishing smell, however, is due to their unique features rather than to the general oily property. The sun is a general cause but its action depends on the nature of the matter it acts upon. The sublunary world has causes of its own which are effective and can explain much that astrologers attribute to the stars. "Thus when grounds manured and enriched by compost, do yield more plentiful crops of Corn, than before; it is plain that we are to ascribe this fertility, not to the influence of the Sun and Stars, but to the fatning of ground by the dung or soyle, seasonably laid upon it, by the careful Farmer." Would Ptolemy and the contemporary astrologers have denied that? Yet, such reasoning proves that there has been a shift in stress from the stars to events in our immediate environment.

Gassendi then goes into a detailed description of the astrological lore, the houses, the planets, the virtues of the signs of the zodiac and all their significances. He cannot of course bring forth any other arguments against these notions than have already been produced in the past, so that all he can do is employ such terms as "the houses ridiculed," "the signs derided," this demolished, or that destroyed. Merely citing these things, he says, makes refuting unnecessary, for they are so laughable. Yet, virtually all his comments had been made before, and so had his questions, such as, Why should Aries be a diurnal sign and Tarus a nocturnal, which had been asked a thousand times over. "Nor can I suppress the Rising of my spleen when I consider the dominion of the Signes over the several parts of Mans body." (p. 46) In Chapter XI, "The Celestial Houses Demolished," he asks: "And if that house, whatsoever it be, which begins to rise, be the House of Life; why should not that which begins to set, be the House of Death? Why is the Eighth House so destructive to Mankind above the rest?"

Equally preposterous appear to him the astrologers' method of weather prediction by such means as the Lords of the seasons, climatic determination by the planets, conjunctions, aspects or opposition. Here and there a new argument wholly unknown to the classical writers makes its impressive debut. "If the Earth suffer so much of alteration from the various aspects of the Moon; it is fit that Jupiter should suffer some alteration from the aspects of his proper Moons, which as they are more in number, so are they swifter in their motions and oftener changed in their configurations." Moreover, these moons should exert the same influence which Jupiter is said to exert on the earth.

As a trained scientist, Gassendi does demand experimental evidence for the beliefs which he finds so curious and gratuitous. He cites instances of famous predictions that went awry. What about the numerous stars discovered by the telescope and which were previously unseen? Surely they too have specific virtues, and the entire list of rules and precepts regarding stellar action must be revised in the light of these new additions. Their rules lack full substantiation and are based on few instances, and are frequently contradicted by experience. True, the new stars may be claimed by them to be too small for discernible influence, but then their number is so large, especially in the milky way. And the Chaldeans not only made few observations but lacked much knowledge and missed out on some basic concepts, such as the eccentric rather than concentric course of the planets, the precession of the equinoxes, and misconstrued as a result the true positions of both the planets and the stars. "Hence, whereas they affirm that their rules are confirmed by frequent Experiments; that is manifestly vain and false, even from this, that they are contradicted by as many, and more Experiments." Thales was not concerned with astrology in order to make money. He cornered the olive market by studying the snow or rainfall of winter and thus knew what to expect. It is Gassendi who apparently is the first to cite the famous words of Kepler that the foolish daughter astrology was not to be despised if by her gains she maintained her wise mother astronomy.

Gassendi ridicules the alibi so often resorted to by the astrologers to the effect that "the fault is not of the art itself but of the artist," or that poor prognostications are due to errors in their calculations. "Again, I cannot but allow them to be somewhat Modest, when they confess their Art to be only Conjectural: and yet they may be accused of great Arrogance, when they boast it to be of equal certainty with the Arts of Physick, Rhetorick, and Navigation. For in these, Human prudence and industry so act their parts, as that the proposed and desired End doth for the most part follow thereupon; and when it doth so follow, the Cause is not immanifest; But in Astrology meer Chance plays the whole game; and the Event foretold doth seldom or never follow; and when it doth follow, the Cause is not (?) altogether obscure and uncertain and every man may give as good a Cause among sublunaries for that Effect, as Astrologers do from the Stars; and so Astrology is not so much a true Art, as meer Lottery, or Guessing at randome. Nor am I in saying this, injurious to those noble Creatures, the Stars, whose true and genuine virtues, whatsoever they be, I most willingly allow them; but it is injurious to them, to dishonour them with the imputation of such power and efficacy, as is incompetent to them, and to make them many times the instruments not only to Mens ruine, but even to all their vicious inclinations, and delectable villanies. . . . We deny not, but God hath endowed the Stars, as all the rest of his Creatures, with some certain Virtues; but we question, whether Astrologers know what those Virtues are; and whether the Faculties, which they ascribe to the Stars, be the same that God gave them, or others meerly imaginary." (pp. 76–77)

To the insistence of the astrologers that there hardly could be another cause to which to refer changes in weather besides happenings in the sky, Gassendi replies that indeed the stars, chiefly the sun, are responsible as general causes for sublunar weather, though there exist also causes among inferior events, by the nature of which the stars "do attemper their influence and accommodate their action." These earthly events that play a part in determining the weather are "eruptions of Flames and Fire, and Vapours caused by them from subterraneous Waters; yeah, Metals themselves," which some claim are generated in the bowels of the earth by solar action but with no evidence to substan-

ASTROLOGY ON THE DEFENSIVE

tiate it. There may be causes within the earth itself that could explain the formation of metals which need not be attributed solely to the sun. And if the moon acts upon the earth then surely the earth acts back upon the moon. Besides, "For as when a room is enlightened by a Flame, from which many small sparks issue forth, no man can discern the particular light, which ariseth from each particular spark, the Air being promiscuously upon the Earth, by their several influences blended or confused together; it is impossible for any man to distinguish their several activities." (p. 81) The sun is bound to be more active because it is of greater apparent diameter, and anyway closer to us, hence his light is more potent.

Forecasting the future can bring only harm to people. And it is folly of astrologers to say that foreknowledge makes it possible to avoid the evils the stars foretell, because what kind of prognostications are they if they can be so easily sidestepped? And how can one determine the exact moment of birth? How is it possible for seven planets to determine in one short moment all that will happen to an individual, years hence or for the rest of his life? How can the planets do that to many infants seeing the light of day at the same moment, and accomplish all they are supposed to whether they are above or below the horizon? If at least they were given more time to act, it would be understandable, or if they took into account "his constitution derived from his Parents." For an accurate nativity one would have to know with great exactitude the latitude and longitude and our clocks and watches are far from good these days. Ptolemy himself knew he could rely on sun dials, hour glasses of either sand or water, and he relied solely on the astrolabe. But what modern astrologer watches over a delivery with astrolabe in hand? And before the work of Tycho one was not aware of the error introduced by refraction, which these astrologers certainly fail to take into account to this day. And are our smallest astrolabes sufficiently accurate for these purposes?

Gassendi considers in detail the answers to these queries usually given by the apologists for astrology, and actually demolishes them one by one. Though most of his arguments have been used before by people who merely disliked astrology as sceptics or for religious reasons, some new ones are added by him which employ the new contributions of science. He also ridicules elections and questions and even medical astrology, in part, as when he doubts that there is a right time for purges.

There can, however, be no doubt that Gassendi's attack upon astrology was definitely in a new vein and represents a point of view which has broken loose from many values and assumptions that motivated the opposition of the past. Besides the addition of science, accuracy and measurement, we discern here and there symptoms of a conscious attempt to explain the psychological reasons for this hunger for divination. More ancient than astrology, he says, are the human evils of vanity, foolishness and credulity, and what is equally important, "In all Ages from the beginning of the World, men have been greedy of knowing things to come; in all Ages there have been Impostors, who complying with the humour of Curiosity have pretended to the knowledge of Future successes, that they so might acquire the reputation of singular wisdom, and procure gain to themselves by the Credulity of others." (p. 120) Wise men of all times rejected the art, especially in Greece, where only the Stoics, "who held even Dreams to be true" were its advocates. (This is, of course, a fiction. Besides, it was the stoics who were the staunchest defenders of science.) The Tetrabiblos, or Quadripartitem, could not have been written by the same genius who wrote the Almagest, hence, it was surely written by an impostor. In this manner Gassendi seeks to destroy "Their Plea of Antiquity, Authority, Reason, and Experience, or Observation."

If he is somewhat overzealous in denying astrology the support of antiquity and authority, he certainly presents a much sounder case when it comes to condemnation on the grounds of reason, experience and observation. Here he musters many novel arguments motivated by the new discoveries, the voyages of the explorers, and above all by the recognition of the supreme importance of forces and events down here below as compared with happenings or forces up above in the heavens. After reading the last chapters of his book, filled as they are with lucidity and soundness, one is obliged to conclude that the vigor of his reasoning gains its sustenance from a shift in values which is making itself felt in the thought pattern of western Europe. The proximate, the small, the immediate, the actual, and the material are assuming greater importance than they had been accorded hitherto, and the remote, glamorous and fanciful is becoming less attractive by comparison, as if the two could not share equal weight. This stress on the immediate and realistic may be responsible for, or is, perhaps a symptom of the weakening of the religious spirit, and is simultaneously a force in attenuating the fear and tension in men which had led to an insatiable curiosity about the future. Apparently the present became all-important.

Gassendi is the first to strike at some of the very foundations of the astrological assumptions. His manner, particularly in the last chapters of his work is reasonable, fair and gentle, especially by comparison with the vulgarities of many modern controversies. He seeks to understand the astrological position and renders it with excessive caution and fairness, and answers it with judicious calmness. "Wherefore it is not to be inquired of the Stars, why an infant is born strong or weak or of a sweet and mild disposition, or of a cholerick and harsh; but collected from the Complexion of his Parents, from the good or evil condition of their seed, from their diet, course of life, and the like. Nor are we to say, that such an Infant was born infected with a foul and contagious disease because the Sixth House was his Horoscope; but because his Mothers Lower House was impure and infectious. Nor that such a man was killed by a Canon shot because his Horoscope was direct to a Quartile of Saturn; but because the Gunner had levelled and discharged his piece directly against him. Nor when a man is slain with a Sword is Mars or any secret Malignity of the Stars ruling his Nativity, to be accused of his death; but the Thief, Souldier, or other person, who is the true Homicide: and so of other accidents." (p. 126)

He admits that the inferior world is under the influence of the superior, but that does not mean that it does not have causes of its own or that it owes all its occurrences to events above. Moreover, and here he strikes at the very crucial point in the logic of astrology, the sun and moon do undoubtedly exert an influence on terrestrial things by virtue of their rays. But why must we assume that just as the sun controls the heat of the year and the moon "the Fulness of the Shellfish," the planets must be endowed with similar action? "Observation teacheth that when the Moon is in Conjunction with the Sun, the marrow in the bones of Animals is diminished; but doth Observation teach that any such effect follows when Mars, Venus, or other Planet is in Conjunction with the Sun or Moon or other Planet?" Astrologers do not know as much about the sky as do plowmen, shepherds or mariners because they live in cities, spend their time indoors and rely upon ephemerides not on direct observations, as these simple folk do.

The sun is not the only source of radiation. The earth may emit cold just as the sun emits heat and these rays may effect the air thereby effecting not only our bodies but also our minds, "by the intercession of the temperament." People do, no doubt, vary in their dispositions and temperaments. Yet what evidence have we that these are really determined by the stars and that astrology has discovered the true relationship?

What experiments and observations did the early or the later astrologers have for their beliefs? The time was inadequate; the Chaldeans report few experiments to say nothing of the wise saying of Hippocrates that experience is fallacious, requiring at best cautious interpretation. Besides, the ancients were ignorant of the true nature of the planets, their relative sizes, their orbits, or the fact that sun-spots may be greater than Venus or Mercury. Their observations lack accuracy with no telescope at their service; and unaware of life under the Equator, they had little knowledge of the reversal of season that it entails.

There are in addition the factors of difference in soil, climate and culture. "Because with us Men very rarely live to an hundred years; is it reasonable thereupon to predict that among the Tovopinambaltij (who commonly attain to twice that age) no Man shall exceed an hundred? And when (as Historians tell us in their Indian relations) the Women of that Country usually bear Children after the ninetieth year of their Lives; shall we give the same judgement of our Country Women, who cease to bear Children before they are fifty? Supposing the Nativity of an European to be the same in all points with that of a Brasilian; must their Constitutions, Lives, Fortunes, Deaths be therefore the same?" (p. 133) How can our astrological findings apply to people of a culture "who hold all things in Common, who neither value nor collect wealth, and who know no such thing as Adultery, Incest, Rape, or Polygamy, but have all women in common," thus betraying the impact of the voyages of discovery. Gassendi is aware of the fact that Ptolemy took these cultural differences into account, but implies that he failed to do anything about them besides warning his disciples, and that in vain.

In addition, there is this eternal dickering and disagreement among the students and practitioners of astrology. Aside from the fact that, as Sextus ab Heminga has shown after carefully examining thirty prominent horoscopes, few if any agreed with reality, we encounter ever so often such incidents as Luther's horoscope by both Cardan and Gauricus. Both these notable astrologers assumed different hours and even years for Luther's birth and both missed the true birthday, which fact did not stop them from producing elaborate prognostications. No wonder astrologers are wrong most of the time, if not always. But the vain and the ignorant love it. "Men therefore being commonly possessed with Hope, Fear, Love, Hatred, or some other passion, interpret all things in favour of that passion and expect that even the Stars should be as much concerned therein, as themselves; and thus they swell themselves with the Air of Phansy, that they may be much greater than indeed they are, and of Gnats be taken for Elephants."

Chapter VII

THE FOUNDERS OF MODERN ASTRONOMY AND ASTROLOGY'S DEMISE

1. The Pre-Copernican Forerunners

THE forerunners of modern astronomy begin to make their appearance some time after the revival of learning, and simultaneously with the reign of astrology. It would seem as though during the thirteenth and fourteenth centuries the scholars of Europe were too fascinated with the rediscovery of Greek science and its proper assimilation to make any significant contributions. But as we have seen, interest in astronomy was maintained consistently. The Sphaera Mundi of Sacrobosco, a concise, simple but matter of fact synopsis of Ptolemy's Almagest, was the basic text around which clustered numerous commentaries. (See The Sphere of Sacrobosco and Its Commentaries by Lynn Thorndike, Chicago University Press, 1949) Written early in the thirteenth century, it acquired worthy commentaries by such outstanding medieval scholars as Michael Scot, Robertus Anglicus, Cecco D'Ascoli and others. Treatises on the quadrant, on the Arabian writers such as Alfraganus, on Euclid, the Almagest, and on diverse technical problems were continuously produced, though admittedly contributions of significance were meager, if any.

In the opinion of most historians of astronomy, the first significant pioneer in the revival of aggressive progress in this science was George Peurbach (1423-1461), professor of astronomy and mathematics at the University of Vienna (1450-1461) and author of a scholarly work entitled Epitome of The Almagest later edited and published by his pupil Regiomontanus, and of a summary of Ptolemy's planetary theory entitled New Theories of the Planets, similarly edited and published. It should be noted that in the true internationalist tradition of the times he also lectured at Ferrara, Bologna and Padua. "Although interested primarily in astronomy and trigonometry, he wrote on arithmetic, but this was merely for the use of students in these branches of science."

(History of Mathematics by D. E. Smith, vol. 1, N. Y. 1923, p. 259) He also compiled a table of sines, made a thorough study of the orbit of a comet seen at Vienna and compiled a work Tables of Eclipses, later edited and published by George Tannstetter, a successor of his in the chair of astronomy and mathematics at Vienna, made famous by Peurbach. Yet, before becoming professor at the University of Vienna, Peurbach was astrologer to Ladislaus of Bohemia. (Die Geschichte der Sternkunde, E. Zinner Berlin 1931, p. 406)

Though many historians regard Peurbach as a landmark in the revival of modern astronomy, it is questionable that such a title is deserved. Since the eleventh century there existed a continuous chain of scholars who kept alive the spirit of science. There was the mathematician, John of Gmunden (1318–1442), the first man to occupy a chair devoted entirely to the teaching of that subject at the newly founded University of Vienna (1365), which was destined to become a mathematical stronghold for many years to follow. He was the author of treatises on sexagesimal fractions, on trigonometry and on the computus. There was also Nicholas of Cusa (1401–1464), the son of a poor fisherman whose career in the church brought him a cardinal's red cap and made him governor of Rome. Besides being Peurbach's teacher, he was the author of numerous tracts on physics as well as mathematics involving such topics as the reform of the calendar, the quadrature of the circle, the theory of numbers, impetus and inertia, the weight of air, and many other topics of vital importance to writers on mathematics and physics of his day. He is justly regarded as a pioneer not only in mathematics but in mathematical and experimental physics, in urging the importance of weights and measurements, and experimentation generally.

In the true spirit of the Church, Nicholas declared the astrologers "fools with their vain imaginings" in their wild interpretations of the story of the Magi and the star of Bethlehem, but in most of his scientific writings he adheres closely to his astrological faith, and to numerology. Even his stress upon measurement is fully permeated with the conventional belief in magic, alchemy and astrology. For example, he believes that the balance will distinguish between various occult virtues, that the weight and color of a patient's urine will aid in diagnosing diseases, lead and gold may weigh the same but be far different from each other in perfection, and that the amounts of sulfur and mercury in metals must ultimately be thus determined. He even introduces weights into the art of weather prediction or of forecasting the fertility of coming seasons. Nor was theological mysticism neglected in his writings. If his friendliness to astrology did not result in professional astrologizing, it might well be because of his conviction that the Alfonsine Tables contained many errors requiring immediate correction.

ASTRONOMY AND ASTROLOGY'S DEMISE 169

Regarded as more crucial in the path of modern science is the pupil and collaborator of Peurbach, Johann Muller, or Regiomontanus (1436-1476), equally outstanding and influential in the fields of mathematics and astronomy. Like his master, he lectured as a young prodigy at Venice, Rome, Ferrara and Padua and later accepted an invitation from the king of Hungary to arrange and evaluate his precious collection of recently acquired Greek manuscripts. The king's sponsorship soon terminated and Regiomontanus moved to Nurnberg, the most cultured city in Germany at the time, famous for its printing presses and scientific interests. He was enthusiastically received there by the citizenry and struck up a fruitful friendship with one of its richest and most learned merchants, Bernard Walther (1430-1504), who supported him for many years, collaborated with him in his labors, and established him in a printing enterprise in which Regiomontanus published not only the works of his master Peurbach, but many other valuable scientific treatises. Though Regiomontanus died at the age of forty, his scientific output was overwhelming. Besides editing the books begun by Peurbach, he authored a pioneering Tables of Sines, the study of a comet, several books on trigonometry and trigonometric functions, tables of stellar and planetary positions which were regarded by most astronomers of his time to be superior to the Alfonsine Tables and even to the Prutenic. Moreover, they contained many original and accurate observations. The Alfonsine Tables of astronomical data were compiled by and under the supervision of the king of Leon and Castile, Alfonso X (1223-1284), an enterprising scholar in astronomy. After conquering Toledo in 1252 from the Arabs he gathered there Jewish and Christian scholars to improve upon the values given in the Toledan Tables which had been gathered in the same city by a Mohammedan astronomer, Arzachel, in 1080 A.D. for the purpose of correcting errors found in Ptolemy's calculations. By the time of Alfonso new errors had been detected in the latter, hence his effort at their rectification. Alfonso is also responsible for the publication of the Libros del Saber, a vast and valuable encyclopedia of astronomical knowledge, mostly from Arab sources. The Prutenic Tables were composed by Erasmus Reinhold in 1551 at the expense of Duke Albert of Prussia hence named Prutenic or Prussian, and were based upon the calculations from Copernicus' De Revolutionibus. In 1667 Kepler issued the Rudolphine Tables, so named after his and Tycho Brahe's former patron and employer, the Emperor Rudolph II of Bohemia.

Besides numerous treatises on astronomy, geometry, improved instruments and physics, Regiomontanus also published many Ephemerides and calendars as well as numerous letters on astrological matters. In 1468 he cast the horoscope of the new university of Pressburg, then under the reign of Matthias Corvinus, king of Hungary, where he apparently lectured, and for which he foresaw a great future. Says Thorndike: "However good a mathematician Regiomontanus may have been, he proved an indifferent astrologer on this occasion, for the new university was of short duration." (vol. IV, p. 420) His correspondence on astrological subjects with James of Speyer, a famous astrologer, is of interest mainly because of the caution with which he discusses or rather evades such dangerous questions as the effect of a possible conjunction on the birth and career of Christ, merely referring to "the virtue of the great conjunction which predicted and signified" His coming, though he did manage to compute astrologically the day of the Passion. His Ephemerides are full of the usual astrological material involving weather prediction, side by side with citing times for bleeding, planting, taking a bath and cutting one's hair. His publishing house issued numerous astrological texts.

Astrological beliefs and labors were part and parcel of the activities of practically all the pioneering contributors to the mathematical sciences, the improvers of instruments and the gatherers of data who crowded the sixteenth century before and after the advent of Copernicus. We might mention only several of the more outstanding ones.

Associated in one way or another with Regiomontanus were Georg Collimitius Tannstetter (1482–1535), Johann Werner (1468–1528), Johann Schoner (1477–1547), and Joachim Camerarius (1500–1574), to mention only a few. Tannstetter edited Peurbach's tables of eclipses and another set by Regiomontanus, issued a work on calendar reform at the request of the emperor Maximilian, edited Witelo's work on optics in collaboration with Peter Apian in 1535, a work on the rising and the setting of the stars in 1511, and a work on geography by Albertus Magnus. As a physician he lectured on astrological medicine at the University of Vienna and published annual astrological predictions. He opposed several astrological writers who predicted invasions, wars and floods as a result of the conjunction of 1524, castigating them as a disgrace to the fair name of astrology. He then proves the dire predictions to have been exaggerated on religious and astrological grounds, and as was often the case with astrological disputants, he proceeds to give his own sound and reasonable predictions based on astrological principles which to us seem wholly indistinguishable from the very assumptions and practices he had just finished condemning in such violent and pious phrases.

Werner was "a priest, who was interested chiefly in astronomy but wrote the first original work on conics to appear in the sixteenth century." (History of Mathematics by D. E. Smith, vol. 1, p. 331) He is the Werner against whom Copernicus wrote a rather harsh diatribe ad-

ASTRONOMY AND ASTROLOGY'S DEMISE 171

monishing him for stating that Ptolemy's observations were often inaccurate and for overlooking the fact that the fixed stars moved faster after Ptolemy than in the period before him. He wrote works on spherical triangles, on astronomical instruments, on geography, the movement of the eighth sphere which Copernicus criticized, and vast observations on the weather with rules for prediction. He was also the author of numerous astrological works, horoscopes, judgments, nativities, cometary prognostications, and conjunctions.

Johann Schoner and his son Andreas (1528-1590) are described by Smith as "perhaps the best known" among the minor German writers on astronomy and mathematics. It is Schoner senior who is the great scholar; he edited many of the manuscripts left behind by Regiomontanus, made numerous and original observations, some of which were used by Copernicus in his De Revolutionibus, and was also a geographer of note. Originally a poor priest, bookbinder and globe maker in the cultural city of Nurnberg, he later became professor of mathematics at the newly founded university of that city. He published treatises on the sphere, on a cylindrical sundial, on geography, on the Spanish and Portuguese discoveries, on the Molucca islands, astronomical tables, a popular book on medicine, though no physician, edited a book by Regiomontanus on the magnitude and true path of a comet, and another on the astronomical instrument, the Saphea, a work of his own on the comet of 1531, and many other works besides, of similar content and notable merit. Yet, he was also the author of a large body of work on astrology. His book on medicine contained the entire lore of medical astrology, and it is likely that he wrote the book in the first place because of his astrological expertness. He cast the horoscope of the Nurnberg university and located the favorable time for its opening, published Ephemerides and a large Opusculum astrologicum (1539) dedicated to two nephews of an astrologer friend of his. The work deals fully with weather prediction by the stars, judicial astrology, elections and nativities. Six years later he published another lengthy work dealing further with judicial astrology and which is embellished with an introduction by Philip Melanchthon (1497-1560) the great scholar, religious reformer, teacher and friend of Luther, and expert in mathematics, astronomy and astrology. Since Schoner was a devoted friend and ardent admirer of Copernicus and had persistently urged him to publish his full work, he points out in this volume, issued two years after the De Revolutionibus, that the Copernican doctrine is in no way antagonistic to astrology. In this same work he analyzes his own geniture and that of Regiomontanus and their fates, to prove the accuracy of the art. Like every other scholar of the time, he criticized the excesses of astrologers, disagreed violently with other writers in the field on one interpretation or another but fully accepted the science and its applications and even neglected to attack superstitious Arabian astrology, as others did merely to reintroduce it in their own fashion. We might say he was somewhat bolder or perhaps old-fashioned in his beliefs. The Spanish Catholic Index of 1559 carried his name for his superstitious belief in nativities.

Camerarius was a close associate of Melanchthon and was also primarily an all around scholar and classicist, and but secondarily a contributor to mathematical and astronomical progress. He edited Theon of Alexandria's commentary on Ptolemy's Almagest, and the Tetrabiblos. Piously devoted to astrology all his life, he was the author of a typically stereotyped book (1576) on divination, rooted wholly in the classical tradition and including full elucidation of oracles, chiromancy, divination from the flight of birds and sacrifices, magic, necromancy, and astrology. He was a great believer in the witches' sabbat and as in a previous work published when he was a young man, in 1532, he accepted wholeheartedly the full complement of medieval or ancient faith in omens, portents and astrological rules.

Among the sixteenth century mathematicians and astronomers there is no single name known to have been in opposition to astrology outside of those who attacked it on religious grounds. Certainly those who made outstanding contributions were practicing astrologers or close to it. Among them may be cited Gemma Frisius, Michael Maestlin, Jacob Milich, Christopher Rothmann, Caspar Peucer (1525–1602) and Erasmus Reinhold, all of them men of exceptional stature even among the great, and of deserved and recognized influence.

Gemma Frisius (1508–1555) whose work was continued by his son Cornelius Gemma Frisius (1535–1577) is regarded by Smith as "the most influential of the various Dutch mathematicians of the sixteenth century." His book on arithmetic, published in 1540 marked a turning point in arithmetical texts and became the equivalent of a best seller because it combined the commercial with the theoretical, previously kept apart by tradition. "It went through at least fifty nine editions in the sixteenth century, besides several thereafter. He also wrote on geography and astronomy, suggesting the present method of obtaining longitude by means of the difference in time, and taking one of the first steps toward the modern methods of triangulation." (p. 341–342) He occupied the chair of medicine at the University of Louvain from 1541 on, and his son succeeded him, adding the chair of astronomy to that of medicine. In addition it should be pointed out that Vesalius states in his De humani corporis fabrica that he together with Gemma Frisius stole bodies off the galleys outside Louvain for dissection. He was a friend of the Copernican theory and wrote several letters to the bishop of Erm-

ASTRONOMY AND ASTROLOGY'S DEMISE 173

land in Prussia where Copernicus lived, urging him to help in getting Copernicus to publish his great work so as to overcome the uncertainties which beset astrology. A few weeks before the appearance of the De Revolutionibus he writes the same bishop that he is still awaiting "with supreme desire that mathematical work of that great man, Nicholas Copernicus," which he feels certain will revolutionize heaven and earth and the universe.

Nevertheless in his treatise on astronomy of 1530 he discusses astrological problems in full; he was also the author of regular astrological Ephemerides, and of a posthumous book entitled the Catholic Astrolabe issued by his son in 1556, and dealing almost exclusively with astrology. His son Cornelius concludes the work with a horoscope of his father.

Like Cornelius Gemma, Michael Maestlin also studied the comet of 1577 and concluded that it had no parallax and belonged to the stellar region. But Maestlin went further and postulated a circular motion for it around the sun, much like Tycho Brahe. Its orbit lay ouside of Venus but it also moved to and fro in a plane perpendicular to that orbit, an idea borrowed from Copernicus whose admirer he was. Michael Maestlin (1550–1620) was a "talented mathematician," as Dreyer puts it, and Kepler's teacher. He was also one of the earliest defenders of the Copernican doctrine and no doubt steered Kepler in that direction. He was the author of an Epitome of Astronomy, a compendium of all relevant astronomical knowledge of the time: a book on the comet of 1577, and another on the comet of 1580. The very fact that all astrological interpretation of the comet is concentrated in the introduction to his first study is telling. In it he points out that he was more attracted to astronomy than astrology because it is more interesting. Since childhood, he writes, he had been fascinated with mathematics and was fortunate that the duke of Wurtemberg supported him so he could devote himself fully to philosophy, science and mathematics. Dukes like him or princes like Alfonso the Wise, of the Alfonsine Tables, are to be admired rather than those rulers who cause the death of thousands to increase their lands or power.

He then proceeds to point out that his observations of the cometary orbit are accurate and better than those previously recorded, commenting that it is too bad that astrologers err in interpreting cometary significances from the unreliable data of the past. Aristotle is wrong in his theory of exhalations, and comets are definitely situated among the stars. The Copernican theory is reasonable and fits his own data best. The book closes with an astrological study of the comet's meaning, and Maestlin starts out in the same manner in which Thurman Arnold plunged into a discussion of St. Thomas Aquinas as legalist over a recent radio program. "It is customary to denounce Communism these days," declared Dr. Arnold, "and I hereby denounce it," and after this brief bow to the times, he proceeded to uphold vague hypotheses related to it. One can hear Maestlin make the same mumbling comment to the effect that it is customary or obligatory these days to condemn astrology or rather its excesses and I hereby do so. But—astrologers, true astrologers that is, know that eclipses and comets bear forebodings of misfortune, and they know it by virtue of numerous observations of the past. He is not quite sure how to interpret the present comet because he has been preoccupied with astronomy lately; but so far as he can see, it is under Venus and warns of the evil menace of the Turks. After discussing many other such forebodings and citing subsequent events which proved their accuracy, Maestlin concludes with an exhortation to his readers to turn to God.

In 1580 Maestlin became professor of mathematics at the university of Heidelberg and published his second cometary study. Again astrology is brought in in the preface and the concluding section. Comets are signs of God's warning to sinners, just as the rainbow is a sign of his kind promise. Unskilled though he is in astrological judgments, it is plain to see that this comet brings far worse tidings than the preceding one, since the former was merely under Venus and this one is of "horrid aspect, sad face, dark funereal obscurity, Saturnine visage, and pale image of death." The bulk of the treatise, however, deals with excellent observations and farsighted interpretations, bearing on the comet's orbit, its properties, and nature. Again proving it to be outside the sub-lunar area, he criticizes the defenders of Aristotle's position and marvels at their stubbornness in the face of irrefutable evidence. The new star of 1572 and the last two comets have convinced him that the Aristotelian concepts are false.

A man highly regarded in his time was Jacob Milich (1501–1559), who was professor of mathematics and astrology at the university of Wittenberg where he had previously received his M.D. He is the author of a frequently reprinted Oration on the Dignity of Astrology in which he makes the usual apologies for that much abused art. Too much is expected of it, he thinks, which is unfair, and he then goes on to prove that its late forecasts were faithfully fulfilled. If only parents moulded the future of their children by the natures given them by the stars, the children would be singularly well adapted to their fates. Milich is also the author of a commentary on the second book of Pliny's Natural History which deals with astronomy and meteorology. In it he expresses the usual astrological beliefs and defends the Aristotelian theory of cometary origin, though he seems fully aware of the newer notion that comets are like planets.

Rothmann, the mathematician and zealous observer of the heavens in the service of the learned Landgrave at Cassel was a life-long correspondent of Tycho Brahe's, as was also his benefactor and co-worker, both of whom were apparently too preoccupied with instruments and observations to bother with astrology. Rothmann was a strong admirer of Copernicus and an early adherent of his system though he also had friends among professional astrologers. Peucer who was the son-in-law of Melanchthon and professor of philosophy, mathematics and medicine at Wittenberg, was much preoccupied with astrology. He still believed in the fixity of the earth and its central location, but regarded Copernicus as the "greatest of all writers on astronomy since Ptolemy." In a book on divination he treats that subject in the conventional manner indulging in astrology, the regular belief in demons, their varied powers and misdeeds. Erasmus Reinhold, similarly professor of mathematics and astronomy at Wittenberg, was the author of the Prutenic Tables, the first tables based upon the Copernican theory, published in 1551 and dedicated to Albert, duke of Prussia. His praise of Copernicus was, of course, boundless and came earliest. He considers him a second Atlas or Ptolemy, though confiding to the reader that he had to rework many of Copernicus' observations and compute others in a somewhat modified manner. Tycho Brahe referred to him as "the illustrious astronomer of our age." Yet, he composed annual predictions and never gave up his conventional interest in all the astrological trimmings and practices. The same can be said of all the astronomical works and authors of the time, with very few exceptions indeed.

2. *The Giants of Modern Astronomy*

A. COPERNICUS AND BRAHE

The inveterate fusion of critical or experimental pioneering with astrology will become clearer when we consider the very giants of modern astronomy namely, Copernicus, Brahe, Kepler and Galileo. Copernicus (1473-1543) was of a retiring personality and busy with a number of other occupations. To begin with, he was canon of the cathedral of Frauenburg, where his uncle Lucas Watzelrode was bishop. After his uncle's death in 1512 he conducted the business of the Chapter and was for a while administrator of the diocese; he laid before the Prussian Estates a proposal for strengthening the currency; he represented the interests of the Chapter before the court of the king of Poland, and practiced medicine throughout the period of his active life, though unofficially, treating particularly his friends and the poor of Frauenburg, the latter gratis. Yet, he must have devoted considerable time to astronomy as well. He was no great observer, since the total number of his observations amount to 27 and "his instruments, which were mostly of his own construction, were far inferior to those of Nassir Eddin and of Ulugh Begh." (A Short History of Astronomy by Arthur Berry, London 1898, p. 96) Not only were his errors greater than Hipparchus could possibly think of tolerating, but in his discussions with Rheticus the latter brings out that Copernicus did not hold accuracy to be of vital importance, and only "rough agreement between theory and observation was all that he could hope to attain." Besides, in his high northern latitudes good observation was impossible, he claimed.

But that Copernicus advanced a theory which was novel and stimulating became known to many interested parties early in his life, though he held no chair, lectured nowhere, and published nothing. As early as 1515 his assistance was sought by a committee appointed by the Lateran Council to consider ways and means of correcting the apparent imperfections in the calendar. Copernicus, incidentally, declined on the ground that the orbits of the sun and moon were too imperfectly known for satisfactory calendar reform to be undertaken at the time. In 1533 "John Albert Widmanstad explained the Copernican theory to pope Clement VII in the Vatican gardens in the presence of cardinals Orsini and Salviati, Iohannes Petrus, bishop of Viterbo, and Matthaeus Curtius, the well-known medical writer." (Thorndike vol. V p. 410) We have already seen that such outstanding mathematicians and astronomers as Gemma Frisius, Reinhold and others looked forward to the publication of his work with great anxiety. Cardinal Nicholas von Schonberg urged him to complete his work as soon as possible, and paid the cost of the printing. The final manuscript of the De Revolutionibus was sent to Tiedemann Giese, bishop of Culm, who in turn submitted it to Rheticus who actually saw the job through. In other words, not only was there no opposition to Copernicus' views but on the contrary, sympathetic anticipation of the fuller text after friendly reception of the preliminary outlines. Moreover, the friendly reception was given to it by Catholic and Protestant leadership and scholars alike, even though Luther is said to have reacted violently against the fool who will upset the world of common sense with his nonsense about rotation and revolution of the earth.

In 1539 Georg Joachim Rheticus (1514–1564) who had just then become professor of mathematics at the newly founded Protestant university of Wittenberg, could no longer check his curiosity concerning the details of the much bruited about Copernican theory, and packed up his belongings and went off to Frauenburg to learn at first hand what he could from Copernicus himself. There had only been available until then a brief essay known as the Commentatriolus which was written by Copernicus and circulated in manuscript to a small circle of friends. Rheticus was received by Copernicus with exceptional kindness and was given the freedom of his house and of his MS and data. After only a few weeks' stay he wrote his famous Narratio Prima in the form of a letter to his old friend and master Johann Schoner. In this brief account Rheticus recounts lucidly and fully the gist of the theory propounded by Copernicus whom he calls "my doctor preceptor" or master, and with whom he lived for close to two years. There can be little doubt that Copernicus read and approved every word of this treatise, written under his tutelage and in his own home, and by a youngster. For these reasons the allusions to astrology contained therein are of interest in mirroring the attitudes of both people. Rheticus wishes to show how beautiful and significant is the epicycle which Copernicus gave to the motion of the earth's deferent.

"I shall add a prediction. We see that all kingdoms have had their beginnings when the center of the eccentric was at some special point on the small circle. Thus, when the eccentricity of the sun was at its maximum, the Roman government became a monarchy; as the eccentricity decreased, Rome too declined, as though aging, and then fell. When the eccentricity reached the boundary and quadrant of mean value, the Mohammedan faith was established; another great empire came into being and increased very rapidly, like the change in the eccentricity. A hundred years hence, when the eccentricity will be at its minimum this empire too will complete its period. In our time it is at its pinnacle from which equally swiftly, God willing, it will fall with a mighty crash. We look forward to the coming of our Lord Jesus Christ when the center of the eccentric reaches the outer boundary of mean value, for it was in that position at the creation of the world. This calculation does not differ much from the saying of Elijah, who prophesied under divine inspiration that the world would endure only 6000 years, during which time nearly two revolutions are completed. Thus it appears that this small circle is in very truth the Wheel of Fortune, by whose turning the kingdoms of the world have their beginnings and vicissitudes. For in this manner are the most significant changes in the entire history of the world revealed, as though inscribed upon this circle. Moreover, I shall soon, God willing, hear from your own lips how it may be inferred from important conjunctions and other learned prognostications, of what nature these empires were destined to be, whether governed by just or oppressive laws." (Three Copernican Treatises, by E. Rosen, N. Y. 1939 p. 121–122) Clearly, astrological belief is here so inextricably interlinked with the study of astronomy that neither Rheticus nor Copernicus see anything unusual in this mode of reasoning.

Rheticus had in fact been a devoted student of astrology all his life. In 1536, at the age of 22, he discussed the legality of astrological predictions and concluded that legislation against mathematici was not aimed at prediction based upon an analysis of natural causes, but was rather aimed at divining on the basis of the situation at the moment of interrogation or at revealing thieves and murderers from the condition of the stars at that moment, which cannot be scientific. In 1542 he published at Wittenberg selections from the De Revolutionibus on the sides of plane and spherical triangles and in the angles. In 1557 Rheticus published the works of Werner and explained in the introduction that the constellations, or rather the planets within them, indicated that year that the Turks would meet with dire disaster. In addition the sphere of the fixed stars showed an anomaly which his great teacher, Copernicus, was the first to detect. Ptolemy was unaware of this irregularity and Copernicus had enjoined him to study this phenomenon which he himself could not complete so as to provide a reliable basis for better astrological interpretations. In 1550 Rheticus published in fact at Leipzig, where he taught from 1542 to 1551, an Ephemeris based upon Copernican principles.

In 1563 there occurred a conjunction of Saturn with Jupiter and some friends of his under the impact of that event, urged Rheticus to undertake a full commentary on the writings of Copernicus. Rheticus launched that task but it remained apparently unfinished. Further, in his correspondence with Ramus, Rheticus expressed his ambition to free astronomy from hypotheses and to purge astrology of its ancient influences which he, presumably as a modern, found most unsatisfactory. It is perhaps for some such reasons that he expressed a strong desire to obtain the full text of Paracelsus' Astronomia and to have worked on a Latin translation of the Archidoxa by the same author. Finally, in the dedicatory letter of his Chorographia to duke Albrecht of Prussia, Rheticus points to the fact that the work is of definite service to astrology.

Tycho Brahe (1546-1601) was certainly one of astronomy's greatest. The remarks one often encounters to the effect that he lacked theoretical skill but was merely an observer, are of the kind only people unfamiliar with science can utter. There were few aspects of astronomy which Tycho's touch left unmodified and a list of his contributions constitutes a complete cross section of the science. Besides improving the accuracy of the instruments already in use, such as the quadrant and the equatorial armilla and introducing the method of graduation by transversals, he began the study of refraction to allow the error it introduced into observations, and established the custom of generally evaluating and allowing for error of all measurements taken. Tycho also introduced the practice of continuous observations rather than sporadic ones taken on important occasions, such as conjunctions or eclipses, and of repeating many measurements by taking observations under different

ASTRONOMY AND ASTROLOGY'S DEMISE 179

conditions. He reexamined the positions of the fixed stars and gathered numerous measurements on the planets. He discovered the irregularity in the motion of the moon, styled variation, and an additional one known as the annual equation, though he left it in an incomplete state of investigation. He also found the oscillation of the moon's orbit to the ecliptic and the variation of its nodes. He reexamined precession and determined its true value; he discarded the bewildering notion of trepidation or a supposed variation in its value. And one should not overlook Tycho's great, revolutionary study of the nova and the several comets, as already discussed, to say nothing of his attractive theory of the planetary system and its service in weakening the grip of the Ptolemaic.

No less arresting is Tycho's record as astrologer. "While occupied with the study of astronomy and occasional observations, Tycho, like everybody else at that time, believed in judicial astrology, and now and then worked out horoscopes for his friends. He even kept a book in which he entered these 'themata genethliaca.'" (Tycho Brahe by J. L. E. Dreyer, Edinburgh, 1890, p. 21) While still a youth of sixteen at the University of Leipzig under the supervision of his tutor Mr. Vedel, whose job it was to guard the young man against the study of astronomy so as to oblige him to cling to the study of law selected for him by his father, Tycho already dabbled in astrology clandestinely. He cast that year the horoscope of Caspar Peucer, Melanchthon's son-in-law and professor of medicine and mathematics at the University of Wittenberg, whither Tycho went in 1566, four years later. Strangely enough, he predicted that Peucer would meet with great misfortune, exile or imprisonment, and be liberated from it at the age of sixty. Indeed, in 1574 Peucer was suspected of Calvinism and thrown in prison where he lingered 12 years, being incarcerated at the age of forty nine and freed at sixty one, good enough for such purposes. "From a lunar eclipse which took place while he was at Leipzig, Tycho foretold wet weather, which also turned out to be correct," says Dreyer.

Interest in astrology was never a secondary matter with Tycho. He was as passionately and as devoutly interested in it as he was in his study and observation of the skies, if not more so, since as we shall see it was a primary passion with him to which the gathering of data was subservient. For example, in his first published work on the nova of 1572, Tycho devotes a section to astrological considerations. The astrological effect of the star, he says, is difficult to foresee because it is so unique, the only precedent for it being the nova of Hipparchus, 125 B.C. But since that ancient nova was followed by tragic times to both Jews and Gentiles, there is no doubt but that similar events are about to occur in our own times, especially since the new star appeared close to the conclusion of a complete period of all the trigoni. The new star is in Aries, where the new trigon will commence, hence it forecasts great political and religious changes. At the start of its career the star looked like Venus and Jupiter, hence its effects will be pleasant; later it resembled Mars, hence it forebodes "a period of wars, seditions, captivity, and death of princes and destruction of cities, together with dryness and fiery meteors in the air, pestilence, and venomous snakes." As Dreyer points out, Tycho's earlier interpretations were on the meteorological side and physical in content. As he grew in confidence he began to regard astrology as dealing more with the effect of the stars on the human mind, and therefore on human actions, an art requiring greater skill and insight.

As was customary, Tycho does not fail to shower abuse on the common prognosticators and promises a work that will revolutionize the science of astrology. Both the Alphonsine and the Prutenic Tables are well off the true positions by several hours. He discusses the importance of calendars and the kind of data they should supply. The book also contains his study of an eclipse of the moon on December 8, 1573, giving all the relevant data from tables and from his own observations. Following the rules of Ptolemy as laid down in his Tetrabiblos, he gives the astrological meaning of the event. The eclipse was in Gemini, hence a human sign which means, that considering the positions of Mercury and Mars, Nurnbergers are in for serious trouble, as are indeed all countries whose rulers were born when Gemini was culminating. The duration of the predicted action will persist for as many months as the eclipse lasted hours, and the results will hit hard all princes and rulers, as eclipses are wont to do, and "as I have observed myself." Tycho then cites evidence of the immediate past to prove the experimental nature of his prognostications. He cites eclipse after eclipse which took place in various signs and in each case the consequences were just what the rules would demand of them. He concludes with a promise to do better work in the future, because neither sneers nor hardships can deter him. Let others glory in military prowess or pride of lineage; let others seek the glamor of courts or gold or the pleasures of gambling and hunting. Though descended of noble lineage on both maternal and paternal sides he puts little stock in such matters and is proud only of things which were actually produced by himself. He will therefore aim at further work of the kind, and happy is he who is more concerned with celestial things rather than terrestrial.

In 1574, when Tycho was only 28 years of age, he was asked by some students at the University of Copenhagen to deliver a few lectures on mathematical subjects, entirely neglected then in the university's curriculum. He consented mainly because the king had asked him to comply with the students' wishes and thus honor the university. He began with an historical introduction in which he pointed out that both

ASTRONOMY AND ASTROLOGY'S DEMISE   181

geometry and astronomy were of great antiquity. Abraham discerned by the stars that there was only one God, and Plato would admit no one who was ignorant of geometry. Hipparchus and Ptolemy were great astronomers of old, and in our own times Copernicus may well be counted a second Ptolemy, a great theoretician and scholar in matters astronomical. His theory is contrary to physical principles in part, and even to mathematical axioms, but it is great nonetheless.

Astronomy is of value to man in that it helps him tell time and exalts his spirit by freeing it from consideration of earthly matters. Its greatest merit lies in its power to interpret the meaning of celestial movements to human fates. To deny the influence of the stars means to disbelieve in God's wisdom. What are the planets for if not to influence the weather, just as the sun determines the seasons, and the moon, the tides and the rise and fall of humors. Besides, past observations have established the nature of planetary action just as they have the effects of the sun and moon. The conjunction of Mars and Venus in certain parts of the sky means rain and thunder, of Jupiter and Mercury storms, and so forth. Some conjunctions in certain positions cause plague, others diverse misfortune. Some people grant the effect of the planets on physical conditions but deny their effect on man. But what is man if not composed of elements and nurtured by the elements? His heart is equivalent to the sun, the brain to the moon, and like the sun and moon they act upon each other reciprocally, and are dependent upon each other. The liver corresponds to Jupiter, the kidneys to Venus, the milt to Saturn, the gall to Mars, and the lungs to Mercury. As to horoscopes they are merely the dictates of experience. Those born under Saturn are inclined to sublime studies while those born under the influence of Jupiter take to politics. "The solar influence makes people desire honor, dignities and power; that of Venus makes them devote themselves to love, pleasures, and music; while Mercury encourages people to mercantile pursuits, and the moon to travelling." (ibid. p. 77)

Tycho then considers all the usual arguments in favor of astrology, citing and refuting all the objections offered, even as did Ptolemy in Tetrabiblos. He cites the same objections and offers the same confutations, mentioning the role of climate, culture, education, the power of God to contravene the signs of the stars, and he even reiterates Ptolemy's caveat that the wise man rules the stars and that man being forewarned might be able to avert threatening evil. Even if he fails it is still good to know the future so as to adapt to its inevitability. In other words, Tycho was in no way original in these matters, but merely lectured on the ordinary astrological credo, unadorned and unrefined. He obviously regarded this aspect of the subject important enough to give it practically all the time available to him, devoting little time to anything else.

In 1576 King Frederick II of Denmark offered Tycho the island of Hveen, near Elsinore where he was building a castle at the time and where Tycho could retire and pursue his astronomical studies undisturbed. Tycho accepted and soon thereafter erected from royal funds a beautiful castle and observatory, Uraniborg, which housed his famous mural quadrant and his other instruments, and where the great astronomer spent his happiest and most active years from 1576 to 1597. The king was a true lover of learning and wanted nothing for his generosity but the advancement of science. The only obligation Tycho did have toward his benefactor was to compose astrological horoscopes and predictions when the occasion required it. In 1577 the king's eldest son was born, Prince Christian, destined later to become one of Denmark's popular kings, and Tycho felt it his duty to work out his nativity. This was an elaborate document in Latin with a German summary at the end, and like all such documents was based on elaborate astronomical analyses and calculations. For that purpose Tycho used the Prutenic Tables though he also gave the positions of the planets according to the Alphonsine merely for comparison. As a conscientious worker Tycho was not quite satisfied with what he had, so he appended whatever observations he had taken himself of Jupiter, Mars, Venus and the sun. Being unorthodox in science, he did not employ a square figure for the horoscope diagram but a circular one. Like his defense of astrology, the horoscope had nothing unusual about it. It read like the thousands of others issued annually by the practitioners. That this was no mean task can be seen from the fact that the horoscope of each of the three princes he composed in time, was "a handsome volume in small quarto, bound in pale green velvet with gilt edges, containing about 300 pages, all written in Tycho's own hand." (Dreyer, p. 153)

Tycho's scholarly biographer and outstanding astronomer, Dreyer, goes out of his way to point out that "Tycho did not take much interest in nor attach any importance to these astrological prognostications." He cites, what he considers as conclusive evidence, the fact that the queen's father had procured two horoscopes for a friend and found that they were far from agreeing with each other. He therefore asked Tycho's advice on the meaning of that irregularity, to which Tycho presumably replied that he is not concerned with astrology but merely anxious "to put astronomy into proper order." Yet, this can hardly be regarded as conclusive evidence because giving the answer requested is troublesome, and Tycho would want to avoid the bother. Also, every student of astrology knew that the art was far from perfect, and in fact, in a bad way on many counts. To begin with, the field was full of charlatans, and every one complained about them; one was not a good astrologer if one failed to do that. Second, men of Tycho's calibre certainly knew that the data were full of holes and that until measurements became more accurate, astrological interpretations were doomed to uncertainty, and diversity of interpretation was inevitable. Besides, it was perfectly natural for such people as Tycho to regard their obligatory horoscopes as chores, and incessantly to complain about them, particularly when they were at work on some vital astronomical problem. We shall encounter the same attitude in Kepler and Galileo. The fact that astronomical problems held more fascination at the time, is no proof that these great scientists did not take astrology seriously. Tycho's very answer to the above question shows that he was in dead earnest about the whole business. He points out that differences in the horoscopes are not surprising, since each had assigned rulership to different ascendants, because one used the Prutenic tables and the other the Alphonsine. The difference between them was nineteen hours for the position of the vernal equinox and that makes all the difference in the world. To top it all Tycho points out that neither the Prutenic nor the Alphonsine tables are correct and what is needed is more data.

B. KEPLER

Kepler's attitude toward astrology is of special interest because of the frequent references to his complaint that astrology must work hard, presumably illegitimately, so as to earn money for the support of dame astronomy. This statement is interpreted by those who quote it as implying that Kepler disbelieved in astrology but pursued it merely to earn a livelihood and thus be in a position to devote his free time and energies to the study of what really interested him, true astronomy. Even a cursory acquaintance with Kepler's life and works gives the lie to this gross historical misconception. The most reliable analysis of this problem is contained in a work by H. A. Strauss and S. Strauss-Kloebe, entitled *Die Astrologie des Johannes Kepler* (Oldenburg Verlag, Munich & Berlin 1926). Besides an introduction of thirty pages, the book contains almost two hundred pages of diverse excerpts from the numerous writings of Kepler which more than any interpretation or analysis reveal the author's thoughts and attitudes. Already in 1895, Norbert Herz in his *Kepler's Astrology* pointed out that this great astronomer and mathematician had honestly adhered to the basic tenets of astrology throughout his life. But Kepler's biographers continued to explain away this fact by means of such comments as the following: "Nowhere does Kepler utter an astrological declaration as his own conclusion, invariably these announcements are wrapped in expressions such as 'The astrologers declare, opine, believe, conjecture, etc.'" Another biographer writes: "Anyone competent to read between the lines will clearly discern that Kepler personally was free from astrological nonsense."

And in saying these things, biographers really felt they were serving the cause of science and truth!

In his own words, Kepler devoted himself to philosophy "with extraordinary anxiety" ever since he was "old enough, to recognize her sweetness." Philosophy to him meant science, religion, mysticism, and above all mathematics. Geometry, together with the lure and romance of numbers and forms, were to him the warp and woof of cosmic beauty, and the hidden pattern of God's designs. "Thus the construction of Kepler's world-temple derived from the treasure-halls of mathematics and philosophy inspired by a God of order, harmony and superhuman wisdom." (H. A. Strauss and S. Strauss-Kloebe. *Die Astrologie des Johannes Kepler*, Berlin 1926 p. 7) But unlike the speculating philosophers of the period, Kepler invariably sought factual evidence for his schemes or hypotheses, accurate data, and mathematical rigidity.

He viewed his belief in astrology in exactly the same light. On becoming instructor in mathematics at a high school in Graz, at the age of 22, he was required to publish annually an almanac containing prognostications concerning weather, harvests, catastrophies, wars, commerce, etc. He took to it with alacrity since he had dabbled in astrology while still a student at Tübingen. Like many another learned astrologer he was not a mere orthodox practitioner, but displayed independence of thought and boldness in criticism where he believed criticism was due. In one of his early almanacs issued in 1598 he writes: "As experience teaches us, that most beautiful gift of God, that noble phenomenon of the divine orbits and their earthly influences, (i.e. astrology) is brought in disrepute by nothing else as much as by the trend of some to claim too much for her through unseemly and superstitious prating, and thus drive the learned away from her. I have therefore ventured during my labors of the last two years, to whittle down such immoderate claims of *astrologia* and to declare that no serious trust can be put in the *Prognostica* attached to the yearly calendars. Rather are they meant as sheer entertainment, to be read particularly by scholarly, thoughtful and peace-loving people, because the art itself possesses no power whereby some events may be foretold specifically rather than in generality." (Ibid. p. 8) Yet it was the specific and particular prognostications the public was clamoring for. This serious limitation of astrology did not deter Kepler from practicing astrology, however. In his Prognosticon of 1604 he even went so far as to state: "The horoscopes of particular individuals, and what man stands to gain from them, as well as Astrological Medicine, a disagreeable and badly contaminated work, I pass over in silence." But that declaration does not hinder him from commenting in almost the same breath: "When something unusual in the heavens arises, emanating either from strong constellations or from new comets,

ASTRONOMY AND ASTROLOGY'S DEMISE

the whole universe perceives it and responds to it, and so do all vital energies of every single thing in nature." To prove that not all sense organs are as yet known to us he poses the question: "Tell me then from a scientific point of view with which eyes the sublunar (earthly) organisms can perceive positions of stars in the zodiac, discern their geometrical juxtapositions known to us as aspects, and learn therefrom how to pursue their prescribed tasks and functions? Did my mother see with her own eyes the stellar arrangements so that she consciously knew to give birth when Saturn, Jupiter, Mars, Venus and Mercury stood to each other in sextiles and trigons? Did she give birth to me, her firstborn, on such a day when as many aspects prevailed, involving Saturn, and Jupiter, as occurred in her own life-span, particularly in quadrature and opposition and at loci occupied in her own history?" Similarly, he asks, how does the anima terrae, or earth soul, know to respond to the heavens' impulses? Conjunctions are endowed with exceptional powers to act upon the earth and so do comets since, "whereas all of Nature and her forces possess the hidden power to detect the aspects of all heavenly rays and be regulated by them, they will, no doubt, detect comets as well."

Kepler stood bravely by the defense of astrology against her detractors, warning them that science in rejecting astrology may be guilty of throwing out the baby with the bath. "Yet for such excesses, astrologers have nobody to blame but themselves. Not only have they through many abuses brought this salutary art into disrepute and suspicion, but they understood so little of its real worth, for which I here stand up, that never knowing the baby, they merely slopped around in the filthy bath." At the age of 23, he assured his teacher Maestlin, that by rejecting the chaff of astrology he could safely retain and enjoy the kernel. At the age of 50, after completing the Rudolphine Tables he writes in the introduction to that great work: "The science of the heavens consists of two parts. The first treats of the motions of the heavenly bodies (astronomy). The second of the effect of these bodies on the sublunar world (astrology)." Kepler had consciously made it his life's ambition to place that second task on a sound foundation, a thankless but worthy ambition. It stood badly in need of his aid, he thought, because it suffered from many gaps and evil practitioners.

In his attempt to purge astrology of its vagueness and exaggeration he denied the power of astrology to foresee the accidental but merely to detect by scientific means the logically consequent. That, incidentally, was the point of view of all scholarly defenders of astrology from the Babylonians to Ptolemy down. The public clamored for the prognostication of things that mattered, the dramatic, the unexpected and immediate, and the emotional pressure sucked the science into its stream and dragged along enough of its practitioners to satisfy its wants. But the more sober ones kept aloof of this popular wave, remained loyal to their scientific caution and declared with Kepler: "That the sky affects man remains unquestioned, but how this action is resolved in its full details is as yet hidden." For instance, it is folly to conclude "that the conjunction of Saturn and the moon will cause one to be swindled by a Jew. Should such a conjunction occur on a Saturday, no one in Prague will be swindled by a Jew, while hundreds of Christians are daily deceived by Jews though the moon can only be in conjunction with Saturn at best once a month." Similarly, he admonishes: "It is sheer nonsense, folly and superstition to claim to foresee that the native's bride will be from this or that country, have such and such a hidden mark on her body, that she will not be faithful to her husband, that she will have so many children, or that the native will have two, three or more wives. Venus, in the house of Saturn, indicates an old lady; in the eighth field a widow; Mars in the house of Venus, and in trigon to the moon, an unchaste woman, while Venus within the path of the sun's rays, a sick one. To such rules of houses and the deductions therefrom concerning human fate and fortune, without regard to human nature and man's intervention, I call a halt and will have none of it."

He did not regard the twelve signs of the zodiac as qualitatively distinct and found he could do all he wanted with the four points of the zodiac, i.e. the east and west intersections with the horizon, known as ascendant and descendant, and the upper and lower culmination points. Similarly, of the twelve "fields" of the horoscopes he rejected all but the four corner ones. When it came to reading the signs of the heavens for what he called "general dispositions," Kepler was no longer timid or skeptical. "To critics like Feselius and his authors I have this to say: That some remarkable predictions concerning such generalities can be derived from the heavens, and that our knowledge is based upon such experience, cannot be denied. Moreover, that the art of deciphering these prognostications can be acquired by anyone who devotes to it as much zeal as the physician does to the study of herbs and their diverse effects, can be daily verified by observation." The positions of the planets and constellations at the moment of birth determine the fate of an individual. "To begin with, I may rightly boast of this experience and truth, that man, in the moment of ignition of his life, when he becomes himself and can no longer remain in his mother's womb, receives the stamp of his character from all the heavenly configurations and light beams converging at that moment upon the earth, which imprint he retains unto his grave, since it fashions his appearance and physique, his conduct, virtues and gestures." Further, "This stamp is imprinted at birth by the mysteriously creative force lodged in the character of the sky upon the native's features, and can, through some as yet hidden instinct, be detected by the observer (of the skies)." That star-injected power, the native guards within him all his life, and whenever these celestial configurations recur, they restimulate his being. But most remarkable is the fact that the initial stellar imprint at birth, possesses a lasting power to guide the life course of the native.

Kepler's practical labors in astrology are found under three headings: weather, international affairs, and individual fates. "With endless patience we see him at work incessantly at his astro-meteorological observations. All through the year he records the weather from one day to the next, eagerly seeking associated earthly factors, more and more his grip to tighten on the elusive elements in his prognostications. Here, too, the sky is not the only determinant. Local, geographic conditions were given by him their due regard. He recognized, for example, the effect of mountains on local weather conditions. But he also describes the action of the subterranean spirit Archeus in bringing about clear weather." (ibid p. 26) Needless to say his earnest labors in this field were not crowned with success and the weather's vagaries defied the prognostications he laid down in his numerous almanacs, which, understandably enough, he always regarded as drudgery. Yet that complaint need not be taken any more seriously than the oft repeated comment of some outstanding concert pianists that they dislike concerts. When his almanacs were attacked or belittled he promptly and vehemently came to their defense.

Though he was not quite orthodox in the belief that different regions of the sky dominated different countries, indicated wars, plagues, rebellions, etc. he nevertheless considered it essential for rulers to carefully watch the signs in the sky. In his prognostication for 1618 he warns: "Whether they regard it necessary or not, all potentates or rulers, particularly those, that have large populated cities, should eagerly see to it that they do not submit with abandon to good times in March and April, carefree and unconcerned," lest May greet them with bad luck and hard times. The signs of the sky are likely to be fickle then, and one had better be careful not to throw fire into dry straw, which admittedly is sound advice under all circumstances. Wisely, too, he warns his readers not to dote upon the intricacies of prognostications, and thus be distracted from looking after one's own conduct and responsibilities. He thinks that "human beings are more differentiated by the stars than by social institutions and habits." Yet fear and anxiety before the stars is folly. Only a philosophic attitude and scientific comprehension of the divine scheme of the universe, afford clear vision and peace.

To understand the complex and ambivalent attitude toward astrology by many of the learned men of the early modern times, one must carefully scrutinize their concepts and their reasoning. One will then observe that the concept which we single out as a unified notion such as belief in astrology, is far from being homogeneous or simple; rather is it most involved and polyvalent, and as intricate in its nature as is happiness or justice. Let us consider Kepler's Introduction to his almanac or prognosticon for the year 1598, which he entitles *Guide to the Four Seasons and Other Significances of the Planets and Eclipses.* Composed for the year of our Saviour 1598.

Learned opinion has it, my noble lords and readers, he says, that there are two kinds of prognosticated events; some stem from natural and perceptible causes, others quite numerous, transpire for reasons unknown and unforeseen by any man. To the latter group belong, among others, miracles and divine revelations, entailing acts that are supernatural. This implies that nature is directed by God to suspend her laws or utterly modify her conduct by His special command. Kepler points out, that the devil also dares reveal in this manner many mysteries to his witches and sorcerers, but his secrets are sheer deceptions, or small pickings which even mortal man can manage to come by. In addition, there are people sorely stricken mentally who can reveal most wonderful occurrences which surprisingly come true. But those astrologers do reach beyond their legitimate ken who seek to prognosticate specific details which in truth their science does not legitimately permit. Unwittingly an astrologer may hit upon accuracy here and there but that will be sheer luck. When questioned, the astrologer himself will fail to account for the reasons behind his success. One is obliged to postulate in such instances that his good fortune may be the product of a mysterious power acting for the sake of the person whose fortune is the issue, rather than for or upon the fortune-teller himself. "It does not, however, follow that another astrologer will be equally lucky, or capable of raising the art to as high a level." There are few such lucky astrologers; besides, many of them tend to regard as correctly foretold events of which they had in reality prognosticated the exact reverse. Or they consider a successful guess one which is only partly so. Moreover, people tend to forget all the failures since they occur so often, while a single guess, being a rare event, is long remembered. Often too, gossip converts a false prophecy into a presumably truthful forecast.

Of the natural arts of forecasting there are many and diverse ones besides astrology, all of which seek accuracy, but with uncertain results. Yet none of these deserves more honor than astrology, since though her strength derives from nature and the heavens, she cannot help the inevitable intrusion of other natural prognosticating skills so that were the astrologer really honest to his trade and wish to speak only of what he knew, he would not be understood, and would be obliged to discourse merely of what he learned in astronomy. These intruding, natural, prognosticating skills are also more certain than astrology because they derive from earthly and related spheres and come closer to specificity in forecasting. Thus, a military expert can foresee victory or defeat, a lawyer the outcome of a suit, a philosopher the effects of changes in government, an aged man the future of his children, a physician the prognosis of a given disease and the farmer the kind of harvest or weather to be expected. Each is more expert in his special field and can therefore do a better job at forecasting in it than the astrologer, since they are presumably fully familiar with the respective factors governing each situation. The astrologer, however, knows only the sky. Hence a good astrologer skilled in worldly events, having at his fingertips the birth-hours of all lords and princes in the realm, may, I will admit, be not quite perfect in specific and particular detail, but be the equal of any in forecasting; but one must not forget that it is humanly impossible to attain satisfactory elaboration in brief statements. Only the by now six and a half thousand-year-old devil can do that. When all is said and done, it is still most difficult to prognosticate reliably in specificity, because in addition to natural causes, there function in the world the powers of man's free will, the free will of good and evil spirits and of the Almighty Lord himself, the effects of which He alone can foresee. Man's will is conditioned by nature, that of the spirits depend on God, who reigns over all, but His reign is mostly in the hearts and minds of men. Also, God's rule is of a general nature of law and order and affects little the specific events in the world, though He can, and in my opinion does it very rarely, intervene in orderly processes through miracles, which override or suspend the laws of nature. Hence, one cannot find in nature the certainty and security in prognostications which many demand of the astrologers. Kindly bear in mind that in the good society one must not exclusively pursue the useful and the profitable, but one must also act for the Glory of God, the delight of man, the enjoyment of peace as well as the pleasure that comes from the contemplation of such things as astrology and God's wonderful schemes and creations. Herewith I humbly submit to you this my fourth Prognosticon of 1597.

Here are the workings of a sincere mind, the mind of a unique genius, also the mind of a medieval scholar. The devil, spirits, miracles, evidence, prognostication, science, witches, respect for learning and disrespect for its abusers, astrology, natural law and probability, critical evaluation and independent thought, all are taken for granted. There is an earnest desire to be critical, fair and reasonable, to discriminate justly between right and wrong and examine arguments and evidence rationally. The outcome seems as strange to us as do the appearances of Ubangi or Zulu women, after hours of labor at self-beautification. Not only the mores but the very mode of scientific thought seems dependent upon the folkways. We might conclude with a sample of one of Kepler's prognostications, bearing in mind that he literally wrote thousands of them in his lifetime.

"My father Heinrich was born on the 19th of January, 1547. Since Saturn was in trigon to Mars and stood in the seventh house, i.e. at the end of the seventh house, everything pointed downward (I presume he was actually born earlier). He (Saturn) brought forth a human being that was foredoomed to misdeeds, proved himself gruff and quarrelsome and met in the end a lonely death. Venus and Mercury only served to augment the evil in him. Jupiter, burning and about to fall, contributed to his misery but also blessed him with a wealthy spouse. Saturn in the seventh house wrought love in him for the mercenary life, gave him many enemies and a marriage of incessant conflict. Jupiter and the Sun both badly situated, seduced him into false and futile lust for superficial honors, leading to disillusionment and frustration and later to restiveness. For the coming year (1589) the aspects bode ill aplenty for my parents. Since both great lights (sun and moon) seem offended as is Saturn in his retrograde motion, it has to transpire that my father treat my mother cruelly and finally desert her for good and die in a strange bed." (ibid. p. 171)

Yet, Kepler has some harsh criticism of Cardan, for the latter's irresponsible astrological excursions. He does not know how good a physician he might be, says Kepler, but he surely is too credulous as astrologer. "He is so full of rash notions that it is practically impossible for him to have paid any serious or critical attention to even one hundredth part of them. He seems to have been carried away with them as if he regarded himself an oracle and thus misuses his calling and exploits people's ignorance, particularly our credulous German ingenues, who swallow it as if bewitched." (ibid p. 153) And Cardan too as we shall see, attacked and chided superstition and credulity with self-righteous vigor and biting vitriol.

C. GALILEO GALILEI

Even Galileo Galilei (1564–1642) still taught and practiced astrology. After teaching for eighteen years at the University of Padua, he accepted in 1610 an offer from Cosimo II, Grand Duke of Tuscany, to become his court mathematician. After one year at this post, however, Galileo wrote to the Grand Duke: "I would wish that to the title of Mathematician his Highness would be pleased to add that of Philosopher, as I have studied a greater number of years in philosophy than months in pure mathematics. And how far I have profited by it, and if I can and ought to merit the title, I hope to be able to show his Highness as often

ASTRONOMY AND ASTROLOGY'S DEMISE

as it is his pleasure to give me an opportunity of discussing such subjects with those whose knowledge is most esteemed." He received the coveted title and was proud of it.

Fahie says in his interesting biography of Galileo: "While the Grand Duke was wont to declare that Galileo was the greatest mathematician in all Christendom, his wife, the Grand Duchess Christine, believed him to be the greatest of astrologers, and at the commencement of what proved to be her husband's last illness, she begged him to correct his horoscope! He did so, and communicated the result in a letter of the 16th of January, 1609, according to which Ferdinando I had still many years to live. Galileo's prognostic was speedily proved to be false, as the Grand Duke died twenty-two days after!" (Fahie, J. J. Galileo, His Life and Work. London, 1903, p. 64)

A survey of the historians and writers who have dealt with Galileo is of interest. Nine out of ten omit reference to his astrological labors, and those who mention it feel obliged to offer an apology. Thus, Fahie explains that Florence, where Galileo lived, was noted for its interest in divination and astrology, and that the latter was a popular subject at the universities of Padua and Bologna, where Galileo had taught.

"No wonder, then, if Galileo, more temporum dabbled in horoscopes; but it is not to be supposed that a mind, which early discarded the trammels of ancient sciences and took nothing on trust or mere authority, could easily have believed in them. We prefer to consider his action in this and other instances, in the light of a pious fraud." (Ibid, p. 65)

This belief is perhaps more unscientific than Galileo's acceptance of astrology. The assumptions that Galileo's astrological work was a pious fraud reminds one of the Nazi general who, when he discovered that his father was of Jewish ancestry, claimed that he was really the illegitimate son of an Aryan halfwit. Pious frauds do not harmonize with the character of a man like Galileo.

At Padua, Galileo lectured to medical students on astrology, which was then considered an indispensable adjunct of medicine. Astrology was centrally anchored in the whole ambit of sixteenth century knowledge and, dominated all intellectual disciplines. Hence Galileo lectured on the accepted astrological relations between the planets, the human organs they governed, and other relevant astrologico-medical topics. William Harvey who, incidentally, was a firm believer in the value of astrology in medicine, is said to have been a pupil of Galileo's, as was Robert Fludd, the famous English physician and astrologer. The three lectures which Galileo gave in Padua on the new star of 1604 attracted over a thousand people; unfortunately, the full text has been lost. Of the origin of the nova, Galileo said, "One might well believe that the star was formed by the meeting of Jupiter with Mars, and with particularly good reason, since the star made its appearance at the place where these planets were in conjunction and at the same time." (F. Arago, Oeuvres Complètes de Galileo, Vol. III)

In subsequent works Galileo declared that new stars, like comets, are products of terrestrial exhalations, though at immense distances from the earth and reflecting the sun's rays. The belief was nearer to the Aristotelian view than that of Tycho Brahe who postulated a celestial origin for novae. Galileo did note, however, that the new star had no parallax.

D. NEWTON, BACON, DESCARTES AND OTHERS

There is a vast array of giants in the history of science whose attitude toward astrology was no different from that of Brahe, Kepler and Galileo. René Descartes was a great physicist, mathematician, mechanistic biologist, anatomist, philosopher, pioneer of the mystic order of Rosicrucians, alchemist, physician and possessor of the Philosopher's stone and elixir vitae, assuring him a life span of a hundred years. Huygens, who made immense contributions to astronomy, physics, mechanics, and mathematics, was a devoted student of astrology and numerology. For example, since the number of planets and satellites had now reached twelve, Huygens was certain that this was the most perfect and sacred of numbers. In his *Cosmotheros*, Huygens remarked that "There are on the earth men of cold temperament who would thrive in Saturn, which is the farthest planet from the sun; and there are other spirits warm and ardent enough to live in Venus."

Francis Bacon, called the father of modern science, chided astrologers for their abuse of the art but looked forward to the day when it would be established on a more scientific basis, and its excesses and malpractice would vanish. Only a reformed and scientific astrology, claimed Bacon, would be capable of predicting wars, plagues, famines and revolutions. "Astrology should rather be purged than absolutely rejected," he concluded. (Francis Bacon, *Advancement of Learning*, World Classics, Vol. I, p. 86) "And of such observations let a just astrology be formed and according to these alone should schemes of the heaven be made and interpreted. Such an astrology should be used with greater confidence in prediction but more cautiously in election and in both cases with due moderation. Thus, predictions may be made of comets and all kinds of meteors, inundations, droughts." (Ibid, p. 89)

In the life and work of Isaac Newton astrology begins to show signs of declining grandeur. Not that Newton questioned the basic astrological beliefs. When he entered the University of Cambridge in 1660 and was asked what he wished to study, he replied, "Mathematics, because I wish to test judicial astrology."

Newton remained an ardent student of alchemy throughout his life, and alchemy, as we shall see was as inseparable from astrology as physics is from mathematics. Among Newton's library were well-thumbed and annotated works by Geber, John Dee, the famous English alchemist and astrologer, and others of their kind. Newton's private physician was Richard Mead, who wrote a book on the effects of the sun and the moon on disease, as popular a subject for medical research at the time as are cancer and nutrition today.

In addition, Newton was a great student of mystical theology, a subject he took as seriously as other aspects of knowledge which his gigantic genius enriched. His *Observations Upon the Prophecies of Daniel and the Apocalypse of John* is, like Kepler's theological works, full of religious fantasy and abstruse symbolism. Christian theology was often closer to Newton's heart than the problems of gravitation and light. When Newton's friend and pupil, Halley, ventured to deprecate his master's excursions into theology, he obtained the sharp rejoinder, "I have studied these things. You haven't." Nor must one forget that the great Napier, the inventor of logarithms, was the author of A Bloody Almanac, a regular blood and thunder astrological prognostication, published in all seriousness as late as 1646–1647, which goes to show that beliefs of that kind die very slowly.

It is hardly necessary to consider what the attitude of the average cultured man of the early seventeenth century was toward astrology. If the learned were universally steeped in it, the average uneducated person guided his life by it. Astrology was as credible and real to the common people as was the existence of God or evil spirits.

In all civilizations astrologers were held in highest respect, often put on a par with priests. True, they were feared but only because of their vast knowledge of celestial forces and the frequent utilization of their alleged powers for sinister purposes. At all events, one avoided incurring the displeasures of any astrologer. This, too, need not seem anomalous. Fear and reverence of astrologers is akin to the attitude of most people today toward scientists. Knowledge is respected and envied, but the scientist is often viewed with distrust and suspicion. Numerous movies, for example, have portrayed him as a rather jittery and unsavory person, hopping nervously about a room crowded with fantastic glassware, flickering lights and sparking knobs, moving pumps and pistons, about to initiate experiments upon some temporarily deserted or lost heroine.

Yet there is also a widespread respect for science especially for inventions such as electrical devices, airplanes, radio, machines and gadgets of all sorts. This esteem for the scientist is genuine, though it has social limitations. Albert Einstein, Madame Curie, Thomas A. Edison or Alexis Carrell may be popular heroes, but the influence which any scientist can exert in the political or social sphere is limited. On the contrary, the scientist is suspect in these fields and often becomes a ready butt for jokes, witness the weird looking, bespectacled professor portrayed by some cartoonists as the symbol of the New Deal.

The position of the astrologer in the later Middle Ages and up to recent centuries was similarly ambivalent. He was feared and respected, but unlike the scientist of today, was far more influential because of the greater respect for learning shown by royal courts, princes, the nobility and church dignitaries. Almanacs were voraciously read, not only for prognostications but for their social and moral wisdom—viz. Franklin's *Poor Richard's Almanac*. The astrological beliefs were so strong, the heavenly signs so apparent and foreboding, and the masses so anxious to know their meaning, that almanacs were best sellers and the utterances of astrologers were held in awe.

The opinions of St. Augustine notwithstanding, the Old and New Testaments possess considerable traces of astrological beliefs. To begin with, the Book of Genesis tells of God creating stars that are lights in the firmament "and let them be for signs." There is the miracle of Hezekiah's pillar, and of Ahaz' sundial, the darkening of the sun at Christ's death, the star of the Magi which gave early church philosophers so much to write about, and other references. Indeed, astrology is almost a universal pattern of folklore, and should perhaps be added to the list of institutions common to all human cultures.

True to its cultural role, literature everywhere is imbued with astrological lore. Chaucer, Shakespeare, Milton, Ben Johnson, Dryden, and almost every poet and writer up to the eighteenth century fully accepted or even dabbled in astrology. As a folklore element, astrology influenced the minds of all people, in all walks of life. To the people of the time, it was plain common sense, and denying the influence of the stars on human life was as bold and blasphemous as asserting that all men are created equal or that man descended from primates.

Chapter VIII

THE PROCESS CALLED CHANGE

1. The So-Called Copernican Revolution

IN the tragedy of Galileo and Pope Urban VIII we are permitted a painful insight into the growth process in scientific ideas and fundamental cultural beliefs. Everybody concerned was caught in a tight trap of belief, failing to realize he was in it; everybody raved and struggled, though some suffered more than others. Ultimately an adjustment was reached and life became normal again. But there are belief transitions that are not quite so violent in their impact and are of interest nonetheless because they reveal other aspects of the mind in the process of change. Thorndike, in his usual manner, and a few other investigators, have given us valuable analyses of astronomical thought after Copernicus, and a summary of their conclusions and evidence will bring out some points of interest.

What was the attitude of the students of astronomy and of the teachers in the field to the new Copernican idea? The reaction of the scholars of the time can be classified under several headings.

There were those who defended the old Ptolemaic theory and opposed the new one as too audacious or unsound. Strangely enough, there were amazingly few such writers among the scientists of the time, contrary to the general notion. For example, Dodoens, author of a little work entitled Cosmography, published in 1548 and another edition in 1584, defends the view that the sun moves around the earth and refutes the idea that the earth can revolve about the axis of the eighth sphere which is the axis of the revolving universe, because the four elements of which it is composed can only move in a straight line. He fails to cite Copernicus in connection with five other points, but shows thorough familiarity with the De Revolutionibus. In the edition of 1584 he states that his Cosmography can serve as introductory to Ptolemy but also to the De Revolutionibus of Copernicus, "a most learned man who dissented from Ptolemy in some hypotheses." He argues on

195

occasion against both these great men and postulates the need for a ninth sphere to account for trepidation.

As typical anti-Copernican villain of modern folklore could serve Michael Stanhufius, who in two books on meteorology issued at Wittenberg in 1562, abusively derided those who God knows on what authority advanced the fantastic notion that the sun stands still and the earth is revolved and moved. Aristarchus of Samos, he says, held such views and Suidas reports that he had two moronic sons, which is precisely what one would expect of such a lunatic. Copernicus' name is not mentioned in the work, however. On the other hand, Barozzi in 1585 refutes the views of Aristarchus and Copernicus, mentioning both by name.

Another author who denies the motion of the earth is Sebastian Theodoricus of Einsheim, professor of mathematics at Wittenberg, whose work on the sphere appeared in 1564. Like Dodoens, he cites Copernicus as an esteemed authority on several occasions but fails to mention him in connection with the earth's motion which he is so busy denying. Moreover, he disagrees with ancient authorities on several scores, indicating that he can have a mind of his own.

Among non-scientific writers may be cited Bodin, the political liberal and father of the idea of a constitutional monarchy, and Paul Minerva, a high church dignitary. Both confuted the idea of the earth's motion as contrary to common sense and religion, respectively. Both mention Copernicus by name and argue against him, though Minerva admits that such improbable theories have intellectual merit, and he speaks highly of Copernicus as scientist and philosopher.

There were also astronomical or mathematical writers who failed to see any conflict or were unimpressed by the difference in interpretation between Ptolemy and Copernicus. For example, Nicolaus Biesius published in 1556 a work on the universe and natural philosophy in which he reports the Copernican system but neglects to state his own opinion of it. In his Meteorological Ephemerides of 1575, Richard Forster, physician and scholar of London, speaks of himself as a faithful student and follower of Ptolemy. He criticized a fellow astrologer for following the Arabs rather than the latter, and also mentions Copernicus with equal adulation as if there were no disagreement between them. Another, though none too careful author, Iunctinus, praises Copernicus for his calculations of the year's length, misinterprets him in another connection, but in his commentary on Sacrobosco's Sphere (1582) still treats the earth as stationary. However, in another work, Speculum Astrologiae, issued in 1573, he estimated the movements of the planets according to observations of Copernicus.

THE PROCESS CALLED CHANGE

That many fairly popular astronomical texts completely overlooked the Copernican speculations, goes without saying. Wolfgang Meurer's Meteorology published two years after the author's death, in 1587, shows no trace of the De Revolutionibus, nor for that matter of the nova of 1572 or the comet of 1577. It does cite many other recent authors but not Copernicus or Brahe. There were many, and popular works too, which continued the old textual material as if nothing had happened.

There were authors who seemingly knew the Copernican theory was important but thought it too advanced for their readers. Robert Recorde, the author of the first algebra text in English, the inventor of the sign for equality, published his Castle of Knowledge in 1556. It was a popular introduction to astronomy and represented the earth at rest, and though it mentioned approvingly the Copernican theory, failed to discuss it because it was "too difficult for this first Introduction." The same was true of Michael Maestlin whose elementary textbook of astronomy was published in 1582 and in which he follows Sacrobosco and Ptolemy, whom he holds in high esteem. The motion of the sphere of the stars he views in the conventional light, but admits that the Copernican scheme would have been simpler. "But since these are the more difficult and require a fuller explanation than can be given at present, we could not present them here." (L. Thorndike, History of Magic and Experimental Science, vol. VI, p. 47) Similarly Jean Pierre de Mesmes whose work, Astronomical Institutions, appeared in French in 1557 considers himself quite a modern and cites many contemporary astronomers who he believes have vastly advanced the science of astronomy. Yet, he warns his readers that he will not discuss Copernicus' arguments against the ninth sphere because it is hardly fair to upset inexperienced minds with new theories. He refers to Copernicus as "another second Ptolemy" but regards his view of the motions of the earth as absurd. The same attitude is shown by Erasmus Oswald Schreckenfuchs who edited an edition of Ptolemy's Almagest in 1551, and wrote an elaborate commentary on Peurbach's New Theories of the Planets in 1556. He refers to Copernicus as "that miracle of nature" who turned everything in astronomy upside down, but his hypotheses require elaborate discussion for which this is not the time nor the place.

There were also attitudes like that of Gemma Frisius whose tract on the astrolabe was published posthumously by his son in 1556. In this work Gemma praises the equations which Copernicus elaborated for the putative inequality in the supposed motion of the fixed stars and takes the opportunity to praise the cleverness and accuracy of the ancients whose data are "the fundamentals of the art." In other words there was no conscious battle between the old and the new; any more than there was an organized battle between the church and science. There were in fact no clear-cut lines that could be drawn between moderns and ancients. The paths of logic cut each other at all angles and in all directions much as they do in our society, as becomes apparent in polls, for example. Some people follow a pattern, the majority don't seem to do so but display a diversity of personal warps and woofs of opinions. Herman Witekind is a relevant example. After complaining that there are too many texts in astronomy and too few readers, he proceeds, of course, to write one and in it defends the belief in a ninth sphere, cites Copernicus for the motion of the fixed stars and the distances of the planets to the earth, and then proves that the earth is stationary and at the center of the universe, giving the stock arguments.

On the other hand there were many astronomers whose attitude to the entire affair was that of little concern for the fancy theoretical superstructure, being interested exclusively in the empirical implications of the new theory. Their point was that the theory is all right if it helps in the matter of tables and positions, and as for the rest, let the philosophers worry their willing heads. Erasmus Reinhold's Prutenic Tables were viewed by many in that light. Generally speaking, they were regarded as superior to the Alphonsine which were based wholly on Ptolemy. Yet there were some who were disappointed in them because their advantage over the Ptolemaic was slight, and they cooled in their enthusiasm for Copernicanism because of it.

Some people had unique and unclassifiable objections. Consider the case of Francis Bacon (1567–1631) the prophet of the method of science according to many moderns and also his contemporaries. He not only "harked back to the time-honored objections" but "at first mild in his opposition, he later became emphatically opposed to it." (The Gradual Acceptance of the Copernican Theory by Dorothy Stimson, Hanover, N.H. 1917, p. 73.) With his distrust of mathematics he "speaks of it as a possible explanation of the celestial phenomena according to astronomy but as contrary to natural philosophy" in his Advancement of Learning (1604). In the Novum Organum published in 1619 he defended the immobility of the earth as the only true theory. Again in his De Augmentis Scientiarum (1623) he discusses the old beliefs in the solidity of the heavens commenting that: "It is the absurdity of these opinions that has driven men to the diurnal motion; which I am convinced is most false." (ibid. p. 73) Bacon's reason for the earth occupying a central position is unique. Besides the common observation of the sky being spherical all around us, there is the fact that "dense bodies are contracted into a narrow compass" and given a spherical shape like that of the universe or the heavens. Hence, it is natural that "the middle of the world be set down as the proper and peculiar place for dense bodies." His main argument against Copernicus, in addition to minor ones, is that the assumptions he advances "are the speculations of one who cares not what fictions he introduces into nature, provided his calculations answer." (ibid. p. 73) Bacon's arguments are entirely free from any reference to the Bible or religion.

There were men like Fromundus who at first supported Copernicus and then retracted because of "the terror at the decree of the Sacred Congregation of Cardinals." His rebuttal to the books of Philip Lansberg and son, both of whom wrote in defense of Copernicus, which he, as publisher, issued in 1631, one year before Galileo's second condemnation, elicited from Galileo the opinion that "of all the opponents of Copernicus whom he had seen, Fromundus was the most sensible and efficient." A year after his condemnation, Galileo in a letter to Gassendi and Diodati writes as follows: "As for Fromundus (who, however, shows himself to be a man of great talent) I wish he had not fallen into what seems to me a truly serious error, although a rather common one, in order to refute the Copernican opinion, of beginning by poking scorn and ridicule at those who consider it true, and then (what seems to me still less becoming) of basing his attack chiefly on the authority of the Scriptures, and finally of deducing from this that in this respect it is an opinion little short of heretical. To argue in this way is clearly not praiseworthy." (ibid. p. 75) If the Scriptures are the works of God, says Galileo, so are the heavens, and one is as glorious as the other. Considering that these words were uttered after Galileo's recantation, they throw a queer light on his possible notions of what the trial and his abjurations were all about.

One thing seems certain. In the words of Dorothy Stimson "Catholic, Protestant, and unbeliever, Feyens, Melanchthon, Bacon and Bodin, all had recourse to the same arguments to oppose this seemingly absurd doctrine." The truth is that it is going too far to designate all opposition to Copernicus as absurd because the reasons given for rejecting him were as different as the people who did the rejecting. Generally speaking, non-astronomical writers were opposed to the Copernican theory and all the four mentioned above (Feyens was professor of medicine at the University of Louvain) belong in that category. Many astrologers were for it and many against, but the same could be said about those students of the heavens who were not conspicuous for their interest in astrological applications. In other words, those modern people who entertain the fiction that there are heroes who stand for progress and villains who believe in opposing it, had better abandon that view in favor of the truth revealing the complexity of the paths and byways of change.

2. Copernicus and His Orbs

That Copernicus in no way overcame the major complexities or all the blind spots of the times, is apparent from even a superficial study of his system. True enough the introduction of the rotation of the earth in twenty-four hours and its annual revolution around the sun, was a most ingenious simplification. The revolution of all the other planets around the sun in their synodal periods served to explain the stations and retrograde motions. Moreover, unlike many others before him, he is aware of the fact that Philolaus did not postulate the revolution of the earth around the sun but the revolution of the earth and sun around the central fire.

In the dedication to his masterpiece Copernicus states that the work took him "not nine years but four times nine years." Although Copernicus was slow about preparing his final work for publication, he had released a brief but detailed treatise of his theoretical conceptions, entitled Commentariolus, which circulated in manuscript form and spread abroad his ideas. It was, in all likelihood, this forerunner which spread the fame of the retiring scholar, who as canon of the Cathedral of Frauenburg in Ermland, Prussia, devoted his spare hours to courageous mathematical speculation, thus reviving the spirit of Eudoxus, Apollonius, Hipparchus, Heraclides or Aristarchus. Already in 1514, twenty-nine years before the publication of his great work and his death, Copernicus was invited by the bishop of Fossombrone to give his opinions on the then urgent question of calendar reform. Characteristically enough, as has already been pointed out, Copernicus declined on the grounds that "he did not think the motions of the sun and moon had yet been sufficiently investigated to allow of a final settlement of the question." In 1533, Pope Clement VII was given a verbal account of the Copernican theory and three years later Cardinal Nicolaus von Schonberg, Archbishop of Capua, "a very liberal minded man and a trusted councillor both of Clement and of his successor Paul III, wrote to Copernicus urging him to make his discovery known to the learned world and begging for a copy of whatever he had written, together with the tables belonging thereto, all to be copied at the Cardinal's expense." (Dreyer, 318)

In 1509 Georg Joachim Rheticus, a young professor at the new University of Wittenberg, paid Copernicus a visit and spent two years with him at Frauenburg studying his opus, a summary of which he later published under the title of Narratio Prima. Copernicus was probably encouraged by the excellent reception of this summary and his great work appeared in 1543, the year of his death.

THE PROCESS CALLED CHANGE

There has been considerable discussion among scholars and historians about the anonymous introduction which Andreas Osiander, a prominent Lutheran theologian of Nürnberg, who supervised the printing, appended to the work. Because of the issues involved the introduction is well worth quoting.

"To the Reader Concerning the hypothesis of this work.

Since the novelty of the hypothesis of this work has already been widely reported, I have no doubt that some learned men have taken serious offense because the book declares that the earth moves, and that the sun is at rest in the center of the universe; these men undoubtedly believe that the liberal arts, established long ago upon a correct basis, should not be thrown into confusion. But if they are willing to examine the matter closely, they will find that the author of this work has done nothing blameworthy. For it is the duty of an astronomer to compose the history of celestial motions through careful and skillful observation. Then turning to the causes of these motions or hypotheses about them, he must conceive and devise, since he cannot in any way attain to the true causes, such hypotheses as, being assumed, enable the motions to be calculated correctly from the principles of geometry, for the future as well as for the past. The present author has performed both these duties excellently. For these hypotheses need not be true nor even probable; if they provide a calculus consistent with the observations, that alone is sufficient. Perhaps there is someone who is so ignorant of geometry and optics that he regards the epicycle of Venus as probable, or thinks that it is the reason why Venus sometimes precedes and sometimes follows the sun by forty degrees and even more. Is there anyone who is not aware that from this assumption it necessarily follows that the diameter of the planet in the perigee should appear more than four times, and the body of the planet more than sixteen times, as great as in the apogee, a result contradicted by the experience of every age? In this study there are other no less important absurdities, which there is no need to set forth at the moment. For it is quite clear that the causes of the apparent unequal motions are completely and simply unknown to this art. And if any causes are devised by the imagination, as indeed very many are, they are not put forward to convince anyone that they are true, but merely to provide a correct basis for calculation. Now when from time to time there are offered for one and the same motion different hypotheses (as eccentricity and an epicycle for the sun's motion), the astronomer will accept above all others the one which is the easiest to grasp. The philosopher will perhaps rather seek the semblance of the truth. But neither of them will understand or state anything certain, unless it has been divinely revealed to him. Let us therefore permit these new hypotheses to become known together with the ancient hypotheses, which are no more probable; let us do so especially because the new hypotheses are admirable and also simple, and bring with them a huge treasure of very skillful observations. So far as hypotheses are concerned, let no one expect anything certain from astronomy which cannot furnish it, lest he accept as the truth ideas conceived for another purpose, and depart from this study a greater fool than when he entered it. Farewell." (Three Copernican Treatises, E. Rosen, p. 24–25)

It is curious that this introduction should have stirred up as much discussion as it did. Many writers regarded Ossiander as an appeaser or as an outright traitor to science. Copernicus, it is said, regarded the motions of the earth as a reality. The fact is that no matter how we look at it, the motions of the earth are a theory by all scientific standards and definitions. True, those of rotation and revolution have been made highly probable, but they are still not facts but inferential explanations. Few historians have anything but harsh words for Ossiander, whose comment stands out as a marvelous statement of the role, value and origin of a theory. He does state that real and irrevocable truth comes only from revelation; but precisely what is one to expect from a theologian of the sixteenth century? Those were Copernicus' ideas as well. Besides, if Copernicus firmly believed in the factual reality of his theoretical constructions, then, as Ossiander points out, he surely believed in a lot of silly fictions such as epicycles and the fantastic and complex "third motion." And if he is to be dubbed a visionary bold re rotation and revolution, he should be called a superstitious knave re epicycles and the "third motion."

Compare the caution of Ossiander with the far more serious fear of theory or hypotheses displayed by the great Newton who, unlike the theologian, escapes all censure. Says Newton in his immortal Principia: "We are certainly not to relinquish the evidence of experiments for the sake of dreams and vain fictions of our own devising." And later on: "But hitherto I have not been able to discover the cause of those properties of gravity from phenomena and I frame no hypotheses; for whatever is not deduced from the phenomena is to be called an hypothesis; and hypotheses, whether metaphysical or physical, whether of occult qualities or mechanical, have no place in experimental philosophy. In this philosophy particular propositions are inferred from the phenomena, and afterwards rendered general by induction. Thus it was that the impenetrability, the mobility and the impulsive force of bodies and the laws of motion and of gravitation were discovered." Thus Newton even bars any hypotheses, while Ossiander rather mildly suggests that since only God knows the real truth, all man can have is hypotheses that explain the facts well and are "easiest to grasp." And Copernicus himself certainly referred to the earth's motions as hy-

THE PROCESS CALLED CHANGE

potheses and not facts. It goes without saying that just as some Greek thinkers began to regard the oft-talked about spheres as real, so some students of Copernicus and even he himself occasionally talked of the motions as real. That is only human and is done apparently quite innocently, just as we still talk of the sun as rising, or of angels and the devil.

The De Revolutionibus is divided into six books. "The first gives a general sketch of the new system and finishes with two chapters on plane and spherical triangles. The second book deals with spherical astronomy. The third discusses the precession of the equinoxes and the motion of the sun (or rather the earth) the fourth the theory of the moon's motion; the fifth the motions of the planets in longitude; and the sixth their motions in latitude." (Dreyer p. 322)

To begin with, Copernicus declares, the universe is spherical "partly because this form, being a complete whole, needing no joints, is the most perfect of all; partly because it constitutes the most spacious form, which is thus best suited to contain and retain all things; or also because all discreet parts of the world, I mean the sun, the moon and the planets appear as spheres; or because all things tend to assume the spherical shape . . ." such as a drop of water. "Therefore no one will doubt that this form is natural for the heavenly bodies." (A Source Book in Astronomy, Harlow Shapley & Helen E. Howarth 1929, p. 1) He then proceeds in the next chapter to cite some factual evidence for the earth's sphericity. The motions of the heavenly bodies are circular. Such a path has no beginning and no end. True the motions of the planets do not appear to be circular. Their courses are oblique to the zodiac and the sun and moon, for example, "are discovered moving now with a slower, now a farther motion. The remaining five planets, moreover, we also see at times going backward and in the transition, standing still. And while the sun moves along always in its direct path, the planets wander in various ways, roaming now to the South, now to the North, wherefore they are designated 'planets.' They have the added peculiarity that they at times come nearer to the earth, when they are called at perigee, then again they recede from it, when they are called at apogee. *Nevertheless it must be admitted that the motions are circular, or are built up of many circles; for thus such irregularities would occur according to a reliable law and a fixed period, which could not be the case if they were not circular.* For the circle alone can bring back to us, through its motion made up of circles, the irregularities of the days and nights and the four seasons; in which several motions are recognized because it cannot happen that the simple heavenly bodies move irregularly in a single circle. For this would either have to be caused by an inconstancy in the nature of the moving force—whether the inconstancy be brought about

ASTROLOGY AND ALCHEMY

by a cause from without or within—or would have to originate in an irregularity of the moving body. But as reason rebels against both and as it is unworthy to assume such a thing concerning that which is arranged in the best of order, so one must admit that the regular motions seem irregular to us, either because the various circles have different poles, or because the earth is not situated in the center of the circles in which the planets move. . . ." (ibid p. 3)

Copernicus then proceeds to defend the possibility of the earth's motion. "Every change of position which is observed is due either to the motion of the observed object or of the observer, or to motions, naturally in different directions of both; for when the observed object and the observer move in the same manner and in the same direction, then no motion is observed. Now the earth is the place from which we observe the revolution of the heavens and where it is displayed to our eyes. Therefore, if the earth should possess any motion, the latter would be noticeable in everything that is situated outside it, but in the opposite direction, just as if everything were traveling past the earth. And of this nature, is above all, the daily revolution." (ibid p. 4)

After arguing that the earth need not be centrally situated he sets out to refute the arguments of the ancients against the earth's revolution. Ptolemy claimed that a twenty-four hour rotation would constitute so violent a motion as to scatter the earth in pieces. Copernicus claims that the immense heavenly sphere, being further away would have to rotate faster and thus be in far greater danger. Actually, he says, friction causes the air to partake of the earth's motion. He even considers gravity with amazing lucidity. "I at least am of the opinion that gravity is nothing but a natural tendency, implanted by Providence in all particles, to join themselves into a whole in the form of a sphere. And it is credible that this tendency is also innate in the sun, moon and other planets by the effect of which they retain their round shape, while they complete their circuits in various ways." He then proceeds to fix the correct order of the planetary orbits from a heliocentric origin. "But in the midst of all stands the sun," he concludes. "For who could in this most beautiful temple place this lamp in another or better place than that from which it can at the same illuminate the whole? Which some not unsuitably call the light of the world, others the soul or the ruler. Trismegistus calls it the visible God, the Elektra of Sophocles, the all-seeing. So indeed the sun, sitting on the royal throne, steers the revolving family of stars."

At this point Copernicus comes up against one of his most difficult and bewildering tasks, which greatly complicates his reasoning. To the ancients and to the astronomers in his day, ideal rotation implied a relationship between bodies like that of the moon to the earth. We say that the moon shows the same face to the earth because its period of rotation is of the same duration as its period of revolution. In other words, whenever a body revolves about a center and shows the same face to that center, we invariably explain it as rotation added to revolution. To the ancient and medieval thinkers the reverse seemed true. Revolution was expected to proceed as if a long rod passed through the revolving body thus making it natural that it present the same side to the center. "Copernicus therefore would have expected the axis of the earth to have continued during the year to be directed to a point a long way above the sun, as if the earth were the bob of a gigantic pendulum. This would have made the celestial pole in the course of a year describe a circle parallel to the ecliptic." Since it does nothing of the kind, but remains fixed or rather, the axis remains parallel to its original position, always pointing to the same place on the celestial sphere, Copernicus was obliged to postulate a compensatory motion "whereby the axis of the earth describes the surface of a cone in a year, moving in the opposite direction to that of the earth's center i.e. from east to west. Hereby the axis continues to point in the same direction in space." He next made this backward motion slightly less than a year thus cleverly accounting for the procession of the equinoxes, and it was also made to explain two erroneous notions of the time which Copernicus shared, namely, one in the supposed irregularity in the motion of the equinoxes, a conclusion based on poor measurement, and the second that the obliquity of the ecliptic also showed irregular change. To explain these three motions of the earth, which he had raised to five, Copernicus resorted to most complex and ingenious schemes. For example, he postulated a pendulum-like motion of the earth's axis which he compounded as the result of two tricky circular motions. He makes use of an old though little known theorem that "a rectilinear motion may be produced by a combination of two circular ones, as when a circle rolls on the interior of another with a radius twice as great, in which case a point on the circumference of the smaller circle will describe a diameter of the greater one." (Dreyer p. 330) He employed eccentrics and epicycles to account for planetary inequalities in speeds and brightness, imposed by not using ellipses as orbits. His course of the earth around the sun is therefore far from the simple picture presented to us in modern texts. He did, however, reduce the number of eccentric and epicyclic circles from some eighty odd to thirty-four.

His picture of the earth's motions is as follows: (Figure 16)

The earth T, according to Copernicus, revolves annually around a center B which is situated near the sun S, but not in it. This center B is not stationary but revolves around another center A in 3434 years, thus accounting for the imaginary variation in obliquity. A, on the other

206   ASTROLOGY AND ALCHEMY

hand, in its turn, moves in a circle around S, the sun, in about 53000 years, thus accounting for the imagined motions of the earth's axis.

The moon's orbit was none too simple either, though considerably simpler than Ptolemy's picture. Instead of one deferent and epicycle, he employed two epicycles. (Figure 17)

The center of the deferent d, is situated in the center of the earth. Upon the deferent moves c which in turn is the center of the epicycle, revolving in the opposite direction. Upon this epicycle is located point a which is the center of the second epicycle upon which the moon is placed.

When it came to the planetary motion Copernicus had a major advantage over Ptolemy in that he employed only one epicycle to account for what was called the first inequality, or motion in longitude which was the orbital inequalities in speed and proximity to earth. He did not

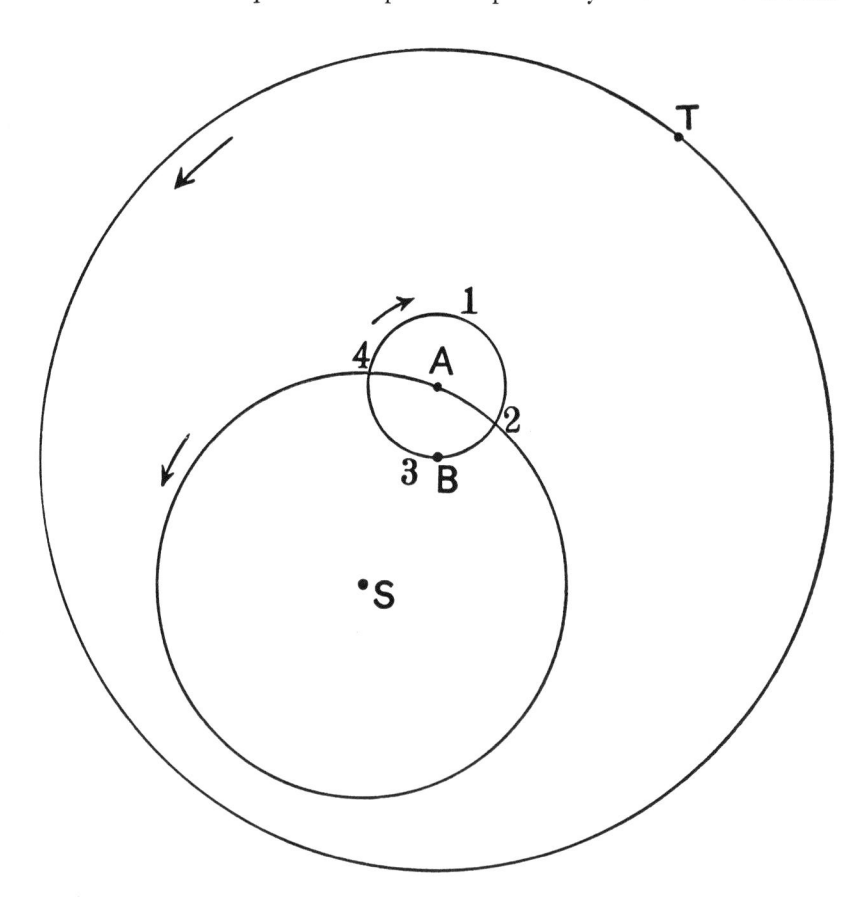

FIGURE 16. THE EARTH "T" REVOLVES ANNUALLY AROUND A CENTER "B," SITUATED NEAR THE SUN "S" (Copernicus)

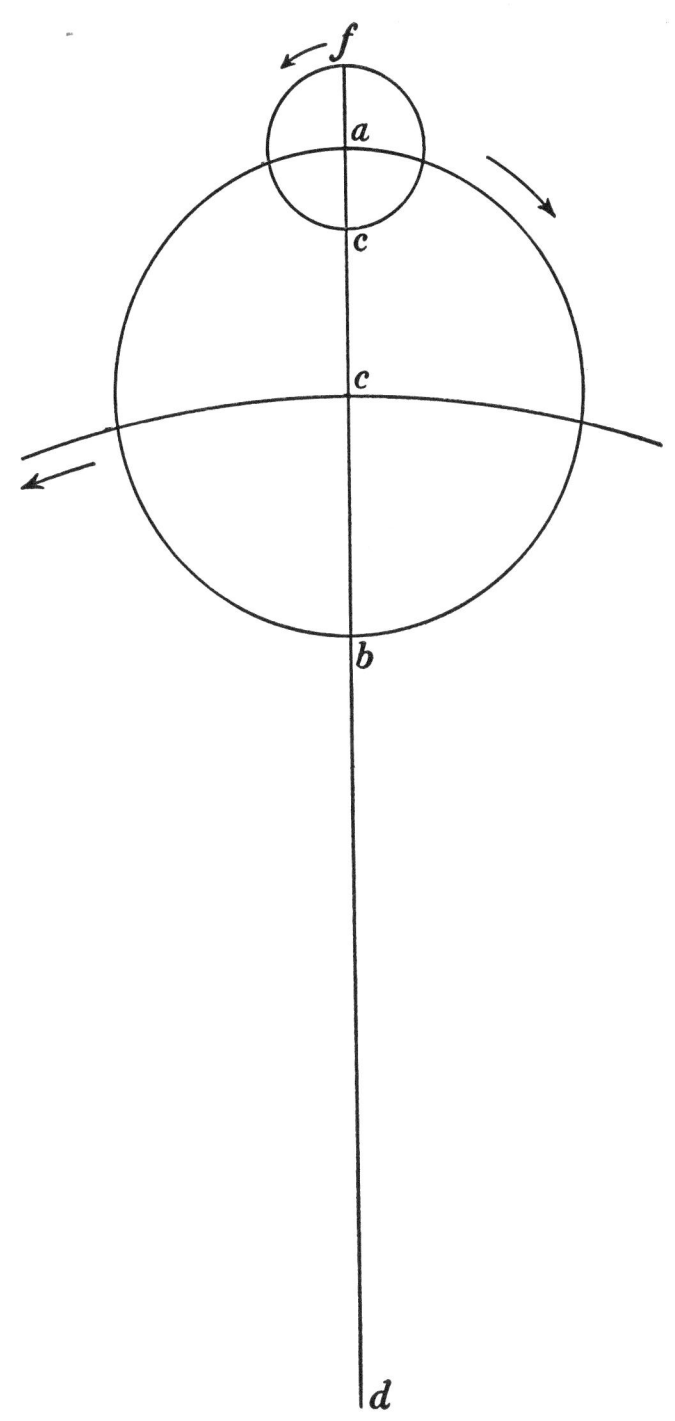

FIGURE 17. TWO EPICYCLES WERE POSTULATED BY COPERNICUS TO ACCOUNT FOR THE MOON'S ORBIT

have to explain the inequality in latitude from the ecliptic, since that was taken care of by the plane of the planet's motion about the sun. He discarded Ptolemy's equant because it violated the principle of uniform circular motion.

The superior planets were also easily accounted for. The earth revolves around the center D. At C is located the center of the eccentric orbit of the center A of the epicycle, and both center and epicycle move in the same direction with the same angular velocity, the planet being at F, I and L in the three positions of the epicycle shown. (Figure 18) The paths of the inferior planets were more difficult to explain and in the case of Mercury, Copernicus is even forced to postulate a pen-

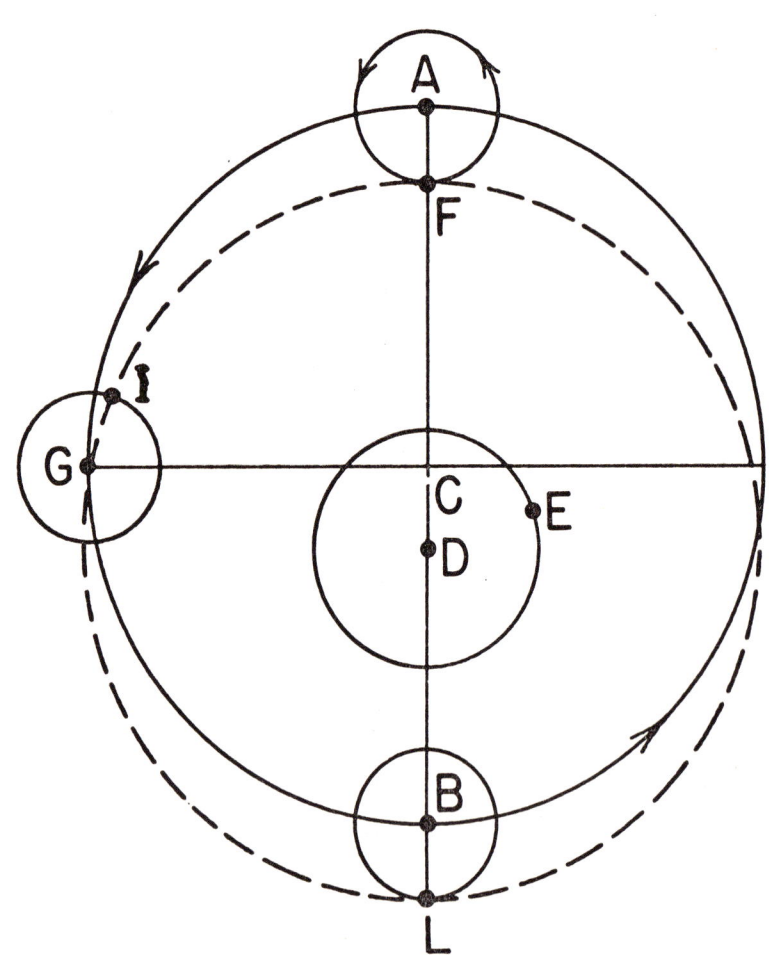

FIGURE 18. PATH OF SUPERIOR PLANET, ACCORDING TO COPERNICUS

THE PROCESS CALLED CHANGE 209

dulum-like motion along a line to the right and left of its mean orbit so as to give that orbit varying radii. Though he here deviates from circular motion, he fails to explain why he does it.

3. Respect for Mathematics

There were some factors in European society during the second half of the sixteenth century which operated both in favor of acceptance of the views of Copernicus and others which pulled in the opposite direction. The main force in aiding the march of new ideas was the strong revival of Platonism during that time, which spelled a gnawing away at the authority of Aristotle. One focus of opposition to the Copernican view came partly from traditionalists and people of little imagination; to whom rotation and revolution of the earth were upsetting concepts, mathematical though they were in nature, and as speculative as irrational numbers and the vague spheres of the ancients to which they did not object. Some opposition came, however, from scientists who could not accept seemingly fantastic concepts that were not only unverified by sensory data but totally contradicted by them.

Violent resistance to the heliocentric theory came from Aristotelian physics and theology. "At the core of that system lay the physical theories of Aristotle and the Aristotelians had adopted the mathematics of Ptolemy only after transforming his abstract constructions into material spheres. The theological dogmas of the church, however, were not so inextricably involved with the old astronomy as to make acceptance of the heliocentric theory impossible. The synthesis of Christian theology and Aristotelian science made by the Schoolmen of the thirteenth century was the chief barrier which prevented the Church from being entirely neutral concerning the true astronomical doctrines. Had the Christian theologians not previously committed themselves to Aristotelian science they would have found no great difficulty in reconciling passages in the scriptures with the ideas of Copernicus. The idea that these passages were interpreted figuratively, as statements of the way things appeared to the common man rather than as scientific truths, had already been invoked when the Church had made a place in its theology for the basic axioms of Greek science. By no other means could the references to the 'four corners of the earth' and to the sun and moon as the 'two great lights' have been brought into accord with Greek astronomy, with its spherical earth and its geometrical proofs that the moon was actually smaller than the planets." (Astronomical Thought in Renaissance England by Francis R. Johnson, Baltimore 1937 p. 94–95).

It is important to bear in mind that the people who had studied Ptolemy were primarily interested even as he was in merely "saving the phenomena" as mathematicians, and cared little for a physical or mechanical basis for the explanations. If a material model was readily available, well and good, and if not, then no matter. Aristotle wrote five hundred years before Ptolemy. During that interval considerable progress had been made, more data accumulated, trigonometry and geometry were much improved, hence little wonder that Aristotle's naive visualization of actual spheres got little recognition either from Ptolemy or his followers. Hence even as the Ptolemaic system grew less and less competent in accounting for the inequalities that piled up as observations expanded and data accumulated, the mathematical astronomers became more amenable to skillful theorems such as super-epicycles or any scheme whatever that helped explain the observed data.

In addition there was the neo-Platonist revival which had swept through the learned world the preceding centuries. While Plato's rich, mystical and bewildering Timaeus was the sole scientific representative of Greek science during the early middle ages, subsequent rediscovery of Aristotle's works and its enthronement by the thirteenth century Schoolmen at the University of Paris, particularly Thomas Aquinas, as a "Natural Theology," forced Plato into the background. Particularly in England, but elsewhere as well, there was some resistance to Aristotelian dogmatism, and adherence to the earlier Platonism never quite slackened its grip. Thus mathematics and experimental science retained their hold on Roger Bacon and Grosseteste who never quite submitted wholly to the wave initiated by St. Thomas. During the fourteenth century the spirit that dominated their thoughts blossomed forth at Oxford in a whole array of mathematicians and experimentalists. (See R. T. Gunther, Early Science in Oxford vol II & F. R. Johnson, Astronomical Thought in Renaissance England. Also A. E. Taylor, Platonism and its Influence) It was therefore no accident that sixteenth century England saw men like Leonard and Thomas Digges, Robert Recorde, the active circle around Sir Thomas More, mostly enthusiastic neo-Platonists, who had not fallen victim to Aristotelian authority and whose minds were open to any interesting mathematical theory or scientific innovation. Hence the amazing speed in the acceptance of the Copernican doctrine in sixteenth century England and even the popularity of the Tychonic scheme, as is ably discussed in Johnson's work Astronomical Thought, already cited. (It should be remarked in passing that the views of Plato and his relation to science expressed in the works here referred to, are diametrically opposed to those advanced by B. Farrington in his Science and Politics in the Ancient World. Unfortunately, the latter work reads more like a political pamphlet than a historical essay.)

Thus it transpired that, insofar as one may generalize, the Platonists welcomed any mathematical simplification, while the Aristotelians necessarily fought tooth and nail any novelty. "Furthermore, the neo-Platonic philosophy included the Pythagorean belief in the fundamentally mathematical structure of the universe. The notion that number was 'the first model of things in the mind of the Creator' and that explanations of material phenomena were to be sought in the harmonious mathematical relationships discoverable in them, was the basis of Pythagoreanism. Hence to the Renaissance neo-Platonist, the simplest and most harmonious mathematical system capable of representing the facts would, by virtue of those very qualities, be closest to reality and consequently the most acceptable system." (Astronomical Thought in Renaissance England, F. R. Johnson p. 95–6) Copernicus himself was strongly influenced by Plato's attitude, as Johnson clearly demonstrates, and Copernicus was essentially a mathematician, not an observer. As Johnson points out, to the mathematicians, the simpler or better explanation quite naturally had the greater appeal and physical support was of secondary import. It is of interest that even Dr. Johnson, who so brilliantly and objectively analyzes the forces operating in the acceptance and spread of Copernicanism, himself retains the notion that "the idea that Copernicus himself had advanced his new theory merely as a mathematical device, and did not consider it physically true" was "a false impression created by the spurious preface inserted in De revolutionibus by Andreas Osiander."

Of interest too, is Dreyer's comment, "If one of the leaders of the church (at least in Italy) at the beginning of the 16th century had been asked whether the idea of the earth moving through space was not clearly heretical, he would probably merely have smiled at the innocence of the enquirer and have answered in the words of Pomponazzi that a thing might be true in philosophy and yet false in theology." (Dreyer p. 352) For that matter, even early in the 17th century Kepler wrote in his Introduction upon Mars as follows: "Now as touching the opinions of the Saints about these Natural Points. I answer in one word, That in Theology the weight of Authority, but in Philosophy the weight of Reason is to be considered. Therefore Sacred was Lactantius who denied the earth's rotundity; Sacred was Augustine, who granted the Earth to be round, but denied the Antipodes; Sacred is the Liturgy (Officium) of our Moderns, who admit the smallnesse of the Earth, but deny its Motion: But to me more sacred than all these is Truth, who with respect to the Doctors of the Church, do demonstrate from Philosophy that the Earth is both round, circumhabited by Antipodes, of a most contemptible smallnesse and in a word that it is ranked among the Planets." (Source Book in Astronomy p. 30) But, continues Dreyer, "the times had changed. The sun of the renaissance had set when in 1527, the hordes of Connetable of Bourbon sacked and desecrated Rome; the reformation had put an end to the religions and intellectual solidarity of the nations, and the contest between Rome and Protestants absorbed the mental energy of Europe. During the second half of the 16th century science was therefore very little cultivated, and though astronomy and astrology attracted a fair number of students (among whom was one of the first rank) still theology was thought of first and last. And theology had come to mean the most literal acceptance of every word of Scripture; to the Protestants of necessity, since they denied the authority of Popes and Councils, to the Roman Catholics from a desire to define their doctrines more narrowly and to prove how unjustified had been the revolt against the Church of Rome. There was an end of all talk of Christian Renaissance and of all hope of reconciling faith and reason; a new spirit had arisen which claimed absolute control for Church authority. Neither side could therefore be expected to be very cordial to the new doctrine." (ibid)

A second source of opposition to Copernican thought stemmed from empirical, or we might say, experimental evidence and was voiced among others by as great a scientist as Tycho Brahe. Whatever other motives might have been involved, these objections had a logic and merit all their own and drew their vigor from the simple demand for observable evidence to support any new and bold conceptions. Tycho found it difficult to picture "the heavy and sluggish earth" moving through space. Then there was the absence of any stellar parallax which meant that there was no discernible displacement of stars as viewed from the extremes of the earth's orbit, six months apart. Aristotle had raised the same objection against theories of motion of the earth in his time, and the argument remained valid. To overcome its force Copernicus postulated that the sphere of the stars was virtually infinitely far removed from the sphere of Saturn so that the orbit of the earth was a point by comparison and hence showed no parallax. But, it had been generally assumed that an outer sphere begins where the inner one terminates, what then occupied the vast space between Saturn and the orb of the fixed star?

Next, how about a stone dropped vertically from a high tower? Should it not fall far from the foot of the tower if the earth rotates or revolves? Moreover a cannon ball fired eastward or westward should have different ranges and velocities. And could thin air really carry along heavy bodies as the Copernican argument maintains? And how could one in all honesty grant the "triple motion" which Francis Bacon too, found so difficult to accept? Besides, the stars, it was believed, were large bodies to which measurable diameters could be assigned at least until the telescope proved them to be mere luminous points. Now even if a third magnitude star, believed to be of a diameter of 65″ showed a parallax "as great as one minute, the star would be as large as the annual orbit of the earth round the sun." Such magnitudes either of distances or diameters one cannot expect to be believed in easily by anyone who looks to evidence in even the crudest possible manner.

The defenders of Copernicus such as Rothmann, a friend of Brahe, could answer all or most of these objections easily enough. He had no trouble with the Scriptural arguments on the general ground that there are many things in the Bible we put no stock in, such as windows in the heavens etc. Next, the earth was no heavier than any other planet and if they revolved, the earth could too. Gravity, according to Copernicus, was a property of all matter which tends to assume the spherical shape and applies to all celestial bodies. The atmosphere, as Copernicus suggested, moved along with the earth. Enormous distances and diameters are possible since who are we to put limits to divine wisdom and power? Rothmann, incidentally, admitted that the third motion was obscure and unnecessary.

Tycho then proceeds to offer his own system of planetary orbits. The earth is stationary with the moon of course revolving around it as well as the sun. All remaining planets, however, revolve around the sun, much as they do in the Copernican system. Hence the Tychonic scheme, as Dreyer puts it, "is in reality absolutely identical with the system of Copernicus, and all computations of the places of planets are the same for the two systems." Tycho retained, needless to say, the scheme of deferents and eccentrics. His course of the moon practically approached modern accuracy because, unlike Copernicus and others before him, Tycho observed the sun, moon and planets regularly and consistently, everywhere in the sky, not just at conjunction and opposition as had been the practice before. "Hereby he succeeded in making the first important step forward since Ptolemy as regards the motion of the moon, so that at his death all the great lunar perturbations were known with the one exception of the secular acceleration of the mean motion, which could only be discovered by the comparison of observations made in the course of centuries." (Figure 19)

No wonder then that some scholars and philosophers were inclined to throw up their hands in dismay and propose that all theoretical speculations and fancy schemes be terminated and a fresh start be made at gathering data. The French mathematician Pierre Ramus (Pierre de la Ramée), Professor of Philosophy and Rhetoric at the Collège Royal of Paris, is the outstanding spokesman of that group. In a work published in 1569 at Basle, the first three books of which constituted a history of mathematics, Ramus complains that astronomy is merely arithmetical

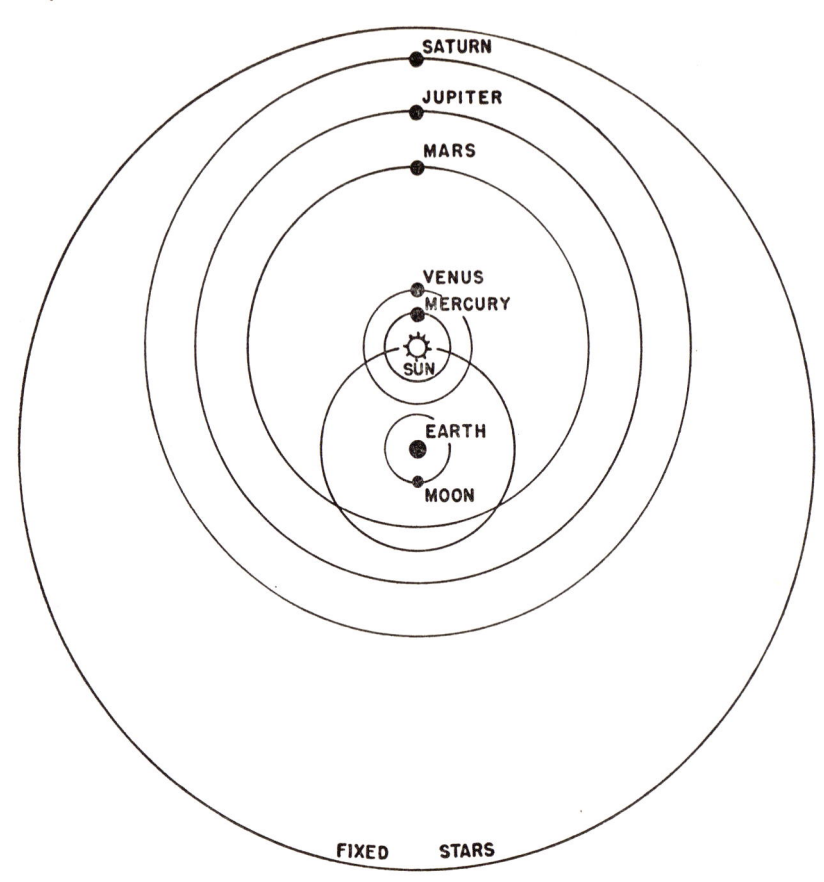

FIGURE 19. TYCHO'S SYSTEM

pursuing of celestial motions and geometrical measurement of dimensions of the celestial spheres. "Astronomy," he concludes, "is involved and impeded by the many hypotheses from which it can be liberated by mathematics." He has but kind words for the Chaldeans and Egyptians who pursued the science of astronomy without hypotheses but founded on observations. Then came Eudoxus with his revolving spheres improved upon by Aristotle and Calippus, followed by the Pythagoreans who introduced epicycles and eccentrics. "Lately Copernicus, an astronomer not only comparable to the ancients but much to be admired, rejected all the old hypotheses and revived those admirable ones which demonstrate astronomy by the motion not of the stars but of the earth. If only Copernicus had proceeded without hypotheses, it would have been easier to work out an astronomy corresponding to the true state of the stars, than, like a giant, to move the earth; and it was to be hoped

THE PROCESS CALLED CHANGE

that some distinguished German philosopher would arise and found a new astronomy on careful observations by means of logic and mathematics, discarding all the notions of the ancients." (Dreyer 368–9)

The year these notions saw the light of day, their author met Tycho Brahe, already famous as a great and skillful observer of the stars. Ramus revealed to him his doubts of the unchallenged assumptions of the past, presumably the sacredness of circularity and uniform motion, but Tycho, glibly considered nowadays a mere observer and improver of instruments and not theoretically conspicuous, replied that a science such as astronomy without hypotheses was impossible. Nevertheless he must have been in full agreement with Ramus' views that astronomy must start anew from the very bottom, gathering accurate data over a long range and working more with them than with imaginary spheres and epicycles. Tycho in turn insisted on the need for hypotheses and proceeded to devote the remaining thirty-one years of his life to the laborious task of gathering the best data astronomy had seen until then, and with the most ingenious instruments.

It was in gathering the data on the orbit of Mars, which four years after Brahe's death permitted the genius of Kepler to plot accurately its course, that Brahe bequeathed to humanity a priceless heritage. From these amazingly accurate observations Kepler ascertained the position of the nodes, i.e. the place where the orbit of Mars crosses the ecliptic, the inclination of his orbit to the ecliptic, and the fact that it did not oscillate, as had been believed, and the conclusion that the plane of the orbit passes through the sun. Kepler naturally assumed heliocentricity and after obtaining his beautiful and consistent results exclaimed that Copernicus did not know of his own riches. Using his great mathematical skill and his fervent, though often ebullient imagination in plotting the course of Mars, Kepler soon discovered that the orbit could not be a circle and "that the apparent change of the diameter of the annual orbit must be caused by the fact that the center of equal distances and the center of equal angular motion were not coincident," and that that was true for the orbit of the earth as well as for the orbits of all planets. This eccentricity, he concluded, was due to a force emanating from the sun, a notion which led to the discovery of his second law, that the line joining the planet to the sun sweeps equal areas in equal times, which means that when the planet is at its perihelion, or nearer the sun it will move faster than when it is farther from the sun or at aphelion. This law plus careful calculation forced him to state "that the orbit of Mars is not a circle but of an oval figure." At some position this oval was circular, at others at 90° to the former, it deviated most from the circular. It was in fact egg-shaped. As we know, it was finally shown to be an ellipse with the sun at one of its foci. Through this discovery a fundamentally new departure was made in astronomical thought, which with one stroke declared obsolete most of the theoretical superstructure of the preceding two thousand years. Ptolemy himself had abandoned the alleged self-evident and inviolable principle of uniform circular motion when he introduced the equant. By a whim of irony Copernicus defended this ancient principle and discarded Ptolemy's innovation, rebuking its author for unorthodoxy. Yet Ptolemy's departure from traditionalism was sterile of results while Kepler's mathematical novelty had consequences of the deepest and widest revolutionary nature. Through it an invisible belief value, a tacit unchallenged principle which harnessed and dragged an irrational loyalty behind it and held reason manacled and enslaved for centuries, was suddenly ruptured beyond repair and redemption. Once liberated the human mind could look back elated and depressed and ask, how could I have been so slow and credulous, and then proceed to further errors and further conquests.

4. *The Fate That Was Galileo's*

The full implications of the Copernican system were first revealed by Galileo, who was a deeply religious man, though circumstances contrived to bring him into opposition to the church and eventually to shake his faith in his own scientific convictions. "I am a zealous and Catholic Christian," he exclaimed, and the idea of questioning or deviating from Catholic doctrine was unthinkable to him. And in 1624, eight years after his first condemnation by the Inquisition, Urban VIII declared, "We have observed in him love of religion and all good qualities worthy of the Papal favor." (J. J. Fahie, *Galileo*, p. 206)

The work of Copernicus was mainly speculative; that of Galileo was experimental and comprehensible to the millions. Copernicus knew that his central hypothesis—the revolution of the earth—was opposed by some staunch supporters of the thought pattern of the time. But as we saw, most people concerned fully realized that his ideas were mathematical, and were judged as such, and that the Ptolemaic system explained the facts fairly well. At one point only does Copernicus indicate his attitude on this issue. In the Introduction to his major work he says: "If there are some babblers, who, though ignorant of all mathematics, take upon them to judge of these things and dare to blame and cavil at my work, because of some passage of scripture which they have wrested to their own purpose, I regard them not and will not scruple to hold their judgment in contempt." These were the only disputatious words Copernicus ever wrote except his few harsh words in his Letter to Werner. He was not only reticent but generally shy. In addition, his theory was in fact merely interpretative and supported by little evidence beyond the desire for simplicity.

Galileo was of a more extrovert type, battling for his beliefs with eloquence and logic, putting his opponents to flight until a force too powerful to be vanquished namely, sanctioned folklore and its Inquisition—forced him to waver and fumble and even to renounce his convictions. A letter from Antonia Querengo to Cardinal d'Este written in 1616, shortly before his first condemnation by the Inquisition, vividly depicts this aspect of his character.

"Your Reverence would be delighted with Galileo if you heard him holding forth, as he often does, in the midst of fifteen or twenty, all violently attacking him, sometimes in one house sometimes in another. But he is armed after such fashion that he laughs all of them to scorn; and even if the novelty of his opinions prevents entire persuasion, at least it convicts of emptiness most of the arguments with which his adversaries endeavor to overwhelm him. He was particularly admirable on Monday last in the house of Signor Federigo Ghisilieri; and what especially pleased me was that before replying to the contrary arguments he amplified and enforced them with new grounds of great plausibility so as to leave his adversaries in a more ridiculous plight, when he afterwards overturned them all." (ibid, p 161) If Galileo's championing of the theory of Copernicus came rather late in life, since he taught the Ptolemaic during most of his stay in Padua, his experimental researches proceeded at a steady pace all the while.

His work in the new science of physics had made him famous throughout Europe, and the eighteen years he spent in Padua were relatively tranquil. His lectures on the new star of 1604, his treatises on Military Architecture, Fortifications, the Sphere, Accelerated Motions, and Gnomics, his invention of the geometrical compass, air thermometer and other apparatus were well received. Then in 1609 he constructed the telescope, and the brilliant astronomical discoveries that followed created a veritable revolution in man's conception of the physical universe.

In rapid succession Galileo announced to the world the true topography of the moon, many hitherto invisible stars, the planets of Jupiter, the ring of Saturn (which Galileo took for planets), the reversed crescents of Venus, and sun spots. Collectively these discoveries challenged the established astronomical conception of a static, circumscribed universe carved out in perfection. Small wonder then that the human mind was staggered by the impact and implications of Galileo's observations and that the defenders of the established belief pattern reacted violently against his interpretations.

It had been assumed that the moon's surface was smooth and polished; Galileo showed that, like the earth, it was irregular. The nobility of the planets vanished under his onslaught as did the notion of the starry sphere. Before Galileo it had occurred to few men that there might be invisible stars. Now, moreover, all the fanciful correlation of visible stars with mystical and abstract symbols of the constellations was laid open to doubt. Furthermore, the number of planets, the magical seven, was in jeopardy, since each planet seemed to be surrounded by other planets. Venus had phases like the moon, and the sun, the source of all light, the essence of purity and perfection, was spotted and rotated about an axis.

Many of Galileo's contemporaries, especially the so-called common people, could not accept these shattering truths and, consequently looked to the Inquisition to suppress their discoverer and uphold the foundations of the universe as they saw it.

How human and familiar are the reactions of some of the writers of the time. Francesco Sizzi, a Florentine, in his book *Dianoia Astronomica* (1611) declared that: "There are seven windows given to animals in the domicile of the head through which the air is admitted to the tabernacle of the body to enlighten, to warm and to nourish. What are these parts of the microcosmos? Two nostrils, two eyes, two ears and a mouth. So in the heavens as in a microcosmos there are two favorable stars, two unpropitious, two luminaries and Mercury, undecided and indifferent. From this, and many other similarities in nature, such as the seven metals, etc. which it were tedious to enumerate, we gather that the number of planets is necessarily seven. Moreover these satellites of Jupiter are invisible to the naked eye and, therefore, do not exist." (Fahie, *Galileo*, p. 103) Another contemporary, Christmann, in his *Nodus Gordius*, asserted, "We are not to believe that nature has given Jupiter four satellites (as Galileo had shown) in order to immortalize the name of the Medici. These are the dreams of idle men who love ludicrous ideas better than our laborious maintenance of the heavens. Nature abhors such horrible chaos and to the truly wise such vanity is detestable." The reference to the Medici derives from the fact that Galileo called the satellites of Jupiter Medicean planets after his benefactor. Even Kepler's teacher, the mathematician Maestlin, the defender of Copernicus and his theory also stated, "I will never concede his four new planets to the Italian from Padua, though I die for it." This idea later formed the thesis of a book by Maestlin. Among those who recoiled at Galileo's claims that unseen satellites revolved about some of the planets, were men like Welser of Augsburg, the greatest mathematician of his day, and Clavio of Rome, both admirers of Galileo. The same attitude was shown by Julius Libri of Pisa and Cesare Cremomino of Padua, celebrated professors.

But, as usual, if there were men who doubted or scorned the evidence which Galileo had seen through his wonderful new telescope, there were also others who were more receptive to new data or concepts.

Kepler, for instance, wrote, "I was sitting idle at home thinking of you, most excellent Galileo, and of your letters when the news was brought me of the discovery of four planets by the help of the double eyeglass. . . . The authority of Galileo had the greatest influence on me, earned by the accuracy of his judgment and by the excellence of his understanding. So I immediately fell to thinking how there could be any addition to the number of the planets without upsetting my Mysterium Cosmographicum, published thirteen years ago, and according to which Euclid's five regular solids do not allow more than six planets round the sun. I am, however, so far from disbelieving the existence of the four circumjovial planets that I long for a telescope to anticipate you, if possible, in discovering two round Mars (as the proportions seem to require) six or eight round Saturn and perhaps one each round Venus and Mercury." (Fahie, *Galileo*, p. 104)

Paradoxically, though the learned and scientific world had many who were antagonistic to the Galilean views, the leaders of the ecclesiastical world, at first, were cordial and even eulogistic. Repairing to Rome in 1611 to obtain the benediction of the church, Galileo found that "even those who discredited his discoveries and dreaded their results, were as eager as the true friends of science to see and hear this wonder of the age."

He expounded his idea in the Quirinal Palace of Cardinal Bandini, and at the request of Cardinal Bellarmine, a commission of church dignitaries was appointed to examine his claims. Their report was complete acceptance of Galileo's evidence, and, as a result, Pope Paul V granted him an audience, expressed his admiration and friendship, and the high and low dignitaries of Rome vied with each other in heaping praise upon him.

But Galileo's triumph was short lived. After the learned meditated a bit over his discoveries they apparently felt either consciously or unconsciously that acceptance of the new cosmology meant the destruction of many cherished views, the crumbling of an entire belief pattern in which they had enjoyed harmony and security. Many became restless and were torn by inner conflict not knowing how to save the old cosmology and accommodate the new.

"An accidental circumstance was the spark which fired the train. One day in December 1613 Father Castelli and other learned men were guests at the Grand Duke's table at Pisa where as usual the Tuscan Court was wintering. The conversation turning on the satellites of Jupiter, Castelli took the opportunity of extolling and expatiating on his master's discoveries. One of the guests, Boscaglia, Professor of Physics at the University, and a peripatetic of the purest water, managed to excite the religious scruples of Cristina, Dowager Grand Duchess, by telling her that all Galileo's telescopic discoveries were true, only the deduction from them of the double motion of the earth must be wrong as the Holy Scriptures were clearly opposed to such a doctrine. Castelli, who had left the apartment, was recalled to answer this objection. At first he deprecated bringing the Bible into the controversy, but as this was unavailing, he resolutely took the theological standpoint and side, the Dowager Duchess standing alone and Boscaglia taking no part. Castelli hastened to apprise Galileo of this incident and added that it appeared to him that the Grand Duchess had merely persisted in opposition in order to draw him out." (Fahie, Galileo, p. 148)

In response to this letter Galileo for the first time attempted to face the theological implications of his doctrine. The Bible, he said, clearly admitted of a different astronomical interpretation from that traditionally accepted. "Who will set bounds to man's understanding? Who can assure us that everything that can be known in the world is already known? . . . I am inclined to think that Holy Scripture is intended to convince men of those truths which are necessary for their salvation and which being far above man's understanding cannot be made credible by any learning or by any other means than revelation. But that the same God who has endowed us with senses, reason and understanding does not permit us to use them and desires to acquaint us in another way with such knowledge as we are in a position to acquire for ourselves by means of those faculties—*that*, it seems to me I am not bound to believe, especially concerning those sciences about which the Holy Scriptures contain only small fragments and varying explanations; and this is precisely the case with astronomy, of which there is so little that the planets are not all enumerated, only the sun and the moon and once or twice Venus under the name of Lucifer. This, therefore, being granted, I think that in discussing natural phenomena we ought to begin with texts from scripture, but with experiment and demonstration, for, from the Divine Word, scripture and nature do alike proceed. And I can see that that which experience sets before our eyes concerning natural effects or which demonstration proves unto us ought not upon any account to be called in question, much less condemned upon the testimony of Scriptural texts, which may (under their mere words) have meanings of a contrary nature." (Bethune, J. L. D., *Private Life of Galileo*, Boston, 1832 p. 75) To illustrate this argument Galileo proceeded to show that Joshua's miracle of making the sun stand still was impossible.

This trend of thought was the very one feared by his followers. Into these paths advocates of the new astronomy like Father Castelli feared to tread. Yet they knew that sooner or later the storm would break.

Thus Fra Paolo Sarpi predicted in 1613 "that the ecclesiastical authorities will change a question of physics and astronomy into one of theology and that to my great grief Galileo, if he wants to live in peace and escape the charge of heresy, will have to recant."

In 1614 two Dominican monks, one a preacher and the other a Professor of Ecclesiastical History, accused Galileo of heresy before the Inquisition. Galileo's letter to Father Castelli was the condemning evidence; this, in reality, was the blind alley to which the new ideas led, namely, that (1) many chapters of Holy Scripture cannot be taken literally; (2) that in discussing natural phenomena the Bible is not authoritative; (3) that biblical commentators err in matters of science; (4) that scripture is authentic only in matters of faith; (5) and that many passages in the Bible require a new interpretation, all of which, incidentally, was true, since the points enumerated follow from Galileo's statement.

So strong were the pressures of common sense and common faith that Galileo was brought before the Inquisition. Fearing the outcome, namely, condemnation of the Copernican doctrines, he told Mgr. Piero Dini that he was preparing a full defense of the new astronomy. The latter advised him "to avoid theology and confine himself to mathematics and physics." As was to be expected, the apologetic treatise, though moderate and humble, only added fuel to the fire.

In this period of intrigue, before Galileo was actually brought to the bar of justice, it appears that his most belligerent opponents were the mass of mediocre if well-meaning citizens, workers, merchants, professors, teachers and ecclesiastics, the type of men who, in many parts of the U.S.A., would defend "keeping the Negro in his place," who threatened the prophets of the Bible, smashed the house of chemist Priestley because of his political views favoring the social aims of brotherhood advocated by the French Revolution, and who dragged the abolitionist Garrison through the streets. The Catholic hierarchy certainly did not instigate the persecution of Galileo. On the contrary, the number of defenders of Galileo in high ecclesiastical circles is amazing; the leading cardinals attempted to moderate the revilers of Galileo and indeed sought to let matters slide.

But Galileo felt that his views must sooner or later come to trial. Had he agreed to be quiescent, there probably would have been no trial. Thus, writing from Rome in February, 1616, a few days before his first condemnation, he said: "My business so far as it concerns myself, is completed. All the exalted personages who have been conducting it have told me plainly and in a most obliging manner, and have assured me that people are fully convinced of my uprightness and honor and of the devilish malice and injustice of my persecutors. As far, therefore, as this matter is concerned I might return home without delay; but there is a question connected with my case which does not concern myself alone but all those who during the last eighty years have advocated in printed words and private letters, in a public lecture and private conversations, a certain theory not unknown to your Excellency on which they are now proposing judgment. In the hope that my assistance may be of use in this matter so far as a knowledge of those truths is concerned, which are proved by the science to which I have devoted myself, I, as a zealous and Catholic Christian neither can nor ought to withhold that assistance which my knowledge affords; and this part of the business keeps me fully employed." (ibid)

On February 26, 1616 Galileo was called before Cardinal Bellarmine to hear of the condemnation by the Holy Office of the Copernican doctrine, which was just the thing he had voluntarily come to Rome to prevent. The Holy Office had declared, the Cardinal informed him, "that the proposition that the sun is the center of the universe and is immobile is foolish and absurd in philosophy and formally heretical since it contradicts the express words of the Scriptures in many places, according to the meaning of the words and the common interpretation and sense of Fathers and the doctors of theology; and secondly, that the proposition that the earth is not the center of the universe nor immobile receives the same censure in philosophy and in regard to its theological truth, it at least is erroneous in Faith." (*Gradual Acceptance of the Copernican Theory*, Dorothy Stimson, p. 58) Galileo was ordered to abandon the condemned opinion and abstain from "teaching, defending or discussing it" under threat of imprisonment. All this Galileo promised faithfully to carry out.

To squelch rumors that Galileo was forced to recant during that private session between him and the Cardinal, Galileo requested of the latter to state in writing exactly what had transpired at their secret meeting. The representative of the Holy Office wrote as follows: "We, Robert Cardinal Bellarmine, having heard that Signor Galileo was calumniated and charged with having abjured in our hand, and also of being punished by salutary penance, and being requested to give the truth, state that the aforesaid Signor Galileo has not abjured in our hand nor in the hand of any other person in Rome, still less in any other place, so far as we know, any of his opinions and teachings, nor has he received salutary penance nor any other kind; but only was he informed of the declaration by his Holiness and published by the Sacred Congregation of the Index, in which it is stated that the doctrine attributed to Copernicus,—that the earth moves around the sun and that the sun stands in the center of the world without moving from the east to the

west, is contrary to the Holy Scriptures and therefore cannot be defended nor held. And in witness of this we have written and signed these presents with our own hand, this 26th day of May, 1616.
Robert Cardinal Bellarmine."
(ibid p. 58)

The Cardinal then reported to the Congregation in the Pope's presence that he had had the interview with Galileo, had given him the proper warning and that Galileo agreed to abide by it. The Congregation then suspended "until corrected" the work of Copernicus, De Revolutionibus and all other books dealing with the condemned doctrine. News of the verdict either traveled slowly or was broadcast reluctantly because two years later we find Fromundus, a late opponent of Copernicanism, writing to Feyens, an early enemy of the doctrine, wondering whether it really was true what he had vaguely heard that the doctrine of Copernicus had been condemned. "Until now, I have known nothing about it; no more have this crowd of German and Italian scholars, very learned and, I think, very Catholic, who admit with Copernicus that the earth is turned. Is it possible that after a lapse of time as considerable as this, we have nothing more than a rumor of such an event? I find it hard to believe, since nothing more definite has come from Italy. Definitions of this sort ought above all to be published in the universities where the learned men are to whom the danger of such an opinion is very great." (ibid. p. 60)

Thus the admonition of the Holy See was apparently reluctant, if not halfhearted. Galileo's books were not interdicted. Cardinal Bellarmine, however, advised Galileo to be cautious, to "write freely but be careful to keep outside the sacristy."

Even after the admonition had been administered Galileo thought that he had enough influence to gain a reversal of judgment; for that purpose he lingered in Rome for a few months. The Ambassador of the Medicis, however, sized up the situation shrewdly when he told the Grand Duke of Tuscany that Galileo "seems disposed to emulate the monks in obstinacy and to contend with personages whom you cannot attack without ruin to yourself. It may any moment be heard in Florence that he stumbled into some abyss or other. However, the heat will probably drive him from Rome before long and that will be the best thing that can happen to him." (Fahie, p. 170) As a final measure Galileo's patron, Cosimo II, ordered him to return. "You have had enough of monkish persecutions and ought to know by this time what the flavor of them is. . . . His Highness . . . would therefore be glad if . . . you would not *tease the sleeping dog any more* and would return here as soon as possible." (Fahie, p. 171)

After an audience with Pope Paul V, who assured him of his admiration and good will, Galileo left Rome.

For sixteen years Galileo carried on his work in relative quietude. In the interval he published *Il Saggiatore*, which received the papal imprimatur in 1623. The book dealt with Galileo's views on comets, which, incidentally, like his theory of tides, was far from correct, but it also discussed the Copernican system in a clever, elusive and non-committal manner. In 1630 he completed his famous work, though certainly not his greatest, the *Dialogues on the Two Principle Systems of the World— The Ptolemaic and Copernican*. After some revisions by the author and hesitation on the part of the censors, this work too received the papal imprimatur.

In 1623 Cardinal Maffeo Baberini became Pope Urban VIII. In some ways it was Urban's accession to the papacy which led to the renewal of Galileo's troubles. Urban, unlike his predecessors, Gregory XV or Paul V was a student of science and a great admirer of Galileo. In 1612 upon receipt of Galileo's work on *Floating Bodies*, Cardinal Barberini told the scientist, "I shall read it with great pleasure, both to confirm myself in any opinion which agrees with yours and to enjoy with the rest of the world the fruits of your rare intellect." (Fahie, p. 184) A year later, upon receipt of the book on sun-spots, he wrote to Galileo in a similar vein. In his conflict with the Inquisition Baberini was of great help to Galileo, since he opposed any punitive measure, or even mild admonition to the man he so greatly admired. In 1620, three years before his elevation to the papacy, Barberini addressed to Galileo some complimentary verses, affirming, "The esteem which I always entertain for yourself and for your great merits has given occasion to the enclosed verses. If not worthy of you, they will serve at any rate as a proof of my affection; while I suppose to add lustre to my poetry by coupling it with your renowned name. Without wasting words in further apologies, I beg you to receive with favor this small proof of my great esteem." (Ibid. p. 185)

Galileo naturally rejoiced at the elevation of his enthusiastic admirer to the papacy and his crusading spirit was revived. Now his dream of getting the church to endorse the Copernican views might be realized. He, therefore, planned to go to Rome and advise the new Pope to take immediate action; "I have in my head," he confessed to Prince Cesi, "plans of no small importance for the learned world and perhaps can never hope for so wonderful a combination of circumstances as the present to ensure their success, at least so far as I am able to conduce to it." To this epistle the Prince replied, "Under the auspices of this most excellent, learned and benignant Pontiff, science must flourish. . . . Your arrival will be welcome to His Holiness."

Accordingly Galileo arrived in Rome in 1624, and had six long interviews with the Pope during which he hotly defended the heliocentric theory and suggested the revocation of the decree of 1616. The Pope listened cordially but promised nothing. Instead, he loaded him with favors, gave a pension to his son, born of an illegitimate alliance, gave Galileo two medals, a number of Agnus Dei and a picture of himself. To Galileo's patron, the Grand Duke of Tuscany, the Pope described Galileo as the scientist whose fame "will shine on earth so long as Jupiter and his satellites shine in heaven."

"We have observed in him not only literary distinction but love of religion and all good qualities worthy of the papal favor. When he came to congratulate us on our accession we embraced him affectionately and listened with pleasure to his learned demonstrations which add fresh renown to Florentine eloquence. We desire that he should not return to his native country without receiving from our generosity manifold proofs of our favor. And that you may fully understand to what extent he is dear to us we give this honorable testimony to his virtue and piety. And further we assure you that we shall thank you for any kindness you can show him; and by imitating or even surpassing our fatherly liberality you will add to our gratification." (Ibid. p. 206) In short, Urban VIII, like many of the ecclesiastical dignitaries, was essentially not hostile to the Copernican theory. Every work of Galileo which defended the Copernican system received the approbation of the Pope, who, on several occasions remarked that the heliocentric hypothesis is not heretical, only rash, that he opposed the decree of 1616, and that he was not averse to the discussion of the Copernican views so long as it was kept on a theoretical level.

And Galileo was as obedient as he thought he should be. In 1630 he completed his *Dialogues on the Two Great Systems of the World* and submitted it to the Master of the Sacred Palace, Riccardi, for permission to have it printed in Rome. The work deals with a discussion involving three men Salviati, Sagredo and Simplicius who meet on four days to consider the relative merits of the Ptolemaic and the Copernican theories of the solar system. The introduction is sufficiently refractory to be thoroughly non-committal. "First I will endeavor to show that all Experiments that can be made upon the Earth are insufficient means to conclude its Mobility, but are indifferently applicable to the Earth moveable or immoveable; and I hope that on this occasion we shall discover many observable passages unknown to the Ancients. Secondly, we will examine the Celestial Phenomena that make for the Copernican Hypothesis, as if it were to prove absolutely victorious; adding by the way certain new observations, which yet serve only for the Astronomical Facility, not for Natural Necessity. . . . I hope that by these

Considerations the World will come to know, that if other Nations have Navigated more than we, we have not studied less than they; and that our returning to assert the Earth's Stability, and to take the contrary only for a Mathematical Capriccio, proceeds not from inadvertency of what others have thought thereof, but (had we no other inducements) from those Reasons that Piety, Religion, the Knowledge of the Divine Omnipotency and consciousness of the incapacity of Man's Understanding dictate unto us. . . ." (A Source Book in Astronomy, by H. Shapley and H. E. Howarth New York 1929, p. 53) His heroes then proceed to argue the first day on the nature of our earth and the other planets; on the second day the daily rotation of the earth is demonstrated; the third considers the problem of parallax, and indicates why it could not be observed at the enormous distance we are from the stars, and argues for the possibility of the earth's annual revolution; finally the fourth day discusses the question of the tides and advances the view that their ebb and flow prove the earth's rotation.

The book was granted permission after lengthy examination and the request that an introduction be inserted stressing the speculative or hypothetical nature of the contents. Because of the outbreak of the plague Galileo had the book printed in Florence which change required a new kind of permission. Riccardi asked to have the book sent to him again and finally full license and approval were granted.

No sooner had the work appeared than the storm broke loose. The arguments given are too petty to be repeated. What is relevant is that the conflict which was brewing in the minds of men who were both scientists and believers in Scriptures, burst into the open and sought rationalized justification for its pathological existence. Naturally, the cultural network of beliefs and emotions embraced by the term faith, won over the solitary intruder of the new astronomical concepts, and the Inquisition concluded that Galileo taught and defended the condemned doctrine. Figuratively speaking, the condemnation was like the cry of a saint who knows he is tempted and doubts that he can resist the ever growing passion. Such situations are more dangerous than dynamite.

The sale of the Dialogues was stopped at a great loss to the printer. Galileo was ordered to Rome and threatened with compulsory transfer in chains if he temporized which he did at first, claiming illness, being indeed in declining health and close to seventy years in age. He finally went on his own in a litter supplied by the Duke after he was convinced his examiners meant business, and stayed in the palace of his friend Niccolini, the ambassador to Rome of the Grand Duke of Florence.

He was questioned four times. There can be no doubt of the sincerity of his claim during the first hearing that he felt he had carried out the full letter of admonition and thought that he had confuted the Copernian theory rather than defended it, had submitted the manuscript without hesitation or reluctance and gladly made all the changes required of him. "With remarkable, in fact unique, consideration, the Holy Office then assigned Galileo to a suite of rooms within the prisons of the Holy Office, allowed him to have his servant with him and to have his meals sent in by the ambassador." (Gradual Acceptance, p. 65) A few days later "they even assigned as his prison, the Ambassador's palace, out of consideration for his age and ill-health." At his second cross-examination Galileo offered to add a day to his Dialogues in which he would further refute the condemned doctrine, adding that he was to blame for his skill in debate if he gave his readers the idea he believed in his hero's cause. On the occasion of the third hearing he submitted a written statement in which he reiterated that he thought he had carried out Cardinal Bellarmine's directions and appealed to his judges "to consider his miserable bodily health and his incessant mental trouble for the past ten months," the exacting journey at his age, his loss of honor and similar afflictions already endured.

His fourth and last interrogation came by order of the pope and under threat of torture. He restated his case that he did not and never had held the doctrine of Copernicus after being apprised of the opposition to it by the Church dignitaries. "As for the rest, I am in your hands, do with me as you please . . . I am here to obey." In conclusion he abjured on his knees in the presence of the full congregation, and promised to denounce other heretics, that is, Copernicans. Since he was a heretic by virtue of his adherence to a doctrine which had been declared contrary to Scriptures, he was sentenced to "formal imprisonment" at the will of the Congregation and to repeat the seven psalms of the penitents for three years, once a week. At his request his sentence was immediately commuted to confinement in his own villa at Arcetri, outside Florence, but no visitors were to be permitted. This point could not have been strictly administered since we know that Milton visited him there in 1638. His sentence and abjuration were this time given adequate publicity by Pope Urban VIII and the universities of all Europe were made fully cognizant of the prohibition.

It is not necessary to conclude with the author of The Gradual Acceptance of the Copernican Theory that Galileo "plainly perjured himself, however fully he may be pardoned for it because of the extenuating circumstances." (p. 68) This statement was made before the work of Freud became widely known and before it was realized that in a subconscious or even conscious conflict of loyalties or incompatible beliefs one is merely gripped in a vise of struggle to which the term perjury is hardly applicable. Caught in the trap of fanatical faiths, both Nazism and Marxism have brought poverty and misery to millions and have not yet learned how to resolve their fantastic perversion of reality and common sense in the adoration of a creed hatched in bitterness and hate and in the absence of objectivity. In the wake of the despair and frustration wrought, for example, by the communist creed and faced with unyielding failure, the Soviets can only rave and kill for sabotage, espionage and deviation. Similarly, the sanctioned beliefs of the people of the seventeenth century, an age of religion, clashed with the oncoming findings of science. In a way it was a fortunate era because the victims of that clash were few, and respect for science and speculation was strong enough to ease the violence of the conflict. Modern times are less fortunate. We know of no victimized scientist in the Soviet Union who was treated with the leniency shown Galileo, whether the victim was economist, sociologist, psychoanalyst, anthropologist, biologist or physicist. Like the churchmen of the 17th century, the Leninists of today are caught in a trap of conflict between their mystical faith in abstractions and the defiance of obdurate reality. Like a youngster who seeks in vain to do things beyond his knowledge and power and beyond what the materials can render, so that he finally resorts to rage and destruction, the Church in 1632 and the Soviets in our own days can only turn to Inquisitorial Indices and occasional imprisonment (1632), to executions and Siberia on a large scale (from 1928 on) as the only outlet to painful frustrations, as the only way of resolving an inevitable conflict.

Some historians of science have been harsh in their judgment. "Why did this master-spirit of the age—this high priest of the stars . . . whose career of glory was near its consummation—why did he reject," asks a modern writer, "the crown of martyrdom which he had himself coveted and which, plaited with immortal laurels, was about to descend upon his head? If, in place of disavowing the laws of nature, and surrendering in his own person the intellectual dignity of the species, he had boldly asserted the truth of his opinions and confided his character to posterity and his cause to an all-ruling Providence, he would have . . . disarmed forever the hostility that threatened to overwhelm him." (Brewster Martyrs of Science, p. 94) " Had Galileo but added the courage of the martyr to the wisdom of the sage; had he carried the glance of hi indignant eye around the circle of judges; had he lifted his hands to Heaven and called on the living God to witness the truth and immutability of his opinions, the bigotry of his enemies would have been disarmed and science would have enjoyed a memorable triumph." (Ibid. p. 95) Had Galileo done all this, he would have enacted a wonderful scene for a Hollywood plot, but hardly anything else. Galileo could not have played the martyr's role, because he never meant to defy church authorities. Had he cast his eye around the room, he would hav

THE PROCESS CALLED CHANGE

seen, as indeed he saw, dignitaries of the church he loved, men he held in fervent respect. Whatever else he may have been, he was a pious Catholic and wanted to remain such. His utmost ambition was not to alienate or attack the church but persuade it to make room for his scientific views. He never dreamed of offending the church, defying its edicts, or weakening its prestige. What he desired proved impossible in his lifetime, because the uprooting of the belief pattern he opposed took much time, subtle undermining and prolonged efforts at readjustment on many fronts. Indeed, though his mission failed, the seed had been cast, and the new astronomical beliefs were launched on their way to ultimate acceptance.

Other historians of science were more conscious of the tragedy of the situation. "It is probable," writes A. Berry in his Short History of Astronomy, "that many of those who were concerned in the trial were anxious to do as little injury to Galileo as possible, but were practically forced by the party personally hostile to him to take some notice of the obvious violation of the decree of 1616." (p. 171) This penetrating historian states further: "There can be no doubt that Galileo was a perfectly sincere member of the Church, and, although he did his best to convince individual officers of the Church of the correctness of his views and to minimize the condemnation of them passed in 1616, yet he was probably prepared when he found that condemnation was seriously meant by the Pope, the Holy Office and others, to believe that in some sense at least his views must be wrong, although as a matter of observation and pure reason he was unable to see how and why." (p. 171) Thus, many historians familiar with the case have felt that the glib condemnation meted out by those who shared the views expressed by Brewster, was not quite the last word, or perhaps, the most reasonable.

What of the learned Pope, Urban VIII, the scholar and scientist? His role too can only be understood in the light of the clash of belief patterns. Urban's primary task was to serve the church and defend her dogmas, particularly in those perilous days of the Protestant revolt and the Thirty Years' War. Doubtless he was attracted to the soundness and appeal of Galileo's views and wished to accommodate them to Catholic doctrine. But he could not. Pressure from thousands of monks and dignitaries especially those unfamiliar with science, clinging to a venerable astronomical system, came down upon him from all directions. Urban knew that he must not only defend the faith, but also avoid internal conflicts, suppress any work which insinuated that the Bible was written by human beings who took superstition for truth and put scientific misconceptions in the mouth of God or His Apostles. The books of Galileo with their vast implications were too dangerous to ignore. Galileo wanted to make his science acceptable to the Church, and Urban VIII, like so many other popes and cardinals, avid of the new learning, had hoped the church could accommodate the new science. But public opinion made that impossible and his own beliefs could not make the adjustment either. His inner conflict could only be resolved in the manner history resolved it.

What other way out for the Pope was there, considering the state of mind of the laity and the vulgar, the professors, scientists and the theologians, including his own? By punishing Galileo, Urban obeyed his conscience and that of the church, though time mocked his mental anguish, resolved his dilemma and accomplished only a few decades later, all that Galileo sought in his pained bewilderment, and failed.

It is not difficult to imagine that before Urban VIII decided to inflict the severest penalties upon Galileo he gave the matter careful thought. He may well have spent sleepless nights castigating himself for catering to his intellectual enjoyment by indulging in or flirting with advanced cosmological theories which in reality only served to confound the faith of the common people which he was called upon by God and Christ to nurture and protect. He must have seen himself as a shepherd who deserted his flock for selfish revelry or Bohemian adventuresomeness. His callous attitude toward the fate of Galileo may well have been an act of remorse and repentance.

That Galileo submitted to the verdict of the Inquisition which forced him to abjure his conviction that the earth rotated and revolved around the sun, can be seen from his utterances during the nine years of his imprisonment. Ten months before his death in 1642 he wrote to his pupil Rinuccini, who had begged his opinion of a recent argument against the earth's motion, and stated that the Copernican doctrine is false beyond a doubt, because it contradicts the Holy Scriptures as interpreted by the greatest Catholic theologians, who declare that the earth is the center of the universe. The Copernican arguments, Galileo added "fall to pieces before the fundamental argument of the Divine Omnipotence." This may or may not have been sincere. "As I hold the Copernican theory to be insufficient," he concluded, "so, that of Ptolemy, Aristotle and their followers appears to me far more delusive and mistaken because its falsity can be clearly proved without going beyond the limits of human knowledge." (Brewster, *Martyrs of Science*, p. 394) Since these systems are all unacceptable, concluded Galileo, philosophers must find a new one which both science and theology can accept. This was the only hope of a man who had attempted to force new concepts into old belief patterns and failed. Such is the tearful road of progress, even in science.

But while the transition from the Ptolemaic to the Copernican theory seemed to be marked with the tragedy of Galileo, the disappearance of

THE PROCESS CALLED CHANGE

astrology from the horizons of science occurred as quietly as a sunset in a sky behind stratus clouds. Except for Gassendi, astrology simply faded away unfought, unmourned and unburied. It did not die in battle, fought by some and defended by others. It simply was dissipated with the march of time and none seems to have missed it. And it would seem that the very people who so ardently defended it, namely Brahe, Kepler and Galileo were the ones who laid the foundations for its demise. It was they who introduced such fascinating and novel concepts as the ellipse, and the telescope, and accuracy, and new instruments, and new concepts—and thereby opened up vast new horizons of endless allure and gratification in results, so that the old had no chance to hold the interest of scholars any longer. All students of astronomy were too busy with the new to bother with the astrological hypotheses or their applications. The old ideas simply lost their grip on the minds of men concerned with the heavens and their wonders. Little did Kepler know that his ellipse would do more to undermine astrology than a thousand logical disputations or a thousand treatises and specious arguments. Thus men who in their lifetime may be arguing lucidly and passionately for a given creed, may through their very labors seemingly unrelated to the issue, prepare the ground for the very denial or destruction of that which their minds and faith defended.

For several centuries modern scientists paid no heed to the few pathetic practitioners of astrology one sees huddled behind curtains in impoverished little stores of our large cities. Occasionally a group of juvenile scientists for lack of anything better to do organize a committee to "expose" these simpletons in the name of progress or science. The majority of scientists merely look at the strange lore and logic of astrology and pleasantly embrace the idea that it had always been folly and stupidity which hung over the minds of man in the past like the primitive chaos hovering over the waters. They fail to see it as a fossil which had had its glorious days and good times, but perished in the mind's struggle for survival and gave place to new adjustments, new assumptions, new hypotheses and new approaches. The modern practitioners have nothing in common with the logic of Ptolemy or Kepler, but the mental labors of the latter and the many other believers in the astrological hypotheses of the past were true soldiers in man's struggle for scientific truth.

FIGURE 20. THE RISE AND FALL OF ASTROLOGY

The object of this graph is to summarize briefly the historical vicissitudes of a belief, in this case, that of astrology. The description of the ordinate as "Extent of Belief Among the Learned" is approximate. It is measured by the number of treatises published on the subject and by its acceptance among diverse authors of the period. Note that astrology swept into Greece despite opposition, but did respond to Christian opposition and apathy, immediately following the spread of the teachings of the Bible. After the Revival of Learning in the tenth and eleventh centuries, Christian opposition proved futile. Hence neither faith nor an organized church will always have their way with advancing or receding belief patterns. In the Christian world of the west, astrology reached its peak at the precise time when the Church was at the peak of its power. Yet, apparently love of the new learning and the impact of fashion proved stronger within the minds of the very supporters and rulers of the Church, than the inherited prejudices against the materialistic and deterministic science come down from a pagan world.

Note again that astrology's second decline, in the seventeenth century, occurs for entirely different reasons than its first fall into desuetude in the fourth century or thereabouts. The forces which obscured or repressed astrology earlier were absorption with religious values, while the forces which caused astrology's abandonment in the later period were equally enthusiastic absorption with the newly-won scientific hypotheses, and the experimental zeal they generated.

The level of popular belief was located on the graph in an arbitrary fashion merely to indicate that the astrological folklore is universal and deep-seated among people everywhere, regardless of its rise and fall among the learned. In the nineteenth century the popular level was significantly depressed but rose again in the turbulent and frustrating years of the mid-twentieth.

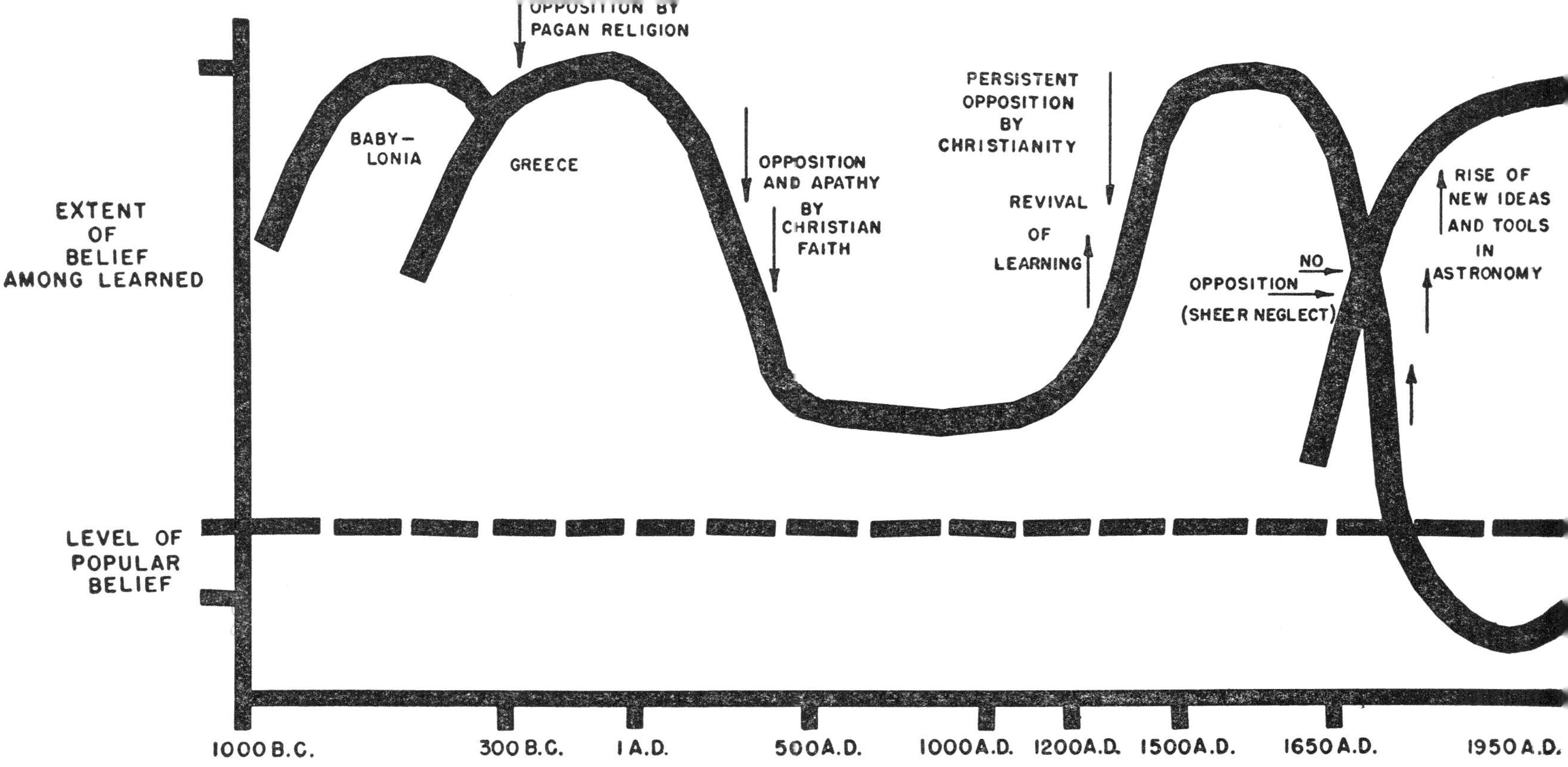
OPPOSITION BY
PAGAN RELIGION
BABY-
LONIA
GREECE
OPPOSITION
AND APATHY
BY
CHRISTIAN
FAITH
PERSISTENT
OPPOSITION
BY
CHRISTIANITY
REVIVAL
OF
LEARNING
NO
OPPOSITION
(SHEER NEGLECT)
RISE OF
NEW IDEAS
AND TOOLS
IN
ASTRONOMY
EXTENT
OF
BELIEF
AMONG LEARNED
LEVEL OF
POPULAR
BELIEF
1000 B.C.
300 B.C.
1 A.D.
500 A.D.
1000 A.D.
1200 A.D.
1500 A.D.
1650 A.D.
1950 A.D.

Book II

THE QUEST FOR THE NATURE OF MATTER

Chapter IX

THE GRAND ROMANCE OF ALCHEMY

1. A Dreamland of Science

THE astrological belief pattern revolved around the assumption of stellar influence upon human fates on earth. Its appearance in several independent cultures indicates that the belief sprang from an innate attitude of man toward celestial phenomena. The sense of wonder and awe evoked by eclipses, the motions of comets and planets, the phases of the moon and the annual courses of the stars elicited in man everywhere particular responses, which jointly with his quest for knowledge and his egocentric view of the world led to the astrological hypotheses. A major factor in strengthening this attitude were the few accurate and useful observations made, such as the correlation between the positions of the sun, stars and planets and the seasons, between the phases of the moon and the tides, the value of the calendar and stellar aid in navigation or travel.

We have seen that for several thousand years the belief displayed amazing tenacity in the face of strong opposition. Essentially, however, the evidence upon which it rested was remote, mediated more by reason and deduction than direct or unequivocal observation and experimentation. The subject to be considered in the following chapters shows different bonds between theory and evidence. In alchemy the observed events were immediate and striking. True, alchemy contained theoretical components derived from such abstract philosophers as Empedocles, Plato and Aristotle, but the facts of water emerging from air or vice versa, the sight of compounds changing color under your very eyes, vapors turning to metal or metals becoming compounds again—these events were undeniable, subject to your control, and dramatic. One might therefore assert that the alchemical principles of unity and transmutation of elements were not only obvious but that they literally compelled acceptance. Unlike astrology, the alchemical theories seemed to be in much closer harmony with direct and unsophisticated observation, and the logic employed seemed wholly secure and sound. The groping for truth under such circumstances and the pitfalls encountered, have therefore something novel to contribute.

The story of alchemy is an extraordinary mixture of nobility and mysticism woven into a plot which is thoroughly scientific and "materialistic." For five centuries, from the fourteenth to the eighteenth, the most gifted students of nature, the most devoted experimentalists and pioneers in chemistry believed passionately in the existence of an elixir of life, a substance which could resurrect the dead and cure all disease, bring perfection to the crippled, restore permanent youth to the senile, bring wisdom to the foolish and virility to the impotent. In addition to these grandiose powers it could also transmute the base metals into noble, silver and gold, and thereby accelerate a process normally catalyzed in the earth's womb by the slower influence of the celestial bodies.

The belief in this compound and its magic powers gathered adherents among rich and poor, among men and women of noble or humble birth. In a Europe of small states it created an international fraternity of learning such as humanity had never seen before. In a world of petty rulers, poor roads, no police force or international law, it stimulated travel and intellectual intercourse on a scale we enjoy today under far more favorable circumstances. The selflessness and devotion its followers displayed, may serve as models to students of science in our own era.

It cannot be said that the nineteenth century was kind or even fair to the alchemists. Saturated with a newborn faith in reason and progress it regarded the alchemists as false prophets, as apostles of superstition to be doubly detested because they sought gold and freely indulged in charlatanism and deception. "The reader, who may wish to amuse himself with the nonsense of our own alchemists, is referred to the *Theatrum Chemicum Britannicum, containing severall poeticall pieces of our famous philosophers who have written the Hermetique mysteries in their own language*, by Elias Ashmole," writes a secretary of the Royal Society of London. (Brande, Wm. Th. Progress of Chemical Philosophy, Boston, 1818 p. 19). Similarly typical is the following: "The so-called 'age of alchemy' is not regarded by scientists with a great deal of pride. During this period . . . the bulk of chemical inquiry was actuated by base and ignoble motives. Chemistry . . . was the servant of avarice and greed," (Coles L. A. The Book of Chemical Discovery, London, 1933, p. 37). Such quotations could readily be multiplied.

This attitude unfortunately still persists, although there were also men like Liebig and others whose historical approach entails much tolerance and understanding. "It is the prevailing ignorance of chemistry and especially of its history which is the source of the very ludicrous and excessive estimation of ourselves, with which many look back on the age of alchemy; as if it were possible or even conceivable that for more than a thousand years the most learned and acute men such as Francis Bacon, Spinosa and Leibnitz could have regarded as true and well-founded an opinion void of all foundation." (Justus von Liebig, Familiar Letters on Chemistry, London, 1851, p. 41). Liebig then proceeds to point out that the views of the alchemists were not only reasonable but, as he says, inevitable. "We hear it said," he continues, "that the idea of the philosopher's stone was an error; but all our views have been developed from errors and that which today we regard as truth in chemistry may, perhaps, before tomorrow, be recognized as a fallacy." And after enumerating many of the hard-won discoveries of alchemy the great chemist concludes: "Alchemy was never at any time anything different from chemistry. It is utterly unjust to confound it, as is generally done, with the gold-making of the sixteenth and seventeenth centuries. . . . Alchemy was the pure science." But in spite of such respected and articulate defenders, the name of alchemy languished in disrepute with the vast majority of chemists who were too busy extolling the new acquisitions of their science, to waste sympathy on their predecessors.

2. Early Chemistry and the Beginnings of Alchemy

It will be informative to steal a passing glimpse at the earliest chemical knowledge. It is known that already in the second millennium B.C. dyes and metals were worked in Chaldea and Egypt. Egyptian drawings portray large scale smelting and moulding of metals in well laid out foundries. Glass production and glass staining were well developed, and even used to imitate precious stones. Colored articles and paintings, metal objects and alloys are found in the excavations of ancient cultures in the Orient besides Egypt where they reached the highest development.

— Papyri found in the tombs of the pyramids, such as the famous papyrus Ebers, dating from before Moses (1550 B.C.) yield reliable information of early chemical knowledge. In this commixture of magic, incantations and medical lore we find items such as the following: "Take of cummia one sixty-fourth part, of birds oil one eighth part, and of milk one part; boil, filter through linen and drink." Observe the regard for quantity in this citation. Yet, along with the directness of the above prescription, an incantation or magical formula would be given for keeping snakes in their holes or for curing some skin eruption. (Ebbel, B. The Papyrus Ebers, Copenhagen, 1937).

— Clearly these records betray considerable chemical knowledge. The medical papyri point to much experience in the isolation of many vegetable, animal and mineral extracts and their utilization in healing. There had also evolved long before the Christian era a rich folklore about the origins and wonders of chemical science. A collection of fables has come down to us known as The Book of Enoch, supposedly written in the first or second century B.C. which claims as its author the biblical Enoch, the father of Methuselah.

The beginnings of the science of alchemy are lost in the untraceable recesses of the past. The wealth and mystery of the legends, so characteristic of the spirit of that science, as well as the custom of attributing one's writings to some historical person of great fame for the purpose of gaining immediate acceptance, have worked havoc with attempts at accurate historical research. Even the origin of the word alchemy is uncertain, although the term was coined by the Arabs as recently as the eighth century of our era or thereabouts. It is claimed by some to derive from the Greek word "chyma," signifying molten things, while others would have it spring from "Khem," the name of the dark soil of Egypt. (The Origin of the Word Alchemy, Ciba Symposia 1, 322, 1940).

Most authorities seem agreed that alchemy evolved in Graeco-Egypt during the early centuries of the Christian era. "As a matter of fact neither in Egypt nor in Greece has any trace of alchemy been discovered till after the Christian era." (Waite, A. E., The Secret Tradition in Alchemy, London, 1926, p. 55). "Despite the universal tradition which assigns to alchemy an Egyptian origin, no hieroglyphic document relative to the science of transmutation has yet been discovered. The Graeco-Egyptian alchemists are our sole source of illumination upon the science of Hermes, and that source is open to suspicion because subject to the tampering of mystical imaginations." (Berthelot, M., Collection des Anciens Alchimistes Grecs. Paris 1888; also L'Etude de la Chimie. Paris 1938 p. 251)

It is nonetheless a fact that the foundations of alchemy, no matter how defined, were being laid in Egypt centuries before the science reached full bloom in Greek-speaking Alexandria and in neighboring cultural centers. Without the practical labors of Egyptian craftsmen and the skills they attained in the working of alloys and ores of gold, copper, silver, tin, lead, mercury and later iron, millennia before the Christian era, no science of alchemy could have arisen whenever it did. Already Theophrastus (315 B.C.) describes the production of white lead in the following terms: "Lead is placed in an earthen vessel over sharp vinegar, and after it has acquired some thickness of a kind of rust, which it commonly does in about two days, they open the vessels and scrape it off. They then place the lead over the vinegar again, repeating over and over again the same process of scraping it till it is wholly gone. What has been scraped off they beat to powder and boil with water for a long time and what at last settles to the bottom of the vessel is white lead." (Treatise on Stones Cited by Partington, J. R., A Short History of Chemistry, Macmillan, 1937, p. 16). Hence numerous chemical processes were known to these workers including reactions which required accurate and refined observation, ingenuity, and appreciation of quantitative proportions.

The so-called Leyden and Stockholm papyri written in Greek around 300 B.C. contain numerous recipes from older Egyptian sources for the production of artificial gems and the manufacture of dyes, cleansing materials and various alloys imitating as nearly as possible the appearance and properties of gold and silver. (Cayley, J. Chem. Educ. 3, 1149, 1936; 4, 979, 1927). In these documents color changes are greatly stressed. There is no mention of trransmutation, and the text resembles notes of an experienced and conscientious artisan. According to one authority these papyri are "an interesting collection of laboratory recipes of the kinds which Diocletian ordered destroyed." (Stillman, J. M., The Story of Early Chemistry, New York, 1924, p. 80). However the truth of Diocletian's edict (296 A.D.) which presumably ordered all alchemical treatises of conquered Egypt to be seized and burned so as to prevent the people from rising up against Rome, has recently been challenged as an invention of later alchemists. (Wilson, W. J. An Alchemical Manuscript by Arnaldus de Bruxella, Osiris 2, 262, 1936).

The true science of alchemy, centering around the basic concept of transmutation, was born from the union of Egyptian practices with Greek philosophy in the flourishing academies and forums of Alexandria. That city which was built by Alexander the Great at the mouth of the Nile in 331 B.C. became for several profitable centuries the hub of Eastern trade and manufacture, the cradle of learning, particularly in science, and the meeting ground of the heritages of Greece, Judea and Egypt. It is from Alexandria that the first Western treatises on alchemy or theoretical chemistry of any kind have come down to us. The oldest documents of the birth of alchemy were found in a famous manuscript now at the library of St. Mark's in Venice, apparently copied about the tenth century A.D., from a third or fourth century MS. This collection of treatises and some later MSS yield us all our knowledge of Alexandrian science, which constitutes a well constructed model and precursor of medieval alchemy.

Leading authorities of Alexandrian alchemy were Democritus, Synesius, Zosimus, Olympiodorus, Stephanus and a few minor figures, all of whom gained the status of ancient authorities to the European alchemists. Democritus, who probably wrote in the second century A.D. was known as The Philosopher and left two authentic works, "Physical and Mystical Matters" and "Book Addressed to Leucippus." Others which he authored have been lost. The former work deals with practical chemical and metallurgical reactions among which already such philosophical statements are found interspersed as "Nature rejoices in nature and nature conquers nature and nature masters nature." (Taylor, F. Sherwood, Origins of Greek Alchemy, Ambix 1, 38, 1937). Parts of this work were entitled the Chrysopoeia or gold-making and Argyropoeia or silver-making.

Zosimus or Zosimos was a prolific commentator and compiler. He cites numerous apparatus first employed by Alexandrian alchemists which he did not devise himself. He ascribes their invention to the Jews, especially the renowned Mary the Jewess, who is reputed to have initiated numerous apparatus and devised new techniques and after whom the sand bath is still named in French, "bain marie." "It may be noted in passing, that in this early age of alchemy women were prominent in the art. Maria the Jewess, the alchemist Kleopatra, Theosebeia, the sister of Zosimos, and Paphnutia the Virgin are mentioned. All four belong to the first three centuries of the Christian era." (Ibid, p. 41).

Among the Alexandrian texts we already meet with a tendency, which later becomes common practice among alchemists, of attributing alchemical interests and activities to heroic figures of history or religion. Spurious compositions bear such titles as "Work of Isis Addressed to Horus," "The Chemistry of Moses" or "Dialogue of Cleopatra and the Philosophers." All texts contain the concepts of unity of all matter, all employ mystic symbolism to describe technical processes and are written in lofty philosophic style. The ancient sign of a serpent devouring his tail, known as Ouroboros, the symbol of wisdom, is encountered with the inscription "All is One," as well as the allegoric use of death and revivification by a magic lotion. These foreshadow the amplifications in which the European followers of alchemy, known as adepts, will subsequently take great delight.

Of special interest are the diagrams of some apparatus appearing in the MS of Synesius assigned to the fourth century and representing distillation, showing round-bottom flasks overmounted with heads which lead into retorts and are placed in ovens. From other Greek texts it is clear that a variety of vessels were being used which had removable or fused heads, glass tubes serving as air condensers, as were also funnels, cylinders, furnaces, spatulas, and other tools. Reactions are cited involving sulphur, metals, their salts and alloys, processes such as distillation, fixation, meaning precipitation, amalgamation meaning crystallization, and calcination or application of heat leading to diverse results. Thus, Zosimos in writing of reactions involving water of sulphur adds the following advice: "On uncovering the alembic, you will stop your nose on account of the odor," implying no doubt the evolution of hydrogen sulfide gas. Methods of employing heat varied from direct use of

THE GRAND ROMANCE OF ALCHEMY

the sun's rays to baths of putrefying manures, hot sand, water and ashes. Charcoal was also used for higher temperatures.

The beginnings of the notion of transmutation and the role of mercury in this process can already be discerned. "Having sprinkled the metal with vinegar, cast on it also white cadmia or magnesia or chalk in order that one metal may be made from another" says Democritus. (Hopkins, J. A., Alchemy, Child of Greek Philosophy, Columbia University Press, 1934, p. 66). "Mercury robs all metals of their appearances . . . whitens all metals and attracts their souls. It refines them and is diffused. Being thus properly disposed and having in itself the principle of all liquidity when it has undergone decomposition, it changes colors everywhere," writes Synesius (ibid. p. 68). He regards mercury as a volatile spirit which can fuse with a non-volatile body or metal. Color indicates the degree of purity achieved by such ennobling action, and the height of achievement is the obtaining of gold, the noblest metal.

Zosimos reveals the more abstract and philosophical aspect of alchemy. Material gold means little to him. He views gold as the highest spirit, the acme of quality which can be attained by the use of an effective coloring principle or ferment. His language is allegorical and mystic. "But our gold which possesses the desired quality can make gold and tint (i.e. transmute) into gold. Here is the great mystery—that the quality becomes gold and then makes gold." (ibid. 71) Silver-making, or transmutation into silver is the first step in the mystic process. Gold-making is the second and last. Colors and their proper sequence in the chain and spirit "penetrate into the depths of the metal," and when "the spiritual substances have taken on a bodily metallic form, the transmutation has taken place." Every metal strives to become gold and can attain its goal with the aid of a ferment or catalyst. "In fact just as yeast, although in small quantity raises a great quantity of dough, so also a little quantity of gold or silver acts by aid of this reagent. . . ." Zosimos cites also Water of Sulphur as a catalyst in the making of gold and silver.

In Stephanus, the seventh century alchemist and teacher at Constantinople, we encounter the poetry, enthusiasm, love of allegory, combined with practical knowledge of chemistry and metallurgy, spiced with religious passion, all of which is so characteristic of later alchemy. "I speak of that which falls from the moon's waning, how it is found, how it is treated and how it has an unburnt nature. O wisdom of teaching of such a preparation displaying the work, O moon clad in white and vehemently shining abroad whiteness . . . for it is white as seen, but yellow as apprehended, the bridegroom to the allotted moon, the golden drop falling from it . . . the unchangeable embrace . . . the god-given work, the marvelous making of gold. . . ." (Taylor, F. S., The Alchemical Works of Stephanus of Alexandria, Ambix 1, 129).

ASTROLOGY AND ALCHEMY

Astrological symbols appear in these texts, as might have been expected, since that association had been made more than a millennium previously in Chaldea and Egypt. In these and related cultures the known metals were kept down to seven, though if it were not for the sanctity of that number the list could easily have become extended. Each planet was said to rule a particular metal and both shared the same symbol. The sun was equivalent to gold, the moon to silver, and mercury, unknown to the early Egyptians, to the planet by that name; Venus was said to rule over copper, Mars over iron, Jupiter over tin and Saturn over lead. Since each planet dominated a day of the week, it logically followed that each day of the week was assigned to a different metal.

Of equal antiquity was the classification of metals into noble and base. The former group included gold and silver. Gold was perfection itself and silver close to it. Mercury was intermediate because of its power to add lustre to other metals. But thoroughly base and imperfect were lead, iron, copper and tin, regarded as nature's stepchildren, striving to attain the status of gold. This notion formed the background for the process of transmutation.

From the Greek philosophers Empedocles, Plato and Aristotle, Alexandrian thought acquired ideas which made significant contributions to the fruition of alchemy. Empedocles had postulated that all natural objects were composed of four basic elements—earth, air, water and fire. This Plato granted. "Out of such elements which are in number four, the body of the world was created." (Timaeus p. 15. The Dialogues of Plato v.2 N. Y. 1937). But he also insisted on the basic unity of all matter. All substances were transient forms of an unknowable and indescribable material substratum. Substances, he claimed, were transmutable one into another. "In the first place, we see what we just now called water, by condensation, I suppose, becomes stone and earth; and this same element, when melted and dispersed, passes into vapour and air. Air again, when inflamed becomes fire; and again fire, when condensed and extinguished, passes once more into the form of air; and once more, air, when collected and condensed, produces cloud and mist; and from these, when still more compressed, comes flowing water, and from water comes earth and stones once more; and thus generation appears to be transmitted from one to the other in a circle." (ibid p. 30) The so-called elements, Plato suggests, "God fashioned by form and number" out of a crude precursor.

The conception of material nature which won a foothold in the Greek thought-pattern was that formulated by Aristotle as a critical synthesis of the teachings of both his predecessors and a balanced compromise of their extreme views. All matter consists of the four elements earth, air, fire and water. These may indeed change into one another because they owe their existence to combinations of the four qualities hot, cold, moist and dry. Fire is hot and dry, air hot and moist, water moist and cold and earth cold and dry. Transference of qualities is indeed constantly taking place in nature.

Moreover the change is not random. "Nothing exists which is not good." "Nature and gold are working towards an end, striving for what is perfect." This process is exemplified by the growth of an oak. Acorns produced by the mature tree are endowed with power for development. Matter possesses predetermined will and power to strive toward a goal.

These ideas became the scientific pattern of the times, an invisible structure of postulates indispensable for reasoning. We too employ such a scaffold, though it is differently constituted. It is easy to see that the juncture of Egyptian knowledge with the attractive philosophy of Greece necessarily led to Alexandrian alchemy, from which the complex but coherent mansion of the medieval folklore of alchemy derived much of its building material. It did it indirectly however, through the mediation of Mohammedan learning.

With the ascension of Christianity to the official faith of the Roman Empire, science and learning disintegrated. In 389 A.D. the Emperor Theodosius ordered the destruction of all pagan schools and temples, thus terminating the life of the famous Serapion of Alexandria and its library, leaving its scholars homeless and schoolless. A similar measure put into effect the same year by Zeno, Emperor of the East, closed the important school of Edessa. A veritable stream of émigré sages and philosophers began to flow eastward to Syria and Persia where they found a welcome refuge. In Europe science declined. "The influence of the church was during that period not conducive to the advance of natural or physical science. Not indeed because of any active hostility to natural science as such, but because of two fundamentals which under the influence of the early fathers as St. Adrian and St. Augustine dominated Christian thought. To the church of that day, this earthly life was only of importance as a discipline and preparation for the life after death. Only those things were worth while which were necessary preparations for life to come. . . . What mattered, therefore, such trivial matters as the nature of the material universe and the laws and causes pertaining to it?" (Stillman, J. M., The Story of Early Chemistry, New York, 1924, p. 140).

This sudden shift in values failed to prove disastrous to science because of the receptivity of Persia and Asia Minor to the influx of the learned refugees. And when in the seventh century the Mohammedan invasion swept the Near East, science again met with good fortune. With uncommon vision and alacrity the rulers of the illiterate Arabian hordes organized academies at their courts and installed men of learning in positions of importance. Physicians, engineers, alchemists, astrologers, mathematicians, philosophers and financial experts crowded the court, and were there held in high esteem. Much has been made of the blind and ferocious fanaticism of the followers of Mohammed, and again and again is the baseless story recounted of the burning of the great Alexandrian library because all wisdom was presumably contained in the Koran. The facts are that nowhere in the history of humanity until the coming of Western democracy does one encounter such sincere religious tolerance, love of learning and freedom in its pursuit, as in the courts of the several Caliphs who ruled the vast territories of Islam after the death of Mohammed. There scholars of various Christian sects such as the Gnostics, Nestorians, Jacobites as well as Jewish savants who had left Alexandria and other Christian centers of learning, found tolerance and freedom, and science found a fertile soil.

Syriac was the official language of these centers, most prominent of which was the Academy of Bagdad, founded in the eighth century. Into Syriac was translated all the riches of Greek and Alexandrian learning such as the writing of Euclid, Archimedes, Appolonius, Ptolemy, Aristotle, Hippocrates, Galen, Theophrastus, and Plato and the alchemical writings of Zosimos and other Alexandrians. In a word the learning of Greece, Rome, and Graeco-Egypt found a home worthy of its grandeur.

Syriac was soon replaced by Arabic, from which most of the ancient authors were translated into Latin during the awakening of the quest for knowledge in Europe in the eleventh century. It was thus that famous oriental names came to dominate the science of alchemy in the western world and add mystery and romance to its high intrinsic appeal. During the middle ages when glamor was a prerequisite for scientific authority the names of Abu Abdallah Jaber ben-Hayyam-al-Kufi, known as Geber (ca 720–813 A.D.), Abou Bekr Mohammed ben Zakariya El-Razi, known as Rhases (866–925), Abu-ali-ben-Abdallah Ebn Sina, known as Avicenna (980–1026), rang with impressive pomp and commanding dignity. And great scholars these men were who kept alive the torch of knowledge until the European awakening. The science they preserved reached the West through Mohammedan Spain, where great Arabian academies flourished and attracted Christian scholars who came to learn and to translate the newly-found wisdom.

The Islamic writers mentioned, and some others, did much to advance alchemy, or the divine art, as it was termed, beyond the Alexandrian level. Geber, whose actual existence is still in dispute but whose works, said to number over one hundred, date back to the ninth century A.D., is typical of the European alchemists that followed him. While displaying strong leanings to mysticism, he is also fully conversant with the laboratory and "made noteworthy advance in both the theory and practice of chemistry." (Holmyard, E. J., The Works of Geber, London, 1928, p. xi). He observed many new substances and reactions and valued experiment highly. His major contribution to alchemy, it is conceded lies in his clarification of the alchemical theories of transmutation, the nature of philosophic mercury and sulphur and their value in the composition of metals, and the use of colors in transmutation. He speaks of the wonder-working transmuting tincture, the powder of projection and the grand elixir. His writings mark the beginnings of full-fledged alchemy in style and contents.

A summary of early Arabian alchemy is contained in a tenth century encyclopedia entitled The Writings of the Faithful Brothers, issued by a society of Arab scholars founded at Barra about 950 A.D. In 1160 the book was publicly burned in Bagdad by the theological authorities but its influence on European alchemy was in no way affected thereby.

Before considering the final philosophy of alchemy as elaborated in medieval Europe on the basis of Graeco-Egyptian and Arabic antecedents, it may be of interest to survey briefly another, though possibly later phenomenon. The development of alchemy in China, which shares numerous features with its western counterpart, presents an intriguing query. Did these two lines of thought stem from a common origin or had they evolved independently? The idea of a happy life after death has been found in many religions and seems to offer a pleasing vision to most people, even in our own time. It is little wonder then, that early in the history of China there evolved the quest for immortal life on earth, a quest sponsored and nurtured by Taoism (6th century B.C.). The idea of attaining immortality soon merged with belief in magical immunity from all kinds of menacing forces such as fire, water, detection by enemies and affliction by disease. These wishful conceptions found their way into the earliest Chinese treatise on alchemy by Wei-Po-Yang written about 142 A.D. This study is marked with the same poetic charm and philosophic depth which characterized many western works. In it are also encountered the habit of secrecy, the notions of primal matter, and the concepts of Yin and Yang or the two contraries, dark and light, evil and good, female and male, negative and positive. "From the interaction of these two contraries all things in the universe were created and controlled in their various manifestations." (Wilson, W. J., Chinese Alchemy. Ciba Symposia 2,595, 1940). In this treatise are also discussed the common metals represented by symbols, such as lead by the dragon and mercury by a tiger. Numerology is found here too, with its occult relationships and meanings.

Popular, life-prolonging recipes recommended proper breathing and gymnastical rhythms. Abstention from the common five foods, hemp, millet, cara, rice and pulse, was regarded as important. Candidates were even exhorted to fast "and inhale air and drink dew," which diet may be augmented by vitalizing substances from the vegetable, animal and mineral kingdoms. In the latter group are mentioned cinnabar, the sulfide of mercury, and another potent immortalizing medicine, gold, which purifies and ennobles. Many of the physical properties of this metal are mentioned. It is also stated that "gold is born under the influence of the moon. At daybreak, receiving magic force from the sun it returns to its mother." Cited in this treatise are such processes as distillation, liquifaction, solidification and color changes in chemical reactions. A recipe is given for the preparation of a gold "pill of immortality" shrouded in the same mystery and beset with the same difficulties which loom so large in the West. The search meets with similar failure, which is slurred over with resort to humility and faith. It should be noted that all these ideas bespeak considerable chemical practice and speculation in earlier periods.

By the third or fourth century A.D. when European alchemy was coming into its own, its Chinese sister science was in full bloom under the leadership of the scholar and alchemist Ko Hung, often referred to as the Chinese Paracelsus. In his works are cited experimenters who anteceded him, their numerous recipes for making gold and silver and the pill of immortality. Yet recipes are also given for the use of tin in gilding or the mixing of arsenic sulfide with sand to make crucibles and furnaces. As in the West, many later Chinese works on alchemy are written in verse. Chinese alchemy offered a meeting ground, even as did Western alchemy, for mysticism, religion, philosophy and romance, employing astrology, magic, numerology, symbolism and allusions to sex, displaying throughout considerable ingenuity and perseverence in experimentation. In the West transmutation of base metals into gold and the search for longevity were preeminent, while in China it was the pill of immortality. "Perhaps it (immortality) failed to appeal to the European alchemists whose Mohammedanism and Christianity promised them immortality anyway." (Lu-Ch'iang Wu and T. L. Davis, Ko Hung on the Gold Medicine and On the Yellow and White. Proc. Am. Ac. Arts & Sci. 70, 221, 1935). Although it is now recognized that the world of antiquity indulged in more commerce and cultural exchange with India and China than has hitherto been suspected, the relationship between Chinese and Western alchemy is still a controversial problem. (Johnson, O. S., A Study of Chinese Alchemy, Shanghai, 1928; Chicashige, Masumi, Oriental Alchemy, Tokyo, 1936). Considerable evidence is available to point to probable paths of diffusion between China and the West through the Arabs and Persians, with whom the Chinese had commercial and cultural intercourse, both before and after the advent of Mohammedanism. And since all reports and texts of European alchemy prior to Arabian influences may be spurious, these claims have to be regarded seriously and weighed with due caution.

3. Alchemical Principles and Aims

The science of alchemy rested upon a congeries of beliefs which remained unchallenged for a number of centuries and which, like astrology, constituted a coherent and logical structure. Most fundamental was the belief in the unity of matter originally developed in Greek philosophy. It was a stimulating conception which infiltrated all alchemical thought, functioning like an unquestioned article of faith. It was inscribed on all diagrams and inserted in all texts. Without it alchemy would have been impossible. It implied that "All things were produced by this one thing by adaptation" and that "nothing in the world dies, but all things pass and change."

Paracelsus begins his short Catechism of Alchemy thus: "Q. What is the chief study of a Philosopher? A. It is the investigation of the operations of Nature. Q. What is the end of nature? A. God, who is also its beginning. Q. Whence are all things derived? A. From one and indivisible Nature. . . . Q. What should be the qualities possessed by the examiners of Nature? A. They should be like unto Nature herself. That is to say, they should be truthful, simple, patient and persevering." (Waite, A. E. The Hermetic and Alchemical Writings of Paracelsus. N. Y. 1894, vol. 1, 289).

If classification is a mark of true science, then alchemy was scientific from the very start. Surely it was a great achievement to have isolated a small group of substances out of the bewildering diversity of rocks and ores, discern in them common physical properties and classify them as metals. The next step was more easily taken, but is sound classification nevertheless. Some metals, namely gold, and silver, were found to be unchangeable in fire. These were called noble or perfect, since repose, like immobile sphericity, were associated with permanence, nobility and perfection. It was also the pattern of the time to regard instability or motion as imperfect, or rather, as striving toward perfection. Hence the other metals were called base; they also tended to lose their lustre and malleability in the fire. They were semi-metals.

Galena, or lead sulfate, which had the metallic lustre and color of lead and was considered a semi-metal, gave off sulphur on heating and yielded true metallic lead. Sulphur was present in iron pyrites and on expulsion yielded metallic iron. Fire was the universal purgative agent; hence that which it expelled was a contaminating earthy substance.

On the other hand fire and heat caused mercury to evaporate and

ASTROLOGY AND ALCHEMY

escape. These events, particularly sublimation, amazed and bewildered the primitive researcher as much as did eclipses or comets. The volatility of mercury suggested to him that when a metal was heated and calcined, i.e. oxidized, the change occurred because something was driven out. Besides, does not a burning fire give the undeniable impression of something ascending, or spirits emitted or released, giving off light and heat in the process?

But these sets of qualities, the ones associated with sulphur and with mercury, were plainly observed to vary with different ores or compounds. What was therefore more reasonable in the light of the times than to assume that both sulphur and mercury were properties of the universal, primal matter which combined in various proportions to yield different products? The term "mercury" designates for us the metal mercury and "sulphur" the elements by that name. But the ancients used these words in the same sense, as well as in a more generalized one to designate *principles*. Mercury stood for the principle of metallicity, hence malleability and lustre, often also for the invisible properties; while sulphur referred to the principle of changeability or to the visible, earthy properties, attacked by fire. Mercury was the positive, the masculine, the ennobling principle and sulphur the negative, the feminine, the contaminating one. To differentiate between the real substances designated by these terms and the abstracted principles, the latter were referred to as the Philosophers' Mercury, or Sophic Mercury and the Philosophers' or Sophic Sulphur. Mercury was the soul and sulphur the body of elements. Fixed mercury was the same as sophic mercury, which meant that the original mercury was heated, sublimated and condensed numerous times so as to free it from impurities, either real or imaginary ones.

Metals varied in their properties and appearance because their substratum of primal matter combined with varying amounts of the two principles to produce them. This aspect of the alchemical creed was an Arabian contribution of Geber's, who expressed it as follows: "The sun (i.e., gold) is composed of most subtle mercury and a bit of purest sulphur, fixed and clear and of a translucent redness; and since this sulphur is not colored as much, hence one component has more color than the other; therefore gold is more or less yellow. . . . When the sulphur is impure, crude, red and pale, its bulk fixed and only a fraction not, and in combination with a crude and impure mercury so that both were about equal, the mixture resulted in Venus (i.e., copper). If the sulphur was little fixed and partly volatile and of an imperfect whiteness —of this mixture Jupiter (tin) will emerge."

Of utmost significance to early experimenters was the phenomenon of color, which was abstracted even as its designation by a noun is abstracted

THE GRAND ROMANCE OF ALCHEMY

by us. It was not adequate to state that silver was white. More satisfactory was it to say that it possessed the principle of whiteness. Similarly, things were sweet because they contained the principle of sweetness. "When a soft object was hardened by mixing it with something harder than itself, it was supposed that the soft object communicated to the mixture a portion of the universal softness that was its attribute, while the hard object carried into the thing formed some part of the universal hardness that existed even if all hard things were destroyed." (Muir, M. M. Pattison. The Alchemical Essence and the Chemical Element, London, 1894, p. 18).

There is nothing strange in this mode of thought. Molière was fully conversant with the spirit of the times when he ridiculed the physician who pompously explained that morphine put the patient to sleep because it possessed the soporific principle. The fact is, we still think in such terms. Moreover, recent research has shown that essentially this is a correct visualization. The sweetness of sugar as well as the action of drugs do seem to depend upon or reside in a specific configuration of atoms within a certain part of the molecule, hence on a specific radical which may be attached to a variety of substances.

What beginner in the study of chemical reactions is not fascinated and intrigued by the wonder of color changes? Who does not under these conditions imagine himself peering into the very womb of becoming, where change and growth prevail and the mysteries of matter are revealed? It is easy, indeed, to picture the feelings of these early experimenters when they poured mercury in the form of a fine shower upon molten sulphur and watched both familiar substances vanish. In their place appeared a black substance. When in turn, this was heated in a closed vessel it was now converted into vapor. The vapor was condensed and yielded a beautiful red solid. These reactions were no different from those of our youngsters or uninitiated adults who use chemical sets for entertainment. They are deeply impressive, nonetheless. To the alchemist color meant something more, however. Besides being an independent quality which could be removed from and added to primal matter, color also possessed moral values. Black, quite naturally, stood for darkness, red for light, and yellow, the color of gold, symbolized nobility. For these reasons color was taken to indicate the state of purity attained by substances on their way toward the peak of perfection, namely, gold.

In the absence of any notion of elements, compounds and alloys the world of change which confronted the alchemist on all sides, pressed steadily upon his consciousness and invited no hesitation. His awareness of unceasing and ubiquitous flux was particularly strengthened by the appeal of Greek philosophy entailing the unity of matter, the four elements and the universal four qualities, of which the interchangeability was common and incontroversial experience. Add to this the innate tendency of man to attribute human values and motives to natural events and, unless firmly on guard, to fuse the moral, romantic and philosophic values of the times with his observations and interpretations, and the alchemical theory of transmutation becomes a logical necessity.

That transmutation took place all about him is quite apparent. "The alchemist made a solution of bluestone (copper sulphate) in water, dipped a piece of iron in this solution, obtained a deposit of copper on the iron, and triumphantly declared he had transformed iron into copper. He boiled water in an open dish and when the water had disappeared he pointed to the earthy matter in the dish as proof of transmutation of water into earth. And the alchemist was justified in drawing these conclusions from the data which he had. He might have concluded that the copper existed in the blue-stone and was drawn out by the iron and that the water he boiled down contained earth which became visible when the water was removed, but had the alchemist come to this conclusion it would have been as much an unverified guess as the conclusion was whereat he actually arrived." (Muir, p. 28)

From such humble beginnings the theory of transmutation evolved into a complex philosophic system. Briefly, it postulated that within the bowels of the earth in earliest times matter seethed and heaved. Through this process nature gave rise to all kinds of base compounds. These were of incipient crudity, monstrosities which nature constantly endeavored to perfect, a task requiring great refinement, time and effort. The creative vat in the center of the earth was linked to a womb, creating feeding and bearing offspring and eternally striving toward their perfection.

"One is obliged to admit that nature never really intended to produce such metals as lead, iron, copper, tin or even silver, which latter is the first stage of perfection, but strove toward the creation of gold (the child of her desire); because this creative force forever seeks in its wisdom to bestow upon its products the last degree of perfection. Failure to achieve this goal and the emergence of corrupt substances in its place are not Nature's fault, but the fault of external circumstances. Hence the existence of imperfect metals signifies that their state is analogous to abortions and monstrosities which come about when nature is hindered in her process, or when she encounters resistance that ties her hands and hampers her normal motions. These obstacles derive from the coarseness which the mercury has contracted amidst the impurity of the womb, where it abounds, or from combining there with poor and combustible sulphur." (Translated from W. Salmon, Bibliothèque des philosophes chimiques—Preface)

THE GRAND ROMANCE OF ALCHEMY

These monstrosities were, however, transitory stages because natural forces were at work undoing the original contaminations and perfecting all metals into gold. An evolutionary drive was on, deep in the bowels of the earth. Substances were transmuted slowly and gradually from crude into pure, and finally into the purest and noblest substance, gold. Thus, inorganic change was a law of nature. "Nothing in the world dies, but all things pass and change."

Whence did the energy come for the evolutionary transformation? According to the alchemical folklore it was supplied by the stars. Celestial bodies were endowed with invisible powers over terrestrial matters and exerted their influence with divine certainty though with extreme slowness. While some alchemists viewed the formation of gold as the final stage, others postulated a cycle evolution in which gold became somehow contaminated anew and thus converted into a base metal to resume again the long path of transformation under celestial influence. Still others, especially Paracelsus, maintained that gold never became impure again but was transformed into stone and minerals which then became the substance of plants and animals. The inorganic was thus believed to evolve into the organic, placed higher on the evolutionary scale.

This continuity between the inorganic and organic worlds was a basic alchemical concept. Changes in metal were likened to changes in a growing embryo. And in the symbolic language of alchemy the vessel in which transmutation was supposed to take place was termed "the philosopher's egg."

During the nineteenth century the alchemical theory of unity of matter seemed laughable. Chemical elements were then held to be unique, irreducible and basic entities, and though Mendeleyev had shown recurrent sets of properties in his atomic table, no one suspected the uniformity in the constitution of all elements. Today, however, the unity of matter is a sound scientific theory based upon the concepts of protons, neutrons, mesons, positrons and electrons, some of the building blocks of all elements.

The keystone of the alchemical credo was the philosopher's stone, the occasionally congealed product of stellar radiation. This was thought to be a substance the preparation of which could bring about the transmutation of imperfect elements into gold by chemical means in the laboratory within a relatively short time. It was endowed with the powers of performing rapidly what the noble celestial bodies took aeons to accomplish. Quite obviously a substance possessing such amazing powers could not be prepared with ease by anyone. Even if one were given a meticulous description of the procedure, one could never achieve the synthesis unless one was learned and wise, fully versed in the art and its oriental lore, in the mysteries of the cabala and in theology. One's character had to be noble and impeccable. One also had to be holy and blessed, as were, for example, Raymond Lully, Albert the Great, Thomas Aquinas and many other great alchemists.

Rich and glamorous grew the folklore of the philosopher's stone. Its very preparation was a sacred process dignified by the name "magnum opus," or the great magistery, the masterpiece. Before approaching this revered task one had to perform the lesser work or minor magistery, which was the transmutation of metals into silver. This process was performed after a white substance known as the white elixir, philosophical mercury, or salts of silver, had been prepared by devious and secretive steps. One then made a projection; that is, one mixed this powder with the base metal and converted it into silver. Transmutation of metals into gold was the goal of all chemical knowledge. To achieve it one had to be in possession of philosophical sulphur and mercury, or salts of gold and silver. This was usually a red powder and was called the red elixir. It was by means of this powder that the crowning glory of the great projection was made. It involved mixing the red elixir with the crude metal to effect its ultimate transmutation into gold.

In reality, the material involved in these euphonious and awe-inspiring processes often consisted of gold trichloride, silver nitrate and mercury trichloride. These compounds were enclosed in a glass matrass, sealed hermetically. This meant that the open glass end was fused in the flame. The sealed vessel was called the philosopher's egg, already referred to, and was kept for long periods of time on a sand bath, a water bath or an athanor, which was a furnace yielding uniform heat. These were referred to in alchemy as the three vessels.

So significant was this function, so much enshrouded in mystery and sanctity as to resemble a strict ritualistic performance in its every detail. The method of heating the philosopher's egg was minutely prescribed, leaving much room for individual skill and ingenuity. Glass in those days was poor, easily broken, and the number of unexploded eggs must have been small indeed. Heating was performed gradually. The temperature had to be maintained first for a specific time at about 150° Fahrenheit, when the glass vessel had to be hot enough for the operator to touch without burning his hand. The second stage required a heat between the boiling point of water and the melting point of sulphur, the third stage just below the melting point of tin, and the fourth below that of lead.

Each step in the execution of the magnum opus was given an impressive name and was further subdivided into smaller divisions. The preliminary period was the *Preparation*. The second one was the *Decoction*

THE GRAND ROMANCE OF ALCHEMY

in the Egg, and the third was the *Fixation and Fermentation* and the last *Transmutation*. The process of decoction itself consisted of (a) conjunction or union of the philosophical mercury and sulphur; (b) putrefaction, when the primary reaction leading to a black color took place, which process was held akin to organic putrefaction from which springs all life; (c) ablution, when the color changed to white and hence indicated the emergence of life; and finally (d) rubification, when the mixture turned red, produced the gold and reached the stage of perfection.

The duration of the decoction had to be considerable so as to simulate as faithfully as possible the periods during which the various planets exerted their influence. To the reign of Mercury were assigned fifty days, to that of Saturn forty, to Jupiter twenty-one, to the moon twenty-one, to Venus forty, to Mars forty-five and to the reign of the sun an indefinite period at the discretion of the alchemist. These rules permitted much leeway however. The colors of substances were considered to be most significant. Similarly, the color of a planet or a comet was regarded as basic in its prognosticating function or general description. A change in color was supposed to betray basic internal changes and mysterious reactions and transmutations. The Graeco-Egyptian alchemists had already assigned names to the various color changes, of which four primary ones were recognized, namely melanosis or blackening, leucosis or whitening, roses or turning violet, and zanthosis or the process of turning either yellow or red. These colors also were assumed to represent the four cardinal points, north, west, south and east, respectively. In addition they also symbolized the elements. White corresponded to air, yellow to water, red to fire and black to earth.

After proper decoction the glass container was broken, the red powder removed and subjected to *fixation and fermentation*, designed to give it the final touches of augmenting and intensifying its powers by mixing it with heated gold. At the very end came the crowning glory of transmutation. A small amount of lead, for example, or tin, was heated in a crucible, and in a mood of deep reverence and ecstasy, a small quantity of the ennobling powder of transmutation, the philosopher's stone, the great elixir, wrapped in wax, was added to it, or, as the alchemists said, projected upon it. On cooling, pure gold was supposedly found in the crucible and the alchemist achieved wide renown as one of the saints of learning and piety and of rare experimental skill. He became an *adept*. No alchemist sought greater honor than that.

The most salient feature of alchemy is its complete fusion of experimental practices with mystical aims and symbols. The alchemists' mode of thought was only a different form of discourse from our own, as different as is forensic phraseology from our ordinary means of expression, or as is poetic language from common prose. Just as lawyers, priests, politicians, diplomats, poets or scientists have evolved today a conventional, professional style and tone, together with a unique mode of thought and formal conduct, even so did the alchemists develop a professional pattern which seems strange and remote to us. But then consider the following stanza by Thomas Campbell:

> Star of love's soft interviews,
> Parted lovers on thee mart;
> Their remembrancer in Heaven
> Of thrilling vows thou art,
> Too delicious to be riven
> By absence from the heart.

To people accustomed to poetry this language is quite understandable. But there are others to whom it seems utterly fantastic and childish. Frequently ridiculed is legalistic or medical language, in fact, any traditionally evolved form of discourse which becomes as natural to the particular profession as a cap and gown to a graduation ceremony, or the wig in a British court.

Viewed in this light the symbolic language of the alchemists loses its exotic nature and becomes a normal human phenomenon. In an age of involved similes and parables in literature, of mystical concepts in religion and philosophy, alchemy, which merged all of these intellectual disciplines into one, necessarily employed them all. In addition, all of alchemy, like all of medicine, was placed under astrological domination. The total effect of this admixture of values, thought and language could lead to nothing else but what we actually encounter. Far from being "an insult to the human understanding," as the prominent historian of chemistry, Ernst von Meyer, puts it, it becomes a valuable document for study and an aid in the understanding of man's quest for scientific thought.

It was customary for learned men of Europe and the Orient then, even as it still is today in many parts of the world, to impress colleagues with riddles and cryptograms. The more symbolic the language and the more ingenious and confusing the style, the wiser the speaker was held to be. It is this love of enigmas and mysticism, together with the belief that alchemical research is noble and belongs exclusively to the elite, that accounts for alchemical symbolism, allegory and secretiveness.

These features and mysteries of the subject combined to create the most romantic and audacious flight into fancy that mankind has ever attempted in any organized manner. The philosopher's stone, or the great elixir, gradually evolved in the minds of the medieval savants into an agent of general perfection. It could cure all diseases, make men invisible, bestow eternal life, restore youth, undo all physical and mental imperfections and create beauty and wisdom at the will of its possessor. For this reason the philosopher's stone was also called the universal medicine, the elixir of life.

Chapter X

THE LITERATURE OF ALCHEMY

1. The Hermetic Museum

THERE is no better means of penetrating the thoughts and aspirations of the alchemical philosophers than through an examination of their literature. True, their writings are incomprehensibly cryptic, in spots too obscure to decipher. But it is also true that many of their chapters contain excellent and ingenious science, and others are as noble and impassioned as the Scriptures. There is in them poetry and an earthy quest for truth; there is simplicity of style and true love of wisdom and knowledge. Moreover, the exhortation frequently heard in our own times for the humanization of knowledge and for closer bonds between the disciplines of science, philosophy or religion on the one hand and the daily needs of man on the other, were not needed in the era of the alchemists. To them man was the object of all nature and of all knowledge.

Most of the original works on alchemy are rare library collections, usually written in Latin, the language of science in the Middle Ages. There are, however, several accessible volumes in English from which the general reader may gain a fairly complete picture of the aims and language of these courageous scholars. Virtually all of these works were published toward the end of the last century in London by the publishing house of James Elliot and Co., which has apparently aimed at specialization in such matters.

The largest collection is a two-volume work edited by Arthur Edward Waite, entitled "The Hermetic Museum, Restored and Enlarged: Most Faithfully Instructing All Disciples of the Sopho-Spagyric Art How That Greatest and Truest Medicine of the Philosopher's Stone May Be Found and Held." The translation was made from a Latin text published at Frankfort in 1678 and contains "Twenty Two Most Celebrated Chemical Tracts." While the two volumes contain many anonymous treatises, they also reproduce works by Nicholas Flamel, Basil

Valentine, Thomas Norton, John A. Mehung, Cremer, Sendivogius, Philalethes, Helvetius and Michael Maier, all of which are famous names in alchemy.

Several of the treatises are illustrated with the symbolic drawings or paintings characteristic of the "divine art and occult science." Without a study of these drawings it is almost impossible to peer into the minds of alchemical scholars and comprehend their ways of thought. These illustrations have the same grandeur and imaginative sweep as their language and ideas.

Most of the works deal with the philosopher's stone, which by its very mystery and broad philosophic horizons has literally inspired thousands of untranslated treatises of similar content. In an intimate talk with the reader the editor states that: "It would be unjust to doubt . . . that of all the arts invented for the use of life by the reason of man that of *Alchemy* is the most noble and glorious. For all philosophers exclaim, as it were with one voice albeit in many languages, that this art is not only true, but (after the Divine Law by which our souls are saved), the best and most magnificent gift bestowed upon man by God; and that it should therefore be investigated with all zeal and with the greatest pains. But as good wine needs no praise, so neither does this art require a herald, for its truth is undoubted and its utility in human life universally acknowledged and shewn forth, not only in the Art of Medicine, in Pharmacy, and many other sciences but more especially in the Art of Transmuting Metals. . . . Different men devote themselves to the study of this science from different motives. The philosopher is impelled by the love of truth, and the thirst after wisdom. He delights in knowledge for its own sake. . . . He has at his command the most effectual means of becoming rich, if he would only use them. But he is fired by the love of philosophy and does not care for the mocking grandeur of fortune. . . ."

The essays expound the unknown nature of the philosopher's sophic mercury and sulphur, the principle of the contraries, the beliefs on these matters of the venerable "sages of the Saracens, Egyptians, Arabs and Persians," and powders employed in the preparation of the elixir, its multifarious but wonderful qualities, and similar relevant topics. Alchemical authorities of preceding periods are freely and piously quoted. Frequently a scene of contemporary life or a philosophical aside find their way into the text, as do also religious and moral contemplations, strewn about in a forest of redundancy, in plain or metaphorical or just so florid language.

There are essays like "The Golden Tract, Concerning the Stone of the Philosophers, by an Anonymous German Adept," which are wordy and merely glorify the Stone in repetitious eulogies, elaborate on philosophic mercury and sulphur and describe in the customary vagueness the procedures to follow. Others, like "The Golden Age Restored," have a literary beauty in their style and content, possessing a fascination all their own. This last work is replete with Biblical quotations, chiefly from writings attributed to Solomon, because the parable on which it is constructed employs some theme from the Song of Songs. The author relates: "As I pondered in my mind the marvels of the Most High and the duty of fervent love to our neighbors, which He laid upon us; I remembered the wheat harvest, when Reuben the son of Leah, found Dudaim in the field, which Leah gave to Rachel for the love of the Patriarch Jacob. Then I was carried forward being plunged in profound thought, to the time of Moses, who rendered potable the golden calf (which Aaron had formed) by reducing it to powder in the fire, throwing it into the water, and giving it to the children of Israel to drink; and I marveled greatly at the wonderful and masterly destruction of the metal by the man of God."

The author then retires to contemplate "the matter further on the morrow" and falls into a deep slumber. He sees a vision, of course, in which Solomon appears "in all his power, wealth and glory, and with him came his whole harem: sixty were queens, eight hundred concubines, and of virgins there was a countless number." An exceptionally beautiful virgin came to stand behind him. Her thighs were like half moons, her navel a round goblet, her breasts two young roes, etc. But "her garments which were rancid, ill-savored and full of venom lay at her feet whither she had cast them. And at length she broke forth into these words: 'I have put off my coat; how shall I put it on? I have washed my feet; how shall I defile them? The watchmen that went about the city found me, they smote me, they wounded me; they took away my veil from me.' Thereupon I fell to the ground with great and ignorant terror." . . . Solomon then approached him and bade him rise, taking the opportunity to deliver an eloquent and mystifying oration on the true beauty of the virgin, who came to him as a gift of nature. He also cheered up the author on that matter of the garments. Their smell, he said, "is to the wise like the smell of Lebanon—but to the ignorant an abomination." Though by that time it seems most of the harem had reached a state of nudity, both Solomon and the dreaming author are still interested in the lone, naked virgin by his side. "If thou art on watch, says Solomon, and makest good use of thy present opportunity, the bloody sweat and snowy fears of this virgin will have power to restore thee, and to strengthen and clarify thy intellect and memory that thy eyes may see the secret wonders of the Most High, the height of the things above, the depth of the things beneath, and that thou mayst clearly understand the powers and operation of all

THE LITERATURE OF ALCHEMY

Nature and of the elements. Thy intellect shall be silver and thy memory golden. The color of all precious stones shall appear before thy eyes; thou shalt know their birth, and separate the good from the bad, the sheep from the goats." They then indulge in a philosophical conversation reminiscent of the Book of Daniel. In the meantime all the virgins have reached the stage of nudity and King Solomon assures the author that "the more their loveliness delights me the less am I deterred by their foul garments."

An ancient lady then appears out of the crowd and introduces herself as the mother of the nude one at his side. After praising her daughter's beauty and virtue, she compliments the author on his choice and his disregard of the foul garments. She reveals to him that the filthy clothes beneath her feet conceal a dowry "lest in the present war she should be deprived of her wealth by soldiers." The senile mother of the virgin was about to give him "the lye of the Sages" with which to wash the garments and "the flowing salt, the incombustible oil, and an inestimable treasure," when she was interrupted by King Solomon, who boastfully declared "the ornaments of my concubines shame the rays of the sun, and the beauty of my virgins the light of the moon. My virgins are heavenly, my wisdom inscrutable, my mind past finding out." The author then vows his love for the virgin, whom King Solomon presents to him to own and cherish, and he wakes to find it was all a dream. "Until the light dawned I was full of subtle thoughts. But when I had risen and poured forth my prayers, behold, I saw the garments of the naked virgin lying by my bedside." But the virgin was not there and he was terrified. He could not look at the deserted garments, and changed his quarters, leaving the garments behind fearing to touch them.

Five years had passed before the author thought of them again. He decided to destroy them in the furnace and change his dwelling. But that night his would-be mother-in-law appeared to him in a dream and "rebuked him with angry words" for neglecting her daughter's garments and the priceless jewels they concealed. Moreover, it seemed he had been the cause of her daughter's death. The author is shocked by the accusations and protests his innocence, since these five years he had not seen her daughter. "All this is true," says the old lady. "Nevertheless thou hast sinned grievously against God and on that account hast not received from me my daughter, or the lye of the Sages wherewith to cleanse her garments. For since thou wert from the first horrified at the sight of my daughter's garments, the planet Saturn, her grandfather, was wroth, and changed her into what she was before her birth." The author pleads his innocence, and the wrath of the ancient lady is palliated. She rewards him for his good intentions in keeping the malodorous garments for five years by revealing a great secret. "My daughter for the great love she bore thee, has left thee under her garments a grey box wrapped in a thick, black, mouldy cloth. With this came a bottle full of lye, and directions: 'Purge that box well of the dirt and bad smell with which the garments have infected it, and then thou shalt want no key, but the box will open of its own accord and in it thou shalt find two things, viz. a white silver casket full of polished diamonds, and a rich robe intertissued with precious solar stones.' All these treasures belonged to my dear daughter and she left them all to thee before she was transformed and perished. If thou wilt skilfully transpose this treasure, carefully purify it, and silently and patiently place it in some warm, moist, vaporous, and transparent chamber, and guard it there from cold, wind, hail, swift lightning, and all outward injury, till the season of the wheat harvest, thou shalt perceive and behold the great glory and beauty of thine heritage."

The author awoke, prayed and immediately proceeded to search for the box, which he duly found. The outside wrapping was so hard, however, that he could not cleanse it with lye or cut it with iron, steel or any other metal. "So I did not know what in all the world I should do and began to think that it was a poisoned cloth and to call to mind the saying of the Prophet: 'Though thou wash thee with nitre and take thee much soap, yet thine iniquity is marked before me, saith the Lord God.' "

So another year passed and "still all my patient toil and thought had met with no success." In despair he took a walk in a garden, fell asleep, and spoke to the ancient woman again, complaining of his failures. "Then she laughed at my simplicity and said: 'Dost thou try to eat oysters or crabs in their shells? Must they not be first prepared by the ancient cook of the planets? I told thee to purify the grey box with the lye I gave thee but not the cloth which is wrapped around it. The latter thou shouldst first have burnt with the fire of the Sages.' For this purpose she gave me some glowing coals, wrapped in a soft cloth from which I was to obtain the subtle fire of the Sages." He set to work with fire and lye, remembering the wise saying, "Fire and Azoth are sufficient for thee." (Azoth is one of the 170 designations of the Philosopher's stone), and "the passage in Esdras (Bk IV): 'And he gave me a goblet filled with fire, and when I had drunk it wisdom grew in me; and God granted me understanding and my spirit was preserved, and my mouth opened, but nothing else was added.' After forty nights I had finished 204 books, of which seventy were worthy to be read by the most wise and were written upon box tablets. I thus continued in silence and hope, as that ancient woman had bidden me do until at last after a long time my understanding, in fulfillment of Solomon's prophey, became silver and my memory gold."

"When in obedience to the directions of the ancient lady, I had skilfully placed the treasure of her daughter in a chamber by itself, and closed it up, I gazed upon those brilliant lunar diamonds and solar rubies, and understood the meaning of Solomon when he says: 'My Beloved is white and ruddy, the chiefest among ten thousand. His head is as the most fine gold, his locks are husky, and black as a raven; his eyes are as the eyes of doves by the rivers of waters, washed with milk, and fitly set; his cheeks are as a bed of spices, as sweet flowers, etc."

He wished to remove the wondrous treasure he had uncovered and cleansed, but recalled the words of Solomon, "'I charge you, O ye daughters of Jerusalem, by the roes and by the hinds of the field, that ye stir not up nor awake my love till he please,' etc. These words enlightened me, and shewed unto me the aim of the wise; wherefore I patiently left the treasure in the chamber and waited till through God's mercy all should have been happily perfected by the operation of Nature and the labor of my hands."

There was an eclipse of the sun soon thereafter "which was terrible to behold, for it began with a misty greenness, somewhat shot over with other colors. . . . Men were full of fear but I rejoiced." The author then cites a few more quotations from the Song of Songs which he incorporates into his parable. "And thus," says the author, "in the name of the Holy Trinity, we will, in these few words, conclude our exposition of the Great Mystery of the Most Precious Philosophical Stone, and of the Arcanum of the Sages."

While some followers of Freud may find a speculative paradise in this fable, it is a fact that both Christian, Mohammedan and Hebrew scholars tirelessly sought to unwrap the hidden meanings of the poetry of love included in the Song of Songs. Our author does it successfully with his task of preparing the philosopher's stone, his message harmonizing well with the main point of the parable, namely, that the hard physical labors pursued in the laboratory with lowly and evil-smelling chemical substances, are well worth the glory and wisdom which crown such efforts.

Another work, "The Sophic Hydrolith," claims to be "a chymical work, in which the way is shewn the matter named and the process described, namely, the method of obtaining the universal tincture." It is an even, quick stepping work, warning against false pretenders and extolling the true philosophers. The "God-fearing chymist and student" is reminded that the true philosophy, that is, alchemy, is a divine and holy Art, achieved not by the might of man but the grace of God." Hence it is a personal gift and must not be revealed to the unworthy. Knowledge of nature is glorious, but does not lead to wealth, as some dupes assume. The author then proceeds by means of numerous enigmas and riddles to unfold the processes which he believes are essential in the preparations of the stone, in this case apparently, metallic mercury.

Other works, too, warn against false teaching and deluded practitioners, charlatans and dupes. In "The Only True Way" the author goes so far as to claim that "most men who nowadays have devoted themselves to this exalted art of chemistry are pursuing a wrong course and are deceivers or deceived. The deceivers are conscious of their own ignorance and try to veil it under an obscure and allegorical style. The less they really know, the more pompous and the more unintelligible do their speculations become." The author then proceeds to ridicule all experiments the puttering chemists so pompously extol. "Can Nature, in the heart of the earth, where the metals do grow and receive increase, have anything corresponding to all those pseudo-alchemistical instruments, alembics, retorts, circulatory and sublimatory phials . . . cobbler's wax salt, arsenic, sulphur, mercury and so forth?"

The author speaks from bitter experience. It is all useless, he says. "For I too toiled for many years in accordance with those sophistic methods and endeavored to reach the coveted goal by sublimation, distillation, calcination, circulation, and so forth, and to fashion the Stone out of substances such as urine, salt, atrament, alum, etc. I have tried hard to evolve it out of hairs, wine, eggs, bones, and all manner of herbs; out of arsenic, mercury, and sulphur and all the minerals and metals. I have striven to elicit it out of aqua fortis and alkali. I have spent nights and days in dissolving, coagulating, amalgamating and precipitating. Yet from all these things I derived neither profit nor pay. I had hoped much from the quintessence, but it disappointed me like the rest."

The Only True Way, then, is to abandon the old methods and seek "the method which Nature herself pursues in the bowels of the earth," by the method which is "digestion by gentle heat." The author is apparently a reformer-homeopath who has antedated modern critics of alchemy with most of their standard arguments against the art, even citing all the motives ascribed to them. In a word, ignorance and malice makes the writers on alchemy complicate the preparation of the Stone and give it a multitude of names. All this is rubbish. "Follow the guidance of Nature: *she* will not lead us astray," is his slogan.

His solution, presented in the same language used by those he condemns, is indeed simple. Use "different varieties of heat," he advises, and above all "natural heating of essences." Pay no heed to the Sages and their operations. "Give them a wide berth." You will be made a fool of, contract dangerous diseases while your possessions will go up in smoke. He is amazed that most practitioners fail to see the simple truth which he so clearly comprehends. What have these adepts gained by their agonizing and costly toil? "Let me beseech you to profit by their heartbreaking experience, and to have done with everything but true Alchemy, which teaches that the substance is brought to perfection and attains the exaltation of elementary fire, by its own light and liquid, by which also imperfect metals are ameliorated because their elementary fire was not properly digested by its liquid. And for the same reason the elementary fire cannot remain for the liquid is separated from the elementary fire by the heat of the ordinary fire and evaporates in the form of white smoke." This kind of language is continued until the author, revolutionary and reformer that he is, is fully satisfied that the matter has been put clearly and simply before the reader. In the course of his elucidating tirade he also explains exactly why the Sages were deluded by the sequence of color, and the causes of their other errors.

Before he is done condemning and reforming he reintroduces most of the processes he has set out to ridicule. "The whole thing is done by a simple process of heating which includes the solution and coagulation of the bodies and also the sublimation and putrefaction. But some writers have substituted for the simple and true essence a certain other essence with which they have deceived the whole world, and involved many persons in considerable losses. . . . It would be better not to publish such writings . . ." he concludes, since they delude people and cause them pain and losses. He pleads with the reader to trust his own observations, condemn the bewildering and confusing phraseology of the ancients and "let the Book of Nature be the most favored volume in your library." He begs forgiveness for upsetting so many cherished ideas, but we must all be honest and truthful and fight deception, and to put it into operation he starts ridiculing and condemning the followers of tradition all over again, constantly repeating his plea for direct knowledge of nature. There is no mercury or sulphur in the womb of the earth, where metals have been seeded and where they grow. Their natural growth must be observed and studied.

In conclusion he discusses the various degrees of natural heat or coction, by which the first Matter "is differentiated into the various kinds of natural bodies. . . . The vegetable nature is that in which the coction is least perfect. . . . The coction of the animal is almost as imperfect as that of the vegetable substance; for its essence is easily burned. The coction of the mineral substances is the most perfect of all because in them the metallic liquid is more closely united (by coction) to its elementary fire. . . . For the liquid of wood is not so completely gained (by coction) to its essence as the liquid of metals is to *its* essence." The author then proceeds to explain why he really disapproves of the traditional approach to color changes. Since the liquid of wood is not metallic, hence imperfectly fused to its essence, it produces a black smoke. Perfected by coction it becomes metallic and issues a white smoke, as when "imperfect metals are melted in the fire. That is why the Ancients said that you must first make the substance black before you make it white. . . . Again they say: 'You must first make it white before you make it red. To make red is to make perfect, because gold and silver have been rendered perfect by coction, their essence being fully united to their liquid and changed into pure fire.'"

The author insists that "the metallic essence is the pure substance which by natural coction must be raised from the lowest to the highest stage of development." For this reason he will have no truck with any of the authorities who believe in sophic sulphur or mercury, because "names do not alter facts: the fact is that the elementary fire must be so united to its elementary liquid by natural coction that they become indivisible. . . . The perfected substance the Ancients have well called Elixir or fire which has undergone a process of perfect coction: for that which before was crude and raw is 'cooked' or digested by the process of coction."

One wonders how many of our own preaching reformers and revolutionaries will appear in this light to future students.

An essay rather frankly entitled "The Glory of the World or Table of Paradise: A most precious book, containing art, the like of which is not to be found upon earth; shewing the truth concerning the true Philosophy and the most noble medicine and priceless Tincture, together with divers other valuable Arts and the instruments required for them," is by comparison, a prosaic description of methods and procedures in the preparation of the stone. Like the other tracts, it is so critical of predecessors, wordy pretenders and braggarts, as to seem almost nihilistic. Yet the thesis manages to ramble along for almost a third of the book, offering directions to follow, true and guaranteed ones, of course. A long section deals with the fire or wisdom of the Sages, among whom are listed many historical, as well as imaginary figures. Thus we read there statements on alchemical topics by Plato, Aristotle, Pythagoras, Parmenides, Theophilus, Mundinus, Socrates, Ananias, Democritos, as well as Hermes, Noah, Nero, Adam, Seth, Abel, Lucas, and others. They all have wise but diverse things to say on putrefaction, coction, calcination, and other phenomena. But they say it poetically, and, as usual in the literature of alchemy, interject considerable philosophic and religious comment of genuine merit. Lengthy explanations of the brief statements by the celebrities cited are included in the work. These abound in imaginative anecdotes about Greek and Biblical figures which retain the charm and spirit of the original cultures that created them.

The Collection also contains the Emerald Table, a classical alchemical article of faith, the origin of which is still controversial, but about which numerous fanciful legends were circulated by adepts. European alchemy obtained it from the Arabs, who in all likelihood had copied it

THE LITERATURE OF ALCHEMY

from the Greeks. (Read J. Prelude to Chemistry, N.Y., 1937, p. 53) The table, also known as the Sinaragdine Table, constitutes the Precepts of Hermes Trismegistus, presumably found engraved upon a stone slab in Phoenician characters. It was located, according to legend, in the tomb of Hermes by Alexander the Great. Others had it that it was Sarah, the wife of Abraham, who took it from Hermes' tomb somewhere near Hebron. Whatever the origin, it was cherished as much as the ten commandments are in the sphere of religion and ethics. The text is typical of the lingo of alchemy.

The Precepts of Hermes, engraved upon the Emerald Table.
1. I speak not fictitious things, but that which is certain and true.
2. What is below is like that which is above, and what is above is like that which is below, to accomplish the miracles of one thing.
3. And as all things were produced by the one word of one Being, so all things were produced by this one thing by adaptation.
4. Its father is the sun, its mother the moon, the wind carries it in its belly, its nurse is the earth.
5. It is the father of perfection throughout the world.
6. The power is vigorous if it be changed into earth.
7. Separate the earth from the fire, the subtle from the gross, acting prudently and with judgment.
8. Ascend with the greatest sagacity from the earth to heaven, and then again descend to the earth and unite together the powers of things superior and things inferior. Then you will obtain the glory of the whole world and obscurity will fly far away from you.
9. This has more fortitude than fortitude itself; because it conquers every subtle thing and can penetrate every solid.
10. Thus was the world formed.
11. Hence proceed wonders which are here established.
12. Therefore I am called Hermes Trismegistus, having three parts of the philosophy of the whole world.
13. That which I had to say concerning the operation of the sun is completed.

Of special interest are three illustrated tracts. The first one is entitled "The Book of Lambspring, consisting of fifteen drawings, each of which is explained by a poem on the page facing it. The work is ushered in by a special poem beginning with the lines:

> And I have clearly set forth the *whole* matter
> That rich and poor might understand
> There is nothing like it upon earth.

To enjoy true philosophy the reader is warned he must cheerfully give both of time and labor. "For you must subject to gentle coction the seeds and the metals . . .

ASTROLOGY AND ALCHEMY

> You will discover and bring to perfection the whole
> work of Philosophy
> Which to most men appears impossible
> Though it is a convenient and easy task.
> If we were to shew it to the outer world
> We should be derided by men, women and children.
> Therefore be modest and secret
> And you will be left in peace and security.

The pictures are, of course, realistically drawn. Yet they generate an atmosphere which, though far from being as lurid as the paintings of the surrealists have a dreaminess all their own. In a way they remind the reader of our contemporary boogie-woogie dances, in which the faces of the youngsters maintain expressions of utter ritualistic seriousness, while the legs are frivolously performing weird movements or the hips voluptuous paths.

In these pictures we note realistically drawn renaissance backgrounds of cities, countryside, lakes, forests, mountains, landscapes and interiors. Yet we are amused or startled by imaginary dragons and unicorns, wise-looking lions or ferocious dogs, gigantic and unidentifiable birds, kings on ludicrously built thrones, perched on lizards, fires and angels walking calmly along the road, or a bearded, respectable king with sceptre, crown and all opening his mouth terribly wide to swallow a young man who is his son.

In "The Golden Tripod" we see two young girls riding on two lions busy chewing each other up, while the girls, unperturbed, hold high in their hands hearts, out of which emerge a sun and a crescent moon. A knight in shining armour standing behind them, swings a long sword, intent on doing irreparable damage. Unlike the previous work, this one shows numerous symbolic drawings, such as the triangle pointing downward, which designates the earth. In it are inserted two circles. Its corners contain the symbols for the sun, moon, and mercury, and above it are Hebrew words. Other realistic and symbolic drawings are in a similar vein.

The "Drawings of the All-Wise Doorkeeper" are even more crowded with symbols, equally bewildering and more mystical, containing real or imaginary beings in unexpected but earnest poses against peace-oozing, naturalistic backgrounds. The poetry of "The Book of Lamb-spring" merely explains in fifteen steps and the usual allegorical language the laboratory procedures to be followed in the preparation of the stone. Both the pictures and the verse employ the customary symbols, such as the king for gold; two enormous and demure-looking fishes reposing half submerged in a quiet lake or bay represent sulphur and mercury within a matrix of primal matter, which by internal coction gives rise to the metals. The poet describes this process as follows:

THE LITERATURE OF ALCHEMY

The Sages will tell you
That two fishes are in our sea
Without any flesh or bones.
Let them be cooked in their own water;
Then they also will become a vast sea,
The vastness of which no man can describe.
Moreover, the Sages say
That the two fishes are only one,
Body, Spirit and Soul.
Now, I tell you most truly
Cook these three together,
That there may be a very large sea.
Cook the sulphur well with the sulphur
And hold your tongue about it:
Conceal your knowledge to your own advantage
And you shall be free from poverty.
Only let your discovery remain a closed secret.

The work entitled "The Golden Tripod" consists of three tracts by Basil Valentine, Thomas Norton, and "a certain Cremer, Abbot of Westminster," respectively, all of which works may be spurious. The first tract is a mine of beautiful parables. Its tone may well be surmised from the opening paragraph.

"When I had emptied to the dregs the cup of human suffering, I was led to consider the wretchedness of this world, and the fearful consequences of our first parents' disobedience. Then I saw that there was no hope of repentance for mankind, that they were getting worse day by day, and that for their impenitence God's everlasting punishment was hanging over them; and I made haste to withdraw myself from the evil world, to bid farewell to it, and to devote myself to the service of God."

He enters a monastery and keeps busy with his devotional duties, yet finds he has much time on his hands which he does "not wish to spend in idleness, lest my evil thoughts should lead me into new sins." Books are his constant companions until a brother dear to him is afflicted with a "severe disease of the kidneys," and he discovers that "none of the many physicians he had consulted had been able to give even momentary relief." The author then decided to try his hand at it.

"As I loved him, I gathered all manner of herbs, extracted their salts and distilled various medicines. But none of them seemed to do him the slightest good." After experimenting with vegetable extracts for six years, he decided to study metals and minerals. One discovery led to another until he arrived at a stage where he easily understood "the nature and properties, and the secret potency, imparted by God to minerals and metals." In the course of his experiments he found a mineral "which exhibited many colors, and proved to be of the greatest efficacy in art. The spiritual essence of this substance I extracted, and therewith restored our sick brother in a few days, to perfect health." In view of his acquired knowledge and dramatic success he decided to write the tract.

Practical chemical knowledge is interspersed in beautiful prose filled with exalted expressions of philosophy, ethics and religion, patterned after the language of the opening paragraph quoted above. Following an introductory section, the metals are described in the usual manner. Thus copper—"Amatory Venus is clothed with abundant color, and her whole body is one pure tincture, not unlike the red color which is found in the most precious of metals. But though her spirit is of good quality, her body is leprous, and affords us permanent substratum to the fixed tincture." Iron is described as "Warlike Mars, a hard, firm, and durable body which is evidence of the generosity of his soul; nor can fire be said to have much power over it." The metals, or planets, then converse eruditely about themselves and their mutual relations, which are somewhat enhanced by the mixed company, since the moon appears as a "beautiful lady in a long, silver robe, intertissued with many waters," and Venus was dressed "in a crimson robe, intertissued with threads of green, and charmed all by the beauty of her countenance and the fragrance of the flowers which she bore in her hand." Then follow the twelve keys which describe the twelve stages in the preparation of the stone, giving directions for the successive processes. Here is a sample of the directions for the initial step:

"Let the diadem of the King (gold or sophic sulphur) be of pure gold, and let the Queen (silver or sophic mercury) that is united to him in wedlock be chaste and immaculate.

"If you would operate by means of our bodies, take a fierce grey wolf (antimony) which though on account of its name it be subject to the sway of warlike Mars (iron), is by birth the offspring of ancient Saturn (tin) and is found in the valleys and mountains of the world where he roams about savage with hunger. Cast to him the body of the King and when he has devoured it, burn it entirely to ashes in a great fire. By this process the King (gold) will be liberated and when it has been performed thrice the Lion (mercury) has overcome the wolf and will find nothing more to devour in him. Thus our body has been rendered fit for the first stage of our work."

A moving style and spirit permeate and brighten the entire text, which cause it to compete in beauty with the best of the Bible. Thoroughly typical is the opening paragraph of the Fourth Key.

"All flesh that is derived from the earth must be decomposed and again reduced to earth; then the earthy salt produces a new generation

THE LITERATURE OF ALCHEMY 271

by celestial resuscitation. For where there was not first earth, there can be no resurrection in our Magistery. For in earth is the balm of Nature and the salt of the Sages."

There is hardly a treatise that does not have a charm all its own. While most of those discussed so far were written either anonymously or by obscure adepts, volume II of the "Hermetic Museum" contains the work of such alchemists as the Englishman, Thomas Norton, also known as Philotethes, Sendivogius, the Pole, the famous Helvetius, and the original editor, Michael Maier, physician to the Emperor Rudolph II of Prague, the grand patron of the sciences.

The works presented in this second volume are even richer than those of the preceding one. They deal with chemistry only about as much as the Scriptures deal with religion. Here we find penetrating comment on the importance of observation and experimentation, incessant pleas to the reader to be critical and not put too much faith in the Ancients, though these same derided Ancients are reverentially quoted by everybody alike. The texts are full of abstract parables, as well as anecdotes dealing with contemporary events, presenting an excellent mirror of social and cultural life and manners throughout the middle ages. The elements of sex and romance enter everywhere and add human vitality and interest to the alchemical contents. There are, in addition, numerous tales of deluded seekers after the stone, their follies and sorrows, bringing out the morals that flow therefrom. The texts also abound in stories of persecution of adepts by ignorant or greedy rulers. If the science they contain may not be worth the trouble of deciphering, as literary efforts some of these works well deserve to be read; their store of folklore, aspirations, fears and superstitions of the times is hardly mustered elsewhere so lucidly and compactly.

A few more points are well worth commenting upon. One of the most striking features is the widespread criticism of past authorities, even though the critic and the Sage criticized share in our eyes the same basic point of view, stemming from common, and by now exploded, assumptions. Thus Cremer, the Englishman, commences his Testament as follows: "I have attempted to give a full and accurate account of alchemy without using any of those obscure technical terms, which have proved so serious a stumbling-block in the way of many students of this Art. I am here describing my own experience during the thirty years which I spent and wasted in perusing the writings of authors whose whole ingenuity seemed to have been concentrated upon the Art of expressing thought in unintelligible language. The more I read the more hopelessly I went astray. . . ."

Sendivogius, the Pole, of whom more later, begins his collection of tracts entitled "The New Chemical Light, Drawn From The Fountain of Nature And Of Manual Experience" with the following words: "When I considered in my mind the great number of deceitful books and forged Alchemistic 'receipts' which have been put in circulation by heartless impostors, though they do not contain even a spark of truth—and how many persons have been and are still daily led astray by them—it occurred to me that I could not do better than communicate the Talent committed to me by the Father of Lights to the Sons and Heirs of Knowledge."

Similarly critical is Philalethes, who writes: "Anyone who has read a few 'Receipts' claims the title of a Sage and conceives the most extravagant hopes; and in order to give themselves the appearance of very wise men indeed, such persons immediately set themselves to construct furnaces, fill their laboratories with stills and alembics and approach their work with a wonderful appearance of profundity. They adopt an obscure jargon, speak of the first matter of the metals . . . etc."

Or consider the following from Michael Maier's "The Secrets of Alchemy." "I had also read the books of those moral philosophers who undertake to prescribe an effective remedy for every disease of the mind. But after giving all these boasted specifics a fair trial, I found, to my dismay, that they were of little practical use. In many cases, the causes of mental maladies appeared to be material, and to consist in an excess or defect of the bile or of some other bodily substance."

Few, indeed, are the adepts who fail to berate most of their predecessors and colleagues, singling out some, however, for special praise. This simulates in every way procedures customary in our own times. It must be admitted that the glib accusation that scientists in the past blindly followed authority is not borne out by the facts.

Part of the current folklore of the nature of the science of the past and the causes of its inadequacy, is presumably its unexperimental approach. This, too, is a modern superstition. Of all people alchemists deserve this false accusation the least. There is hardly an author who fails to stress repeatedly the value of persistent experimentation and more experimentation. The contemporary defenders of science who so boldly condemn speculation and theorizing, comparing such activities adversely with the true nobility of patient and lowly labor in the laboratory might very well spare their oratory, since they are merely plagiarizing in hackneyed words what many alchemical writers expressed in beautiful prose.

Not only were most alchemists revolutionaries in ideas and interpretations, but in processes and instruments as well. Writes Thomas Norton in his "Ordinall of Alchemy": "The Ancients describe a special furnace for use in every stage of our Art, devised differently according to the bent of their minds. Many of these however are quite unsuitable, some being too broad, others too high, and others out of harmony with the requirements of Nature. Some of the furnaces described in these books may be rejected, seeing that they are the inventions of men who only appeared to be, but were not really, Sages. Of the furnace which can be most highly recommended you will find a pictorial representation in this volume. One which was unknown to the Ancients, I am proud to call my own invention. I set it up, in the first instance, at a very considerable outlay. But its advantages more than make good its cost. It is so constructed that sixty different chemical operations, for which diverse kinds of heat are required, may be carried on in it at the same time, and a very small fire of only a foot square supplies a sufficient degree of heat for all these processes." Equally unfounded is the fable supported and circulated by some modern scientists that alchemists were interested in gold. There is not a single work or a single comment which does not bear eloquent testimony to the contrary, or which does not speak with contempt both of such accusations, as well as of those "puffers" or charlatans who enter the Art for material gain.

2. *The New Pearl of Great Price*

No different are the works compiled under the title "The New Pearl of Great Price" similarly edited by Arthur Edward Waite. Here are gathered the writings of the earlier apostles of alchemy, such as Michael Scotus, Rhasis, Albertus Magnus, St. Thomas, Raymondus Lullus and Arnoldus de Villa Nova, originally published in 1546 "as written by Bonus of Ferrara and edited by Janus Lasinius." John Read, in his "Prelude to Chemistry" says of it: "This is one of the early printed works on alchemy, and it was issued from the Aldine press with the sanction of Pope Paul III and the Venetian Senate." This author is, however, unfair in citing some instances of belief in magic cited in it, as evidence that: "It contains some extraordinary statements which must have caused even the most fire-hardened adept to reach for his salt-box." Virtually all alchemical writers, like all great astronomers, physicians, biologists, explorers, poets and philosophers of those days, believed that some animals were generated in fire, others in clouds and still others in putrefying substances, to say nothing of their believing firmly in evil eye and witchcraft. The explanation cited in the text: "These generations depend on the fortuitous combination of the same elements by which the animal or insect is ordinarily produced," was unctuously repeated as late as the nineteenth century by some moderns.

Essentially this collection is a chip of the old block, displaying in a general way the same features as the tracts of the Hermetic Museum. It is characterized by elaborate apologies for the art in the form of debates or discourses between an alchemist and his antagonist, in which all possible objections are enumerated and their pointed thrusts parried by the rational, open-minded, yet determined friends of alchemy, with whose argumentative powers the authors seem fully satisfied. One work contains the usual illustrations consisting of a series of woodcuts portraying the usual alchemical procedures by means of the same figures, but with distinctive skill and imagery. Generally speaking, these earlier essays are more practical and are less concerned with moral, social and philosophic comments than the later products.

3. *A Golden and Blessed Casket*

A third collection similarly issued by Waite is a work entitled "A Golden and Blessed Casket of Nature's Marvels Concerning The Blessed Mystery of the Philosopher's Stone" by Benedictus Figulus of Utenhofen, as usual in alchemy, a rather legendary personage whom the editor describes as a "strange alchemist who . . . is otherwise distinguished as poet, theologian, theosopher, philosopher, physician. . . ." There are few outstanding alchemists who could not rightly claim to be thus described. "The Golden and Blessed Casket" contains several tracts by Alexander von Suchten, whom Waite identifies as the famous Alexander Seton, or the Cosmopolite, whose life will be told in a subsequent section.

Figulus is a pupil and admirer of Paracelsus, hence the material he has gathered leans toward the medical aspects of alchemy. It is of interest that many alchemists did not regard the Elixir as a substance capable of effecting immortality, but rather the optimal longevity. Thus writes Alexander von Suchten in his "A More Complete Exposition of This Medical Foundation For the Less Experienced Student": "For just as man, through disease and other causes, often fails to reach to the appointed limit of life, so, on the other hand, by removing these impediments, he may prolong life to the utmost limit set him." The present collection is dull or prosaic by comparison, lacking the literary, philosophic and scientific glamor of the other works. The same may be said of "Collectanea Chemica," a small volume of a few tracts. It contains a brief treatise entitled "The Secret of the Liquor Alkahest," written as a catechism on the subject. These works, too, lean toward medical interests and the essay on the Alkahest shows considerable experimentation on urine, such as analyses of its salts, its relation to blood, and changes in its composition with the state of health. It seems both blood and urine can, after considerable treatment, be made to yield the alkahest.

Of special interest are the writings of Edward Kelly, generally claimed to share with Cagliostro the title of arch-charlatan of alchemy, an unscrupulous fraud and impostor. It is precisely because these accusations are based on considerable, even if incomplete, evidence, that his writings are worth looking into.

The work begins with a long poem entitled "Sir Edward Kelly's Work" and is signed with the initials E. L. Its purpose may well be gathered from the opening stanza:

> All you that fain philosophers would be
> And night and day in Geber's kitchen broil,
> Wasting the chips of ancient Hermes' Tree,
> Weening to turn them to a precious oil,
> The more you work, the more you lose and spoil,
> To you, I say, how learned soever you be,
> Go burn your books and come and learn of me.

The poem then guides the reader along the winding road leading to the successful preparation of the philosopher's stone, employing the customary symbols. The last two stanzas announce the completion of the Work:

> Your Jupiter standing red hot on the fire
> So soon as your medicine upon him is cast,
> Presently standeth so hard as a wire
> For when he is fixed and melteth by blast.
> And of all your working this is the last;
> Then let it by test or strong water be tried
> The best gold and silver no better shall hide.

> Mercury crude in crucible heated
> Presently hardeneth like silver anealed
> And in the high throne of Luna is seated,
>   Silver or Gold as medicine hath sealed,
> And thus our great secret I have revealed,
> Which divers have seen and myself have wrought
> And dearly I prize it, yet give it for nought.

Whatever Kelly's character, his two essays, "The Stone of the Philosophers" and "The Humid Path" bespeak average alchemical intelligence, though of no marked originality, but also of no exceptional cupidity or superficiality. They were written in prison to mitigate the unrelenting attitude assumed by his erstwhile benefactor, Emperor Rudolph II. The works do betray full familiarity with the subject treated. They abound in quotations and constitute an excellent summary of the alchemical hypotheses in simple language. Kelly speaks of himself as a martyr of the art. "I venture to hope, however," he writes, "that my life and character will so become known to posterity that I may be counted among those who have suffered much for the truth," a hope which was to be in no way fulfilled.

Kelly's clarity of exposition is praiseworthy. For example, to explain to his reader how mercury, sulphur and salt (a later addition) are essential parts of all metals without being physically detectable in their common forms, he writes as follows: "For as the numbers 2, 3, and 4, are the foundation (of other numbers), though they themselves consist partly of units and partly of each other, as, for instance 12 contains within itself 3 times 4, 4 times 3, 6 times 2, and 12 times 1, which are nevertheless all lost in its own proper name—so Mercury, Sulphur, and Salt exist sometimes singly, sometimes in couples, and sometimes jointly in mineral bodies. And as 3, the fourth part of 12, consists of 3 units, or of 2 and 1 unit, while it is included in 4, which exceeds it by 1 unit, so some minerals which derive their motive force from a simple union of fire, water and earth (which union, as aforesaid, constitutes Mercury) have no affinity with Sulphur or Salt, the perfection of which arises from the addition of air, the fourth element."

The art of making gold is not everything in the world. "Men who have a mere practical knowledge of Alchemy know how to make gold, but the same are not Sages. They cling desperately to the particular method which they have been taught, and decry everything else as false and unscientific, since they do not know the universality of the substance, nor the different ways of manipulating it. They think their one little branch is the whole tree of Philosophy, and thus have obscured the entire garden of the Hesperides with the fumes of their ignorance. There is another class of men, whom I call rationalists or dogmatists, who have reduced the universal science to rules and have laid down codes of weight, quantity, time, etc. as of general application though they apply only to particular cases. The third class are the Methodists. . . . They tell in simple and every-day language the most momentous mysteries of our Stone." The latter are the empirics who over-simplify and have no true regard for universals and are therefore guilty of several theoretical heresies.

A few general comments on alchemy and the alchemists are now in place. It is clear that the pursuit known by that name is as different from the intellectual or practical disciplines of our time as are the social or political outlooks of the respective periods. The science of the Middle Ages was a mixture of philosophy, religion, art, poetry, romance and mysticism. The values of separation and specialization were not appreciated because the cultural pattern of the times made such an approach impossible. It is likely that there was not enough content in each branch of investigation to make specialization possible or desirable. It is also arguable that the growth of scientific knowledge in later centuries led to proper respect for specialization, which, in turn, cleared the road for rapid progress by eliminating the free miscibility of aims and values exploited by alchemy with the resulting confusions. This, in turn, it may be claimed, changed the medieval pattern into its current form.

A full explanation is as difficult in this case as it is in all complex social phenomena. It is a fact that in the Middle Ages there prevailed a philosophy of nature which linked chemistry to astrology and medicine and all of science to philosophy and religion. The alchemists regarded themselves as true philosophers and sages prying into the mysteries of nature. God was part of nature and of man's spiritual strength and eliminating or segregating the religious element was unthinkable. The entire pattern was a firmly cemented unit, and no concepts could flourish beyond its bounds. The transition to modern thought required centuries and constitutes a synthesis of the efforts of numerous scholars and the consequences of many trends.

It is the complex symbolism of alchemy which today seems to stand most in the way of mutual understanding between modern and medieval science. Its novelty and exotic imagery invite facile ridicule, and its total incomprehensibility attracts the modern chemist as much as the cabala or Plato's Timaeus. But this is due to the difference in language and mode of thought rather than subject matter. The alchemists needed symbols just as badly as the modern chemist, and for the same purpose. An average student of poetry will feel at home with the poetic similes of all times, but will find the symbols of modern chemistry completely foreign. One will be as justified in ridiculing or in condemning alchemy. It is a fact nevertheless that the creation of symbols indicates progress in knowledge and specialization, and is a feature of every prospering science. (Lüdy, F., Alchemistische and Chemische Zeichen, Berlin, 1928)

What does contribute to the bizarre and cryptic nature of the alchemists' language is the mysticism they injected into their symbols. But this was definitely part of the thinking of the times, just as were parables and repetitiveness part of the language of the Scriptures. It was this facet of alchemy which permitted multiplication of names and symbols, thus undoing the economy aimed at.

Another disturbing element to us, is the custom of assigning activity and passivity, or masculinity and femininity, to metals and qualities. This principle of contraries, which is encountered in Chinese alchemy as well as in Occidental, seems to have been a helpful concept, and is strongly advocated by some modern philosophies, e.g. dialectical materialism. Many of the alchemical statements on the action and reaction of contraries should readily be accepted as the pinnacle of philosophic and scientific wisdom by the proponents of that philosophy. The assignment of masculinity and femininity to gold and silver or water and earth, is no more licentious than the division of all ideas, forces or events into pairs of theses and antitheses, so enthusiastically exalted by some contemporary scientists who follow the folklore of dialectical materialism. Viewed with this in mind, one may be in full agreement with Davis when he states that "from earliest times the mind of man has grasped tangible and formulated Nature by means of two opposite qualities and a third by which the opposites are mediated, reconciled and included." (Davis, T. L., Annals of Med. Hist., 6, 280, 1924) Father, Son and Godhead, or Thesis, Antithesis and Synthesis, or the "Egyptian 'Ankh, the symbol of life, is a combination of male and female." Even positive and negative electricity and charged particles of matter may well be vestigial, historic residues. Sexual symbols for the designation of contraries have definitely vanished in our culture, but other symbolic dichotomies persist and perform valuable service.

Chapter XI

THE ALCHEMISTS IN PURSUIT OF WISDOM

1. The Earlier Apostles

THE true fascination of alchemical aims emerges most convincingly from the private lives of alchemists, lives devoted to a noble cause in a spirit of rare altruism and loyalty. In an age when religious fervor made thousands of men and women abandon all earthly pleasures for devotional meditation, scientific pursuits matched that faith by producing an equally impassioned love of learning and research. Nothing can better describe that age than the lives of these knights errant in quest of something loftier than the holy grail, namely, the philosopher's stone, the great elixir, the universal panacea.

Just as alchemy was a congeries of empirical and speculative values and theories in chemistry, philosophy, religion and science, so were the records of the lives of the alchemical disciples a farrago of fact and fancy, of history and romance. But historical accuracy is in this case relevant only to the biographer. From our point of view it matters little whether a person like Alfarabi actually was a great musician, or whether the alchemist Flamel left Spain in March or August. What does matter is the setting which writers of the period assigned to these heroes of alchemy and in what colors the thinking and reading public wished to see them painted. The lives of the alchemists constitute the intellectual folklore of the time, enjoyed and created by the ignorant and learned alike. Similarly, Horatio Alger stories injected the values of a specific period into a literary mold. Each period of each culture invades its art and literature in a basically similar fashion. The middle ages like our own times, created its own heroes and idols and fashioned romances around them, as we do today in our fashion.

Because alchemy became a skeleton in the closet to modern science little effort was put into the study of it, with the result that critical evaluations of the field are few. Several historical accounts have been relied upon for the material of this chapter besides the original works themselves. Most useful have been "L'Alchimie et les Alchimistes" by Louis Figuier, Paris, 1860, a rather unsympathetic study, and "Lives of Alchemystical Philosophers, Based on Materials Collected in 1815," compiled in a more friendly and scholarly attitude by A. E. Waite, London, 1888, and a later work by the same author entitled "The Secret Tradition in Alchemy," London, 1926.

The alchemical masters of Graeco-Egypt, Synesius, Democritus, Zosimos, Mary the Jewess, Cleopatra, Hermes and others, became the founding fathers and saints of the later sages and adepts. In an age in which the general revival of learning dazzled the awakening mind of Europe with the wisdom of Greece and Rome, this fervor was fully understandable. This was an age in which the opinions of Aristotle, Pliny, Galen and Ptolemy held unchallenged authority in all matters of knowledge and truth. The alchemists thus merely added their own idols to the revered four masters.

As luck would have it, the next development of alchemy occurred in Oriental lands which provided a fascinating background for fancy and romance. Of this constellation the brightest star was Geber, whose works have already been cited in the preceding chapter. So numerous are the legends spun around him that it is virtually impossible to segregate truth from fiction.

"With the characteristic prodigality of the Middle Ages," says Waite, "no less than five hundred treatises have been attributed to the Arabian adept." Geber became the oracle of the later alchemists, as can be attested by the large number of spurious works attributed to him. As already stated, the "Sum of Perfection," to which the real Geber can justly lay claim, contains the foundation of the notion of the philosopher's stone, as well as considerable knowledge of practical chemistry.

Typical of the legends which embellish the lives of the Arab alchemical scholars is the story of the adept Alfarabi. He lived at the beginning of the tenth century, and like all alchemical fathers, was reputed to have been the wisest man of his age and to have travelled extensively for the purpose of gathering opinions of philosophers concerning nature's marvelous secrets. Many great sovereigns sought to retain him at their courts but he spurned such offers. He visited Mecca not for religious but for philosophic reasons. On his way home through Syria he chanced to stop at the court of Sultan Seifeddoulet, the renowned patron of learning. While this great monarch sat discoursing in a grand hall surrounded by his courtiers and savants, the wise Alfarabi entered in travelling clothes and silently sat down beside him. Everybody in the hall was shocked and the guard was ordered to arrest the stranger. Calmly Alfarabi dared them touch his person and face the consequences.

He then turned to the Sultan and quietly announced that the ruler was apparently unaware of his guest's identity or he would have treated him with due honor instead of vulgar threats. At this the Sultan became interested and entered upon a long conversation with the stranger. They discussed science and philosophy, and the stranger displayed such eloquence that he charmed the entire audience. He proved himself the possessor of vast knowledge of alchemy, astrology, theology and philosophy, and outwitted all who dared debate with him. It occurred to one courtier to ask him whether he also knew music, and humbly Alfarabi requested that a lute be brought. He played. His melodies were at first so tender that the court shed bitter tears. Then he changed his theme and made everyone within earshot dance and laugh. He then returned to a sad tune and again there was lamentation.

After this performance the Sultan could do nothing but implore him to stay. But Alfarabi refused. He was out to find the philosopher's stone and gather opinions and secrets from the wise the world over. Nothing on earth could divert him from his true quest. He departed and soon thereafter met his death at the hands of highwaymen. He is alleged to have written many notable books which are lost.

Another famous Arabian name revered by the medieval alchemists was that of Rhasis, a celebrated physician and chemist. In his youth his major interest lay in music and sensual enjoyment. At thirty he embarked upon a more serious career and mastered the science of medicine, surpassing all practitioners of his time in knowledge and skill. He was generous, noble and kind to the poor. He journeyed in many lands for the acquisition and exchange of knowledge with famous men of learning. He wrote a treatise on transmutation for his friend the Emir Almansour, Prince of Khorassan, who recompensed him handsomely. The potentate then desired to witness a transmutation, to which Rhasis consented, provided an adequate laboratory was equipped for the purpose. The Emir ordered one built and supplied with instruments and materials. The eagerly awaited experiment failed, and the noble and aged savant was furiously belabored by the Emir's minions. A blow on the head blinded him, and the rest of his days were spent in poverty. He died in the year 932 A.D.

Another Arab hero of alchemy was Avicenna, born in Bokhara 980 A.D. He was a great physician and a man deeply learned in philosophy, theology and the ennobling mysteries of the occult sciences. His fame spread far and wide and reached the ears of the Sultan Magdal Doulet, who invited him to his palace. Convinced that Avicenna's reputation was fully deserved, he promptly appointed him Grand Vizier. For a while Avicenna performed wonders as healer, advisor, astrologer and man of great wisdom. But evil soon came his way. Tempted by the powers of his office, his flesh weakened, and he gave himself up to a life of debauchery. He managed to write, however, numerous books, among which were seven treatises on the philosopher's stone. His loose habits led to inefficiency, which soon provoked the Sultan's ire. He was dismissed from his high office and died in his early fifties.

Frequently cited is the name of Morienus. He was born in Rome in the twelfth century but settled in Egypt at an early age and acquired vast knowledge of chemistry and physics. As a youth he heard of a famous Alexandrian philosopher Adfar, and left home for that dream city of learning. The great Adfar took him in apprenticeship, and together they studied happily and arduously. Upon Adfar's death Morienus travelled to Jerusalem where he became a recluse, sharing his isolation with a devoted pupil.

It transpired that the private papers of his master, Adfar, fell into the hands of the wise and studious Sultan of Egypt, Kalid. These papers portended to contain the secret of transmutation which, however, the Sultan failed to decipher. He publicized his failure to the sages of Cairo and offered a magnificent reward to anyone able to extract the secret. Many attempted but none succeeded.

The news reched Morien the hermit, who immediately proceeded to Cairo. It was not the reward he was after but the opportunity of fathoming the full knowledge of his beloved master, of converting the great Sultan and of exposing false pretenders. Morien came and conquered. He not only unraveled the master's secret but performed a transmutation, placed the elixir in a vase upon which he inscribed, "He who possesses all has no need of others." Though he won the Sultan's friendship and admiration, he returned to his solitary retreat.

Kalid was downcast and angered at the departure of the sage. He decreed capital punishment for false pretenders and asked his counsellors to search the land for the retiring adept. All efforts were vain until one day while the Sultan was hunting, his favorite slave, Galip, discovered an old man praying by the wayside with whom he fell into conversation. To his delight he learned from the old man of a great scholar who led a solitary life outside Jerusalem and for whom nature held no secrets, particularly with regard to transmutation. He had, in fact, come to Egypt to inform the Sultan of this man's existence and the scope of his wisdom. He was presented to Kalid, who warned the stranger that death awaited him if his clue proved false. Accompanied with an armed escort the old man and the loyal slave, Galip, journeyed to Jerusalem and brought Morien before the Sultan. He was, of course, recognized, and all was joy. Morien sought to convert the Sultan to Christianity but failed. Their friendship persisted unshaken in spite of it, and together with the slave Galip they studied all aspects of alchemy. Their con-

THE ALCHEMISTS IN PURSUIT OF WISDOM

versations are reported in a book entitled "Liber de Compositione Alchemiae" by Morien.

It would have been impossible for the romantic heritage of alchemy to by-pass such renowned figures as Albertus Magnus or St. Thomas Aquinas. Although much authentic information is available about them, alchemy succeeded nonetheless in weaving into their lives the usual glorifications. Since alchemy rarely invented heroes but merely imposed a cloak of romance upon deserving scholars, Albert and Thomas were ideal figures for it.

It is recounted that Albert desired some land upon which to build a monastery. The owner of the selected site was a William, Count of Holland, who for some reason refused to part with it. Albert invited him and his court to a magnificent feast while they were passing through his home town, Cologne, which happened during a particularly cold spell in midwinter. When they arrived at Albert's domicile they were surprised to see the tables set in the garden, though the ground was snow covered and the Rhine frozen over. The prince refused to sit down, but Albert insisted that all would be well. Knowing Albert's magical powers, the prince and his courtiers finally acquiesced. No sooner had they taken their seats than things began to happen. The dark clouds vanished, the snow melted away, the ice was unbound in the river, the sun shone bright and warm, the trees were covered with leaves, flowers sprang up everywhere, and larks and nightingales chirped merrily from the boughs. The prince was deeply impressed and gave Albert the desired land. The deal and repast over, the weather returned to its wintry normalcy.

The heroes of alchemy were not only endowed with the power to transmute metals. Other alchemical goals were never neglected. Thus, Artephius, a famous alchemist of the thirteenth century, a contemporary of Albert, and the author of two treatises, one on the philosopher's stone and the other on the prolongation of human life, was reputed to have lived more than a thousand years. He was supposed to be none other than Apollonius of Tyara, a legendary magician described by Philostratus, alleged to have lived a century or so after Christ. Similar fables adorned the life of Alain de Lisle, known in church annals as the "universal doctor." He too was supposed to have mastered the elixir vitae. At the point of death in his fiftieth year he availed himself of his elixir and prolonged his life by sixty more years.

Perhaps most prominent among the early or classical alchemical heroes were Arnold of Villanova and Raymond Lull. Like most alchemists, they were expert and renowned physicians. Arnold, as was habitual with the learned men of the time, had travelled widely and was acquainted with most medical and alchemical authorities of his day. Born in

Villanova, Spain, in 1254 (Milano and Montpellier have also been cited as his birthplaces), he studied medicine and taught at the University of Paris, the fame of which was greatly heightened by his stay. He, too, is reputed to have mastered the elixir of life, and the philosopher's stone. He is the author of a "Treatise on Medicine" written for the benefit of Pope Clement V but never delivered, probably because death intervened. He is also the author of several alchemical treatises, among which "Thesaurus Thesaurorum," "Speculum Alchemiae" and "Perfectum Magisterium" achieved wide fame.

While Arnold enjoys the usual halo of alchemical glory, he does not quite achieve the majestic stature of Lull, his pupil and friend. Waite says of him, "Raymond Lully united the saint and the man of science, the philosopher and the preacher, the apostle and the itinerant lecturer, the dialectitian and the martyr; in his youth he was a courtier and a man of pleasure, in mature age he was an ascetic who had discovered the universal science through a special revelation from God; after his death he was denounced as a heretic, and then narrowly escaped beatification as a saint."

Raymond Lull, Lully or Lullus, was born in 1235 of an illustrious family in Majorca, where his father had received land from John I, King of Aragon, for aid in liberating the Balearic Isles from Mohammedan rule. As often happens in legend, Raymond's mother had been sterile for many years but was finally delivered of her only son in response to fervent prayer. Though the father wished to imbue Raymond with love of learning, the boy's impetuosity and frivolity were too strong to overcome, and he became page to the king in line with his determination to enter upon the career of a soldier. He soon became Master of the Palace and later Seneschal of the Isles to King James II of Aragon. Surrounded by the gay life of the court he yielded to temptation and indulged in promiscuity, much to the disapproval and chagrin of his beautiful, virtuous and wealthy wife, Catherine, whom he otherwise greatly respected and cherished. It happened, however, that he soon fell madly in love with a beautiful and cultured lady named Ambrosia Eleonora de Castello de Gênes, whose husband did not hold any particularly important office at the court. He pursued her with much poetry and implored her with fervent tears, but the lady would have none of his passion. On one occasion he followed the pious lady on her way to Mass and rode his horse into the church, thus causing a scandal. He wrote the lady an apology, spiced with a love sonnet, to which she replied with a letter written in her husband's presence. In it she praises his poetry and his talents, professes her love and respect for him, assures him she will never be his and implores him to employ his talents in better ways. This only served to heighten Raymond's love and hopes. He neglected his official duties and continued to pursue the lady.

According to one version, while wandering one day dejected near Ambrosia's house he spied her bathing in the garden. He promptly wrote a poem to the delicacy of her physical beauty, particularly her breasts. To his great delight his verses provoked an immediate response from Ambrosia, who broke her usual silence by desiring to speak with him. When they met she told Raymond that he was acting in a way wholly unbecoming so wise a man, and that instead of indulging his passions, he should devote himself to higher things worthy of his talents. Since he praised her bosom in noble verses, she exposed it, and Raymond then saw that both her breasts were stricken with cancer and gave off an offensive odor.

"Look on what thou lovest, Raymond Lull," cried Ambrosia with tears in her eyes. "Consider the condition of this wretched body in which thy spirit centers all its hopes and pleasures and then repent of thy useless attempts; mourn for the time which thou hast wasted in persecuting a being whom thou didst fondly deem perfect, but who has so dreadful a blemish! Change this useless and criminal passion into holy love, direct thine affections to the Creator, not to the creature, and in the acquisition of eternal bliss take now the same pains which thou hast hitherto vainly spent to engage me in thy foolish passion."

He left the woman he loved a changed man. He renounced his past sins and levity and swore to follow Ambrosia's advice. He divided all his wealth among his family and the poor, and, after making a few pilgrimages, he lived for ten years in seclusion, devoting all his time to God, theology and alchemy. He also studied Arabic because he decided to devote part of his life to the effort of converting the Mohammedans, then in the process of being driven out of Spain. He was favored by a vision of Christ, as a result of which he was conscious of "a perfect spiritual illumination" and became instantaneously capable of reasoning powerfully on all subjects. At the age of forty he terminated his seclusion and set out in search of learning and to solicit aid in his determination to fight Mohammedanism. He miraculously escaped death when a Mohammedan servant of his sought to assassinate him in order to forestall the menace to his religion. Though wounded, Raymond reluctantly overpowered his would-be slayer and handed him over to the civil authorities.

Lull spent some time in Paris practicing alchemy with Arnold of Villanova. By that time he had written many books and treatises on medicine and alchemy which had brought him universal acclaim. He became known as one of the holiest and wisest men in Christendom. Because he had prepared the philosopher's stone, the great panacea and elixir vitae, he became a great healer and master of perfection. But in the midst of his glory he realized that only part of his goal had been reached, and he therefore undertook a journey to Rome and visited the Pope concerning his second goal in life, the conversion of the Mohammedans. After many difficulties he embarked for Tunis.

There he was warmly greeted by numerous Arabian physicians, alchemists and scientists who had read his books, admired his knowledge and revered his mastery over alchemical mysteries. Raymond took advantage of his prestige and began to preach Christianity with fiery intensity in market places, or wherever he had an audience. For insulting Mohammed in a bazaar he was finally arrested, tried as an infidel and condemned to die. However, a prominent Arabian priest and scholar pleaded for clemency and Raymond was pardoned with the caveat that he never set foot again on Mohammedan territory. He thereupon left Tunis and settled in Naples in 1293, where he continued his experimental studies of alchemy and medicine with great success. By that time he had written and published about five hundred books on a variety of subjects, such as rhetoric, grammar, theology, ethics, law, politics, physics, astronomy, chemistry and medicine. Most of them are still extant, though it is not an easy matter to decide which are authentic and which the customary medieval imitations. The works ascribed to him display great knowledge and a sound critical attitude remarkably free from imaginary embellishments that pervade many other alchemical writings of the period. In 1294 he again repaired to Rome to induce the Pope to send missionaries to Mohammedan lands for the conversion of the infidels. He succeeded in persuading the Pontiff to found colleges where Oriental languages were to be taught, the better to achieve his goal. Since the Pope would do no more than that, Raymond embarked upon a customary medieval tour. He wandered from place to place, debating, learning, lecturing, preaching and confuting heretics. He was respectfully welcomed wherever he went; great honors were showered upon him by lay and church rulers. He sought the aid of many kings in organizing a new crusade, but failed. He visited Africa a second time and converted many Mohammedans, though he was finally arrested and tortured. On being released from prison he set sail for Pisa, which he finally reached after meeting with shipwreck not far from port. After recovery he continued his travels and his past activities.

It is reported by some that in his later life Lull was invited by Edward, the King of England, to supervise the mint. Raymond does refer to his stay in England in his "De Transmutatione Animae Metallorum," which is no conclusive evidence. He is reputed to have transmuted thousands of pounds of gold in the Tower of London. This gold was intended for use in a crusade against the Turks.

But Raymond Lull was dissatisfied because his religious mission was undone. He left London and reached Rome, where he urged upon the Pope some practical reforms aimed at successful combatting of the Moslem menace. He also made an appearance before a church council held at Vienna in 1311. Among other things he proposed the banning of the writings of Averroes, then held in high esteem in all Christian schools. Little seems to have come of his mission and efforts, and after staying two years in Rome, Lull set out again for Africa to convert the Saracens. No sooner did he land at Brigia (or Tunis) in 1314 than he began to preach the gospel of Christ which so enraged the devout Mohammedan populace that they immediately stoned him to death. His body was brought back to his native land by Genoese fishermen and he was buried in a church at Palma, at public expense and with great honors. His tomb became a shrine, working miracles.

These are but small samples of representative accounts of the lives of the earlier students of alchemy. In the absence of novels, fairy tales, theatres or popular journals, the medieval mind merged all such human cravings for romance and literature into tales about its alchemical heroes.

That alchemists were selected as heroes is significant. It shows the great respect for science maintained in those days as compared with our current culture. The scientist was a man of vast learning who mastered great mysteries, who could create the philosopher's stone, make gold out of lead, cure disease and bodily defection and affect rejuvenation. But that era was also an age of deep religious faith and sentiment. Hence all alchemists, as in fact all medieval men of learning, were philosophers and theologians preoccupied with debates and conversions. Little wonder then that popular fancy painted the alchemist as it did. Since this folklore was the work of human beings, love, sin, retribution and penitence were necessarily infused into whatever plot was available.

2. *Typical Alchemists of Later Years*

The roll call of alchemists comprises every famous name of the Middle Ages. From Roger Bacon, the author of *The Mirror of Alchemy, The Admirable Power of Art and Nature in the Production of the Philosopher's Stone*, the novelist and poet Jean de Meung, author of the famous *Roman de la Rose*, *The Remonstrance of Nature to the Wandering Alchemist* and *The Reply of the Alchemyst to Nature*, to Pope John XXII, who had a laboratory at Avignon, learned and reputedly wealthy due to his knowledge of transmutation, alchemy claimed adepts in all walks of life, the best and the most alert men of the time, outstanding as practical, philosophical or romantic figures. It was Pope John XXII, the alchemist, who issued two Bulls against false pretenders in the field, presumably to rid it of unworthy amateurs more interested in gain than truth.

It was during the lifetime of this Pope that Albertus Magnus laid down the following eight commandments in his De Alchimia:

"1. An alchemist must be discreet and reticent; he must be secretive about his findings and knowledge.

2. He must dwell far from human habitation and his home must contain two or three rooms designated as his workshop.

3. He must carefully choose the seasons and hours for his labors.

4. He must be patient, assiduous and perseverent.

5. He must perform and master according to the rules of the art the processes of trituration, sublimation, fixation, calcination, solution, distillation and coagulation.

6. He must avail himself exclusively of glass vessels and glazed pottery.

7. He must be sufficiently affluent to afford all expenses his operations may demand.

8. He must avoid having any relations with princes or sovereigns."

These commandments have earned the unique distinction of being the only set of rules actually put into practice by those to whom they were addressed.

The later apostles of alchemy were more specialized in their professional interests. Also, their tales of heroic deeds underwent a change in stress. Primary place was accorded to the philosopher's stone and chemical labors, rather than religious zeal. True, religion and its social values, wisdom and love of mankind, were never divorced from the alchemical ideal. But with the advance of practical toil in alchemy, the pivotal center became the process of transmutation. The lives of the later alchemists illustrate this shift.

Nicholas Flamel was a Frenchman born about 1330 either in Paris or Pontoise of very poor parents. At an early age he became a public scribe, being proficient in painting, poetry and the sciences. He was industrious and capable and supplied his clientele not only with letters but also with appropriate poems or drawings, or even advice. His reputation grew and his business prospered, so that in a fairly short time he owned many establishments, including bookstands for the sale of copies of famous manuscripts, and conducted as well classes in cultural enlightenment for Parisian nobility and courtiers. He married a widow who seems to have been equally learned, energetic, and possessed of a handsome dowry, and together they built up a large business in cultural articles from which they grew richer year by year.

Flamel had a remarkable dream. An angel appeared to him holding a most impressive antique volume in his hand and addressed him thus:

"Nicholas Flamel, behold this great volume. You understand nothing thereof, nor do many others to whom it will remain unintelligible, but one day you shall discern in its pages what none but yourself will see." Flamel reached out for the book but it vanished, together with its bearer. He retained nonetheless, a good picture of it in his mind and thought of it continuously with great longing and regret. As a result of this vision, Flamel and his wife Pernella, became interested in the hermetic arts and practiced alchemy in a laboratory they built in their home. In spite of his extensive business he found time to pursue the philosopher's stone and the grand elixir with the usual intensity, and his bookstores, offices and home were gathering places for adepts in the art, veritable scientific forums and academies.

Day in, day out, they hoped for the return of the angel or some other harbinger of the grand secret. They had almost abandoned hope when one day Flamel happened to buy an ancient volume for two florins from some itinerant scholar in need of cash. He casually put it aside after admiring its curious appearance. A few hours later he was suddenly struck by its resemblance to the book he had seen in his dream. He rushed over to it and was amazed to find it the very book the angel had held in his hand. The book was most unusual, being made of tree bark covered with Greek texts inscribed with a steel instrument and containing three times seven leaves. Each seventh leaf had beautiful drawings. The first showed a serpent swallowing rods, the second a cross with a serpent crucified, and the third showed fountains in the desert surrounded with serpents. "Upon the first of the leaves was written in capital letters of gold, Abraham the Jew, Priest, Prince, Levite, Astrologer, and Philosopher, to the nation of the Jews dispersed by the wrath of God in France, wisheth health." The wrath of God was invoked upon anyone "that should look in to unfold it, except he were either Priest or Scribe." The text consoled the Jews and advised them to wait patiently for their Messiah. It then proceeded to describe the process of transmutation of metals "to the end that he might help and assist his dispersed people to pay their tribute to the Roman Emperors and some other things not needful here to be repeated."

Flamel did not know whether he was worthy enough to dare read the book, but he finally perused it. He was awestruck with its scholarly exposition of transmutation. The procedure, the vessels and experimental technique were lucidly described. However, of the prima materia there was not one word except an insinuation that it was painted and described symbolically somewhere in the volume. The text was interspersed with numerous diagrams such as Mercury attacked by Saturn, a colorful and strange flower on a tall mountain swaying in the wind amidst leaves of purest gold, fantastic trees growing in streams of milk, a King directing his soldiers to kill infants, collect their blood and pour it into a bathtub in which Sol and Luna were bathing. In addition, many pages of the book were covered with strange hieroglyphics. Other pages were filled with some ancient oriental script.

There was also much in the Latin text Flamel did not understand. The figures and signs of the book he had copied on the walls of his chamber. Many mocked him, but one Anselm, a scholar in physics and alchemy, took a strong interest in the mystery-laden volume. Anselm discussed many sections and processes with Flamel, who never actually let him see the book. Flamel followed his suggestions, devoting twenty-one years of his life to the suggested experiments but all in vain. The incomprehensible text proved an insurmountable obstacle. His good wife Pernella finally advised him to find some learned Rabbi to help him, because the consensus of experts had it that, although it contained much Latin, it was an old Hebrew book kept in the temple of Solomon and removed from there at the time of the destruction of Jerusalem by Titus. It should be noted that the Jews played a major role in the revival of medicine, astronomy and alchemy in Europe during the Dark Ages, though later legislation kept them out of the universities, thus banning them from the sciences they were instrumental in introducing. The learned world attributed to Jews great knowledge of the mysteries of nature, of numerological secrets revealed in the cabala, and extraordinary medical skill as well as magic powers.

There were no Rabbis in Paris then because the Jews had been banished from France some time previously by Philip Augustus. Flamel, therefore, bade adieu to his good, though childless, wife and counsel, and betook himself to Spain in search of a Rabbi, leaving the book of Abraham safely locked at home. Two years he spent in that land of learning until he finally met a converted Jew, a most learned physician and alchemist named Canches, who proved to be the right man. No sooner did he grasp the idea of the book than he was beside himself with joy, abandoned all he held dear and set out with Flamel for Paris to study the ancient tome and its great mysteries. "Our voyage was prosperous and happy," writes Flamel. "He most truly interpreted unto me the greatest part of my figures, in which even to the points and pricks he could decipher great mysteries, which were admirable to me." Their friendship was unfortunately cut short by an adverse fate. When they reached Orleans the Jewish savant died of a sudden illness, in great mental agony at seeing the end of his days when about to cast eyes upon the greatest and most sacred book in alchemy.

Alone and disconsolate Flamel continued his homeward journey and reached his wife Pernella considerably wiser than he had left her. Clinging desperately to each utterance of his Spanish friend, he resumed the

THE ALCHEMISTS IN PURSUIT OF WISDOM 291

study of the book, and after unceasing efforts at experimentation he finally succeeded in making a projection on mercury and obtained pure silver on January 17, 1382. A few months later he converted a large quantity of mercury into purest gold. At last he gained the secret of the philosopher's stone and won the battle of transmutation. The grand elixir was his. He was master over longevity, disease, corruption and imperfection.

In spite of all his pursuits of learning, of practical alchemy and the mysteries of Abraham's ancient text, Flamel grew fabulously prosperous and was counted the richest man in France. Many had it that his great wealth came from his alchemical experimentation. In reality one could not indulge freely in alchemy unless one was immensely rich. Like a true adept, however, he lived a simple life in humble dress and home, without ostentation or luxury.

Long before he and Pernella reached old age they had spent a large part of their fortune on charity. He endowed most liberally a famous church near his home and seven others in the kingdom, built fourteen hospitals and three chapels and contributed funds to many worthy institutions in Paris. He caused alchemical paintings to be placed on numerous monuments, which was attested to by many historians. He published numerous treatises on alchemy, such as *The Philosophic Summary* and *Le Désir Désiré*, which achieved great popularity. Flamel enjoyed great fame in his later years. The most celebrated doctors of Europe came to his humble dwelling to pay him homage, and King Charles VI of France sent a special representative to greet him. He is believed to have died in 1419. His fame and honor left a deep imprint on alchemy, and fables of his vast learning and his nobility of character persisted so long that even in 1816 a house in Paris suspected of having been inhabited by him was bought by a nineteenth century gold seeker who ransacked every wall in the prosaic quest for hidden gold presumably left by the alchemist. All Flamel's wealth was bequeathed to the poor in his testament.

Equally wealthy and philanthropic was George Ripley, the famous English alchemist, author of some twenty-four volumes on the subject, most prominent of which is the one published around 1477 and dedicated to Edward IV, King of England, and entitled, "The Compound of Alchemy; or the Twelve Gates Leading to the Discovery of the Philosopher's Stone." These gates, incidentally, are calcination, solution, separation, conjunction, putrefaction, congelation, cibation, sublimation, fermentation, exaltation, multiplication and projection. Ripley was the canon of Bridlington and considered one of the most learned men in England of his day. He spent twenty years traveling on the continent, particularly in Italy, and was a friend and counsel of Pope Innocent VIII and master of ceremonies of the papal household. He spent the last years of his life in England, was extremely wealthy and donated sums of money thought fantastic in those days for religious purposes, among them an annual sum of one hundred thousand pounds sterling to the orders of The Knights of Malta and of Rhodes to fight the Turks.

A pupil of Ripley was Thomas Norton of Bristol, author of "Ordinall of Alchemy." After a long search, Norton spent forty days with the famous master, was initiated into the fullest mysteries and was rewarded with the "disclosure of the bonds of nature." Ripley "refused to instruct him in the process from the white to the red powder, lest the divine gift should be misused in a moment of passion." By hard work and dexterity Morton mastered that process himself. Twice on the eve of success he met with tragic setbacks. Once his tincture just about to be perfected, was stolen by his servant, and the second time the final elixir was stolen by the wife of the Mayor of Bristol, who subsequently grew in wealth and endowed many churches and colleges.

More typical of alchemical legends is the story of Thomas Dalton, who lived around 1450, as abbot in Gloucestershire. Suspected of possessing the philosopher's stone, he was taken by Squire Thomas Herbert from his abbey and brought before King Edward. Another of the king's squires testified upon oath that Dalton had made him a thousand pounds of good gold in less than twelve hours. Dalton then informed the king that he had destroyed the transmuting powder because it invariably proved a harbinger of evil to its owners. He had not made it himself but had obtained it from an adept. The King ordered his release and sent him home with travel expenses, but he was waylaid by Thomas Herbert, his original accuser, imprisoned in the castle by Gloucester and ordered to prepare the philosopher's stone.

For four years he persisted in refusing to betray his master's instructions. He was finally taken to be beheaded, preferring execution to divulging the secret to princes or strangers whose devotion to alchemy was doubtful. Herbert, his tormentor, had him released however, at the eleventh hour, weeping freely at the display of loyalty and his own failure.

Informative are the life and labors of Bernard of Treviso, or the Good Trevison. Born of wealthy Italian nobility in 1406 at Padua or Treviso, he devoted himself to the study of alchemy from the early age of fourteen to the day of his death at eighty-five. At fourteen a copy of Rhasis fell into his hands. The boy was so fascinated with the beauty and wisdom of its contents that with the book before him he spent the next four years of his life in a laboratory he built himself in his father's castle. These experiments cost him eight hundred crowns. He then spent two years more studying the works of Geber, at which task he squandered two thousand crowns. The end of that period found him an eager and

THE ALCHEMISTS IN PURSUIT OF WISDOM 293

mature student of alchemy ready to master transmutation. He therefore set out to find the philosopher's stone.

Like all esoteric sects, the alchemists too had a strong group loyalty, knew one another within accessible regions, enjoyed each other's company and held long discussions over questions of little concern to the uninitiated. It thus happened that Bernard's spacious home became the meeting ground of all alchemists in the neighborhood. The only difference between alchemists and other sects was that while other sects argued incessantly, the alchemists argued between experiments, so that some work ultimately was accomplished.

Among his friends there was a Franciscan monk with whom Bernard became especially intimate and whom he selected as his full time collaborator. At first they went after the universal alkahest which they thought to be the "rectified spirits of urine." They worked with alcohol, which they redistilled numerous times "till they could not find glasses strong enough to hold it." They next began work on human feces, believing that it must possess some health sustaining compounds. They investigated a variety of subjects in search of the transmuting tincture. Twelve years passed and the two friends still labored untiringly at their crucibles, alembics and furnaces, day and night; their recreation consisting of discussions with the crowd of alchemists that always filled the house.

Besides gaining a reputation as a learned, skilful and energetic alchemist, Bernard became known as well as the "good Trevison" because of the generosity he showed toward needy scholars in the art. He supported a whole retinue of traveling companions who chose his castle for a prolonged stay. His house was a university, dormitory, hostel and clubhouse, all in one.

When his friend the monk died, Bernard acquired a new collaborator, a magistrate of the city of Treviso, an ardent seeker after alchemical knowledge. Their first scientific feat was the isolation and purification of common salt from seawater. They believed such salt to possess great transmuting powers, since so many wonderful things happen in the sea, where life is sustained and gold is formed. Bernard bought a house on the shores of the Baltic Sea, built himself a laboratory and set out to crystallize salt and study its reactions and properties. Finding no alteration in the properties of the salt after repeated crystallizations, they despaired of success and cast about for another approach.

These chemical studies had kept Bernard at his vessels and furnaces until he reached the age of forty-six, and he decided to visit various laboratories in Germany, England, France, Spain, Italy, Arabia, Egypt and other lands. He traveled with a retinue of dependents and hangers-on whom he supported. When the sage he visited was in economic straits, Bernard handsomely replenished his empty coffers and spoke words of encouragement to those who were despondent. When he found that some alchemist happened to be engaged in an interesting problem, Bernard would remain, assist in the experiments and await the outcome.

He settled down in one locality in France for eight years to investigate the chemical properties of eggs in the hope of discovering the elixir there. In collaboration with another monk, Maître Geofroi de Lemorier, who had mastered a hitherto unknown process, he boiled two thousand eggs, separated the shells, whites of egg and yolks, and studied the composition of each. The shells were calcined in the fire, the yolks and albumin were putrified in horse manure, and the resulting mixture distilled thirty times. They thus obtained a white and red liquid but remained dissatisfied with their value as precursors of the stone.

He then worked with copperas, a sulphate of iron and vinegar, aided by a sage who was also a great theologian. They calcined a sulphate for three months and then placed the product in vinegar previously eight times distilled. This mixture was then distilled in an alembic fifteen times daily for a year. The experiment would have been continued had not Bernard been stricken with a high fever for fourteen months. After recovery he sought out the company of a famous alchemist in Germany named Master Henry of Vienna, who in private life was confessor to the Emperor Frederik III. Since he was reputed to have found the philosopher's stone, Bernard set out to pay him a visit, accompanied, of course, by his dependents. Having arrived in Vienna, Bernard made a sumptuous feast in honor of Master Henry to which were invited all the adepts of the capital.

At the banquet Bernard and Henry met and were much taken with each other, finding they not only shared many interests in common, but also possessed kindred temperaments. They vowed each other eternal friendship and decided to collaborate in experiments on transmutation. All those present contributed gold to that cause, the total collected amounting to a considerable sum. Bernard and Henry worked the next few months side by side, but were unsuccessful. The crucibles were not strong enough, they explained.

The disappointment felt by Bernard was so acute that he decided to lay off transmutation for a time. For exactly two months he kept his promise, to the great delight of his family, but he realized at the end of that period that it was an impossibility, and he resumed his labors with greater fervor. He continued his travels and visited Greece, Palestine, Arabia, Persia and England, a peregrination which lasted four years. He visited many convents where he experimented with monks of reputation in the science. These travels and experiments cost him about thirteen thousand crowns, which he raised by selling one cherished heritage after another. He then returned to his estate only to find that his family, which had always looked upon him as a madman and spendthrift, had managed to deprive him of his rapidly dwindling wealth and his title to the remaining estates. These relatives made claims, and obtained writs which made him practically a pauper, at least until one or two of said relatives died. He retired to the island of Rhodes to meditate and write but met a monk there who had equally long experience in alchemical labors. They were both poor and could not afford to build a laboratory, and so they satisfied their interests by reading and discussion.

After a stay of a year or two on the island, Bernard met a merchant who had known his family and who advanced him eight thousand florins on the security of the lands he might some day inherit. He returned to alchemy with great fervor, not only because he had felt the misery of being kept away from it for lack of funds, but because he was getting old and felt impelled to hurry. For three years it is reported he stayed in his laboratory, never undressing, combing his beard or resting any more than was imperative. Still he was unsuccessful, and as usual decided that there must be some step in the process he had not quite mastered or followed with required precision, some mystery he had not unravelled with the necessary perfection. For a few years they withdrew from experimentation and reread all the valuable books on transmutation. He finally conquered the secret of transmutation by following those sayings of the philosophers which attained universal acceptance. The last few years of his life were spent in quiet enjoyment of the greatest reward life could offer: possession of the philosopher's stone and its use in several transmutations. Bernard died in 1490 at the age of eighty-three and left posterity many books and a saintly reputation. He was the author of the *Natural History of Metals, Verbum Dimissum, De Natura Ovi*, and many others. In his last book he concludes that the secret of philosophy was contentment with one's lot because unattainable goals may be too painful and disappointing. His own failure he explained away with the usual rationalizations of deluded adepts.

One did not, however, have to be a count and as wealthy as Bernard of Treviso to be an ardent devotee of alchemy. The lure of wisdom, like the call of the arts, recognized no barriers of wealth, race or nation. It was not even completely selective with regard to temperament and honesty. Just as it appealed to rich and poor, noble and commoner, it also beckoned to some honest and truly altruistic individuals, as well as to greedy and deceitful ones. The latter were, however, few in number.

A famed authority in alchemy is one known as Trithemius, born near Treves in 1462. He is particularly noted as the first writer to mention the story of Faust and the devil. Like many another alchemist, he was suspected of magic and gained fame as a miracle worker, sorcerer and ruler over the arcane and dark forces of nature. Unlike Bernard, he was a poor boy, the son of a vine grower who died when the boy was seven, bidding his wife take good care of their child. This the mother did not do. She remarried and permitted the step-father to treat the boy miserably. Abused and half starved, he was made to labor in the vineyards without obtaining the very rudiments of an education. When he reached his early teens the desire for an education grew so strong in him that he stayed up nights learning the alphabet, Latin and Greek. In this laudable effort he was aided by a kind neighbor, but finally ran away from home after obtaining some money which his father had willed him, and settled at Treves. There he devoted his time exclusively to preparation for the University. He then decided to pay a visit to his mother, but was overtaken by a heavy snowstorm near Spannheim and sought refuge in a neighboring monastery, where he had to remain several days until the storm subsided. Trithemius was so pleased with the quiet of the monastery that he renounced the world and joined the order. He was so liked and respected that he was unanimously elected abbot after two years.

He reorganized the chaotic affairs of the monastery and made the monks do useful work such as copying valuable ancient and contemporary manuscripts. In this manner he acquired an amazing collection of works in history, theology, philosophy and science famous throughout Europe. He built himself a laboratory and became addicted to alchemy and magic, on which subjects he wrote several books. He is claimed to have achieved transmutation and mastered cabalistic lore and impenetrable secrets of numerology.

A fair description of sixteenth century alchemy is given in the autobiography of the French alchemist Denis Zachaire, a scion of a noble family of Guyenne, where he was born in the year 1510. He was sent to the university of Bordeaux under the care of a tutor who happened to be a seeker of the grand elixir and a dreamer after transmutation. Under the name of Denis Zachaire, the author of *Opusculum Chimicum* relates as follows: "I received from home the sum of two hundred crowns for the expenses of myself and master; but before the end of the year, all our money went away in the smoke of our furnaces. My master, at the same time, died of a fever, brought on by the parching heat of our laboratory, from which he seldom or never stirred, and which was scarcely less hot than the arsenal of Venice. His death was the more unfortunate for me, as my parents took the opportunity of reducing my allowance, and sending me only sufficient for my board and lodging, instead of the sum I required to continue my operations in alchymy.

"To meet this difficulty I returned home at the age of twenty-five, and mortgaged part of my property for four hundred crowns. This sum was necessary to perform an operation of the science, which had been communicated to me by an Italian at Toulouse, and which, as he said, had proved its efficacy. I retained this man in my service, that we might see the end of my experiment. I then, by means of strong distillations, tried to calcinate gold and silver; but all my labour was in vain. The weight of the gold I drew out of my furnace was diminished by one-half since I put it in, and my four hundred crowns were very soon reduced to two hundred and thirty. I gave twenty of these to my Italian, in order that he might travel to Milan, where the author of the receipt resided, and ask him the explanation of some passages which we thought obscure. I remained at Toulouse all the winter, in the hope of his return; but I might have remained there till this day if I had waited for him, for I never saw his face again.

"In the succeeding summer there was a great plague, which forced me to quit the town. I did not, however, lose sight of my work. I went to Cahors, where I remained six months, and made the acquaintance of an old man, who was commonly known to the people as 'the Philosopher': a name which, in country places, is often bestowed upon people whose only merit is, that they are less ignorant than their neighbors. I showed him my collection of alchymical receipts, and asked his opinion upon them. He picked out ten or twelve of them, merely saying that they were better than the others. When the plague ceased, I returned to Toulouse, and recommenced my experiments in search of the stone. I worked to such effect that my four hundred crowns were reduced to one hundred and seventy.

"That I might continue my work on a safer method, I made acquaintance, in 1537, with a certain Abbé, who resided in the neighborhood. He was smitten with the same mania as myself, and told me that one of his friends, who had followed to Rome in retinue of the Cardinal d'Armagnac, had sent him from that city a new receipt, which could not fail to transmute iron and copper, but which would cost two hundred crowns. I provided half this money, and the Abbé the rest; and we began to operate at our joint expense. As we required spirits of wine for our experiment, I bought a ton of excellent vin de Gaillac. I extracted the spirit, and rectified it several times. We took a quantity of this, into which we put four marks of silver, and one of gold, that had been undergoing the process of calcination for a month. We put this mixture cleverly into a sort of horn-shaped vessel, with another to serve as a retort; and placed the whole apparatus upon our furnace, to produce congelation. This experiment lasted a year; but, not to remain idle, we amused ourselves with many other less important operations. We drew quite as much profit from these as from our great work.

"The whole of the year 1537 passed over without producing any change whatever; in fact, we might have waited till doomsday for the congelation of our spirits of wine. However, we made a projection with it upon some heated quicksilver; but all was in vain. Judge of our chagrin, especially of that of the Abbé, who had already boasted to all the monks of his monastery, that they had only to bring the large pump which stood in the corner of the cloister, and he would convert it into gold; but this ill luck did not prevent us from persevering. I once more mortgaged my paternal lands for four hundred crowns, the whole of which I determined to devote to a renewal of my search for the great secret. The Abbé contributed the same sum; and with these eight hundred crowns, I proceeded to Paris, a city more abounding with alchymists than any other in the world, resolved never to leave it until I had either found the philosopher's stone, or spent all my money. This journey gave the greatest offense to all my relations and friends, who, imagining that I was fitted to be a great lawyer, were anxious that I should establish myself in that profession. For the sake of quietness, I pretended, that such was my object.

"After travelling for fifteen days, I arrived in Paris, on the ninth of January 1539. I remained for a month, almost unknown, but I had no sooner begun to frequent the amateurs of science, and visited the shops of the furnace-makers, than I had the acquaintance of more than a hundred operative alchymists, each of whom had a different theory and a different mode of working. Some of them preferred cementation; others sought the universal alkahest, or dissolvent; and some of them boasted the great efficacy of the essence of emery. Some of them endeavored to extract mercury from other metals to fix it afterwards; and, in order that each of us should be thoroughly acquainted with the proceedings of the others, we agreed to meet somewhere every night, and report progress. We met sometimes at the house of one, and sometimes in the garret of another; not only on week days, but on Sundays, and the great festivals of the Church.

"'Ah!' one used to say, 'if I had the means of recommencing this experiment, I should do something.' 'Yes,' said another, 'if my crucible had not cracked, I should have succeeded before now'; while a third exclaimed with a sigh, 'if I had but had a round copper vessel of sufficient strength, I would have fixed mercury with silver.' There was not one among them who had not some excuse for his failures; but I was deaf to all their speeches. I did not want to part with my money to any of them, remembering how often I had been the dupe of such promises.

"A Greek at last presented himself; and with him I worked a long time uselessly upon nails, made of cinnabar, or vermillion. I was also acquainted with a foreign gentleman newly arrived in Paris; and often accompanied him to the shops of goldsmiths, to sell pieces of gold and silver, the produce, as he said, of his experiments. I stuck closely to him for a long time, in the hope that he would impart his secret. He refused for a long time, but acceded, at last, on my earnest entreaty, and I found that it was nothing more than an ingenious trick. I did not fail to inform my friend the Abbé, whom I had left at Toulouse, of all my adventures; and sent him, among other matters, a relation of the trick by which this gentleman pretended to turn lead into gold. The Abbé still imagined that I should succeed at last, and advised me to remain another year in Paris where I had made so good a beginning. I remained there three years; but notwithstanding all my efforts, I had no more success than I had had elsewhere.

"I had just got to the end of my money, when I received a letter from the Abbé, telling me to leave everything, and join him immediately at Toulouse. I went accordingly, and found that he had received letters from the King of Navarre (grandfather of Henry IV). This Prince was a great lover of philosophy, full of curiosity, and had written to the Abbé, that I should visit him at Pau; and that he would give me three or four thousand crowns, if I would communicate the secret I had learned from the foreign gentleman. The Abbé's ears were so tickled with the four thousand crowns, that he let me have no peace, night or day, until he had fairly seen me on the road to Pau. I arrived at that place in the month of May 1542. I worked away, and succeeded, according to the receipt I had obtained. When I had finished, to the satisfaction of the King, he gave me the reward I had expected. Although he was willing enough to do me further service, he was dissuaded from it by the lords of his court; even by many of those who had been most anxious that I should come. He sent me then about my business, with many thanks; saying, that if there were anything in his kingdom which he could give me—such as the produce of confiscations, or the like—he should be most happy. I thought I might stay long enough for these prospective confiscations, and never get them at last; and I therefore determined to go back to my friend, the Abbé.

"I learned, that on the road between Pau and Toulouse, there resided a monk, who was very skilful in all matters of natural philosophy. On my return I paid him a visit. He pitied me very much, and advised me, with much warmth and kindness of expression, not to amuse myself any longer with such experiments as these, which were all false and sophistical; but that I should read the good books of the old philosophers, where I might not only find the true matter of the science of alchymy, but learn also the exact order of operation which ought to be followed. I very much approved of this wise advice; but, before I acted upon it, I went back to my Abbé of Toulouse, to give him an account of the eight hundred crowns, which we had in common; and, at the same time, share with him such reward as I had received from the King of Navarre. If he were little satisfied with the relation of my adventures since our first separation, he appeared still less satisfied when I told him I had formed a resolution to renounce the search for the philosopher's stone. The reason was, that he thought me a good artist. Of our eight hundred crowns, there remained but one hundred and seventy-six. When I quitted the Abbé, I went to my own house, with the intention of remaining there till I had read all the philosophers, and of then proceeding to Paris.

"I arrived in Paris on the day after All Saints, of the year 1546, and devoted another year to the assiduous study of great authors. Among others, the 'Turba Philosophorum' of the 'Good Travison,' 'The Remonstrance of Nature to the Wandering Alchymist,' by Jean de Meung; and several others of the best books; but, as I had no right principles, I did not well know what course to follow.

"At last I left my solitude; not to see my former acquaintances, the adepts and operators, but to frequent the society of true philosophers. Among them I fell into still greater uncertainties; being in fact, completely bewildered by the variety of operations which they showed me. Spurred on, nevertheless, by a sort of frenzy of inspiration, I threw myself into the works of Raymond Lulli and of Arnold de Villeneuve. The reading of these, and the reflections I made upon them, occupied me for another year, when I finally determined on the course I should adopt. I was obliged to wait, however, until I had mortgaged another very considerable portion of my patrimony. This business was not settled until the beginning of Lent, 1549, when I commenced my operations. I laid in a stock of all that was necessary, and began to work the day after Easter. It was not, however, without some disquietude and opposition from my friends who came about me; one asking me what I was going to do, and whether I had not already spent money enough upon such follies. Another assured me that, if I bought so much charcoal, I should strengthen the suspicion already existing, that I was a coiner of base money. Another advised me to purchase some place in the magistracy, I was already a Doctor of Laws. My relations spoke in terms still more annoying to me, and even threatened that, if I continued to make such a fool of myself, they would send a posse of police-officers into my house, and break all my furnaces and crucibles into atoms. I was wearied almost to death by this continued persecution; but I found comfort in my work and in the progress of my experiment, to which I was very attentive, and which went on bravely from day to day. About this time, there was a dreadful plague in Paris, which interrupted all intercourse between man and man, and left me as much to myself as I could desire. I soon had the satisfaction to remark the progress and succession of the three colours which, according to the philosophers, always prognosticate the approaching perfection of the work. I observed them distinctly, one after the other; and next year, being Easter Sunday, 1550, I made the great trial. Some common quicksilver, which I put in a small crucible on the fire, was, in less than an hour, converted into very good gold. You may judge how great was my joy, but I took care not to boast of it. I returned thanks to God for the favour he had shown me, and prayed that I might only be permitted to make such use of it as would rebound to His Glory.

"On the following day I went towards Toulouse to find the Abbé, in accordance with a mutual promise that we should communicate our discoveries to each other. On my way, I called in to see the sage monk who had assisted me with his counsels; but I had the sorrow to learn that they were both dead. After this I would not return to my home, but retired to another place, to await one of my relations whom I had left in charge of my estate. I gave him orders to sell all that belonged to me, as well movable as immovable—to pay my debts with the proceeds, and divide all the rest among those in any way related to me who might stand in need of it, in order that they might enjoy some share of the good fortune which had befallen me. There was a great deal of talk in the neighborhood about my precipitate retreat; the wisest of my acquaintance imagining that, broken down and ruined by my mad expenses, I sold my little remaining property that I might go and hide my shame in distant countries.

"My relative already spoken of rejoined me on the first of July, after having performed all the business I had entrusted him with. We took our departure together, to seek a land of liberty. We first returned to Lausanne, in Switzerland, when, after remaining there for some time, we resolved to pass the remainder of our days in some of the most celebrated cities of Germany, living quietly and without splendour."

Thus runs the statement of one who claimed to have mastered "the grand work." From his account one can obtain an intimate view of alchemical thought, motivation and life. The final fate of Denis Zachaire has a rather tragic anti-climax. After he had definitely mastered transmutation, Zachaire realized the power he possessed. He prayed "God enlighten me and through His Holy Spirit, grant me the power to use it to Your praise and Glory." But he soon forgot that prayer and abandoned himself to a life of pleasure and passion, though in late middle age. He finally fell in love with a beautiful young girl with whom he settled in Cologne in 1556. Here tragedy overtook him. The young cousin he mentions who had been with him all the time, served him not only as companion and secretary, but also as apprentice. Not being a true scholar, he had planned to steal the secret from Zachaire and reap its glory. One night when Zachaire lay drunk after one of his usual evenings of dissipation, his cousin killed him and escaped with his books and manuscripts as well as his wife, with whom he had been clandestinely intimate for some time. Zachaire's death caused a great stir in Germany, was commemorated in a poem by the laureate of the court of Rudolph II, but the murderer and his attractive accomplice were never apprehended.

The material in the above quotation is based entirely on the elegy of the court poet, de Delle, and is no doubt more drama than history. The entire account has recently been put in a rather unique light by the chemist and scholar, T. L. Davis, who suggests that the book attributed to Zachaire is, in reality, a satire by an unknown author on alchemy and its delusive goals. "Indeed," says Davis, "he seems (the unknown author) to have done for alchemy what Cervantes and Don Quixote did for knight errantry." (T. L. Davis, "The Autobiography of Denis Zachaire: An Account of an Alchemist's Life in the Sixteenth Century." Isis 8, 287, 1926). However, this interpretation seems somewhat extreme. It was as common for alchemists to despair of success as it is for modern teachers to belittle the value of education and deplore their choice of the profession, neither of which attitudes is indicative of true doubt or disbelief. Similarly, satires on physicians or alchemists do not speak for genuine skepticism of the sciences involved.

Interesting and spectacular is the story of Doctor John Dee and Edward Kelly. Dr. Dee was one of the most learned men of his times and an admirable person. Born in London in 1527, he was educated at the University of Cambridge, where he distinguished himself as a capable and diligent scholar. His major interests lay in mathematics, alchemy and astrology. Suspected of sorcery and magic, he left Cambridge and resumed his studies at the University of Louvain, where he engaged in alchemical research and achieved some fame. He returned to England at the age of twenty-four, and, through the influence of a friend, was received at the court of King Edward VI, who rewarded him for his erudition with an annual pension of one hundred crowns. He settled in London as a practicing astrologer, was suspected of heresy during the reign of Queen Mary, spent a few years in prison, though acquitted of a charge of attempting to murder the queen, and was finally liberated in 1555. He subsequently became astrologer and advisor to Queen Elizabeth, who held him in high esteem.

Like most astrologers and astronomers, he practiced alchemy on a large scale, even as did Newton or Tycho Brahe. His assistant was one Edward Kelly, a sincere devotee of alchemy, but a person possessed of an adventurous imagination and enterprising courage. Kelly had been a notary at Lancaster or London, a great student of old English, Welsh

THE ALCHEMISTS IN PURSUIT OF WISDOM 303

and Anglo-Saxon, as well as a collector and translator of ancient documents. It seems that Kelly, whose real name was Talbot, went in for forging old deeds, the language of which he knew so well. He was caught and punished and had his ears cut off as a lesson to others. He wore a skull cap with side flaps to cover his mutilation, which gave him an intriguing appearance.

He quit his native village and sought a hiding place in Wales. At the inn where he stayed an old manuscript was submitted to him for identification. He recognized in it an old alchemical treatise on transmutation, since he had done some alchemical experimentation on the side. He learned from the natives that the old document was discovered in a tomb of a bishop who had been a great adept. Because of the high reputation this bishop had gained in that occult science and the belief that he had mastered transmutation and amassed great quantities of gold, his tomb was raided. The manuscript and two ivory bottles were all that was found in it. One of the bottles broke and proved to contain a heavy red powder, most of which was lost. The other bottle contained a white one. Kelly gladly bought the manuscript and the powders and betook himself to London to see the famous Dr. Dee, who declared the text a most valuable though veiled revelation in the science of transmutation, and the two powders nothing else but the philosopher's stone. Kelly became Dee's assistant and pupil, and the two set to work transmuting base metals.

Dr. Dee happened to have been interested in spiritualism for some time, and Kelly aided him by holding discourses with ghosts. He became in fact the intermediary between the invisible beings and the enthusiastic Dr. Dee. The two went after the occult on a large scale, employed crystal gazing and experimented with numerous forms of necromancy. Dr. Dee, with the help of Kelly, held regular sessions with a special angel, Urich.

The fame of Dr. Dee had spread to the far corners of the continent. For example, a wealthy Polish nobleman named Laski, Count Palatine of Siratz and Sendomir, came to England for the purpose of visiting the court of Queen Elizabeth. He was received with great honors, and the Earl of Leicester was assigned to guide him through the impressive sights of the land. Since the Count Palatine proved to be a man of great erudition and an admirer of alchemy, he was taken to Cambridge and Oxford. How great was his disappointment when he learned that Dr. Dee was not connected with either University! Where he came from Dee represented England's cultural glory. Needless to say, a meeting between the famous doctor and his admirer was promptly arranged; the two met and held a most learned conversation, at the termination of which the visitor was invited to dine at the alchemist's home. But it seems that Dr. Dee was quite poor because he applied to the crown for financial aid wherewith to entertain his noble guest. His wishes were complied with and Queen Elizabeth gave him twenty pounds.

Count Laski and Dr. Dee became greatly enamored of each other; the count not only showed the greatest respect for Dr. Dee's astrological and alchemical knowledge and achievements, but also for his and Kelly's experiments in magic and successful mastery of spirits and prognostications. He invited them both to pursue their experiments in his castle in Poland, promised them full freedom and all necessary expenditures. He had been a dabbler in alchemy himself and had a well equipped laboratory. Being a lover of science, he wished, like all rulers of the time, to have men of learning connected with his court. Dr. Dee and Kelly were so taken with the charm and wisdom of the Polish nobleman that they accepted his offer, and gathering their belongings as well as respective families, they travelled for four months until they finally reached the Count's palace.

Under the Count's supervision and with his assistance, they worked away at transmutations and related experiments for several years. As luck would have it, the Count's prodigal habits led him to sell most of his estates and face serious financial difficulties. He therefore advised his scholars to transfer to Prague, the seat of the Emperor Rudolph II, the patron of Tycho Brahe and Kepler, the friend of alchemists and astrologers and of all culture and science, who he hoped might take an interest in them.

The available accounts of Kelly and Dee are so divergent as to be irreconcilable in many details. It is difficult if not impossible, to decide upon the truth. Much of the material must be regarded as folklore, as an expression of prevailing attitudes, rather than history.

It seems that, to impress the Emperor, Kelly decided to make use of his red powder, perform a few projections with it and effect transmutations. He distributed the formed gold as souvenirs and became the most celebrated alchemist in the Empire. Kelly and Dr. Dee performed a transmutation in the presence of many scientists at the house of Dr. Hayeck, the Emperor's physician.

Rudolph II was raised in Spain at the court of Philip II and from early boyhood showed scientific curiosity and aptitude. After becoming emperor he settled in Prague and devoted all his time to astrology and alchemy rather than government and war, entrusting such tasks to ministers. His court teemed with astrologers and alchemists. Among the latter were Dierbach, Jean Franck, Sebald Schweitzer, Martin Rutzke, Sendivogius and the court poet, Mardock de Delle. It was Rudolph's custom to invite all alchemists to his court and test their skill. If they impressed him favorably and passed the tests, they received gifts and titles and remained to follow their calling. The tests were witnessed by all the men of the court, most of them sound and reliable observers. Yet all asserted on several occasions that transmutation had been definitely effected and obtained samples of the transmuted gold.

According to some accounts, Dr. Dee and Kelly visited many other courts. Their fame spread throughout Europe and reached England, to the delight of Queen Elizabeth. Rudolph II was so impressed with Kelly's erudition that he made him court alchemist and bestowed upon him the coveted title of Marshal of Bohemia. While attached to his court Kelly and Dee seem to have visited King Stephen of Poland on several occasions and served him in many capacities. They also collaborated with Marshal de Rosenberg in some alchemical experiments. This dignitary was extremely wealthy and supported the two alchemists in the hope of discovering the elixir of life, because he was more interested in the immediate benefits of rejuvenescence than perfection of gold. It seems the three worked together for four years and would have spent more time at this absorbing problem had not a quarrel arisen between Dee and Kelly.

Contact with royalty was practically always loaded with hazards to alchemists, if they were unwise enough to disregard the warning of Albertus Magnus. Like many another alchemist, Kelly was imprisoned, it is claimed, because of his refusal to divulge the secret of preparing fantastic amounts of gold for the imperial treasury. Here the accounts are somewhat unclear, but it seems that he finally demanded the right to prepare a substantial amount of powder if he was to perform a transmutation. He was granted his liberty for that purpose, and in collaboration with Dr. Dee toiled frantically but without success. Exasperated by recurrent failures he happened to kill George Henbler, the Emperor's messenger assigned to guard him, and was imprisoned a second time and put in chains.

It is difficult to state how long his incarceration lasted, but it was during that interval that he wrote, in 1596, his treatise entitled *The Stone of the Philosophers*, dedicated to Emperor Rudolph II. Kelly's book, as we have seen, is an excellent summary of the status and the philosophy of alchemy in his day, belying statements that he was an ignoramus and a charlatan. Contrary to Kelly's hopes, the book brought no reprieve. Dr. Dee in the meantime had managed to get Queen Elizabeth sufficiently interested to intercede with the Emperor on Kelly's behalf and demand his liberation as an English subject. This demand was refused, and Kelly lingered on in jail. In 1597 some friends or admirers aided him in an attempt to escape, which, however, ended tragically. While lowering himself by a rope from the window of the fortress that was his jail, Kelly fell from a considerable height and died.

While Kelly was still a prisoner of the Emperor, Dr. Dee returned to London in great splendor, with coaches, retinue and guard. He went straight to Queen Elizabeth's palace and was assured of Her Majesty's indulgence and patronage. He devoted himself to alchemy, but it seems that after a few years he was reduced to poverty and applied to the Queen for aid, which was granted for a period of several years. Finally a commission was appointed to "inquire into his circumstances." He was later granted a pension by the Queen, which he drew until the accession of James I, who cancelled it. He was also made Chancellor of St. Paul's Cathedral and in 1595 warden of the College of Manchester, in which city he died in 1608.

3. The International Propagandists

The folklore of alchemy is not without its apostolic heroes who wander about the world preaching its truths and using the methods of direct evidence to convert the skeptics and cynics. Such a man was Sethon or Sethonius, also known as Scotus. He was presumably a Scottish gentleman who lived on the eastern coast of Scotland in a town named Seatown, whence his name. In the annals of alchemy his name is The Cosmopolite, because of his extensive travels and international activities on behalf of alchemy.

The story has it that in 1601 a Dutch captain, Jacob, or James Haussen and his crew met with shipwreck on the eastern coast of Scotland and were saved from drowning by Sethon, who, on seeing their ship founder, set out in a rowboat and rescued the men in the nick of time. He put them up in his home and became particularly friendly with Captain Haussen. The Scotsman was a practitioner in alchemy, but did not let it be known at the time. His guests soon left him, and Sethon subsequently received many warm letters from Haussen, begging him to pay a return visit to Holland, where he, Haussen, wished to reciprocate the kindness shown him. Sethon had decided to travel anyway for the sake of his alchemy and made Holland his first stop. There he visited his friend. He was so pleased with the hospitality extended him that he decided to make a projection and permit his friend to witness a transmutation. The news of that mysterious performance soon spread because the captain was given the considerable lump of converted gold to have and display. Thus his fame preceded him to Amsterdam and Rotterdam, where he also made some spectacular projections.

He next travelled through Italy and Switzerland. A famous professor of medicine at the Swiss University of Fribourg, Wolfgang Dienheim, describes in his book, *De Minerali Medicina*, how, returning from Rome to Germany in 1602, he found himself side by side with "one singularly spiritual in appearance, tall, thin, with face full of color, of sanguine temperament, and having a brown beard cut in the style of France. He was dressed in black satin and had only one servant who was readily distinguishable by his red hair and red beard. This man was Alexander Sethonius." When they finally arrived at Basel, Sethonius said to him, "You will recall that during our journey you have attacked alchemy and the alchemists. You will recall as well that I promised to answer not by demonstrations (arguments) but by a philosophic act. I am expecting someone else whom I wish to convince at the same time because it is my task to silence all opposition to this art and terminate all doubt." The other personage was a well-known Swiss physician, Jacob Zwinger, professor of medicine at Basel. Crucibles and furnaces were prepared as well as all other necessary materials and apparatus. Sethonius touched nothing but conversed amicably with the two learned men. He later dictated various procedures which they faithfully executed. The two skeptics were stupefied to find the lead converted into gold at the end of the decoction. But Sethonius said: "Now, gentlemen, where are your pedantries; you have observed the factual truth and she is more powerful than anything else in the world, yea, even your sophistry." He divided the gold between the two humiliated but enlightened converts. The author speaks bitterly of those who still dare question the truth of transmutation after what he had seen with his own eyes and which he is willing to affirm under oath and proclaim to the world.

We then find Sethonius in Germany. To a well-known goldsmith of Strassbourg named Gustenhover appeared a man who gave his name as Hirschborgen (in reality it was Sethonius) and who asked for permission to work in his shop. This granted, the stranger gave the goldsmith a red powder, the meaning and value of which he taught him in the course of his stay.

Gustenhover rejoiced in the gift and performed a few projections, knowledge of which spread through the city. The town council appointed a committee to investigate the matter. This committee of three leading citizens witnessed several transformations, vouched for their truth and described the amount and degree of purity of the gold obtained. The news then reached Rudolph II, the Hermes of Germany, whose interests in newcomers in alchemy never flagged. He sent a delegation to Strassbourg to bring the alchemist to his court. Gustenhover performed his transmutation most successfully before Rudolph II, who was sufficiently impressed to demand of him the secret of preparing the powder. In vain did the poor goldsmith relate how he obtained it. Rudolph, driven frantic by his own failures, treated this amateur alchemist, who was not a true philosopher but a mere "puffer," as he did Kelly. He threw him into prison until he was ready to reveal his secret. Gustenhover attempted an unsuccessful escape and spent the rest of his days chained to a wall of Rudolph's dungeon. Sethon, also known as the Cosmopolite, continued his missionary work, although it led in some cases to tragic consequences. But then what is one life or even several when it comes to the need for truth's defense? He appears next at Frankfort on the Main, where he made the acquaintance of a merchant to whom he gave some red powder as a parting gift and instructed him in its use. The merchant performed several successful projections but apparently without tragic involvements.

At Cologne Sethonius had his redheaded servant wander about town, checking on names and reputations of alchemists. They finally selected one among them to board with. Subsequently we hear of a stranger who entered an apothecary and demanded some lapis-lazuli. He started a conversation with the two customers who happened to be in the shop, one an ecclesiastic and the other an old druggist. One of them remarked that though Cologne had many alchemists, few seemed to have discovered the great mystery of transmutation. When the stranger stated his belief in transmutation all present laughed. Sethonius then departed in silence.

The next day he bought some glassware in the same apothecary shop and requested permission to test it. Casually he performed all the steps involved in transmutation and finally made a projection, transforming into gold in the presence of a number of witnesses. One goldsmith among them was not readily convinced and demanded a repetition. In the meantime he stealthily put some zinc into the crucible, which would confuse matters by preventing the gold from forming. Sethonius made the projection and the gold appeared nonetheless.

There lived nearby a very learned man, a surgeon of great repute, a respected citizen who was known as an obdurate disbeliever in alchemy. Sethonius contrived to meet him on the pretense of discussing some medical matters. It seems Sethonius was himself quite a physician. Using medical discourse symbolically, Sethonius finally performed a transmutation in the presence of the skeptic. There were a few ironworkers in the goldsmith's shop where the two had met, and Sethonius, after talking to them, wished to demonstrate how to convert iron into steel. In reality they found it converted into gold. The local doctor, named Master George, was impressed. He asked Sethon how he dared to be so overt in his labors, did he not fear that princes would pursue him and compel him to make gold for their treasuries? Sethonius said he was on guard against such a possibility. "Besides, should a prince ever seize me I shall suffer a thousand deaths rather than reveal my secrets." Master George was a good convert and voluntarily spread the truth with avidity and caution.

Sethonius made converts wherever he went. He visited Dresden, Hamburg and Munich. In the latter city he met and eloped with a beautiful young lady, the daughter of a local merchant. Not long after his marriage he was invited to demonstrate his truths before the Elector of Saxony, which he accordingly did by sending his redheaded assistant there to perform. Like Rudolph II, this Elector, Christian II, was also interested in alchemists, but unlike the former he was more dominated by the desire for the product, not for the knowledge of the process. He lured Sethonius to court and acted very kindly toward him at first, but soon threw him into prison where he was subjected to the usual tortures because of his refusal to divulge the secret of transmutation. But though maimed and crippled he would not betray a science in which secrecy was a major principle. He was then thrown into a special dungeon and was carefully guarded.

There lived in Dresden at the time a well-known Polish chemist named Michael Sendivogius, famed for his mastery of dyeing. Like other practicing chemists he was an alchemist. He made his debut on the stage of history by taking a deep interest in the fate of the Cosmopolite and vowing to aid him at all cost. Through the influence of his friends he obtained permission to see the prisoner, who, in spite of his wretched condition, displayed enough character to convince his visitor of his nobility and his devotion to alchemy. Sendivogius revealed to the prisoner the plans for his escape and asked his cooperation. This plan was that Sendivogius pretend to offer his services to the Elector and suggest that by frequently visiting Sethonius and befriending him, he would seek to extract from him the secret. In the meantime they would both carefully prepare for an escape. The Cosmopolite was too happy for words and promised his future liberator all he desired, by which the latter understood the revelation of the grand secret, since this was all he desired in life. Sendivogius went home to Cracow to sell his estates and returned with the cash to Dresden to begin his campaign for aiding in the escape of the learned victim of the Elector. He bought a house near the prison with the Elector's permission, in order to see the prisoner as frequently as possible. He became acquainted with the guard, who frequently called at his house, ate and drank and became quite intimate with the host. At last the day for action arrived. He had given a lavish party that day for all the officers and soldiers of the guard and saw that they feasted and drank well. Everything else had been prepared with the help of Sethonius' beautiful and devoted wife, who never tired of working with Sendivogius on behalf of her unfortunate husband. When the soldiers had passed out dead drunk, they took the prisoner on a stretcher because he could not move, hurried home with him to make him unearth the elixir he had hidden, and, taking whatever baggage they had prepared, they sped in a postchaise with four horses toward the Polish border, never stopping until they reached Cracow.

In the safety of that city Sendivogius asked for his prize, the grand secret. Sethonius replied, "Regard to what state I have been reduced for refusing to betray my science. These broken limbs, this decrepit corpse speak of my faith to my duty which I plan to uphold in the future." Revealing the secret would be a great sin, he said, and advised his liberator to demand it of God.

Sendivogius was patient, hoping to achieve his objective by kindness rather than anger. He did not have to wait long, because Sethonius died in 1604 as a result of the torture he had endured for science. He asserted until his death that if his illness were only due to natural causes his powder could have cured him in no time at all. But it was incapable of healing cut nerves and broken organs. He did, however, leave to Sendivogius the residue of his powder, the manuscript of his book, *Twelve Treatises,* or *A Treatise on Nature,* and his young widow. The recipient made use of all three and fairly. He published Sethonius' book a year or two after the author's death, married his widow and set out with the powder upon the stormy career of an alchemist.

Sendivogius was born in 1566, the natural son of a Polish nobleman. As a young man he displayed great interest in chemistry, doing successful researches in the dyeing of materials and the nature of pigments. The exploration of mines and ores of Poland was another favorite subject with him. But before meeting with Sethonius his interest in alchemy had been theoretical and immature, and he had achieved no special distinction in it. He knew enough to desire the secret art of preparing the philosopher's stone, and it was in search of this scientific truth that he staked all his wealth, risked his good name with the Elector of Saxony, and his very life. When Sethonius died without revealing the grand secret, Sendivogius was heart-broken. It seems that he married the Cosmopolite's widow in order to get from her whatever information she might possess on the subject. He searched all the belongings of the deceased, all his notes and manuscripts, but in vain. The powder he found had been hidden in some part of the carriage and more was sewn in the clothes of his valet.

He did however succeed in performing several successful projections and became famous. He received requests to visit all the royal courts of Europe but chose to visit the learned Rudolph II first. He was well received at Prague and gave the emperor some powder with which the latter himself successfully converted some lead into gold. The emperor was beside himself with joy and gave Sendivogius the title of Imperial

Counsellor and an impressive medal. He offered him the post of court alchemist, but Sendivogius preferred his freedom and refused, remaining, however, on most friendly terms with the Emperor. From Prague Sendivogius set out to visit his own Sigismond, king of Poland, who wished to witness a transmutation. On the way he was ambushed by the soldiers of a local prince and imprisoned until he would divulge the secret of preparing the stone. He managed to escape, according to the story, quite bare, having used his clothes for a rope by which to lower himself from the prison tower. He sent word to the Emperor of the maltreatment he had received. Rudolph immediately ordered the guilty prince to apologize to Sendivogius, restore his property and give him some vast estate in recompense for the inconvenience suffered. The order was executed and Sendivogius reached Warsaw. He performed more projections and his fame spread further. The Duke Frederick of Wurtemberg pleaded with King Sigismond to permit his subject to come to his court. Permission granted, Sendivogius departed for Stuttgart, was enthusiastically received and was given many honors and even a principality.

Now, Frederick had as his court alchemist, a certain Count de Muhlenfels, who had started out in life as a domestic to an alchemist named Daniel Rappolt and later became barber to the Emperor. He associated with alchemists and picked up enough knowledge on the fly to be presented to Rudolph II and perform projections before his chief steward, Jean Franck. Rudolph honored him with the title of Count and gave him some minor presents. He then came to Frederick as a full-fledged adept and became his court alchemist.

This count wished to obtain the grand secret from Sendivogius as much as the latter had wished to extract it from Sethonius. His methods were, however, somewhat cruder. At first he was obsequious and friendly. Next he warned Sendivogius that the duke was duping him with kindness in order to win the secret from him. This seemed reasonable enough and Sendivogius set out stealthily en route that night, which was exactly what Muhlenfels had expected. He pursued him at the head of some twelve armed men and arrested him in the name of the duke. He deprived Sendivogius of his elixir, a small amount of which he carried in a golden box, his medals, his cap studded with diamonds, and a lengthy manuscript.

While the following year shows Muhlenfels to be still popular, nothing is heard of Sendivogius, who is believed to have pined in some fortress prison. His wife managed, however, to reach Poland and appeal to the king for help. The fate of Sendivogius was reported to the Emperor Rudolph, who suspected the duke of complicity in the crime and commanded him to appear at the court and deliver Muhlenfels as well. Both orders were, of course, obeyed. The duke returned everything that had been taken from Sendivogius, diamonds, gold, medals and manuscripts, but not the elixir, which he claimed he knew nothing about. Muhlenfels was condemned to death by the duke and the sentence carried out with great pomp to appease the Emperor, as well as remove a witness against the duke, who, it seems, had in reality been an accomplice. This happened in 1607.

For the next eighteen years still nothing is heard of Sendivogius. He seems to have lost interest in transmutation and directed his efforts toward the medicinal angle of the elixir. Numerous stories are told about his later exploits. It is claimed by some that he became a charlatan and extorted money from several Polish noblemen on the pretense of pursuing his studies; that he consciously feigned transmutations though his powder was gone; that he became a great healer and druggist; that he became a forger and sold false coins to the Jews of Poland. Others have it that he tired of the glory and dangers of alchemical renown and pursued his studies in the quiet of his estates, pretending to be poor and stricken with a horrible disease so as to keep away the inquisitive, especially kings and princes. The latter account is by far the more reasonable. Certain it is that it was during that period that Sendivogius wrote several treatises on alchemy which are still extant.

There is one account of an alchemist which has a truly happy ending, and that is the story of John Frederick Bötticher, born in Saxony in 1682. He was an apothecary's apprentice in Berlin, a brilliant youth of great promise, when a famous alchemist named Lascaris, playing the same role of a wandering apostle as Sethonius, gave him some grand elixir and bade him study alchemy and convert the unbelievers. Bötticher abandoned his job as well as his hopes of studying medicine and went in for transmutation.

He enjoyed the usual flight to fame. He performed notable transmutations in Berlin in the presence of reputable alchemists. But when he heard that King Frederick Wilhelm I of Prussia wished him to demonstrate at the court, he escaped from Berlin in the nick of time. He wanted to keep clear of the courts. He hid with an uncle, a professor at Wittenberg, an alchemist too, but was demanded of the town by the King. Since the Elector of Saxony, August II, who was also King of Poland, claimed him too as his subject, Bötticher chose the latter evil and went to live in Dresden.

He performed a transmutation before the Elector, who bestowed upon him the title of Baron and showered him with gifts. Bötticher forsook his studies and decided to enjoy the fruits of his reputation. He built himself a gaudy home, decorated with gold and silver, entertained royally and abandoned himself to feasting and revelry. He soon lost court favor and provoked the wrath of his ruler. Upon the order of the Elector he was imprisoned, not in a dungeon, however, but in a laboratory where he was forced to synthesize the magic powder of transmutation for the Duke, his erstwhile rescuer.

The wandering apostle, Lascaris, then appeared again on the scene, regretful that through his proselytizing, one so able met so tragic a fate. He succeeded in persuading a mutual friend, a young doctor named Pasch, to go to Dresden and help in Bötticher's release or escape. Pasch went to Dresden only after Lascaris proved to him that he could make as much gold as was needed either for bribery or ransom. Pasch relied upon some titled relatives at Dresden who held influential positions at the court. However, when he revealed his plans to them, they would hear nothing of such risky affairs and would not even intervene for an audience with the Elector. They argued that if offered a high ransom the Elector would be certain to refuse, thinking that Bötticher was worth it because he could make gold. Pasch then decided to liberate the victim all alone.

He too, like Sendivogius, installed himself in a house near the prison and managed to make contact with the prisoner and befriend the guard. Early in the progress of the plot, however, he was suspected of foul play and thrown into the fortress of Sonnenstein and Bötticher was removed to the tombs of the castle of Count Tschirnhaus. After spending ten miserable years in prison, Pasch attempted an escape in which he fell down an embattlement and was severely injured. Some fugitive companion carried him to the border and he reached Berlin safely but in poor health. He managed to have an interview with Frederick of Prussia, who promised to help him, but he died of his wounds within six months.

Bötticher's new prison was also a laboratory. His master Count Tschirnhaus, was himself a scientist and a practical researcher in various aspects of natural philosophy. While Bötticher was busy in his laboratory seeking a formula for the philosopher's stone, the price of his liberation, Count Tschirnhaus worked in his own more spacious rooms trying to perfect methods for the production of porcelain that would match the best in China. Until the seventeenth century China and Japan held full monopoly over the production of porcelain-ware and controlled the European market. Many European rulers and tradespeople sought ways and means of competing in that trade. Contrary to the notion that feudal lords were not concerned with trade and manufacture, the Elector of Saxony and King of Poland appointed the Count of Tschirnhaus to organize and supervise researches in that direction.

The two scientists, the captive and his guard, became friends. The learned count finally induced Bötticher to abandon his search for perfection, alkahest and elixirs, and employ his talents in a practical direction. Because he was a prisoner and in constant proximity to his master, and because he wished to make better and stronger crucibles and probably desired freedom as well, and perhaps also because he had much time hanging on his hands while waiting for decoctions and rectifications, Bötticher consented.

The result is now well known through the name of Dresden China. In 1704, after having devoted himself to the task for two years or less, Bötticher discovered not only the secret of making the finest transparent porcelain, but also of stained varieties. The Elector was mightily pleased with Bötticher and permitted him to continue both his researches on the elixir and ceramics at Dresden, where he also supervised a factory, though under constant guard. The processes employed in the ceramic factories were generally more carefully watched than modern formulae for secret weapons.

As is well known, the trade in Dresden China brought more prosperity to Saxony than all alchemy could create. Bötticher was appointed chief over that industry, after the death of Tschirnhaus in 1708, and received from the Duke the latter's titles and lands, as well as a pardon. After regaining his freedom, he never returned to his alchemical love but led, instead, a gay and merry life, dying in 1719 at the age of thirty-seven.

4. *Truth and Martyrdom*

It has been mentioned on several occasions that the accounts of the lives of the alchemists here given are not in all likelihood historically accurate because data are lacking for any attempt at verification. Rather should these accounts be regarded as literature. The kind of lore and romance a culture or a period create, are, after all, the most truthful barometer of how people think and what values they cherish.

What is characteristic of alchemy is its fusion of concepts and goals, based on the failure to realize that perfection is a relative and not an absolute term, that gold is perfect only because we choose to call it so, and that a substance which even could produce gold from lead, need have no power whatever to cure disease or bring about the other miracles assigned to it. We have seen that the chemical portions of the alchemical philosophy seemed plausible and "logical" at the time, but that much relevant knowledge lay still hidden in the primal mists of untested thoughts and future experimentation. Lack of awareness of relativity of values and the need for the avoidance of false extensions or identifications still exist as potent encumbrances to knowledge and hinder clarity in many fields.

It should also be borne in mind that not all alchemical writers dis-

THE ALCHEMISTS IN PURSUIT OF WISDOM

played this confusion in a uniform manner. Thus, in his scholarly and perspicacious study of fifteenth century alchemy, W. J. Wilson, in a paper already referred to, points to the scientific spirit of alchemy in that era, adding that "of theological influence there is rarely a trace." There were individual differences among the practitioners, and there were differences in aspects stressed at particular periods. Egypt evolved the empiric knowledge and Greece supplied a philosophy. The succeeding Arab scholars expanded the previously formed combination. The early Middle Ages took over the entire heritage, stressing on the whole the experimental component at first. The sixteenth and seventeenth centuries seem to have singled out the philosophic implications and developed contempt for sheer "puffers," interested in nothing but gold. Yet they never neglected their alembics and furnaces. Similarly, Chinese alchemy stressed the elixir and immortality, while the Occidental science neglected the latter entirely and began the pursuit of the former in later years, after indulging in straightforward experimentation at first.

No science can boast as many martyrs as alchemy, whose devotees would rather die than betray their procedures. Thus, in 1483 Louis von Neus died in jail in Warburg for refusing to reveal the secrets of transmutation; in 1570 Albrecht Beyer was assassinated by murderers who wished to obtain his secret, in 1575 the Duke of Brunswick and Luxemburg burned in an iron cage the woman alchemist Marie Ziglerin for having given that prince a prescription for transmutation which failed to work. Bragadino was hanged in Munich in 1590, George Honauer in 1597 at Wurtemberg, von Krohnemann in 1686, Gaetano in 1709 in Prussia, von Kelttemberg in 1720 in Poland, and David Beuther was alleged to have committed suicide in prison because he could not produce the elixir demanded of him by his pupil, the Elector August of Saxony. Many other less renowned heroes can easily have their names added to the list. It was even dangerous to use the elixir for curative purposes. Thus Sienbenfreund, who possessed it and successfully cured people with it, was followed around Europe by a Scotsman whom he had cured and who with the aid of three medical students waylaid and killed him and robbed him of the powder.

Albert the Great expressed it correctly in explaining one of his commandments: "If you are unfortunate enough to be known to kings and princes you shall be pelted with their foolish questions; 'Well Master, how goes the Work, When do we see some good results?' In their impatience for results they will dub you cheat, good-for-nothing, etc., and be generally annoying and scornful. And if you are not lucky to obtain good results in the end you will receive the full brunt of their fury. If contrariwise, you succeed, they will keep you in permanent captivity to oblige you to work for their benefit." This was wisely said presumably in the thirteenth century and was certainly true as long as alchemy lasted.

While there were many princes with high regard for science who even worked with crucible and alembic, there were many others who prohibited alchemy and persecuted its adepts. Pope John XXII issued an edict against it in 1317, King Charles V of France prohibited it entirely, and a chemist, Jean Barillon, discovered to have had a laboratory, was executed in 1380. Henry IV of England and the Council of Venice also proscribed it. Yet, in spite of these efforts to throttle it, it ultimately won the day, and all laws aimed at stemming the progress of alchemy rapidly fell into desuetude.

Astrology taught us that a pattern of thought may maintain itself for thousands of years, especially if it is an abstract theory, and can easily be made to agree with observed facts by the Procrustean bed of logic and rationalization. All signs of contradictions were smoothly swept aside by reasonable enough excuses, reasonable because similar modes of thought have stood us in good stead elsewhere and proved correct. The pattern of astrological beliefs remained intact until a number of factors contributed to its abandonment or its replacement by another set of assumptions and values.

In alchemy the situation is somewhat different. Here a set of beliefs induced the most learned and brilliant men of the age to perform costly experiments, employ the maximum of patience and obtain elusive results. And yet men went on and on laboring, studying, suffering and dying for the unproved primary assumptions, bravely explaining away failures. Unlike astrology, the field lay close to or even wholly within the confines of experimentation. Yet the road was long and rocky, and victory, as we shall see, came about wholly indirectly and by slow degrees.

The setup for verification was ideal. And yet observe what happened. When the experiment, which lasted years and exacted much money and labor came to naught, one never concluded that the philosophy of the science or its principles were wrong, but that the experimenter had made a mistake. This is often a legitimate enough assumption, since men are fallible and the art was truly beset with difficulties and most apparatus used was imperfect. Even today transmutation is not an easy process, and with the best cyclotron failures still occur. Yet, in the case of alchemy explaining away of indubitable facts became the only proof for an inspiring and costly theory.

On the other hand, one must not assume that the claims of some alchemists to have brought about transmutations were complete inventions. The fact is that the powder termed the great elixir or the philosopher's stone contained some gold which in the process of decoction was

THE ALCHEMISTS IN PURSUIT OF WISDOM 317

deposited as the pure metal. The quantities claimed to have been obtained were certainly exaggerations. But this need cause little wonder. Equipped with a philosophy deeply rooted in the culture, well-knit in consistency and emotional appeal, and devoting years of labor to the final hope of achieving a transmutation, the alchemist who at last found some gold in the crucible after months or even years of patient waiting for the decoction to complete its sacred processes, could hardly be expected to worry about such a minor matter as quantity. The lore and ritual of transmutation, its mystical elaborations and deeply religious implications enveloped the process in so much romance and glory that the joy aroused in the adept's heart at the sight of the smallest glitter of gold in the philosopher's egg, was enough to bring tears to his eyes and cause his knees to bend in prayer. The fact that his elixir worked meant that he was master over the greatest ambition of mankind, that he could bring about all the miraculous transformations the philosopher's stone could effect, that he could cure disease, rejuvenate the old, make the blind see and bring happiness to those stricken with misery. Besides he was an adept, one of the few elect.

As an example of some of the evidence, we may cite the following statement from Geber: "I have seen copper mines in which small pellets of this metal were carried away, the streams running through the mines. After these streams had dried up the copper pellets remained in the dry sand three years. I examined them at the end of that period and noted that they had been baked and digested by the sun and were changed as a result into pure gold. By imitating nature we can produce the same transmutation." The facts Geber observed were no doubt true. Pellets of copper were present and so were ingots of gold frequently found in copper mines. He failed to see the gold pellets at the beginning of the three-year period, but did notice them at the end. The notion that the copper had changed into gold seemed the only reasonable one in view of current and unquestioned hypotheses or assumptions.

A curious argument cited by alchemists in defense of their views was the following. Upon tabulation of all the compounds and metals found in ores one could easily arrange them in an ascending scale of purity from the crudest to the noblest by the ease of their transmutability. What the evidence might have amounted to was that various ores were found to possess different amounts of gold, obtained at the conclusion of a decoction. But to the alchemical mind it was obvious that this arrangement offered incontrovertible evidence of an evolutionary scale from the lowest and basest metal to the highest, that the very existence of intermediate stages proved the truth of the evolutionary process presumably catalyzed by the stars. One can even picture them searching for missing links, a quest which on the basis of their assumptions and interpretation, was bound to be successful.

In addition, the methods of assaying gold were such as to account for the frequent statements by reliable witnesses that they had found pure gold where in reality only alloys could be expected. We may recall here that the celebrated Robert Boyle was believed to have brought about a transmutation by dissolving gold in acqua regia containing antimony trichloride. He obtained in reality a considerable amount of silver, which he accepted as experimental verification of change. As it often happened, few of the substances employed in the reactions were pure. Analyzing for impurities was unknown, and the antimony trichloride no doubt had a high percentage of silver admixed with it. In the absence of analytical chemistry this was inevitable. The sulfide and chloride of antimony were likely to be contaminated with gold or silver salts, which after the severe treatment deposited the pure metals.

And Robert Boyle was not the only one. Guyton de Morveau, the father of chemical classification, also announced as late as 1786 that silver fused with arsenic is converted into gold. As in the previous instance his observation was correct. It was proved later that the silver he employed was auriferous. Hence, as in most cases, neither fraud nor deception was involved but the mode of operation of the human mind and the state of knowledge. When some of our current theories will be viewed in the light of historical perspective, surely men of the future will wonder how we could have failed to see the true explanation that begged acceptance; how we used the facts to prove assumptions which should have been questioned rather than reiterated, and how failure to know one minor item could sustain us in error.

That transmutation could not be easily questioned is only reasonable. Every beginner in chemistry finds the subject far more bewildering than many another science. By merely mixing solutions, dissolving and combining compounds and observing results, one encounters the whole array of confusing phenomena which confounded the early pioneers for over two thousand years. It is a pity we cannot perform a social experiment in ideational development by taking a few bright boys and girls uncontaminated by our present theories and let them set off on a voyage of chemical exploration. You might as well blindfold a stranger in a room and expect him to gain a clear conception of the layout in a few minutes. The devious route taken by chemistry betrays nothing but the workings of the human mind in its groping for truth in its quest for science. The efforts constitute our own behavior as seen at a distance. They are an image of ourselves, as any culture is a nuclear replica of our own.

5. *Alchemical Contributions to the Science of Chemistry*

It is sometimes maintained that a theory which is incorrect cannot lead to productive ideas or to new discoveries of fundamental import. We have already seen that this notion is thoroughly contradicted by the astrological pattern of thought. Not only has astrology been the womb in which modern astronomy grew and matured, but it was the very medium which evolved a mode of approach, a set of assumptions destined to destroy its progenitor.

Fumbling about with matrasses and aludels, blue and green vitriols, dragon's blood and red elixirs, the alchemical workers were nonetheless busy mixing chemicals and observing results. That apparently was sufficient. It seems to suffice for man to be in contact with things and meddle with reality on the basis of one theory or another, in order to accumulate more and more knowledge by stumbling upon something here and there. Time then does the rest. Time gnaws at the most intricate and resistant patterns, weakens a spot here and punctures a hole there, permitting new views to penetrate, ultimately to form completely changed designs. Little wonder then that the contributions to our chemical knowledge during the alchemical period are considerable.

To begin with, alchemy greatly enhanced the employment of quantitative methods in chemical experimentation. Quantitative procedures had been in vogue, of course, before alchemy ruled, but the latter's aims certainly pointed to them more sharply, even if for unique reasons. So strong is the hold of an established belief that the human mind will twist and wrangle, blame others and even himself, explain away and perform all kinds of rationalizing gyrations to retain rather than question, to defend rather than reexamine. And so it happened that when a devout and perseverent alchemist found no gold in his philosopher's egg, he never thought of blaming the objective or the principles underlying his efforts. Instead he would blame his lack of care, impatience, his inaccurate weights, or an oversight in some planetary influence. Back he would go to his chemicals, furnace and crucibles, and start his labors anew, improving his technique. He would question every procedure but never the basic belief where the trouble really lay.

It was during the alchemical period that the properties of solvents such as acqua regia, nitric, hydrochloric, sulfurous and sulfuric acids, various alkali and ammonia water were greatly advanced. Bismuth, antimony, arsenic, compounds of zinc, the oxides, chlorides and nitrates of several metals, iron salts, acetates and carbonates of lead and other metals, salts of ammonium and sulfur were found and their properties fully revealed.

Equally impressive was the progress made in chemical manipulation, in knowledge of reactions as well as chemical apparatus. The preparation and distillation of alcohol, the processes of precipitation, sublimation, calcination and crystallization, as well as the process of cupellation of gold and silver, that is, removing impurities by means of lead and thus purifying the two metals, of concentration of solutions and the preparation of the alkaline metals and salts, all these were achieved with the aid of many valuable innovations in method. Such chemical advances as the reduction of metallic oxides, the invention of means of coloring silver, the discovery of phosphorus while seeking for the philosopher's stone in the human body, the coloring and staining of textiles, the preparation of excellent porcelains, of ammonium carbonate by distillation of urine, and hundreds of reactions in the preparation of salts and elements, acids and alkali, decomposition and recombinations, required great ingenuity and patience. "The secret art of chemistry is more possible than not. Her mysteries reveal themselves to those adepts who invest labor and tenacity; but what triumphs await those who succeed in lifting a corner of the veil hiding nature's mysteries." Thus spoke Rhazis more than a thousand years ago.

Such were the goals of another age. Inspired and fascinated, men worked and fussed and muddled along. Are our goals less inspiring and less fascinating, and are we responding altogether differently? May not the future find our goals also amusing and naive, though probably in different ways? We think not, but then neither did the alchemists consider themselves knights errant in search of a will-o'-the-wisp. They wielded sound logic and nursed little suspicion of the light in which the future would view them.

Chapter XII

IATRO-CHEMISTRY AND PHLOGISTON

1. Paracelsus—Portrait of a Rebel

WHILE many of the alchemists discussed in the previous chapter went about their pursuit of the elusive transmutation and its tinctures, a new idea rose imperceptibly to a dominant position in chemical thought. The idea was not entirely new, but constituted a new stress, a new outlook on aims and values. This new thought was a sudden efflorescence of the idea of the universal panacea and the role of alchemy in the art of healing.

The nature of the transition, as well as the contents of the new philosophy, can best be gleaned from the life and writings of Paracelsus. It was he who founded this new outlook in chemistry or medicine, and in many ways his life was symbolic of his contribution. His career reflected the conflict resulting from the impact of the new ideas upon the established pattern of classical alchemy.

A famous quotation from the writings of Paracelsus is "that the object of chemistry is not to make gold but to prepare medicines." This does not imply that he was opposed to the belief in transmutation. On the contrary. He not only shared all the views of the alchemists, but also their attitudes and interests. Philippus Aureolus Paracelsus Theophrastus Bombastus von Hohenheim shared as well the intense religious feeling that characterized Lull, Albertus, Denis Zachaire, Flamel, Galileo, Kepler, Brahe, Newton and Boyle. This sentiment rivalled in strength his devotion to the science of medicine, which equalled that of Hippocrates, for whom he showed little regard, or Galen, whom he berated, or of Ambroise Paré, who later became an admiring student of his works. In his writings and his actions he also displayed the traits common to the great alchemists—sincerity, loyalty, perseverance and courage.

Paracelsus possessed a personality typical of a rebel. He was cocksure and conceited, derisive of revered authority and contemptuous of his colleagues, violent in his denunciations and calumny, rambunctious, vituperative, impulsive, unsocial, and yet fired with deep sympathy for humanity, and with bold idealism. He was also blessed with vast erudition, rare originality and deep insight. He typified inspired adolescence at its best or at its worst: adolescence which is certain of the tyranny and blindness of the elders and of its own exclusive grasp of truth.

Born in 1493 to a Swiss physician plying his trade at Einsiedeln near Zurich, then as now a famous place of pilgrimage and harboring a Benedictine monastery, he received an early training in the sciences related to medicine. His father taught chemistry as well as medicine at a mining school maintained by the owners of the famous lead mines near Augsburg. He had a laboratory at his home, as was the practice then of anyone at all interested in science.

At seventeen Paracelsus was enrolled at the University of Basel, aiming at a medical degree, but apparently remained there only a short time because, as an admiring, if none too critical, biographer said, "He soon became conscious that he had nothing to gain from their dull reiteration of aeon-old formulas which his intellect disowned." (Anna M. Stoddart, Life of Paracelsus, London, 1911). He left Basel and went to study with the alchemist Trithemius, the abbot of Spannheim mentioned in the preceding chapter. He must have found his master much to his liking since he shared with him two passions, love of science and religious devotion. He was initiated by him into those aspects of arcane learning for which Trithemius was famous.

They soon separated and Paracelsus wandered to the silver mines of Schwatz in the Tyrol, where he continued his schooling at first hand in the industrial process of chemistry, never neglecting his experimental interest in alchemical studies. He worked there ten months and then continued his travels from land to land, visited famous teachers, physicians and scientists, as well as mines and laboratories. "A doctor cannot become efficient at the universities; how is it possible in three or four years to understand nature, astronomy, alchemy or physic?" says Paracelsus. "A doctor must be a traveller," he adds, "because he must inquire of the world. Experiment is not sufficient. Experience must verify what can be accepted. Knowledge is experience." (ibid. p. 12) "I have heard repeatedly from those experienced in the laws that it is written in the laws that a physician must be a traveler. This pleases me very well for the reason that diseases wander hither and thither as wide as the world is and do not remain in one place. If one will know many diseases he must wander also. . . . Not merely to describe countries as to how they wear their trousers but courageously to attack the problem as to what kinds of diseases they possess. . . . The English humors are not the Hungarian, nor the Neapolitan, the Prussian. . . ." (Stillman, J. M., Paracelsus. Open Court, 1920, p. 18)

He travelled to Vienna, Cologne, Paris, Montpellier, the seat of a famous medical school, Bologna, Padua, Salerno and Ferrara, all famous centers of learning, and then through Spain and Portugal. He next went to England and then to the Netherlands, where he became barber-surgeon to the Dutch army. From there he continued his travels through Denmark and Sweden, serving in both countries as army surgeon. He also visited Prussia, Poland, Lithuania, southeastern Europe, Southern Russia, which he calls Tartary, Turkey and probably the Near East.

Wherever he traveled he studied, observed and worked as a surgeon. Wherever he sojourned for any length of time he treated rich and poor, and won great renown for miraculous cures. He learned from the Saracens the lore of their saints, sought out the numerous Jewish physicians and astrologers to learn the secrets of the cabala. He spent time with veterinarians and old women who gathered herbs for superstitious remedies, watched their methods and learned their art. "The universities do not teach all things so a doctor must seek out old wives, gypsies, sorcerers, wandering tribes, old robbers and such outlaws and take lessons from them." "My travels have developed me; no man becomes a master at home, nor finds his teacher behind the stove. For knowledge is not all locked up, but is distributed throughout the whole world. It must be sought for and captured wherever it is. . . . And I testify that this is true concerning Nature; whoever wishes to know her must treat her books on their feet." (Stoddart Life of Paracelsus, p. 74)

Wherever he went he visited mines, analyzed their ores, observed processes, lingered for a while and had his eyes everywhere. He visited mineral springs and analyzed the salts remaining after distillation and noted similarities and differences. His curiosity was unquenchable not only in the healing arts, but also in whatever applied to chemistry and metallurgy. He practiced what he believed, namely that "A doctor must be an alchemist. He must therefore see the mother earth where the minerals grow and as the mountains won't come to him, he must go to the mountains. How can an alchemist get to the working of nature unless he seeks it where the minerals lie? Is it a reproach that I have sought the minerals and found their mind and kept the knowledge of them fast so as to know how to separate the clean from the ore, to do which I have come through many hardships." (ibid., p. 75) Elsewhere he says, "The pillar of true medicine is alchemy. Unless the physician be perfectly acquainted with and experienced in this art, everything that he devotes to the rest of his art will be vain and useless." (A. E. Waite, The Hermetic and Alchemical Writings of Paracelsus, vol. I, Alchemy, the Third Column of Medicine, p. 148)

In 1526, at the age of thirty-three, he was invited to the chair of the University of Basel. This in itself was something unusual and indicates that conservatism is not always vigilant or consistent. Paracelsus had no recognized training or degrees, though he had published several books and described himself on the title-page as "the highly experienced and most famous Doctor of Philosophy and of both Medicines," the latter referring to medicine and surgery. He probably knew Latin but lectured in German, a most revolutionary innovation in those days. He dressed simply and shunned the silk and satin, the staff and swagger of the profession. His lectures were simple and adapted to large audiences, lucid and challenging, disrespectful and braggardly, but replete with the vast stores of his knowledge and varied experience.

Besides being lecturer at the University, Paracelsus was also appointed town physician by the City Council. In both capacities he could only provoke strong antagonism by his intolerance and readiness to deride and condemn. This he did with great gusto in blaring and pompous language, ridiculing with venom and bragging without bounds, respecting none but "nature, God, truth," and himself, and always denouncing authorities. He was a *rebel*. He declares that "evil spirits as Geber in The Sum of Perfection, Albertus Magnus, Aristotle the chemist (not the peripatetic Philosopher) in The Book of the Perfect Magistery, Rhasis and Polydonus; for those writers however many they be, are either themselves in error or else they write falsely out of sheer envy and put forth receipts whilst not ignorant of the truth." (A. E. Waite, Hermetic & Alchemical Writings of Paracelsus, vol. I, p. 48, The Aurora of the Philosophers). Elsewhere he states: "For man is assuredly born in ignorance so that he cannot know or understand anything of himself but only that which he receives from God and understands from Nature. He who learns nothing from these is like the heathen teachers and philosophers who follow the subtleties and crafts of their own inventions and opinions. Such teachers are Aristotle, Hippocrates, Avicenna, Galen and the rest who based all their arts simply upon their own opinions. Even if at any time they learnt anything from nature they destroyed it again with their own fantasies, dreams and inventions before they came to the final issue. By means of these, then, and their followers nothing perfect can be discovered." (Concerning the Spirit of the Planets, ibid, p. 72).

While it is true that different periods offer different tyrannies to rebel against, the antics of the rebel and his logic seem to remain fairly uniform. Those he opposes are fossils and their theories are based on mere opinion and fantasy; his own are bursting with novelty and truth, the very vision of right, the voice of reality and of experimental verification. Moreover, those rebelled against are (a) either innocent and sincere but misguided and deluded, or (b) have ulterior motives such as profits, domination, or envy. Yet, as fate would have it, the modern student reads both Galen and Paracelsus, the reactionary and the rebel, with tolerant or contemptuous smiles, and views their great battle with a feeling of amazement at human folly and passion.

Paracelsus' intentions at Basel were no doubt of the best. Imitating Luther, though a devout Catholic, he posted an announcement of his lectures on the blackboard of the University. In it he invited in a most democratic manner all and sundry to attend them, stated his faith in "research, experiment and experience," rather than "the teachings of the ancients," extolled faith in God and the lofty nature of medicine, condemned its study from books, berated degrees and classical languages and praised his own knowledge, his approach and remarkable cures. Two weeks after his arrival he saw some students build a bonfire in front of the University on the occasion of the feast of St. John. It is said he cast Avicenna's Canon of Medicine into the fire, saying, "Into St. John's Fire, so that all misfortune may go into the air with the smoke," which is probably the basis for the common legend that he made a bonfire in which he destroyed copies of Galen, Avicenna and Aristotle. It could as well be true, because the legend truly portrays his attitude.

No wonder, then, that Paracelsus could not retain his position at Basel. While at first popular with the students, his classes were deserted after a few months when opposition to his stay at the University became clamorous. He upbraided and abused the medical profession, the surgeons and apothecaries, and ridiculed all authorities. In his *Book Paragranum* he makes his point clear: "Follow after me Avicenna, Galen, Rhasis, Montagnana, Mesue. Follow you me and not I you, ye from Paris, from Montpellier, from Wirtemberg, from Meissen, from Cologne, from Vienna, from the Danube, the Rhine, and the Islands of the sea; Italy, Dalmatia, Sardinia, Athens: Greek, Arab, Israelite, follow you me and not I you: of you will no one survive, not even in the most distant corner. I shall be monarch and mine will be the monarchy, which shall bind all your countries. . . .

"I tell you the down on my chin knows more than you and all your writers, my shoebuckles are more learned than Galen and Avicenna, and my beard has more experience than all your universities. God will make other doctors who will understand the four elements and magic, the Kabala, which to you are as cataracts in your eyes; they will be geomantists, adepts, archei, spagyrists; they will possess the arcana, they will have the tinctures. Where will your foul broths be then? Who will then redden the thick lips of your wives and wipe their sharp little noses? The devil with a hunger-napkin." (Stoddart, p. 145, 147)

Surely this attitude towards the profession and its authorities was not conducive either towards the making of friends or attracting students. From the beginning to the very end of his stay at Basel, Paracelsus had difficulties, disputations and squabbles, not only with the medical profession of that prosperous and cultured city, but with its governing Council, his colleagues at the university, and the students. The very fact that Paracelsus had been invited to Basel is ample proof that the governing council was sufficiently impressed by his reputation to defy tradition and offer the chair of medicine and surgery to one who did not even have a medical degree. Yet a few months after Paracelsus had begun to lecture he had everyone against him.

He soon arrived at open conflict with the medical profession and his colleagues at the university. Someone had affixed a letter written in perfect Latin on the doors of the Cathedral, two churches and the new Exchange. This letter was purported to have been written by Galen out of hell, in defense of his medical achievements and against the incessant attacks by Paracelsus. The letter is well worth citing in full because it constitutes the defense of the old-fashioned physicians who were so violently defamed.

*THE SHADE OF GALEN AGAINST THEOPHRASTUS,
OR RATHER CACOPHRASTUS*

Hear, thou who dost soil the glorious renown of my name.
A talker to thee, an idiot am I, in good sooth?
Thou sayest of Machaon's art, I hold not the feeblest experience,
Or having it, failed in practice expert to employ it.
Unbearable! have I not known the commonest simples?
Onions and garlic and hellebore, well do I know them.
Hellebore I send unto thee, a cure for brains that are addled:
I send it as well as all others which benefit fools and the witless.
True 'tis, I know not thy mad alchemical vapourings,
I know not what Ares may be, nor what Yliadus,
Know not thy tinctures, thy liquors divine of Taphneus
Nor Archeus, thy spirit preserver of everything living in all things.
All Africa bears not so many portentous creations.
And yet, thou nonsensical fool, thou contendest in parlay with me!
Art thou itching to measure with mine thy weapons in wrath,
Thou who answeredst nothing to Wendelin's well-reasoned word?
I doubt me if thou art worthy to carry Hippocrates' wash-pot
Or even art fit to give food to my swine or to herd them.
Hast thou made thyself pinions that fell from the wings of a crow?
Thy glory is false and abides scarce a moment in view.
Hast thou read? Thou shalt lose what in cunning of speech thou hast won
And thy works of deceit will bring thee to poverty's pain.
What wilt do, thou insane, when within and without thou art known?
Good counsel it were to hang thyself up by the neck.
"Let us live," doth he say, "we can always change our abode;

If imposture avail not, some other adventure I plan:
What if a second Athenas, a universe new I proclaim?
Not one of the audience I speak to can so much as guess what I mean.
The stygian law here forbids me to speak with thee further today.
Enough for thee now to digest! Reader and friend, fare thee well!
                                                    Out of Hell.

Prompt with unbounded abuse of others, Paracelsus was most sensitive to criticism. He riled at this attack, appealed to the City Council and composed lengthy replies to his "enemies." The refusal of the City Council to do anything by way of apprehending the authors of the lampoon, combined with the unfavorable verdict in a trial for a prize he thought he had deserved, caused him to launch as bitter an attack as he was capable of against the authorities. Fearing imprisonment, he fled Basel in the dark of night less than two years after his arrival.

He resumed his interrupted course of travel. We find him now in Alsace, then Germany, Austria, and Switzerland continuing his studies, his associations with the prominent figures of the time, his use of cures which in the public eye seemed to have assumed legendary dimensions, and the publication of books on the variety of scientific subjects which absorbed his encyclopedic mind.

He settled for a while near Nuremberg where most of his books were being published, but trouble, or "persecution," followed him. He came into conflict with the censor, who banned the publication of all his future books at the insistence of the medical faculty. He continued to write, nevertheless, and found publishers elsewhere, but many of his works had to be published posthumously. A part of his subsequent life was devoted to evangelistic or missionary work. He wandered through the Swiss countryside preaching the Bible and healing the poor. He finally settled at Salzburg, where he died in 1541, leaving his medical books, medicines and implements to a local physician, and most of his property "to his heirs, the poor, miserable needy people, those who have neither money nor provision, without favor or disfavor; poverty and want are their only qualification." It seems what he left behind was more in the nature of spiritual goods than material, but the gesture is indicative of his character, nonetheless.

The bulk of the writings of Paracelsus is incomprehensible to the average scientist of today. But pretentious and bombastic as his style may seem to us, his books are interspersed with amazing bits of general and technical wisdom. Surely the trend of his thoughts was in what seems to us now as the right direction, and his keen intellect peered into aspects of medicine or chemistry which were to loom large in later years and prove most stimulating to all biological science. Yet our task is not to deliver a final judgment, but note what his life and character contribute to the study of the nature of a rebel; one of those people who are allegedly the standard-bearers of progress, the ill-recompensed pioneers of new ideas.

How far does a rebel depart from the period he lives in and how large a sector of his culture pattern is he at all capable of viewing critically, let alone attempt to reform? Paracelsus presumably marks a revolutionary turning point in chemistry and medicine. The dominant belief pattern of natural science at the time entailed transmutation, the four qualities, and the two or three properties of elements, astrology and its relation to the organic and inorganic worlds and human fates, demonology, necromancy, magic, numerology, and other concepts. Which of these did Paracelsus challenge and on what grounds?

We may begin with astrology. Much has been said by admiring biographers about his opposition to astrology. Thus Anna M. Stoddart claims that he "contests the prevailing belief that the stars affect men from their birth to their death." We have seen elsewhere that virtually every astrologer condemned and upbraided other astrologers for their errors. It is true, to cite the author's own and lengthy quotations, that in his Paramirum, under the heading Ens Astrale, he writes: "The stars control nothing in us, suggest nothing, incline to nothing, own nothing. They are free from us and we are free from them. But note that without the heavenly bodies we cannot live; for cold, warmth and the consummation of what we eat or drink comes from them. . . . But observe: if a child which has been born under the luckiest planets and stars, and under those richest in good gifts has in its own character those qualities that run counter to those gifts, whose blame is it? It is the fault of the blood which comes by generation. Not the stars, but the blood brings that about." (Stoddart, p. 185) Paracelsus means to point out here that when those "born under the luckiest planets and stars" fail to display the characteristics expected of them, it is because of differences in blood. Astrology had always granted power to heredity or race, hence this is hardly evidence for scepticism toward astrology.

Further in the same section he writes: "The stars have their own nature and properties just as men have upon the earth. They change within themselves; are sometimes better, sometimes worse, sometimes sweeter, sometimes sourer, and so on. When they are good in themselves no evil comes from them; but infection proceeds from them when they are evil. Now observe that the stars surround the whole world just as its shell does an egg; the air comes through the shell and goes straight to the earth. Then observe that those stars which are poisonous taint the air with their poison so that where the poisoned air comes, at that place maladies break out according to the properties of the stars: the whole air of the world is not poisoned, only a part of it according to the property of the stars. It is the same with the beneficent properties of the stars: that too is Ens Astrale: the vapor, exhalation, exudation of the stars mingle with the air. For thence come cold, warmth, drought, moisture, and such like according to their properties: Observe that the stars themselves do not act; they only infect through their exhalations that part of the meteoron by which we are poisoned and enfeebled. And in this manner the Ens Astrale alters our body for good or evil. A man whose blood is hostile to such exhalations becomes ill; but one whose nature is not hostile is not hurt. He too who is finely fortified against such evils suffers nothing because he overcomes the poison by the vitality of his blood or by medicine which combats the evil vapors from above. Observe then that all created things are opposed to men and men are opposed to them: all may hurt men and yet men can do nothing to them."

Paracelsus challenged every segment of generally held beliefs. According to most authorities and his own confession, he read little and held most of his predecessors and contemporaries in uniform contempt. Yet wisely does Stillman call attention to "a very characteristic habit of Paracelsus, of explaining generally accepted beliefs of his time by some plausibly rational theory," his ever-seething, rambunctious, usually perspicacious and stimulating rebelliousness.

Paracelsus' acceptance of every basic principle of astrology is as plainly visible in his writings as is the sky in an open field. Like his complete acceptance of alchemy, it fills and saturates every idea of his, every thought and argument. One can choose any of his books and find that it underlies all his writings much as faith in God fills the works of St. Thomas Aquinas or the religious writings of Newton. But it was not in the nature of Paracelsus merely to accept a given custom or belief. He was too original a thinker, too critical and restless, a mind too individualistic in his thoughts and manner to do that. He rejoiced in demolishing the accepted, though often only to restate it in his own fashion. At least one may say that historical perspective justifies our viewing it in that light. No doubt those living at the time considered him a thorough-going iconoclast.

"Let not the astronomer deny that magic is astronomy, nor yet refuse the name to divination, nigromancy and the rest. All these things are comprehended under astronomy as much as is astrology itself. They are natural and essential sciences of the stars and he who is acquainted with them all, he is worthy to be called an astronomer. But albeit these sciences are sisters, they have heretofore been ignorant of their relationship, which it is important to recognize, so that one may not be despised by the other." (Preface to the Interpretation of the Stars, Waite, vol II, p. 282)

On the other hand, he is fully aware of Ptolemy's slogan, "The wise man rules the stars." Elsewhere he writes: "The signs of physiognomy derive their origin from the higher stars. . . . The wise man can dominate the stars and is not subject to them. Nay, the stars are subject to the wise man and are forced to obey him, not he the stars. The stars compel and coerce the animal man, so that where they lead he must follow; just as a thief follows the gallows, a robber the wheel, etc." (Concerning the Nature of Things, Waite, vol. I, p. 174)

As we have seen, this was the typical compromise between stellar determinism and free will. Paracelsus' courage leads him even to state that "man . . . can free himself from a malignant planet and subject himself to another better one, from slavery pass by virtue to freedom, and rescue himself from the prison of an evil planet, so also the animal man who is the son of Sol, Jupiter, Venus, or Mercury, can withdraw himself from that benignant planet and subject himself to Saturn or to Mars. . . . It is not to this that a bad star or a bad parent has led him. Had he not been foolish and wicked, he would not have left to the stars so unquestioned a dominion over himself, but he would have struggled against them."

True to the beliefs of the time, Paracelsus is the author of an opus entitled "Interpretation of the Comet Which Appeared in the Mountains in the Middle of August 1531, by the Most Learned Master Paracelsus." In it he foretells of coming bloodshed, social upheavals, deaths of many illustrious men, awesome wars and plagues. It goes without saying that he shared all the pervading beliefs in the close connection between medicine and astrology. In his customary manner he frequently, but always vehemently berates his contemporaries for failing to understand this vital connection, and for disobeying its dictates.

Clearly then, Paracelsus is not a rebel in astrology but a reformer aiming at its strengthening and at giving it an invincible rationale. If we are to label such conduct, we would have to call him in the spirit of modern symbolism a "reactionary." His rebelliousness and general nonconformism were merely surface turbulence and fanfare.

His attitude to alchemy was also typical of the period. His alchemical works are too numerous to cite, and his total acceptance of alchemy is too fundamental to be singled out. Dozens of his works deal with transmutation, the tincture of the philosophers, the mercury or sulphur of metals, their generation, and many other such alchemical concepts. His Short Catechism of Alchemy (Waite, vol. I, p. 288) may deviate mildly from the usual alchemical beliefs, but never in fundamentals.

It is his avidity to belittle the views and efforts of others that gives one the impression of true revolutionary ardor. He often laughs at alchemists and refers to them as "fools who thresh empty straw." These and even more abusive flurries must not be taken to mean, however, that he in any way questioned any alchemical belief or the basic principle of transmutation. On the contrary, he bragged that he had performed it on many occasions. Thus his student and assistant Franz writes in a letter published in 1586: "One day he said to me: 'Franz, we have no money' and gave me a gulden bidding me go to the apothecary, to get a pound's weight of mercury and bring it to him. . . . Then he placed four bricks so close together on the hearth that the air below could hardly escape and shook the mercury into a crucible, which he set upon the bricks bidding me lay burning coals about it. . . . After a long time he said: 'Our volatile slave may fly away from us, we must see what he is doing.' As we came in, it was already smoking and flying away. . . . Then he said: 'Take out the pincers and cover the crucible, make up the fire and let it stand' . . . we forgot what was in the crucible for half an hour when he said: 'We must now see what God has given us; take off the lid.' . . . 'What like is it?' said he. I said 'It looks yellow, like gold.' 'Yes,' he said, 'it will be gold.' . . . It was gold. Then he said: 'Take it and carry it to the goldsmith over the apothecary's and ask him to give me money for it.' This I did. The goldsmith weighed it . . . and fetched money in a flat purse made of cardboard which was full of Rhenish guldens and said: 'Take this to your master and say that it is not quite enough, but I will send him the rest when I get it.'" (Stoddart, p. 252) Elsewhere he states: "And from such has arisen the opinion that a change can be made in metals and that one substance can be transformed into another, so that a rough, coarse and filthy substance can be transmuted into one that is pure, refined and sound. Such discoveries I have attained in various kinds, always connected with attempts to transmute into gold and silver."

Paracelsus' acceptance of the full alchemical creed is basically as orthodox as it could possibly be. The Hermetic and Alchemical writings of Paracelsus, edited by A. E. Waite in two volumes totaling 800 pages, hardly encompass all his authentic works on the subject. But these are sufficient to prove the point. Paracelsus was in every way a regular, orthodox, typical chip-of-the-old-block alchemist, a great chemist with vast practical experience but fully steeped in alchemical language and ideas as spoken and conceived at the time. His pupil and amanuensis, Oporinus, in a rather candid letter written after his master's death, records, "He always had a fire glowing in a corner of our room on which either his alkali, or his Oleum sublimati, or the King praecipitati or arsenical oil, or Crocus martes or his wonderful apodeldoc or whatever else, was stewing." (Karl Sudhoff, Paracelsus, Leipzig, 1936, p. 47)

As a matter of fact, his numerous alchemical writings present an excellent portrait of the man and his relation to the belief web of his times.

For example, in a work entitled The Treasure of Treasures for Alchemists, he presents a typical receipt for the preparation of the Green Lion. "Take the vitriol of Venus, carefully prepared according to the rules of the Spagyric Art, and add thereto the elements of water and air which you have reserved. Resolve and set to putrefy for a month according to instructions. When the putrefaction is finished, you will behold the sign of the elements. Separate and you will soon see two colors, namely, white and red. . . . Work upon this tincture by means of a retort and you will perceive a blackness issue forth. . . . Rectify until you find the true Green Lion which you will recognize by its great weight. . . . This is the tincture, transparent gold. . . . This is true and genuine Balsam, the Balsam of the Heavenly Stars, suffering no bodies to decay, nor allowing leprosy, gout or dropsy to take root." (Waite, vol. I, p. 38)

This is fairly typical alchemical language. But no sooner does Paracelsus complete this matter-of-fact paragraph, than he launches the following tirade: "O, you hypocrites, who despise the truths taught you by a true physician, who is himself instructed by nature, and is a son of God himself! Come then and listen, impostors who prevail only by the authority of your high positions! After my death, my disciples will burst forth and drag you to the light, and shall expose your dirty drugs wherewith up to this time you have compassed the death of princes, and the most invincible magnates of the Christian world. Woe for your necks in the day of judgment! I know that the monarchy will be mine. Mine, too, will by the honor and glory. Not that I praise myself: Nature praises me. Of her I am born; her I follow. She knows me and I know her, etc., etc." (ibid, p. 39) After this harangue, the point of which is not clear, he says, "But I must proceed with my design," and goes on with the usual alchemical lingo about red Sol and sulphur of Sol congelating in a pelican and yielding the Tincture of the Alchemists.

Yet, there can be little doubt that Paracelsus contributed significantly toward new ideas in chemistry. He conceived rightly all events in nature as being chemical in nature. He states, "For the baker is an alchemist when he bakes bread, the vine grower when he makes wine, the weaver when he makes cloth. Therefore whatever grows in nature useful to man—whoever brings it to the point to which it was ordered by nature, he is an alchemist." (Stillman, J. M., Paracelsus, Chicago, p. 37.) This was a novel and useful point of view.

As a reformer in chemistry his contribution lay in the inclusion of compounds of mercury, antimony, lead, arsenic, copper, bismuth, iron, and zinc among the remedies of the period. He also introduced opium. He did not make any basic discoveries, though it is claimed that he was the first fully to describe metallic arsenic, zinc, and bismuth, which be

IATRO-CHEMISTRY AND PHLOGISTON

called half metals because of their lack of the lustre and ductility of the true metals. Paracelsus is also said to have improved methods of amalgamating copper and was the first to reveal the true difference between sulfuric acid and alum, to have discovered the chloride and sulphate of mercury, calomel, the flower of sulphur, and several other compounds as well as many reactions. He certainly did much to augment the use of minerals in medicine.

His theoretical contributions, including his violent deviation from the past, are small except for the inclusion of salt as a property of elements in addition to mercury and sulphur. He records his ideas at length on the relationship of metals in his Concerning the Nature of Things. "Know, then, that all the seven metals are born from a threefold matter, namely Mercury, Sulphur and Salt, but with distinct and peculiar colorings. . . . These three substances he (Hermes) names Spirit, Soul and Body. . . . But it must not be understood that from Mercury, and any Sulphur and any Salt, these seven metals can be generated, or in like manner, the Tincture of the Philosopher's Stone by the Art and the industry of the Alchemist in the fire; but all these seven metals must be generated in the mountains by the Archeus of the earth." (Waite, vol. I, p. 125) Elsewhere in the same work he states, "For all that fumes and disappears in vapors is Mercury; all that burns and is consumed is Sulphur; all that is ashes is also Salt," which, in reality, cannot be regarded as either new or a particularly profitable concept. One must therefore agree with Stillman that, "The great service of Paracelsus to chemistry was not in any epoch-making discovery nor in any development of theory of permanent value, but in opening a new and great field for chemical activity in the application of chemistry to the preparation of mineral and vegetable remedies." (Stillman, p. 108). At best this is only partly true, since mineral and vegetable remedies are as old as man. Paracelsus merely laid greater stress on them. Since none of his concoctions had been tested, his vituperative cocksureness was wholly uncalled for and unjustified. Nevertheless, his ravings served a useful purpose as viewed in historical retrospect. Yet, a contemporary of his, writing under the name of Basil Valentine, no doubt left a far greater imprint on the science of chemistry and without all the bombast and fanfare!

Somewhat less tangible was his contribution to medical theory and practice. There is no doubt that he was a great healer, an amazingly keen observer, and possessed of much medical common sense. Yet, the opinion of medical historians of his influence on the course of medicine is strongly divided. Stillman gives an excellent summary of this matter in his book. It might be of interest to present here a general outline of his medical theories.

In his "Book of the Three Principles, their Forms and Operations," he develops the value to medicine of his three principles, Mercury, Sulphur, and Salt. In each organism there proceeds a threefold operation: cleansing or eliminating through salt; breaking up, or consuming through sulphur and carrying away through mercury. All proper processes are supervised by an Archeus. The proper coordination of these three functions means health, their disharmony, disease. Disease is also brought about by the superfluity in the body or by a shortage of one of these principles. Hence there are some diseases which must be cured with salt, others with mercury, and still others with sulphur.

"The three substances are in the four elements, or mothers of all things; for out of the elements proceed all things; from earth come plants, trees and all their varieties; from water, metals, stones, and all minerals; from the air, dew and manna; from fire, thunder, flashes of light, snow and hail. And when the microcosm is broken up and destroyed, part becomes earth, and so wonderful that in brief time it bears the fruit whose seed has been sown therein, and this the doctor should know. Out of the broken body, too, comes the other element, water; and as water is the mother of the minerals, the alchemist can compound rubies out of it. And the dissolution too gives the third element, fire, from which hail can be drawn. And air too ascends with the rising of the breath, just as dew forms inside a closed glass. There is another transmutation after these, and it yields every kind of sulphur, salt and mercury. How necessary is it therefore to make visible the microcosmic world, for it contains much that is for a man's health, his water of life, his arcanum, his balsam, his golden drink and the like. All these things are in the microcosm; as they are in the outer world, just so are they in the inner world."

There are mercurial diseases, sulphurous and salt diseases. Since like cures like, a time-honored medicinal slogan, these diseases must be cured by their corresponding principles. Hence, there are three basic diseases and three basic medicines, though that is putting it simply. The substance mercury is manifold, and complex, hence the mercuric diseases are manifold. Diseases due to disturbances in the body's mercury or its corruption are gout, mania, frenzy, pustules, syphilis, leprosy, and many others. These are to be cured by treatment with mercury. On the other hand, mercury may exist as a mineral, as a wood, or as a plant. The same is true of salt and sulphur. Hence a physician must know minerals and diseases. And each time Paracelsus reaches a conclusion like the one above, of which he is exceptionally proud, he pauses for a parenthetical remark about the folly and chatter of "those old fiddles Avicenna, Mesue, Galen, Aristotle and the rest." "There are in the human body a salt of fire, a salt of borax, a salt of arsenic and many others. There is no theorizing about them as the ancients did, or learning about them as the philosophers did, for the sores and wounds have their laws and there is nothing to be built on conjecture and fancy." "There are wide differences between what the ancient doctors taught and what we here teach, and therefore our healing art widely differs from theirs. For we teach that what heals a man also wounds him and what has wounded will also heal him." "Therefore, it is reasonable to ridicule the old theories with their causes, reasons and the like. And those who follow whither they lead may be even more ridiculed, etc."

These great revolutionary theories of sulphur, mercury and salt were the truths he fought for, the truths which he hoped to see replace the falsehoods of those ignorant and deceitful fools Hippocrates, Aristotle and Galen. The Galenic doctrine, the one accepted by the medical profession of the time, stressed the four humors—phlegm, blood, yellow bile and black bile. A proper balance among these humors spelled health, disharmony meant disease. Medical diagnosis and analysis involved detection of the humor that caused the disturbances, and all treatment was directed at restoring the allegedly disturbed balance. The revolutionary theory of Paracelsus was different, of course. But precisely how significant does the difference seem to us? Was the rebellion really a battle for truth? Was the violent and prolific abuse hurled by the rebel, the voice of a misunderstood prophet or the ravings of a braggart, perpetually hurt, perpetually demanding more sacrifices to his Ego?

His Excellent Treatise deals with advice to physicians containing nothing that had not been said by Hippocrates or Galen or many others, for that matter. His Paramirum deals with diseases that arise from foulness or poisons contained in food, diseases ascribed to the action of the stars, diseases arising from natural causes such as foul elements or natural humors, diseases arising from evil spirits and magic, and diseases sent by God as punishment for sin. Digestion is pictorially described, and the author's famous homeopathic philosophy is generously expounded. "Each desires its own like, the sweet desires the sweet, the bitter desires the bitter, each in its degree and measure, as those held by the plants sweet, sour and bitter. Shall the liver seek medicine in manna, honey, sugar or in the polypody fern? No, for like seeks its like. Nor in the order of anatomy shall cold be a cure for heat or heat for cold. It would be a wild disorder did we seek our cure in contraries. A child asks his father for bread and he does not give him a snake . . . what blind man asks bread from God and receives poison? If thou art experienced and grounded in anatomy, thou wilt not give a stone for bread."

Digestion is pictured as a complex chemical process presided over by an Archeus or chemical demon which breaks down the ingested food and separates the digestible from the indigestible. The former he converts into nourishment and blood; the latter he discards. The archeus is independent of the human will. Should he fail in his tasks, disorder and disease follow. A similarly fortuitous chemical idea, which we consider prophetic and far sighted today because it happens to resemble modern trends, is Paracelsus' concepts of *tartarus*. By Tartarus is meant a thickening of the juices, a precipitation of solids causing thereby certain diseases, such as stiffening of limb movements, or kidney and liver disorders, depending on the location of its formation.

The fact that many authoritative historians of medicine regard Paracelsus as having exerted some influence upon medical thought and practice must be taken into account. Of vital relevance to our discussion is Stillman's comment: "It is very difficult to justly balance the progressive and reactionary influences he exerted upon the progress of medicine—and naturally, therefore, authorities differ upon this question. Thus Neuburger appreciates the value of the accomplishments of Paracelsus, yet doubts that he is to be considered as a reformer of medicine in the sense that was Vesalius or Paré (his contemporaries): that is, he laid a foundation-stone of importance and the real value of much of his thought required the later developments of modern scientific thought for its interpretation. His aim was to found medicine upon physiological and biological foundations, but the method he chose was not the right method, and his analogical reasoning and fantastic philosophy of macrocosm and microcosm were not convincing and led nowhere. The disaffection and discontent with conditions in medicine produced by his campaign can, thinks Neuburger, hardly be called a revolution. That was to come later through the constructive work of more scientific methods." (ibid, p. 128).

Surely the moral to us must be that less rebelliousness and a little more humility were called for. The new ideas proved centuries later to be quite right, and hence deservant of stress at any time. They had in fact been previously suspected to some extent. They began to take form many years after Paracelsus, but in a manner in no way affected by his works. Some historians claim that his influence was reactionary because "by discarding and condemning all the ancient authorities, thinks Magnus, Paracelsus assailed not only the corrupted Galenism of his time, but did much to discredit the positive achievements of the Greeks." (ibid, p. 130) Hence such labels as revolutionary and reactionary are often wholly misleading.

His beliefs in sorcery, magic, and necromancy were as deeprooted as those of any learned or common man of the period. Like everyone else, he was critical of many ideas and practices, but never of the basic assumptions of the times. Many magicians worked for evil and availed themselves of the aid of the devil. Hence, magic, sorcery, and necromancy are displeasing to God and must not be resorted to. Besides, it is foolish to rely upon the devil, because in the long run he is not as powerful as some think and only God is truly omnipotent, omniscient, and omnipresent. "Do you really believe that the devil in his own might can make a charm so that no one shall be able to wound or stab me? That is impossible; no one but God can do that. The devil can create nothing, not so much that an earthern pot cannot be broken, far less a human being. He cannot even extract the smallest tooth, far less heal a sickness." (Stoddart, p. 258) He did believe that evil spirits of men have magical powers to cause disease in innocent victims, and he devoted a section of his Volumen Paramirum to an abstruse discussion of these unfortunate phenomena.

He believed that the spirit present in each body along with the soul may be coerced by the will of the man who is their master to attack the spirits of other persons and thus do them bodily harm. However, if the attacked spirit is strong enough, the aggressor may be repulsed and even injured. He also believed that the devil was able to induce in man an evil environment, favorable to the entry of disease. It is true, he denied the efficacy of some charms and amulets. Those charms which owed their powers to witchcraft and the devil he condemned with his characteristic virulence. "It is fantastic to suppose that written characters can make either friendship or enmity." Yet he was the discoverer and proponent of healing amulets composed of different metals. One particularly favorite type he named Electrum Magicum. Great healing powers were attributed by him to precious stones and he used them in numerous charms which he called Gamathei. He was a great believer in the medicinal value of the bezoar stone, a name given to any solid, abnormal formation in the internal organs of animals, and regarded by all physicians of the Middle Ages as a most marvelous remedy for a variety of diseases. Since he considered himself the greatest living scholar of the cabala, it goes without saying he was a strong believer in all numerological theories of the time. Thus his assistant, Oporinus, writes: "As a purge he gave a precipitate of theriaca or of mithridate or simply the juice of cherries and grapes in the form of granules (about the size of the droppings of mice) and he was careful always to give them in uneven numbers (1, 3, and 5). He was bitterly opposed to the polypharmacy which prevailed so widely in his day." In addition, he nurtured a strong faith in the world of fanciful spirits as envisaged by the Teutonic tribes. He recognized spirits of fire, earth, air and water, imps, gnomes and hobgoblins, dryads and familiars, astral spirits of plants and animals, telepathy, omens and similar concepts.

Like a true rebel, Paracelsus had one guiding obsession. "Alchemy is to make neither gold nor silver; its use is to make the supreme essences and to direct them against diseases." All physiology was to be explained as chemistry, and chemistry was to be the handmaid of medicine. This change of stress is not as startling as it may seem. The belief that the philosopher's stone had arcane powers, could cure all ills, establish physical and mental perfection, effect longevity and even bring about rejuvenescence, had been part of alchemical lore long before Paracelsus. It was believed that the chemical potency of the philosopher's stone could catalyze health-restoring processes and dissolve harmful impurities.

To Paracelsus, the value of chemistry in medicine loomed so large that he refused, for instance, to concede any importance to anatomy, which, even prior to the publication of Vesalius' *De corporis humani fabrica*, had been making considerable headway. He dismissed the subject with the statement, "To dissect was a peasant's manner of procedure." Though he wrote a book entitled "Greater Surgery," it is difficult to imagine that he could have made any significant contribution to that subject.

Like the behaviorists of our own day who minimized truly psychological phenomena and stressed the role of physiology in psychological problems, he too had a slogan that was so all-embracing as to contain more than a mere grain of truth in it. To the behaviorists every aspect of behavior was physics and chemistry, a basically correct but often irrelevant and limited assertion. To Paracelsus, everything was chemistry. His appeal, too, was to experiment and science. He condemned the theoreticians, just as the behaviorists fulminated at the introspectionists, and both gave specific explanations of things they "sensed" but knew nothing about. Nevertheless, both were stimulating.

The books of Paracelsus contain a maze of privately sanctioned terms, such as Adrop, Azane, or Azar for the principle of wisdom, Azoth for that of creation, Cherio for the quintessence or the virtue of a body, Derses for the breath of the earth which promotes growth, and many others. "He deals in his writings with many subjects for which our modern language has no appropriate terms. He therefore invented a great many words of his own to express his meanings and only a few of his words have attained the right of citizenship in our language. To facilitate the study of the works of Paracelsus, his disciples Gerhard Dorn, Bernard Thurneysser, and Martin Ruland composed dictionaries to explain the meaning of such curious terms. The one compiled by Ruland, entitled 'Lexicon Alchemicum,' Prague 1612, is the most complete." (Hartman, F., The Life and the Doctrines of Paracelsus, N. Y., 1932, p. 29).

It is hard to conceive of any other writer of the period whose views are permeated with magic to a higher degree than those of Paracelsus. Magic is the very foundation of his way of thought. He defines it as wisdom, "the conscious employment of spiritual powers to produce visible effects, as of the will, of love, of imagination. . . ." The virtues or quintaessentia of his remedies share with plants and animals and their organic compounds certain life-giving values, certain medicinal powers.

We are forced, then, to conclude that in retrospect Paracelsus differed very little from his predecessors and contemporaries. The rebel as an innovator can at most seek to modify or make a small dent upon the total pattern of a belief. In view of the slow rate of change of such patterns, hence of the rate of progress in any specific field, a small dent is a good record for any single being. The drama that accompanies the work of rebels may not at all be due to economic resistance by vested interests, as postulated by some authors—(Stern J. B., Social Factors in Medical Progress, New York, 1927), but to the sheer emotionalism and egocentricity of the rebel, mingled with the general inertia displayed by cultures at all times. It is claimed by some writers that the chemical work of George Agricola, a quiet contemporary of Paracelsus, was far more revolutionary in its consequences than all the sizzlings of the Paracelsian school. (Agricola, George, De re metallica, London, 1912, translated and edited by H. C. Hoover and L. H. Hoover).

2. *The Fate of a Movement*

Yet Paracelsus did lay the foundations for a new school of thought; witness his fanatical and militant followers. In the field of chemistry he brought about a shift that was stimulating, nonetheless, and led to some valuable finds. For example, he prescribed mercury for syphilis. His reason for that treatment was his fanciful theory of the balance of mercury, salt and sulphur. Though the term mercury implied a quality, he was nevertheless led to believe that metallic mercury should be added, thus actually initiating an effective remedy. Similar remedies involved arsenic, zinc and other metals for equally fantastic reasons. A vast number of his recipes were, however, as ineffective as his reasons were ridiculous. The fact that one in many proved useful makes for progress. Desirable results are noted more often than not, and the good medicine is retained.

The school of thought Paracelsus founded boasts some prominent chemists and physicians, while there are few, if any, great chemists among its opponents. Thurneysser, Turquet de Mayerne, Quercetanus, Croll, Mynsicht were its early defenders, Libavius and Angelus Sala, two outstanding chemical contributors, Van Helmont, one of the most brilliant scientists of all time, and such leading chemical investigators as Sennert, Glauber, de le Boe Sylvius, Tachenius, and Willis were on its list of adherents.

All of these high-ranking chemists, whose lives extended until about the second half of the seventeenth century, when the iatro-chemical philosophy was supplanted by another, believed that chemistry should be the handmaiden of medicine. Yet this must not be taken to mean that the alchemical views were entirely in disrepute. Far from it. Without a single exception all those named believed in transmutation and in the rest of the alchemical credo. The new fashion merely dictated that more attention be paid to the medical aspect of chemistry than to the philosophical one of transmutation. Thus Thurneysser was quite an alchemist, and though he enjoyed a great reputation as a healer and was court physician to several German princes, he performed famous transmutations while travelling in Italy. Libavius, Sala, van Helmont, and all the other supporters of Paracelsus also claimed to have performed projections, believed in potable gold, the grand elixir, etc.

On the other hand, most of the chemists named above who were also famous physicians, accepted and defended the views of Paracelsus without necessarily discarding the old cures. Thus Turquet de Mayerne, a famous French physician and Professor of Chemistry at Paris, used chemical remedies praised by Paracelsus as well as Galenic prescriptions. For merely defending Paracelsus, the Medical Faculty of Paris, that scientific body which persecuted more physicians and scientists than all the Inquisitions and tyrants of the Middle Ages, had him dismissed from his chair and forbade him to practice medicine. He escaped to England, where he became the personal physician of James I and II.

With the passage of time there gradually germinated in the minds of some supporters of Paracelsus a critical attitude towards much of what the master had taught. Libavius, faithful alchemist and the discoverer of many chemical reactions and practical measures such as glass staining, defended the theories of Paracelsus but exposed many weaknesses. The same is true of Angelus Sala, another pioneer in chemical research.

The giant of iatrochemistry is Johann Baptist van Helmont, born in Brussels in 1577, the scion of a wealthy family of Belgian nobility. He studied philosophy, science, and theology at Louvain, then returned home and married a rich Brabantine lady. He lived a secluded life on his estates, pursuing chemical researches and devoting much time and energy to charity and benevolence.

Though a firm believer in transmutation and the alcahest of Paracelsus, he was strongly skeptical of the medicinal value of potable gold. Though he regarded Paracelsus as supreme master, he nevertheless rejected the Aristotelian four elements which Paracelsus held as basic. His reasons were Aristotle's paganism and the fact that fire was not an independent element, but a quality of many substances. Similarly, earth was no element because it was formed by water. He also rejected in its entirety Paracelsus' basic theory of the three principles because he claimed their presence could not be demonstrated in animal organisms. "He assumes there are two primitive elements, air and water." (Stillman, J. M., The Story of Early Chemistry, N. Y. 1924).

He regarded water as the most significant component of all matter. His evidence for this conclusion comes from a rather ingenious experiment. He placed in a large flower pot 200 pounds of dried earth and planted in it a young willow weighing five pounds. The plant was protected from dust and supplied with rainwater each day. The tree grew, of course, and after five years was found to weigh 164 pounds, while the earth when dried was found to have lost only two ounces. Obviously, reasoned van Helmont quite logically though falsely, the increment came from the added water. Besides, marine fish, too, he said, grew large in water.

He was the originator of the term gas. Though it had been known previously that "airs" existed which had properties that differed from those of common air, it was not until van Helmont's work that such airs were isolated and the concept made clearer. He also is responsible for many other valuable observations in chemistry as well as in medicine, as for instance the fact that a volume of air is smaller after a body burns in it, or that a metal can be differently combined in various compounds and be recovered without having lost its identity, thus undermining the very basis of the belief in transmutation. Nevertheless, he was a strong adherent of the full alchemical folklore and claimed to have made gold on many occasions.

Though hardly agreeing with Paracelsus on major issues, he admired greatly his approach. He realized the limitation of his chemical theory, which lay in its vagueness, and he set out to make it more concrete, at least to his satisfaction. Instead of making the three principles responsible for health and disease, he postulated a theory resembling an acid-alkali equilibrium in the juices of the body. He held fermentation responsible for growth, development, and the production of nourishing juices in the blood. Fermentation is accelerated by gastric acid and animal heat, as is digestion. The acid of the stomach is neutralized by the alkali of the gall in the duodenum. When the acid is not properly neutralized by the all-powerful Archeus, disease ensues, since the acid penetrates other parts of the body. Different diseases imply accumulation of acid in different parts of the body, and a list follows indicating which diseases are due to acid in different organs. He shared with Paracelsus a deep faith in the occult and the mystical and encumbered digestion with an Archeus of somewhat greater powers and deeper spiritualism than the postulate of Paracelsus. Since digestion is an important process in human physiology, the Archeus is an important spirit often dominating even the workings of the brain.

He also rejected the Tartarus of Paracelsus and postulated the cause of urinary calculi to be ordinary precipitation of crystalline salts from urine. He was also critical of a large number of the new chemical remedies which he had found harmful, and suggested many of his own, some of which proved efficacious.

It is also of interest that van Helmont, though more cultured and refined than Paracelsus, shared many of the features of the latter's personality. He was almost as cocksure and braggardly, as mystical and religious, as broadsided and humanitarian, as sharp an observer and clever an experimentalist, as superstitious, as self-righteous, as abusive of others and as great a healer as was Paracelsus. Is this a coincidence, a mark of the times, or a common feature of gifted rebels?

As stated, van Helmont ascribed the causes of all disease to a disturbed Archeus. Hence his philosophy of healing was aimed at pacifying or rectifying that biochemical spirit. He relied much upon dietetics and "upon acting on the imaginations of his patients. He considered certain words as very efficacious in curing the diseases of the Archeus. He admitted the existence of the universal medicine. . . . Mercurials, antimonials, opium, and wine are particularly agreeable to the Archeus, when in a state of delirium from fever." (ibid., p. 192).

Two great chemists belonging to that period, whose work may be claimed to have contributed to the philosophy of iatrochemistry were Johann Rudolph Glauber (1604–1670), and de le Boe Sylvius (1614–1672). Both were physicians and believers in the philosopher's stone, transmutation and the alcahest. Yet their major concern was with the role of chemistry in the physiology of health and disease. Both were critical of some aspects of the iatro-chemical attitude, but gullible of others; both sought to solve most medical problems by explaining them in terms of acid-base, fermentation, alkaline acridity, action of humors, distillation, precipitation, and digestion with the same nonchalance that behaviorists explained problems of behavior as physics and chemistry or conditioning, or as modern Marxists explain all current social and political situations by invoking Wall Street, Imperialism and Big Business. "In the human body he (Sylvius) saw nothing but a magma of humors continually in fermentation, distillation, effervescence or precipitation; and the physician was degraded by him to the rank of distiller or brewer." (ibid., p. 196). Every function, every disease, was readily reduced to a chemical explanation which, if it failed to be specific and verifiable, was at least sizzling with enthusiasm and hope in the promise of the new science of chemistry. Of interest, also, is the fact that both these gifted iatrochemists shared many of Paracelsus' characteristics.

IATRO-CHEMISTRY AND PHLOGISTON

Yet neither was as spiritualistic, mystical, or as fanatically religious as their master.

In spite of the pugnacity and competence of its adherents, of the appealing truth of its basic philosophy, the novelty of its ideas and the medical successes accomplished by some of its new cures, iatro-chemistry offered a solution for everything. The iatro-chemists claimed to be thoroughly scientific with their glib juggling of acid, base, Archeus, fermentation, tartarus, digestion, precipitation, humors, balance, and many other such terms, but failed, nevertheless, actually to analyze a single physiological system illustrating any of these principles. The contributions they did make were as random-begotten as those of the alchemists, and came merely by dint of muddling along.

After a hundred and fifty years of talk of acid, alkali, fermentation, digestion, and similar concepts, chemical research brought to the fore some useful information on these subjects. Chemistry was being steadily enriched, in spite of the heated arguments. New problems emerged and helped seek out their own solutions. A new generation of chemists arose, as it were, which became interested in the rapidly expanding horizons of chemical phenomena per se, and cared little for the presumable subservience of all chemistry to medicine. A change of outlook in chemistry was thus set afoot without battles and revolutions. As with the inception of iatro-chemistry, there occurred no complete displacement of the old, but merely a new stress, a new attraction, a new path branching off from the old and familiar one.

It may be worth observing that the very fortress the rebels stormed, namely, the medical profession with its time-honored empirical remedies, emerged fundamentally unperturbed and undismayed by the attack. Of interest also is the fact that van Helmont, with all the deep regard he entertained for Paracelsus, proved to be a potent factor in undermining his master's prestige by his violent refutation of the three principles, the very basis of the Paracelsan philosophy. Similarly, by proving that metals when dissolved in acids were not destroyed or transformed, but could be recovered in their original state, van Helmont laid the foundation for the destruction of one of his own cherished beliefs and inspirations, namely, transmutation. Thus what one rebels against, one may fail to destroy or even weaken, and what one believes in and defends, one may by one's own labors undermine and destroy.

3. New Trends, New Troubles

Iatro-chemistry, like alchemy, faded out of the picture, and, according to historians, experimental chemistry took its place. It did not succumb in battle, a decrepit old stronghold of reaction battered by the vigorous and enthusiastic blows of a rising tide of reason. Like astrology, it was merely left by the wayside because a new attraction made its appearance. However, some belief patterns do make their exit in battle, often a sham battle over a philosophy grown senile and obsolete, and the phlogiston theory to be considered now may serve as an interesting example. It is true that Robert Boyle (1627–1691) and Herman Boerhaave (1688–1738) did advance some telling opposition to iatro-chemistry or, for that matter, to transmutation of elements also. In his Preliminary Discourse Robert Boyle states his position: "After having gone through the common operations of that art and coming seriously to reflect upon them, I thought it a pity that instruments which might prove so serviceable to natural philosophy should be so little employed to advance it. I saw that several chymists had, by a laudable diligence, obtained various productions and hit upon many more phenomena, considerable in their kind, than could well be expected from their narrow principles; but finding the generality of those addicted to chymistry to have had scarce any view, but to the preparation of medicines, or the improving of metals, I was tempted to consider the art, not as a physician or an alchymist but a philosopher. And with this in view, I once drew up a scheme for chymical philosophy; which I should be glad that any experiments or observations of mine might any way contribute to complete." p. XXVI–XXVII (Philosophical Works by Robert Boyle, London, 1725, Preliminary Discourse, Ed. P. Shaw, 3 vols.).

Generally speaking, however, neither Boyle nor any other great scientist sought to combat the concepts of transmutation. There was merely a shift in interest, as Boyle points out.

The case of phlogiston is of interest because it is our first instance of a theory which was the object of controversy for about three decades, with the correct theory emerging victorious. Many students succumb to the facile idea of picturing this conflict as a replica of the mythical battle between St. George and the dragon, hence as a bitter struggle between Lavoisier and the childish, befuddled defenders of the phlogiston theory. In reality the conflict between the followers of Lavoisier and the phlogistonists has an entirely different moral. It reveals that the proponents of phlogiston were brilliant men and great innovators who were fully aware of all the facts which Lavoisier's theory explains, to our view far better than their own, but who sought very hard to harmonize all new evidence with the older view. It will be seen that the older view did not collapse at once, simply because it had deep roots in a larger philosophy which required some time to be disrupted. It similarly required time for many new ideas cherished by the phlogistonists to become fully absorbed into their philosophy and be properly conceived. All this requires time rather than mere knowledge, logic or brilliance.

Let us review the controversy briefly so as to note these issues.

One of the beliefs of alchemy, as we have seen, was the philosopher's sulphur, by which was understood the combustible property of substances. It was a logical step of early chemistry to look upon fire or combustion as a process in which a combustible substance or principle bound by the body, was released. Substances which could not burn were regarded as devoid of the element fire.

Two brilliant chemists of the latter seventeenth and early eighteenth centuries, Johann Joachim Becher (1635–1682), Professor of Medicine at the University of Mainz, and his pupil, George Ernst Stahl (1660–1734), Professor of Medicine at the University of Halle, formulated the concept of phlogiston which served as an explanation and a bone of contention for chemists for several generations. The concept of phlogiston was particularly clarified by the writings of Stahl, who defined it as the principle of combustibility. It is explained as follows by T. E. Thorpe in his Essays in Historical Chemistry. (London, 1902, p. 41)

"Let me attempt to give you some other notion of this Phlogistic Theory. A piece of wood burns; a piece of stone does not. Why is this? 'Because,' answers Stahl, 'the wood contains a peculiar principle of inflammability: the stone does not. Coal, charcoal, wax oil, phosphorous, sulphur—in short, all combustible bodies—contain this principle in common. To this principle (which, indeed, I regard as a natural substance) I give the name of Phlogiston. I regard all combustible bodies therefore, as compounds, and one of their constituents is phlogiston: the differences which we observe in combustible substances depend partly upon the proportion of the phlogiston they contain, and partly upon the nature of the other constituents. When a body burns it parts with its phlogiston; and all the phenomena of combustion—the heat, the light, and the flame—are due to the violent expulsion of the substance. This phlogiston lies at the basis of all chemical change: all chemical reactions are so many manifestations of parts played by phlogiston.' If zinc be strongly heated it takes fire and burns with a beautiful greenish flame, and a white or yellowish-white substance remains behind. 'Phlogiston,' says Stahl, 'is here making its escape. Zinc is composed of phlogiston and the white earthy powder, which I term the calx of zinc (zinc oxide), now becomes visible.' . . . In heating the lead the calx had, to begin with, a yellow colour, and then it became red by the prolonged action of the fire. The change in the colour affords a measure of the rate of the expulsion of the phlogiston.

"We all know that if a candle is burnt in a limited amount of air, the flame will shortly be extinguished, although no change apparently takes place in the air. This was explained, according to Stahl's doctrine, by supposing that air had an affinity for phlogiston, and that in the act of combustion the phlogiston was transferred from the candle to the air. Gradually, however, the limited amount of air becomes saturated with Phlogiston—that is wholly phlogisticated—and combustion accordingly ceases. In like manner, if a mouse is placed in a confined volume of air, after a time it experiences difficulty in breathing and eventually is suffocated, although the bulk of the air remains the same. The act of breathing, therefore, is nothing else than the transference of phlogiston from the animal to the air, which gradually becomes phlogisticated and is thereby unable to support respiration. To this doctrine of phlogiston, originally broached as a theory of chemistry, nearly every European chemist for upwards of half a century after its author's death gave an implicit adherence."

As J. W. White points out in his excellent volume The Phlogiston Theory, Stahl did not quite picture phlogiston to be a natural or material substance. On the contrary, he insisted throughout that it is "a principle," though no doubt he would have preferred it as material substance had he believed he had enough evidence for it. He had no such evidence and he knew it. It was present in combustible substances, charcoal being particularly rich in it. Metals give it off to the atmosphere when they burn and are converted into calces, or oxides. When such calces are heated in the presence of charcoal, the latter gives off its phlogiston to the calx which is then reconverted to the metal it came from. The liberation or loss of phlogiston by metals on burning is aided by nitre, because "with phlogiston it is kindled to rapid conflagration." It is abstract heat, found in winds, clouds or lightning, rising skyward but ever returning earthward. It is not quite the same as heat but merely the Phlogistic Principle. In a word it was an abstract concept temporarily helpful in symbolizing a complex and puzzling set of processes. It is not fire but an essential component of it; it is the cause of color; and it is not a concrete substance either in pure or combined form, hence it is imperceptible to the senses. It does not escape from the atmosphere and cannot be destroyed.

It is however a fairly general occurrence in science that an idea postulated originally merely as a scheme or as a vague concept becomes, in the course of its day to day exploitation by succeeding thinkers, endowed with real and material existence. That apparently was the fate of phlogiston which Stahl quite wisely left in midair encased in all the vagueness that made it somehow valuable. True, some of Stahl's followers appreciated and retained their master's idea. J. H. Pott (1692–1777) for example, insists that phlogiston cannot and should not be

IATRO-CHEMISTRY AND PHLOGISTON 347

thought of "in terms of number, extent or weight, owing to the subtlety of its component particles." After all, he argued, "when I say Light or Fire everyone understands what I mean, although no one can give either an entirely satisfactory definition including all its properties." Nevertheless, in his work The Properties and Effect of Light and Heat he proceeds to propound the view that phlogiston is a substance in inseparable combination with other substances, pervading the entire universe, filling the atmosphere as well as the animal, vegetable and mineral worlds, though it combines poorly with water. Those elements which contain more phlogiston give off more heat when attacked by acid. But this was only a beginning. Soon each writer on the subject began to inject into the concept more and more concreteness, which process seemed inevitable unless one was constantly on guard against such a temptation. This trend culminated in the writings of Scheele who definitely regarded phlogiston as a substance having weight, testifying thus that the materialist trend had won over Platonic vagueness. "Phlogiston is a true element and a quite simple principle. (2) By the attractive powers of certain materials, it can be transferred from one substance to another; these substances then undergo important changes so that they not infrequently thereby become able, through the action of the heat lodged between their particles, to pass into fusion or into elastic vapor: and in this respect it is the chief cause of smell. (3) It very often brings the particles of substances into such a position, that these attract either all or only certain rays of light or even none at all. (4) In the transference from one substance to another it does not impart to the latter either light or heat. (5) But with fire and air this element enters into such a subtle union that it penetrates very easily through the finest pores of all substances. There thus results from this union the matter of light as well as the matter of heat. In all these unions the phlogiston does not undergo the slightest change and it can be separated anew from the last union. Phlogiston cannot possibly be obtained by itself alone, since it does not separate from any substance, however loosely it may be united with it, when there is not another present with which it is in immediate contact." (Carl Wilhelm Scheele, Chemical Treatise on Air and Fire; Collected Papers p. 137 London 1937) Clearly then even Scheele was far from naive in his claim that phlogiston was an element. Besides, after discussing the possibility of separating phlogiston from metallic earths he remarks: "Who does not see that a wide field for new and fine experiments is here open before us?"

It had been known for some time independently of and long before the phlogiston theory was advocated, that air was essential to combustion. Robert Boyle (1627–1691) had even demonstrated in his Relation Betwixt Flame and Air, at about the time when Stahl was born, that common combustibles could not be ignited in a vacuum, which he was one of the first to work with. As early as 1674, when Stahl was only thirteen, Boyle had already suggested that air was not an elementary body but "a confused aggregate of effluviums from such differing bodies that, though they all agree in constituting by their minuteness and various motions the great mass of fluid matter, yet perhaps there is scarce a more heterogeneous body in the world." (White, p. 27) The importance of air in the production of flame had been stressed with perspicacity by Jean Rey (1575-1645), Robert Hooke (1635-1703) and John Mayow (1643-1679) besides Boyle. It was conceded by all that air absorbed the phlogiston issuing from the burning metal or candle or in breathing and could become saturated with it. Nitre, which we know as an oxidizing agent, the phlogistonists regarded as a substance which possessed a special affinity for phlogiston, thus speeding calx formation. "The more phlogiston a metal contains the more heat is also there." (Scheele p. 174)

"Fire," says the same author, "this product of chemistry which is so wonderful, shows us that it cannot be generated without air." Its complex nature is examined by him with meticulous scrutiny.... "The flame of charcoal arises, therefore, when the heat present amongst the red-hot charcoal unites with the phlogiston of the charcoal, and a part of the aerial acid (carbon dioxide) with the ashes. It cannot take fire immediately because the fire air (oxygen) present among the charcoal is already saturated with the phlogiston of the charcoal; it must therefore ascend, when this air meets with the open air: consequently, the red-hot pieces of charcoal if there are wide spaces between them, must appear to burn on the surface." (Scheele p. 174)

Both Scheele and Priestley, who had discovered oxygen independently, were fully aware that fire air was used up in combustion and that the remaining foul air had less weight and volume than the original air. "If the Fire does not yield during combustion a fluid similar to Air, after the spontaneous extinction of the Fire, air is diminished between a third and a fourth of its bulk.... From the above experiments it likewise appears that a given quantity of Air can be united to or saturated as it were only by a certain quantity of phlogiston.... Therefore Air is composed of two different fluids, the one of which attracts not the phlogiston, and the other has the quality of attracting it, and this latter fluid makes between a third and a fourth of the whole bulk of the Air. What becomes of this last kind of Air, after it unites with the phlogiston, is a question which ought not to be decided by surmises, but by new experiments." (White p. 95) Hence Scheele's great amazement when he found that the air remaining after combustion was lighter even though it had presumably gained in phlogiston. He therefore concludes that in "the union of Air with the inflammable principle, a compound is formed,

IATRO-CHEMISTRY AND PHLOGISTON 349

so subtle as to pass through the fine pores of the glass, and disperse all over the Air." After all, light and heat did precisely that, and why not this phlogiston-fire air combination?

Priestley first obtained his oxygen from the oxide of mercury and was unaware of the fact that the gas constituted a part of the air. He called it dephlogisticated air because it allowed things to burn so well in it, which meant that it combined so avidly with phlogiston. It did that because it had so little phlogiston to begin with, hence its name dephlogisticated air. Air in which a substance had burned was called by the same token phlogisticated air. Plants kept in such vitiated air restored to it its dephlogisticated state since plants seem to remove the phlogiston accumulated in such air by the emanation of bodies which had burned in it. In his Observations on Respiration and the use of the Blood, Priestley presents many such acute observations all logically explained in this reverse phlogistic manner, imbued with startling consistency.

The great Cavendish too adhered to the phlogiston theory and also with his eyes open and his mind clear. After he became acquainted with Lavoisier's theory he admitted that "the phenomena of nature might be explained very well on this principle, without the help of phlogiston." He further admitted that "it will be very difficult to determine by experiment which of these opinions is the truest, but as the commonly conceived principle of phlogiston explains all phenomena, at least as well as Mr. Lavoisier's, I have adhered to that." (Experiments on Air.) This from the man who had just discovered the composition of water in a series of brilliant experiments. He was somewhat critical of Lavoisier because of the latter's theory of acids which, Lavoisier claimed, must contain oxygen because the few he had studied contained it. Cavendish knew that hydrochloric and tartaric acids did not lose their acidity upon combining with phlogiston, that is, upon loss of oxygen.

It is essential to bear in mind that few chemists had identical notions of the nature of phlogiston. Because of its vagueness as a principle each chemical philosopher fitted it to his own mold within the framework of its functional realm. And the speculations around it were many, because the problems and the difficulties were many, and the gaps in knowledge wide and numerous.

Another set of facts which seems to us incompatible with a logical defense of phlogiston is the matter of calcination, or the formation of oxides. In terms of the phlogiston theory, when a metal on heating loses phlogiston, a calx is formed. As we say it when a metal combines with oxygen it forms an oxide. Conversely, when a calx was heated it gained or absorbed phlogiston and became a metal. In our terminology the oxygen is driven off from the oxide, leaving the metal behind. Now, it had been common knowledge even before the era of phlogiston that when metals became calces they gained in weight. If phlogiston was at all material in nature, the opposite effect should have been expected. The phlogistonists were fully conscious of this problem and sought to explain it in many ways.

Even Geber who presumably lived in the eighth century A.D. seemed to be aware of the fact that lead gained in weight upon becoming converted into its oxide, minium, when burnt in air. It was surely noticed by the alchemists of the sixteenth century such as Cardan, Scaliger, Fuchsius, Libavius, Caesalpinus, and above all the French chemist Jean Rey (1575–1645). The latter's experiments were most accurate and even took cognizance of the importance of air displacement to the process of weighing as demonstrated by weighing a loose mass of feathers and the same compressed into a ball. Rey even asserted and proved that when a calx is formed, its gain in weight comes from the air which combines with the metal. However a chemist named Otto Tachenius in his Hippocrates Chimicus published in 1668 took issue with this notion on the ground that if the increase in weight of the calx came from the air it should vary with the seasons. In the winter when the air is dense, a calx should gain more than in the summer when the air absorbed is less dense. And since calces weigh alike in all seasons it clearly cannot be claimed their increased weight is derived from air. A bright idea ahead of the time can thus be logically arrested. Like Robert Boyle at about the same time, Tachenius explains the gain in weight on the basis of the influx of fire particles into the metal. To Tachenius it was an acid from the flame. Why Boyle rejected the notion that air was the contributing source to the gain in weight is a mystery. Perhaps the gain by fire particles was merely more attractive and shut out any other possibility.

There were outstanding workers in the field who brushed the problem aside and made no attempt to face it. Others like Juncker postulated that phlogiston possessed negative weight or the principle of levity. Bodies which it pervaded appeared lighter than they actually were and after the phlogiston left them they showed their true weight which appeared to us as if it were a gain. Because some historians of science operated on the notion of the ignorance and stupidity of the past, this levity argument became the symbol of the phlogistonists' folly and immaturity, and is cited in all text books together with Giordano Bruno's martyrdom as a pioneer of Copernicanism and the Church's obdurate opposition to all science.

Another attitude was that of Baumé who in his Chimie Experimentale et Raisonné, elucidated the processes in this manner. Fire is lighter, of course, than the metal. The calx gains in weight on combining with the fire. Hence the calx has a lighter specific weight. "During calcination the metal loses much inflammable material in the form of smoke: this is

IATRO-CHEMISTRY AND PHLOGISTON

naturally of some weight. How comes it then that, in spite of this loss, there yet may be an augmentation of weight as great as that which one often encounters when dealing with metallic bodies, viz. about twelve pounds of calx for every ten of metal? I reply to this that the increase in absolute weight that is observed is due to the fact that a greater quantity of fire enters into the calx than that of the phlogiston which is dissipated or lost during the process. For the rest, it is certain that each type of metal augments in a constant manner its absolute weight during calcination. I realize however that many difficulties yet await explanation. It is difficult, for example, to find out in what state this fire is combined thus in metallic calces." (White p. 84)

Juncker's negative weight idea found favor with few workers. Scheele called attention to the common observation that phlogiston united with air (that is as the remaining nitrogen) made the air less ponderous, but felt obliged to comment that "However, since phlogiston is a substance (which always supposes some weight) I very much doubt whether this hypothesis be founded on truth." Priestley too rejected the idea with the observation "That phlogiston should communicate absolute levity to the bodies with which it is combined, is a supposition that I am not willing to have recourse to, though it would afford an easy solution of the difficulty." He therefore considered this gap in knowledge one of the most serious challenges of the time and consoled himself by stating: "But neither do any of us pretend to have weighed light, or the element of heat, though we do not doubt but that they are properly substances capable by their addition or abstraction, of making great changes in properties of bodies, and of being transmitted from one substance to another." (White p. 86)

The fact is there was hardly a single phlogistonist who failed to mention the gain in weight of calces and then either brushed it aside or suggested some kind of explanation of which they did not seem too sure. There was hardly a single explanation that pleased anyone beyond its originator and there were therefore as many explanations as there were writers.

There is one more point of special interest. By the time Lavoisier appeared on the scene the quantitative method had been deeply rooted in chemistry. Even the concept of chemical combination had been laid down, though not as clearly and convincingly as it appeared after it was polished off by Lavoisier. As we have seen, there was a general feeling that phlogiston did not explain many phases of the baffling chemical problems of the times and Lavoisier's rejection of phlogiston would have stood out as a truly revolutionary feat had he not smuggled in through the back door the concept of caloric. All of which need in no way serve to minimize Lavoisier's monumental contribution, however.

Nor must it be presumed that the new theory of Lavoisier, the one which is still the foundation of our own chemical knowledge, was not given proper consideration by the defenders of the old. In a series of elegant experiments Lavoisier had proved that combustion, respiration, and oxidation meant combination with oxygen which was a gaseous component of air. Priestley was no fanatic or narrowminded partisan, but the phlogiston concept constituted the warp and woof of his mind. He considered carefully the antiphlogistonist view just as Ptolemy examined the possibility of the earth's rotation. "Of late," he writes, "it has been the opinion of many celebrated chemists, Mr. Lavoisier among others, that the whole doctrine of phlogiston is founded on mistake. The arguments in favor of this opinion, especially those which are drawn from the experiments Mr. Lavoisier made on mercury, are so specious that I own I was myself inclined to adopt it." (T. E. Thorpe, Essays in Historical Chemistry, p. 48).

Both Priestley and Cavendish were convinced that they rejected Lavoisier's views on good grounds. Writes Priestley: "Mr. Lavoisier is well known to maintain that there is no such thing as what has been called phlogiston; affirming inflammable air to be nothing else but one of the elements or constituent parts of water. As to myself, I was a long time of the opinion that his conclusion was just and that the inflammable air was really furnished by the water being decomposed in the process (of passing steam through a red hot iron tube thus forming hydrogen). But though I continued to be of this opinion for some time, the frequent repetition of the experiments with the light which Mr. Watt's observation threw upon them, satisfied me at length that the inflammable air came from the iron." (ibid., p. 49). Priestley's experiments were always ingenious and led to numerous discoveries. Yet, in so far as all his thought was dominated by the theory of phlogiston, they could lead to no orderly conception of chemistry and practically lost their merit in the morass of a false foundation. Yet he reasoned and tested experimentally each hypothesis and each conclusion.

And every new discovery which Priestley hit upon only strengthened his phlogistonist views instead of weakening them. For example, when he heated oxides of lead in a cylinder filled with hydrogen, he found that the gas volume decreased and metallic lead was produced. We know now that the decrease resulted from the combination of the released oxygen with some of the hydrogen to form water. But according to the antiphlogistonist views, oxygen should have been given off with resulting increase in the total gas volume. And so Priestley remarked quite honestly: "I viewed this process with the most eager and pleasing expectation of the result, having at that time no fixed opinion on the subject. . . . Seeing the metal to be actually revived, and that in considerable quantity, at the same time that the air was diminished, I could not doubt but that the calx was actually imbibing something from the air; and from its effects in making the calx into metal it could be no other than that to which chemists had unanimously given the name of phlogiston." (Thorpe, p. 45). Precisely what is wrong with this reasoning except the fact that the future proved it wrong?

He regarded these observations as conclusive evidence that the metal resulted from a combination of calx with hydrogen or pure phlogiston. He realized that the metal should weigh more than the calx, if this were so. But it weighed less, and, as usual, the mind could readily supply an explanation. Part of the calx, he argued, was sublimed away by the heat. "Were it possible," he concludes, "to procure a perfect calx no part of which should be sublimed and dispersed by the heat necessary to be made use of in the process, I should not doubt but that the quantity of inflammable air imbibed by it, would sufficiently add to its weight." (ibid., p. 47) Again, the explanation was not supernatural or stupid, but within the realm of probability. Lavoisier was fortunate in approaching the problem under different circumstances, thus peering into a corner which revealed what proved later to be the truth. He was not equally fortunate with his conclusions on the oxygen content of all acids and his theory of caloric.

Moreover, accusations of ignorance, poor observation or inadequate reasoning are of little aid in understanding the true nature of the difficulty. Quite unjustly Berthelot states: "Priestley, the enemy of all theory and of every hypothesis, draws no general conclusion from his beautiful discoveries which he is pleased moreover, not without affection, to attribute to chance. He describes them in the current phraseology of the period with an admixture of peculiar and incoherent ideas and he remained obstinately attached to the theory of phlogiston up to his death." (ibid., p. 152). The character of Priestley, his vast erudition and interests and his philosophic scope could not be more flagrantly misconstrued. His own words uttered years before are the best reply to Berthelot's accusation. "It is always our endeavor, after making experiments, to generalize the conclusions we draw from them, and by this means to form a theory or system of principles to which all the facts may be reduced and by means of which we may be able to foretell the results of future experiments." (ibid., p. 152). Or "My conjectures concerning the course of these appearances are as yet too crude to lay before the Society. My present ideas . . . are that together with other observations which I shall lay before the public, they afford some foundation for supposing that the nitrous acid is the basis of common air, and that nitre is formed by a decomposition of the atmosphere. But it is possible I may think otherwise tomorrow. It is happy, when with a fertility of invention, sufficient to raise hypotheses, a person is not apt to acquire too great attachment to them. By this means they lead to the discovery of new facts and from a sufficient number of these the true theory of nature will easily result." (Douglas McKie, Antoine Lavoisier, London, 1935, p. 184).

Of course, Lavoisier saw it through. But then not every brilliant man hits upon the right combination of circumstances to facilitate his disruption of a particular belief trap. Accepting or breaking the trap is in itself no sign of genius. An original and gifted mind may work most ingeniously within the confines of a given pattern while often a second-rate mind may somehow manage to break it, for many psychological and accidental reasons. Thus many professional sophists and sceptics questioned astrology while scientists and scholars accepted it. The same was true of alchemy or witchcraft. More often than not it is the layman who mocks learning and philosophy, and is a cynic and iconoclast because he views all scholarship with suspicion. Similarly, empiricists opposing any generalizations whatever, may oppose a particular one much in fashion at the time, for no sound reasons, and be judged in the future as great visionaries.

The views of Lavoisier were at first opposed by most outstanding scientists of the day. Of special interest is the fact that Lavoisier, the great liberator and revolutionary in chemistry, was opposed by a political revolutionary, Marat, an amateur scientist, whose treatise on combustion was rejected with ridicule by the Academy. Understandably, the frustrated and embittered Marat declared: "Lavoisier, the putative father of all the discoveries which are noised abroad, having no ideas of his own fastens on those of others, but incapable of appreciating them he abandons them as readily as he adopts them and changes his systems as he does his shoes." (ibid., p. 277) Apparently when it fits the situation, changing one's views is considered derogatory, even by a revolutionary. Upon other occasions not changing them is held up to ridicule.

The brilliant Cavendish weighed carefully the new hypothesis of Lavoisier in his meticulous and pedantic manner. After giving a full and honest summary of Lavoisier's views he concludes: "It will be very difficult to determine by experiment which of these opinions is the truest; but as the commonly received principle of phlogiston explains all phenomena at least as well as Mr. Lavoisier's, I have adhered to that."

To Lavoisier invariably the credit is given for the discovery of oxygen. Yet it is a fact that it was Priestley who discovered it before him and told Lavoisier about it when he saw him in Paris, stating what oxides he obtained it from, how his experiment was done, and what the properties of the gas were. No doubt Priestley's phlogistic reasoning seems topsy-turvy to us. But the fact that he should have discovered oxygen, as did also another pioneer phlogistonist, Scheele, independently of him, and that Cavendish should have discovered nitrogen and the composition of water, are indeed of interest. All three geniuses were confirmed phlogistonists who gave the anti-phlogiston theory of Lavoisier serious and critical consideration, but were obliged to deny its validity. All three were aware of the relevant facts, of the increased weight of the calx (oxide), of the properties of oxygen regarding combustion and respiration, of the role of air and its mixed composition, and of all other arguments used by Lavoisier to prove his now well-established theory. All three were most accurate and ingenious experimenters, making constant use of the quantitative method with the greatest skill. Thus Cavendish records the percentages of nitrogen and oxygen in air as 79.16 and 20.96, respectively. Similarly, Priestley, who like Cavendish, weighed and measured whatever could be so handled, found water to consist of 7.75 parts of oxygen by weight to 1.0 of hydrogen. The modern figures are 7.93 to 1.0. Scheele's experimental genius and insight are universally admitted.

In attacking the phlogiston theory with faultless clarity and perfect experimental evidence, Lavoisier made two significant observations concerning the prevailing opposition to his views. After refuting one by one the arguments of the phlogistonists he writes: "All these reflections confirm what I have advanced, what I intended to prove, what I am going to repeat again, that chemists have made phlogiston a vague principle which is not strictly defined and which consequently fits all the explanations required of it; sometimes the principle has weight, sometimes it has not; sometimes it is free fire, sometimes it is fire combined with earth; sometimes it passes through the pores of vessels, sometimes these are impenetrable to it; it explains at once causticity and non-causticity, transparency and opacity, color and the absence of color. It is a veritable Proteus that changes its form every instant." (ibid., p. 229).

Although this comment was provoked by Macquer's loose reasoning rather than the sounder arguments presented by Priestley or Cavendish, it was nevertheless correct. Its truth is not limited to phlogiston but to all belief patterns man tries to defend, both true and false ones. And man usually defends everything he believes in for some interval of time, which may vary in extent from one day to several thousand years. Man has rationalized about beliefs which have proven to be false and about beliefs which have stood the test of time.

Lavoisier adds further, "For, we cannot repeat it too often, it is neither Nature nor the facts she presents but *our own reason* that deceives us." The world is not divided into geniuses and fools, far-sighted revolutionaries and victims of prejudice, of blindness, and "vested interests." It is our own reason that forms our shackles, though it is also our reason which leads us to the truth.

The battle of the phlogistonists was lost. The next generation had accepted the victor so casually that to this day the phlogistonists are vaguely remembered by students of chemistry as incompetent and incomprehensible fools who hampered scientific progress for a short while and wallowed in their errors because of poor logic or failure to employ or appreciate the quantitative method which makes for true science.

It will be of interest to conclude this discussion of temporarily consistent thinking which the advance in knowledge forced to disintegrate, with an example from no lesser a scientist than Antoine Lavoisier. Here is a pioneer of science, one of the greatest of pioneer experimenters and defiers of tradition. There are few scientists who understood the scientific method as well as did Lavoisier. His Elements of Chemistry was a revolutionary work which systematized the entire field of chemistry and laid the foundation for its orderly development by introducing marvelous lucidity into a field permeated with chaos up to the date of its publication. In the Preface to this work Lavoisier states with exceptional succinctness and clarity the meaning of the scientific approach. "In commencing the study of a physical science, we ought to form no idea," he declares, "but what is a necessary consequence, and immediate effect, of an experiment or observation." (Elements of Chemistry Part I, Edinburgh, 1790, p. XVI). He is aware of the pitfalls of false generalizations. "Imagination . . . which is even wandering beyond the bounds of truth, joined to self-love and that self-confidence we are so apt to indulge, prompt us to draw conclusions which are not immediately derived from facts; so that we become in some measure interested in deceiving ourselves. Hence it is by no means to be wondered, that in the science of physics in general, men have often made suppositions, instead of forming conclusions. These suppositions, handed down from one age to another, acquire additional weight from the authorities by which they are supported, till at last they are received, even by men of genius, as fundamental truths." Which surely could not have been better stated.

Hence our reasoning must be as critical as possible and it is our duty to be vigilant on that score, guarding ourselves against error and temptation. "We must trust to nothing but facts; these are presented to us by Nature, and cannot deceive. We ought in every instance, to submit our reasoning to the test of experiment, and never to search for truth but by the natural road of experiment and observation." Moreover, "I have never deviated from the rigorous law of forming no conclusions which are not fully warranted by experiment."

Yet all this detailed and excellent knowledge of what constitutes strict

IATRO-CHEMISTRY AND PHLOGISTON

scientific reasoning is no guarantee against error, or rather against doing something which later scholars will regard as examples of the very opposite of what the method of science demands. That this is so Lavoisier proves in the very succeeding chapter, in Chapter I following the preface. He considers the expansion of bodies with heat and their contraction with cold, and explains it on the basis of attraction and repulsion between molecules. Different equilibria levels are reached at different temperatures between these two forces. Greatest attraction results in the solid state, intermediate, in liquid and greatest repulsion in the gaseous state. But, concludes Lavoisier, "it is difficult to comprehend these phenomena, without admitting them as the effects of a real and material substance, or very subtle fluid, which, insinuating itself between the particles of bodies, separates them from each other; and, even allowing the existence of this fluid to be hypothetical, we shall see in the sequel, that it explains the phenomena of nature in a very satisfactory manner." Repeatedly insisting that "we are not obliged to suppose this to be a real substance," he equally insistently refers to it as an elastic fluid, a repulsive cause, and names it caloric, which in all scientific honesty, must be distinguished from light, "though we do not therefore deny that these have certain qualities in common, and that, in certain circumstances, they combine with other bodies almost in the same manner, and produce, in part, the same effects."

No sooner is this concept thrown into the maelstrom of thought than it becomes quite real, just as the concept of revolution postulated by Copernicus had to be taken seriously by him and others even though it was first proposed as a mere mathematical explanation. Lavoisier too wishes the caloric to be a mere speculative hypothesis of operational service. But corruption lurks in the mind once a concept is advanced and a name is given it. In the next paragraph we discover that caloric can escape through any vessel, and must therefore be studied factually and abstractly. "It is in these things which we neither see nor feel, that it is especially necessary to guard against the extravagancy of our imagination, which forever inclines to step beyond the bounds of truth, and it is very difficultly refrained within the narrow line of facts." This statement sounds as if it were a truly subconscious admission of the very sin which Lavoisier is committing at the very moment. The caloric is put through the mill on a variety of claims and visualizations. It can vary in quantity, it vanishes by combining with such substances as ether or alcohol, it can become a vapor, it is the solvent in which the molecules of a substance in the gaseous state are really suspended, it is like sand filling the spaces between tightly packed "small spherical leaden bullets," it consists of particles that "are endowed with great elasticity and have a great tendency to separate from each other," it consists of "free

FIGURE 21. THE VICISSITUDES OF ALCHEMY

This graph demonstrates schematically the rise of alchemy, its progress and vicissitudes, and its final replacement by or fusion with modern chemistry.

Alchemy originated close to the time of the inception of the Christian Era with the confluence of the practical knowledge of Egypt and the intensive speculations concerning the nature of matter by the philosophers of Greece. This led to the first efflorescence of alchemical thought in Alexandria and its sphere of influence. The subsequent decline or neglect of all science which was brought on by the rise of Christianity affected alchemy as much as it did astrology. Alchemy too is similarly resuscitated during the period of the Revival of Learning, early in the second Christian millennium. The first wave of enthusiastic and practical labors was followed by a time of concentration upon diverse, derivative speculations. This speculative, mystical and religious trend soon dissolves and is replaced by iatro-chemistry in which experimentation still plays a significant role. In the course of time, fruitful hypotheses are advanced and modern chemistry is launched. Alchemy is dropped by the wayside, iatro-chemistry loses its interest.

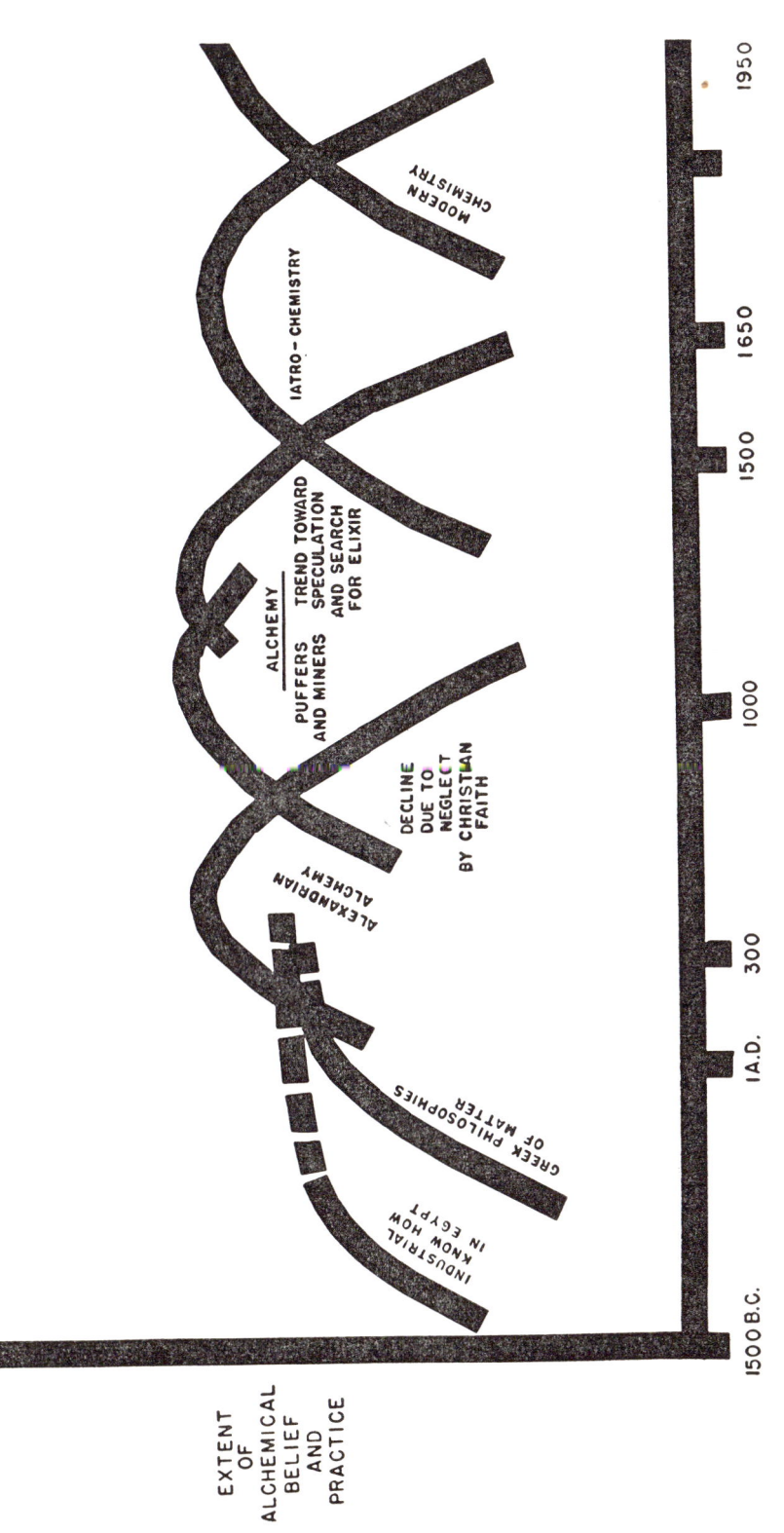

EXTENT OF ALCHEMICAL BELIEF AND PRACTICE

INDUSTRIAL KNOW HOW IN EGYPT

GREEK PHILOSOPHIES OF MATTER

ALEXANDRIAN ALCHEMY

DECLINE DUE TO NEGLECT BY CHRISTIAN FAITH

ALCHEMY
PUFFERS AND MINERS

TREND TOWARD SPECULATION AND SEARCH FOR ELIXIR

IATRO-CHEMISTRY

MODERN CHEMISTRY

1500 B.C.　1 A.D.　300　1000　1500　1650　1950

caloric" which cannot be collected and studied and of "combined caloric" which exists in combination with other bodies and certainly cannot be isolated or studied, when "disengaged from the surrounding bodies." It can be in motion and thus produce the sensation of heat, "the change which takes place upon the thermometer, only announces a change of place of the caloric in those bodies." Moreover the particles of caloric "make an effort to separate themselves on every side . . . and mutually repel each other." But "it is perhaps, more natural to suppose, that the particles of caloric have a stronger mutual attraction than those of any other substance, and that these latter particles are forced asunder in consequence of this superior attraction between the particles of the caloric." Little wonder that caloric could explain so many things. And all this from the man who so rightly mocked the concept of phlogiston as a chimera which could assume a multitude of forms to suit its manipulators, be a material substance on one occasion, an evanescent spirit on another, have weight in one situation and levity elsewhere, etc. It goes without saying that with the passage of time and the advance of research, the concept of caloric had to go the way of phlogiston and the two discarded spirits might well huddle together in limbo. But such is the nature of reason, and such are the vicissitudes of progress.

GLOSSARY

Alkahest—a term used by the later alchemists and Paracelsists to designate an imaginary substance possessing the powers to dissolve all kinds of elements, compounds and ores. Hence a universal solvent.

Ambient—that which surrounds, hence the enveloping matrix. In astrological language the atmosphere enveloping the earth, events occurring in that atmosphere, and particularly the moon, influencing all events in this sublunar world.

Apogee—the position of a celestial body in which its orbit happens to place it furthest from the earth. It is particularly applied to the moon but in the Ptolemaic system could also be applied to the sun.

Ascendant—an astrological term designating a celestial position above the horizon.

Ascension—the act of rising of a celestial body above the horizon.

Astrolabe—An ancient instrument employed for taking the position of sun and stars, used as well to project the celestial sphere on the plane of the equator.

Belief-trap—A belief pattern which is so deeply established in the culture, or in the warp and woof of one's beliefs, as to offer great resistance to any criticism or modification.

Calx—a term used by alchemists to designate an oxide of a metal. Rust (iron oxide) was the calx of iron.

Cardinal points—are the four directions.

Celestial axis—the imaginary straight line passing through the heavens and around which the stars seem to revolve in their daily motion completing a full cycle in twenty-four hours. The polar star is the northern end of the axis.

Celestial equator. When the plane of the earth's equator is extended heavenward to cut the celestial sphere in half, it forms an imaginary circle at the intersection with the heavens. This circular line is the celestial equator.

Clepsydra—A water clock used in ancient Greece and Rome. Water from a tank, kept full to overflowing from a mountain stream, was permitted to run into a tank on which floated a wooden base with a pole at its center. As the tank filled the float rose. On its pole was an indicator which pointed at a chart with the number of the hours on it, thus indicating the time.

Circumpolar stars are stars which are so near the celestial north pole, or south pole, as never to set below the horizon. The further away one is on earth from the equator the more such stars there are.

Concentric—Celestial bodies which revolve about a common center, or any orbit describing a circle around a central point.

Conjunction. When two celestial bodies are seen in the same longitude of the zodiac they are said to be in conjunction. For example, the new moon is always in conjunction with the sun. A conjunction is said to be *superior* when the celestial body is on the side of the sun most distant from the earth, while *inferior conjunction* refers to a similar position on the side of the sun nearest the earth, hence between the sun and the earth.

Critical days refers to a superstitious belief of the past, according to which certain days were supposed to be destined to bring evil luck.

Culmination—the point or time at which a heavenly body crosses the meridian. Also the highest and lowest points of altitude attained by a celestial body in its daily motion in the sky.

Decoction—the act of boiling some substance within a solvent for the purpose of dissolving it or some of its components. Also used for the resulting solution. An alchemical term.

Deferent—an imaginary circle around the earth traveled by a point which served as the center for a smaller circle known as the epicycle, which was the actual orbit of the planet.

Demonology—the belief in demons, hence also the belief in witchcraft.

Direct motion—the motion of a planet in an easterly direction against the stars as opposed to its apparent daily motion from east to west, due to the earth's rotation.

Eccentric—the circular motion of a celestial body around a center which was remote from the earth, so that the planet came at one point nearest the earth and at another furthest from the earth.

Ecliptic—an imaginary great circle of the celestial sphere drawn through the middle of the zodiac which marks the apparent path of the sun among the stars.

Elections of days—the act of consulting an astrologer concerning the most propitious day on which to initiate a certain act or perform some deed.

Elixir—the alchemists' goal, the philosopher's stone. Actually the term had two meanings representing the two aspects of alchemy. First, it was employed to signify the powder or solution which could transmute the baser metals into gold. Second and later, it came to mean a solution which could perfect the imperfect, restore health, rejuvenate the aged, and mend the cripples.

Ephemerides, plural of ephemeris, a diary, an almanac, or a calendar. During the middle ages it was a book of gossip, wisdom, forecasts and an all around substitute for newspapers, movies and radio commentators. It is also employed in astronomy to designate a set of tables giving the positions of celestial bodies for the various times or days of the year. In this sense it is an astronomical almanac.

Epicycle. Epi meaning upon, the word refers to the motion of a planet in a small circle around a center which itself moves in a circular path around some other center. See Figures 10 and 11.

Equinox—the two days of the year, approximately March 21 and September 22, when the sun crosses or is on the celestial equator. From September to March the sun will be seen against the stars below the equator, and the second half of the year above it.

Four Elements—the belief of the ancients that all matter consisted of four components: Earth, Water, Air and Fire. By these terms they meant principles rather than the realities with which the words are related in ordinary experience. Thus, earth meant the solid state, air meant gaseous, water liquid, and fire, heat and energy.

Four humors. Similarly, medicine of the time believed that the body contained four humors: blood, phlegm, yellow bile and black bile, all of which had to be in perfect harmony for normal health.

Four qualities. All matter was believed to possess four qualities: hot, cold, moist and dry. Thus, objects were either hot and dry, hot and moist, or cold and dry, etc.

Free will—the belief of all religions, monotheistic as well as pagan, that man has freedom to choose, that his mind or soul have some independence and power of their own, hence can decide to act or believe one way or another, pray or sin etc.

Gems were believed, until relatively modern times, to have magical powers in healing and in other situations.

Generation and Corruption. According to Aristotle, all earthly, hence sublunar bodies, were composed of the four elements and were subject to changes either of corruption or generation. Celestial bodies were composed of a primary element, a fifth substance, or quintessence, and were not subject to changes of any kind.

Genethlialogy is the science of casting nativities or of elaborating horoscopes. By noting the positions of the planets at the precise moment of birth, astrologers believed they could foretell a person's character and fate. Such forecasts were called horoscopes or nativities. The subject or client was the native.

ASTROLOGY AND ALCHEMY

Heliacal rising of a star. The sun moves eastward against the stars and completes the circle in one year. When the sun is in a given constellation, the stars of that constellation will not be seen, since they are hidden by the sun's rays and are out in the daytime. As the sun moves eastward out of such a constellation, its stars begin to be seen at dawn. The first time a star is thus seen after having been blotted out by the sun, is called its heliacal rising, its emerging from the sun's light.

Homocentric—circles or spheres possessing a common center.

Horoscope—the forecast of a person's fate and personality as interpreted from the positions of the celestial bodies at the moment of his birth.

Iatro-chemistry—the study of chemical processes from the vantage point of the belief that the aim of chemistry is to be at the service of medicine.

Images—special drawings or designs believed to have magical powers, especially effective on certain objects.

Incantations—the uttering of certain words and phrases believed to have great magical powers and spoken in a ritual manner in order to attain some objective, raise spirits or mobilize demons.

Inequality in latitude—irregular motion of the planets along different arcs of their orbits as measured on their plane of revolution, or in degrees of longitude, measured from the point of the vernal equinox, for example.

Inferior planets—Mercury and Venus, whose periods of revolution are shorter than that of the earth.

Interrogation—the custom of asking an astrologer to determine by the stars the time, advisability, or consequences of some planned deed.

Irregularity of planetary motion—see Inequality

Line of apsides—the major axis of the elliptical orbit of the moon around the earth. It is a line joining the positions of the moon at perigee and apogee with the earth. This line revolves eastward once in about nine years.

Lunar calendar—a calendar based entirely on the moon as is the Mohammedan calendar that has no regard for the sun, hence for the tropical year.

Lunation—the period of a synodic revolution of the moon around the earth, which means from new moon to new moon.

Luni-solar calendar—one which counts its months from new moon to new moon but adds on extra days, now and then, to keep the months tied to the seasons, hence to the tropical year, determined by the sun. The Jewish calendar is a luni-solar one, while the Christian calendar is a solar one based on the sun exclusively.

Mathematici—a term designating in antiquity people who studied the mystical properties of numbers. Before the Arabic numerals were adopted, numbers were represented by letters. Hence such individuals prognosticated by equating the numerical values of names and words. A general term for fortune-tellers and even magicians.

Mathesis—the science of mathematical learning which, as explained above, involved the magic powers of numbers.

Medical astrology. Until about two centuries ago physicians assumed that the body and its functions were under the influence of the constellations. All medical treatment had to be attuned to stellar and planetary positions.

Meridian, celestial—an imaginary great circle drawn in the heavens, joining the north and south poles of the sky and crossing the zenith as well as nadir. Noon is the moment when the center of the sun crosses that line in the southern sky.

Native, nativity—see Genethlialogy

Nodes—the points where a celestial body such as the moon intersects the ecliptic in the course of its revolution round the earth. The two nodes are not permanent against the stars but slide westward, completing a cycle in 18.6 years.

Occult—any quality or property hidden from human eyes or understanding, hence concealed or mysterious. The term is not always used in a "supernatural" or magical sense, though often forced into that category.

Opposition. Two heavenly bodies are in opposition when they are 180° apart in longitude. A planet is said to be in opposition when the earth is directly on a line joining it to the sun and in between the two. Thus the moon is in opposition when full.

Orbs—hollow, imaginary spheres postulated by the Greek astronomers as carriers of the planets which were presumably attached to their equators.

Panacea. The later alchemists believed that their philosopher's stone, decoction, or powder of transmutation, was a panacea or a cure for all diseases.

Parallax—the apparent change in the position of an object when viewed from two different places. Since comets were believed to be sublunar, they were expected to show parallax against the stars when viewed with the unaided eye at different hours of the night, or at the same moment from different positions.

Perigee—the point on its orbit at which a celestial body such as the moon is nearest the earth.

Philosopher's egg—the vessel in which the alchemists performed their final processes in the solemn procedure of transmutation.

Philosopher's stone—the substance which was believed by the alchemists to be able to perform the sought-for process of transmutation. It was the symbol of chemical power, of nature's developmental energy, the congealed radiation of the stars, which in its slow flow acts on the crude matter in the earth's womb to purify base metals into nobler ones. Hence in the crystalline, concentrated form it can perform a transmutation in a much briefer period. Many other great powers, both healing and perfecting, were in time attributed to it.

Phlogiston—the fire principle, or the ability of a substance to give off fire. Hence the matter or principle of combustion.

Precession is the conical movement of the earth's axis, or the westward sliding of the equinoxes along the ecliptic, completing a full cycle in 26,000 years.

Projection—a term designating the final step in the alchemist's labor at transmutation in which the wonderful powder, the red elixir, or philosopher's stone, was mixed with the heated metals to culminate in the production of gold.

Retrogression—that part of a planet's orbit in which it appears to be moving for a short period in a direction opposite to that it had previously pursued for a longer time. Normally a planet seems to be moving eastward against the stars. In the retrograde period it reverses its direction and moves westward for a while, then resumes its eastward course.

Sidereal day—time reckoned by the diurnal motion of the stars, hence the time from a given star's crossing the meridian until a second crossing. Sidereal means pertaining to stars.

Solstice—the points on the ecliptic at which the sun reaches, in its annual path, the greatest northerly or southerly distances from the celestial equator. Hence June 21 and December 21.

Spagyric art—a term designating alchemy or iatro-chemistry.

Stations or stationary period. Before a planet initiates its retrogression it appears to stand still. Similarly, before reversing its direction from retrogressive to direct, it appears to be stationary.

Sublunar—any object or event occurring on earth or within the region between the sphere of the moon and the earth. This region was distinct from that beyond the moon which was celestial, divine and subject to other laws.

Superior planets—planets having a longer period of revolution than the earth.

Synodic month—the month as reckoned by the conjunction of the moon with the sun, hence from new moon to new moon. The synodic period of a planet is the interval between two successive conjunctions of a planet with the sun, as seen from the earth.

Syzygy—the two points in the orbit of a planet where it is in opposition and conjunction with the sun.

Trepidation—the belief of ancient and medieval astronomers that the eighth sphere, that of the stars or firmament, underwent a slow wavering. Such a motion was postulated to account for the changes in the motion of the axis of the world.

Zodiac—the belt of constellations, which the sun traverses in its annual trip in the sky. The moon and the major planets also have their orbits in this belt. The ecliptic runs in its center. The zodiac extends about eight degrees north and south of the line of the ecliptic. The ancients divided this belt into twelve portions of thirty degrees each and ascribed to them signs of animals, hence the name zodiac. Today all but Libra, the scales, are names of animals.

INDEX

A

Abbé 297
ablution 255
Abraham 181
Abraham the Jew 289
Abraham Judaeus 106
abstention from food 247
Academia de Secreti 156
Academy 246, 354
acid-base equilibrium 341
acqua regia 318
Adelard of Bath 81
adept 255, 259, 303, 317
Adfar 282
Adrian VI 150
Advancement of Learning 191
aether 44
Africa 287
Against Fate 74
Agricola, George 339
agriculture 4
Alain de Lisle 283
Albert, Duke of Prussia 175
Albertus Magnus 90, 143, 170, 254, 273, 283, 288, 315, 324
Albumasar 89, 104, 106
Alcabitius 104
Alcahest (alkahest) 274, 293, 340
Alchemical Essence and the Chemical Element 251
Alchemical Manuscript, An 241
Alchemical Works of Stephanus of Alexandria 243
Alchemistische und Chemische Zeichen 277
alchemists 115
Alchemy, Child of Greek Philosophy 243
L'Alchimie et les Alchimistes 280
Alcibiades 79
alcohol 293, 320
alembic 242
Alexander the Great 15, 17, 241, 267
Alexandria 37, 40, 240
Alfarabi 279, 280
Alfonso V 121

Alfonso X 169
Alfraganus 167
Alger, Horatio 279
Alkindi 106
almagest, 10, 40ff, 46, 167, 172
almanac 184, 194
Almansour, Emir 281
Alphonsine Tables 109, 148, 168, 169, 173, 180, 183, 198
amalgamation 242
ambient 51
ambivalent attitude to astrology 187, 194
  to learning 154
Ambrosia 284
amulets 337
Anaxagoras 15
Anaximander 21
Andalo di Negro 108
Angel 289
Anglicus, Robertus 167
Annals of Medical History 278
Anselm 290
Anthropology vii
Antichrist 99, 111
Antiochus I 17
antipodes 211
Antonio, Pedro ???
aphelion 215
Apian, Peter 130, 170
apogee, 36, 201
Apology, An 146, 152
Apologia 178
apostles of Alchemy 288
apparatus 316
Appolonius of Myndus 125
Appolonius of Perga 37, 47, 200, 246
Appolonius of Tyara 283
apsides 41
Apuleius Romanus 127
Arabia 60
Arabic 246, 285
  learning 81ff
Arabs 157, 169, 196, 240, 248, 266, 280
Arcanum of the Sages 263
Arcetri 227

369

INDEX

Archbishop of Lyons 105
Archeus 187, 326, 334, 341
Archidoxa 178
Archimedes 31, 246
Arelius Fuscus 19
Aristarchus of Samos 29, 31, 40, 196, 200
Aristotle 21, 22, 28, 68, 88, 122, 144, 147, 173, 209, 214, 237, 244, 246, 280, 324, 335, 340
Aristotle the Chemist 324
arithmetic 172
armilla, equatorial 178
Arnold, Thurman 173
ars mathematica 106
Artemidonius of Parium 126
Artephius 283
Arzachel 169
ascendent 102, 183, 186
ascension 61
Asclepios 64
Ashmole, Elias 238
aspects 57
assumptions 164, 170
Assurbanipal 12
Assyria 106
astrolabe 61, 134, 163, 197
astrological medicine 65, 91, 95, 98, 108, 184, 330
Astrologie des Johannes Kepler, Die 183
L'Astrologie Grecque 122
Astrology and Religion among Greeks and Romans 14
Astronomia 178
Astronomical Institutions 197
Astronomical Thought in Renaissance England 209
astronomy 5, 14, 53, 172, 181, 183, 202, 214, 319
atheism 15, 141
atlas 175
atoms 251
Augustine, St. 75ff, 194, 245
Augustine of Trent 103
Augustus 16
Aurelian 18
Aurora of the Philosophers 324
Averroes 89, 114, 287
Avicenna 89, 114, 246, 281, 324, 325
Avignon 287
Azoth 262

B

Babylonia 4, 6ff, 37
Babylonian Astrology and the Old Testament 11
Bach, J. S. 13
Bacon, Francis 100, 192, 198

Bacon, Roger 91, 94, 144
Bagdad 247
Ball, Franz 15, 64
Baltic Sea 293
Bandini, Cardinal 219
bans against alchemy 316
Barberini, Cardinal Maffeo 224
Barozzi, Francesco 155, 196
Bartholomaeus, Amotosinus 150
Bartholomew of England 86
Basic Works of Aristotle 22
Basil 74
Basil Valentine 259, 269, 333
basilisk 117
Baumé 350
Bayle, Pierre 136
Becher, Johann Joachim 345
behaviorists 338
belief patterns 355
belief trap 46, 354
belief web 129
Bellarmine, Cardinal 219
Benatius, Jacobus 149
Bernard Sylvester 83
Bernard of Treviso 292
Bernard Walther 169
Berosus 15, 17
Berry, A. 229
Berthelot, M 240, 353
Bethune, J. L. D. 220
Beuther, David 315
Beyer, Albrecht 315
bezoar stone 337
Bezold, Carl 15, 64
Bible 11, 74, 149, 213, 220, 270, 327
Bibliothèques des Philosophes Chimiques 252
Biesius, Nicolaus 196
birth 61
Bishop of Fossombrone 107
Black Death 103, 108, 110, 111, 149
Bloody Almanac, A 193
Boccaccio 108
Bodin, Jean 196
Boerhaave, Herman 344
Bologna 191
bonfire of books 325
Book Addressed to Leucippus 241
book burning 106
Book of Chemical Discovery 238
Book of Lambspring 268
Book of Perfect Magistery 324
Book Paragranum 325
Boscaglia 219
Bötticher, John Frederick 312
Bouché-Leclercq, A. 122
Boyle, Robert 318, 344
Bradwardine, Thomas 151

INDEX

Bragadino 315
Brahe, Tycho 109, 122, 130ff, 157, 158, 169, 173, 175, 178ff, 212ff, 302, 304
Braude, William 238
Brett, G. S. 159
Brewster, D. 228
Bristol 292
Bruno, Giordano 350
Bulls, Papal 148, 151, 154, 156, 287
Burke, Robert Belle 95
Busch 133

C

Cabala 133, 145, 254, 277, 290
Caelsalpinus 350
Caesar, Augustus 65
Caesar, Julius 24, 65
Cagliostro 274
Cairo 272
calcination 242, 349
calendar 5ff, 133, 152, 180, 237
    Julian 102
    reform 107, 134, 168, 176, 200
Calippus 27, 214
caloric 351, 356ff
Calvin 152
calx 345
Camerarius, Joachim 154, 170
Campanella, Thomas 157
Campbell, Thomas 256
cancer 285
Canches 290
Cannae 70
Canon of Medicine 325
Canons of a Table of Proportions 109
Canopus 21
Cardan, Jerome 130, 155, 166, 190, 350
Carneades 64, 69, 136
Carrell, Alexis 193
Castelli, Father 219
Castle of Gloucester 292
Castle of Knowledge 197
catalyst 243
Catholic Astrolabe 173
causation 123, 201
causes, general and particular 160
Cavendish 349
Cayley, J. 241
Cecco D' Ascoli 96, 103, 167
Celestial Motion, On the Commensurability or on the Incommensurability of 114
Celestial Physiognomy 156
censor 327
Cervantes 302
Cesi, Prince 224
Chaldea 4, 6ff, 239
Chaldeans 65, 69, 161, 165, 214

chance 73
characteristics, national 59
Charius 337
charlatans 182
Charles VII 107
Charles VIII 105
chemical advances under alchemy 319, 320
Chemical Education 241
Chemical Treatise on Air and Field 347
Chemistry of Moses, The 242
Chigashige, M. 248
Chimie Experimentale et Raisonné 350
China 247, 313
Chinese Alchemy 247
Christ 74, 100, 107, 150, 177, 285, 287
    birth of 96, 144, 170
    horoscope of 143
Christian II, Elector of Saxony 309
Christianity 286
    and astrology 93
    opposition to astrology by 72ff, 104
Christmann 218
chronometers 4
Chrysostom, St. John 74
Church vii, 96, 99, 110, 146, 154, 168, 209, 219, 245
Cicero 23, 29, 69
Circe 16
circles 203
Cirvelo, Pedro 151
City of God 75
claims of alchemists 316
classification 249, 318
Clement V. 284
Clement VII 150, 176, 200
Cleopatra 242, 280
clepsydrae 61
clock, mechanical 114
coction 265
Cohen, M. R. 44
Collectanea Chemica 274
Coles, L. A. 238
Collection des Anciens Alchimistes Grecs 240
Collection of the Most Celebrated Astrologers, A 106
Cologne 283, 308
Colombo 150
color 243, 250, 255
Colson 11
Columbus 151
combustion 345ff
Comet of 1577, The 129
comets 93, 108, 119, 121ff, 158, 171, 173, 330
commandments of alchemy 288
Commentariolus 176, 200

INDEX

Commentary Upon the Sphere 91, 99
communism 143, 173
communist creed 228
compass, mariner's 86, 117
  geometrical 217
Compendium of All Judicial Astronomy, A 108
concentric spheres 24
conception 61
Conciliator, The 96
Concerning the Nature of Things 330
Concerning the Spirit of the Planets 324
condensers 242
Confessions of Cyprian 73
Configuration of the Qualities, On the 116
Congregation, Sacred 199, 222
conic sections 47
conjunctions 104, 108, 119, 148, 178, 181, 186
Constantine the Great 79
Constantinople 74
constellations, qualities of 57ff, 113
Copernicus 43, 137, 150, 157, 169, 170, 172, 175ff, 195ff, 200ff, 357
copper 270
corruption 88, 113
Corvinus, Matthias 170
Cos 17
Cosimo II 190, 223
cosmogonies 20, 90
Cosmographia 155
Cosmography 195
cosmology, new and old 219
  of Ptolemy 40ff
Cosmopolite 274, 206ff
counter-earth 22
Cracow 309
Cremer 259, 269
Cristina, Grand Duchess 220
critical attitude toward alchemy 272
critical days 120
crusade 286
culmination 32, 186
culture viii, 3
Cumont 6, 14
cupellation 320
Curie, Madame 193
cyclotron 316
cylinders 242
Cyprian 73
Cyprus 29
Cyrenaica 60

D

Dalton, Thomas 292
Daniel, Book of 261
Daniel of Morley 83

Darwin 3
Davis, T. L. 248, 278, 302
d'Este, Cardinal 217
De Alchimia 288
De Anima 91
De Caelo et Mundo 91, 124, 132
de Delle, Mardock 302, 304
De Divinatione 69, 77
De Humanis Corporis Fabrica 172
De Minerali Medicina 306
de Mesmes, Jean Pierre 197
de Morveau, Guyton 318
de Muhlenfels, Count 311
De Mutatione Aeris 106
de Petrasancta, Michael 149
De re metallica 339
De Rerum Varietate 155, 192
de Rosenberg, Marshal 305
De Revolutionibus 171ff, 195ff, 203ff
debauchery, life of 282
decree of 1616 225
decoction 255, 307
Dee, John 131, 302ff
deferent 36, 177, 213
della Porta, Giovanni Batista 156
Delphic Oracle 116, 139
Democritus 21, 67
Democritus (alchemist) 241, 280
demonology 149, 328
demons 84, 87, 100, 116, 140, 146, 151, 156, 158, 175
depression 58
Descartes, René 159, 192
descendant 186
Desmarets, Arnold 146
destiny 15, 53, 93
determinism 15, 19, 64, 107, 157, 330
devil 139, 188, 189, 295, 336
diadem 270
dialectical materialism 277
Dialogue of Cleopatra and the Philosophers 242
Dialogues of Plato 244
Dialogues on the Two Principle Systems of the World 224
dials 72
Dianoia Astronomica 218
Diderot 136
Dienheim, Wolfgang 306
Dierback 304
digestion 335, 341
Digges, Leonard 210
Digges, Thomas 131, 210
Diocletian's edict 241
Diodorus 141
Diogenes 136
Dion Cassius 11
Dionysius de Rubertis 103

INDEX

discoveries 4, 164
discussions of alchemists 293
disease 274, 287, 322, 334
disputations 149
Disputations Against Astrology 143
dissection 152, 338
divination 6, 14, 69ff, 91, 93, 134, 151, 156, 158, 164, 172, 175, 191
Divine Comedy 98
Dodoens 195
dogma 209, 229
Don Quixote 302
Dorn, Gerhard 338
Dostoyevsky 101
Drabkin, D. 44
Drawings of the All-Wise Doorkeeper 268
dreams 89, 99
Dresden 309
  china 314
Dreyer, J. L. E. 23, 29, 41ff, 131, 179, 203, 211ff
drugs 116
dyeing 310

E

Early Science in Oxford 210
earth, circumference of 29
  sphericity of 29
earthquakes 122
Easter 152
eccentric 34, 213
eccentricity 215
eclipses 7, 23, 45, 108, 110, 138, 140, 174, 178, 180, 237, 263
ecliptic 8, 12, 23, 25, 27, 28, 57, 205
Edessa 245
Edison, Thomas A. 193
Edward IV, King of England 286, 291
Edward VI, King 302
eggs, chemical experiments with 294
Egypt 4, 5, 11, 13, 16, 239, 241, 280
Egyptian Theory 29
Egyptians 54, 214
Einsiedeln 322
Einstein, Albert 193
elections of days 77, 93, 151, 163
elements, four 56, 81, 118, 144, 195, 244, 328, 340
Elements of Chemistry 356
Elijah 177
elixir of life 238, 254, 266, 282ff, 310ff
Elizabeth, Queen 302
ellipse 43, 215, 231
Elysium 20
Emerald Table 266
Empedocles 21, 237, 244
empirics 354

encyclopedia 169
encyclopedists 86
Endymion 67
Enoch, Book of 240
Ens Astrale 328
Eudoxus 14, 24ff, 141, 200
ephemerides 133, 143, 169, 170, 173
ephemeris 178
epicycles 36, 177, 201
Epigenes 68, 125
epilepsy 62
Epitome of Astronomy 173
equant 41
equator 165
  celestial 11
equinoxes 10
Erastus 158
Ermland, Bishop of
Esdras 262
Essays in Historical Chemistry 345
L'Etude de la Chimie 240
Ethiopians 59
Euclid 23, 47, 167, 246
evolutionary process in alchemy 317
Exafranon 102
exaltation 58
Excellent Treatise 335
exhaustion, method of 23
Experiments on Air 349
explaining away facts 316
Exodus 11, 23ff, 214

F

faculty of theology 105
Fahie, J. J. 191, 216ff
Familiar Letters on Chemistry 239
Farrington, B. 210
fascination, on 116
fate 53, 64, 73, 74, 79, 186
Faust 295
Favorinus 71
fear of astrologers 193
Feselius 186
ferment 243
fermentation 254, 341
Feyens 223
Figuier, Louis 280
Figulus, Benedictus 65, 274
fire 340, 345ff
Firmicus, Julius Maternus 78
first cause 118
fixation 242
Flamel, Nicholas 258, 279, 288
floating bodies, on 224
flood, 149
Flood, Robert or Fludd, Robert 159, 191
Florence 223, 226
foetus 91

374 INDEX

folklore 194, 217, 240, 272, 279, 287, 304
forecasting 163, 168, 174, 189
Forster, Richard 196
fortune 96
fortune-tellers 79
fossils viii
Fossombrone, Bishop of 200
Fountain of Nature 271
Franck, Jean 304, 311
Franciscan monk 293
Franklin 194
Frauenburg 175, 200
Frederick II 90, 182
Frederick III, Emperor 294
Frederick, Duke of Wurtemberg 311
free will 64, 77, 93, 99, 114, 156, 189, 330
French Revolution 221
Freud 227, 263
Frisius, Cornelius Gemma 131, 172
Frisius, Gemma 172, 197
Fromundus 223
Fuchsius 350
funnels 242
furnaces 272

G

Gaetano 315
Galen 65, 74, 81, 148, 152, 246, 280, 321, 324, 335
Galileo 3, 135, 136, 152, 157, 190ff, 195, 216ff
  abjuration of 227
Galileo, His Life and Work 191, 216
Galip 282
Gallicius 156
Garcia, Pedro 147
Garrison 221
gas 341
Gassendi, Pierre 159ff
Gauricus 166
Geber 193, 246ff, 280, 324
Gemma, Cornelius 131
Geneology of Astronomy, The 109
generation 88, 113
Generation and Corruption, On 122
genethlialogical 61
genethlialogy 73
geniture 171
genus 94, 98, 145, 147
Geoffrey of Meaux 108
Geofroi de Lemorier 294
geography 60, 152, 170, 172
geometry 40, 151, 181, 184, 201, 210
Gerard of Cremona 82
German 324
Germany 307
Gibralter 29
Giese, Tiedeman 176

Giovanni, Francesco Pico della Mirandola 147
glass, production 239
Glauber, Johann Rudolph 342
Glory of the World, The, or Table of Paradise 266
gold 243ff
  assay 318
Golden Age Restored, The 260
Golden and Blessed Casket, The 274
Golden Tract, The 259
Golden Tripod, The 268
gravity 204
Greece 4, 13ff, 241, 380
Green Lion 332
Gregory of Nyssa 74
Grosseteste, Robert 210
Gradual Acceptance of the Copernican Theory 198, 227
Great Comet of 1680, The 135
Gregory XV 224
grip of a belief 319
group loyalty of alchemists 292
Growth of Physical Science 32
Guide to the Four Seasons 188
Guido Bonatti 96
Gunther, R. T. 210
Gnostics 246
Gustenhover 307

H

Hades 20
Hexaemeron 74
Hagecius 131
half-meals 333
Halley 193
Halley's comet 121
harem 260
harmony, celestial 92
Harrox 135
Hartman, F. 338
Harvey, William 3, 191
Haussen, James or Jacob 306
Hawarth, H. E. 203
Hayeck, Dr. 304
heat 56, 115
Heath, Sir Thomas 40
Hebrew 290
heliacal rising 10
Helikon 24
heliocentric theory 32, 202ff, 215, 225
Hellman, C. D. 217
Helvetius 259
Henry of Hesse 113, 117ff
Henry of Vienna 294
Heraclides of Pontus or Heracleides 29, 40, 200
herbs 269

INDEX

Hercules, pillars of 29
heresy or heresies 146, 152, 154, 221, 276, 302
Hermann of Dalmatia 82
hermaphroditism 86
Hermes 64, 79, 240, 266, 280
Hermetic and Alchemical Writings of Paracelsus 249, 323
Hermetic Museum 258
Hero 155
Herz, Norbert 183
Hicetas of Syracuse 23
hieroglyphics 290
Hildegard of Bingen 83
Hipparchus 15, 39, 79, 176, 179
Hipplytus 74
Hippocrates 75, 148, 152, 165, 246, 321, 324, 335
Hippocrates Chimicus 350
hippopede 26
historians of science 228
History of Magic and Experimental Science 66, 73, 78, 81, 83, 95, 102ff, 197ff
History of Mathematics 168
History of Planetary Systems 23
history of science viii
holy grail 279
Holland 306
Hollywood 19, 228
Holmgard, E. J. 247
Homer 20, 71
homocentric spheres 24, 26
Honauer, George 315
Hooke, Robert 348
Hoover, L. H. 339
Hoover, H. C. 339
Hopkins, J. A. 243
horoscope 16, 67, 75, 86, 93, 107, 150, 152, 165, 179, 182, 191, 196, 200
Horus 242
houses 160
humanism 145
Humid Path 275
humors, four 335
Huygens 192
Hveen 182
hypotheses 201, 214, 237, 254

I

iatro-chemistry 340ff
images 93
immortality 247
incantations 116
incubi 85, 99
Index 154, 172, 222
India 4, 22
inequality in latitude 39, 208
inequality in longitude 28, 37, 206
Innocent VIII 291
Inquisition 96, 98, 152, 154ff, 216ff, 340
inquisitor 106, 147
insanity 62
instruments 170, 175, 178, 182, 281
Interpretation of the Stars 329
interrogations 151, 178
intolerance of Paracelsus 324
Introduction to Astrology 91
Introduction to the History of Science 90
inventions 4, 354
iron 270
irregularity of planetary motion 37
Ishtar 7
Isis 242
Iunctinus 196

J

Jacobites 246
James of Speyer 170
James II of Aragon 284
Japan 313
Jastrow, Joseph 10, 14
Jeans, James 32
Jehan de Guignecourt 107
Jerusalem 11, 290
Jewish physicians 323
Jews 11, 157, 186, 246, 289, 312
John de Meung 287, 300
John de Murs 109
John of Bassigny 110
John of Eschenden 111
John of Gmunden 168
John at Indagine 148
John of Paris 103
John of Salisbury 83
John of Saxony 104
John of Spain 82
John I, King of Argon 284
John XXII, Pope 287
Johnson, F. R. 209
Johnson, O. S. 248
Joshua 220
Judea 4, 241
judicial astrology 171, 192
Julius Firnicus Maternus 78
Julius II 154
Juncker 350
Jupiter 7, 18, 26, 56, 87, 108, 161, 178, 181, 217, 225, 255

K

Kalid, Sultan of Egypt 282
Kardaja 109, 134
Kelley, Edward 274, 302ff

Kepler 27, 122, 133, 136, 157, 162, 169, 173, 183ff, 211, 215, 304
Kidenas 15
King 270
king of Babylonia 9
Kirch, Guttfried 136
Kleopatra, Cleopatra 242
Ko Hung 248
Ko Hung on the Gold Medicine and on the Yellow and White 248
Koran 245

L

laboratory 247
Lactanius of Gaul 74
Ladislaus of Bohemia 168
Lamarckism x
Lansberg, Philip 199
Lascaris 312
Lasinius, Janus 273
Laski, Count 303
Lateran Council 176
Latin 246, 258, 290, 324
latitude, celestial 59
latitude, motion in 24
laureate 302
Lavoisier, Antoine 31, 344, 349, 354ff
Leibnitz 239
Lenin 52, Leninists 228
Leo X 150
Leucippus 20, 241
leucosis 255
Libavius 339, 340, 350
Liber de Compositione Alchemiae 283
Libra 8
Liebig, Justus 238
Liebler, Thomas (Erastus) 158
Life and Doctrines of Paracelsus 338
Life of Paracelsus 322
Lion 270
Lives of Alchemystical Philosophers 280
London 286, 302
longevity 291
longitude 172, celestial 59
Longo, Giovanni Battista 156
Lorenzo de Medici 147, 150
Louis de Langle 107
Louis XI 105
Louis XIV 135
Lüdy, F. 277
Lull, Lully or Lullus, Raymond 254, 273, 283, 300
lunations 12
Luther 171, 176, 325, birth 166
Lutheran Reformation 154
Lydus, John Laurentius 127
lye of the Sages 261

M

machines 95
Macquer 355
Macrobius 29
Maestlin, Michael 131, 172, 197, 218
Magi 74, 91, 168, 194
magic 16, 73, 79, 84, 91, 100, 107, 146, 154, 168, 296, 302, 328
magic natural 116
magistery 254
magnet 91, 117, 147, 158
Maier, Michael 259, 271
malleability 250
Malta, Knights of 292
Manetti, Giannozzo 121
Manilius 16
manuscript copying 296
Marat 354
Marmarica 60
Mars 7, 18, 27, 56, 87, 108, 153, 181, 186, 215, 255, 270
Marsilio, Ficino 107
Martianus 87
martyrdom 314
Martyrs of Science 228
Marx 52
Mary, Queen 302
Mary the Jewess 242, 280
Mathematical Composition (*Almagest*) 46
mathematici 16, 73, 74
  legislation against 177
mathesis 73, 78, 79
Maximilian, Emperor 170
Mayow, John 348
McKie, Douglas 354
McKeon, R. 22, 122
McLean 11, 12
Mead, Richard 193
Mecca 280
Medea 16, 154
Medici 218
medicine, alchemical 274
  astrological 91, 95, 98, 103, 148, 163, 170, 171
medicine, science of 321ff
Medieval Attitude Toward Astrology 122
Mehring, J. A. 259
Melanchthon, Philip 171
melanosis 255
Menaechmus 47
Mendeleyev 253
mercuric diseases 334
Mercury 7, 18, 26, 34, 43, 56, 112, 181, 208, 218, 255, 270
mercury 243

INDEX

meridian 31
Messiah 289
metallicity 250, 323
metallurgy 243
metals 162, 244, 249, 270
  and calces 346
  and planets 244
Metaphysics 91
Meteorological Ephemerides 196
Meteorology 28, 124, 197
metoposcopy 133
Meurer, Wolfgang 197
microcosmos 218
Milich, Jacob 172
Milton 227
Minerva, Paul 196
mines 310, 317, 322
Mirror of Doctrine 89
Mirror of History 89, *of Nature* 89
missing links 318
mithridate 337
Mohammedan 4, 177, 245, 285
Mohammedanism 285
molecule 251
Molière 251
monsters 150
monstrosities 252
moon 7, 10, 11, 55ff, 67, 145, 161, 170, 181, 213, 217, 243, 270
More, Thomas 100, 210
Morienus 282
Moses 74, 242, 260
Moslem menace 287
Muir, M. M. P. 251
Muller, Johann 169
Munosius 131
Muse, Geometry 114, Arithmetic 114
mysteries 292, 295
Mysterium Cosmographicum 219
mysticism 256, 277

N

Napier 193
Narratio Prima 177, 200
native 62, 186
nativities 51, 61, 78, 86, 115, 156, 163, 165, 172, 182
Natural History 16, 66
Natural Questions by Adelard of Bath 81
Natural Questions by Seneca 67, 125
Navarre, King of 299
nazism 143
Nechepso, King 17, 64, 79
Neckam, Alexander 83
necromancy 100, 303, 328
neo-Platonism 210ff
neo-Pythagoreanism 16

Nero 125
Nestorians 246
New Chemical Light 271
New Pearl of Great Price 273
New Theories of the Planets 167
Newton, Isaac 3, 135, 192, 202, 302, 329
Nicolo di Paganica 103
Nicholas of Cusa 168
Nicolas Oresme 113ff
Nifo, Agustino 149
Nigidius 76
Nilsson 12
nodes 179, 215
Nodus Gordius 218
Noltius 133
North Africa 60
Norton, Thomas 259, 269, 271, 292
nova 130ff, 179
Novum Organum 198
numbers, magic 16
numerology 17, 168, 247, 296, 328

O

Oasis 60
obliquity of ecliptic 205
Observations on Respiration and the Use of the Blood 349
Observations Upon the Prophecies of Daniel etc. 193
occult sciences 281, 303
occult virtues 85, 116, 118, 149, 158, 168
Oeuvres Complètes de Galileo 192
Offusius, Joannes Francus 153
Okeanos 20
Olympiodorus 241
omens 68, 134, 172, 337
On Divination 70
On The Error of Profane Religions 78
On The Heavens 28
On The Properties of Things 87
Only True Way, The 264
opium 332
Oporinus 331
opposition (of Mars) 32
opposition to astrology 104, 113ff, 143ff, 157
Opus Maius 94, 95
Opusculum astrologicum 171
Opusculum Chemicum 296
orbits of planets 21ff
Ordinall of Alchemy, The 272
ores 240, 249, 310
Oriental Alchemy 248
Origen 74
Origin of Greek Alchemy 242
Origin of Word Alchemy 240
Osiander, Andreas 201
Ouroboros 242

INDEX

oxidation 352
oxygen, discovery of 354

P

Padau 191, 217, 292
pagans 138, 139
Palma 287
panacea, universal 279
Panaitros 65, 126
pantheism 15
Paphnutia 242
papyri 239, 241
Papyrus Ebers 239
parable of the virgin 260ff
parables 271
Paracelsus 158, 178, 249, 274, 321ff
  and alchemy 330
  and astrology 328ff
  as discoverer 333
  and magic 338
  and medicine 333ff
  as reformer in chemistry 332
  and remedies 339
  and his school 339
  and spirits 337
  and superstition 336
  and surgery 338
  travels 323, 327
parallax 130ff, 173, 192, 212, 226
Paramirum 328
Paré, Ambroise 321, 336
Paris 151, 290, 298ff
  medical faculty of 340
Parlement of Paris 105, 152
Pasch, Dr. 313
Passover 11
patristic writers 73
Pau 299
Paul III 150, 200, 273
Paul V 219, 224
Paul of Middleburg 107
Paulmier, Pierre 152
Pedro Alfonso 82
Pensées Diverses sur la Comète 136
perigee 36, 201
perihelion 215
Pernella 289
persecution 101, 154ff, 221, 271, 300, 327
Persia 9–10, 245
Persians 248
pestilences 119, 121, 150, 158
Peter of Abano 96, 106
Petit, Pierre 135
Petosiris 17, 64, 79
Petramellarius, Iacobus 149
Peucer, Caspar 154, 172, 175, 179
Peurbach, George 130, 167, 168
Philalethes 259, 271

Philip Augustus 290
Philolaus 21, 22, 200
philosopher's egg 254
philosopher's stone 239, 253ff, 274ff, 282ff, 303, 310
Philosophical Works of Robert Boyle 344
Philosophy of Gassendi 159
Philostratus 283
phlogiston theory 344ff
Phlogiston Theory, The 346
Physical and Mystical Matters 241
Physical Science 126
physics 30, 123, 217
physiognomy 156, 330
Pico della Mirandola 143
Pigghe, Albert 151
Pierre d'Ailly 144
Piero Dini 221
pigments 310
Pisa 219, 286
Place of Magic in Intellectual History of Europe 64
plagues 119, 121, 150, 181, 226, 297, 300
planets 7, 18
  their qualities 56
  powers 63
  moved by love 107
Plato 15, 23, 79, 138, 144, 210ff, 237, 244, 246
Plato of Tivoli 82
Platonism 209
Pliny 16, 66, 81, 174, 280
Plutarch 24
Poland 310
Polydonus 324
polytheism 17
Pompey 11
Pomponazzi, Pierre 211
Poor Richard's Almanac 194
pope 110, 147, 157
porcelain 313
Posidonius 16, 30, 65, 75, 126
positions 57
Pott, J. H. 346
powder of transmutation 292, 303, 310
Prague 304
precession of equinoxes 39, 65, 161, 179, 205
precipitation 242
prediction 110, 138, 151, 156, 157, 161, 170, 175, 178
Preliminary Discourse 344
Prelude to Chemistry 267
preparation 254
prescience 99
Priestly, Joseph 221, 348
prima materia 289

primitive man 3
Primitive Time Reckoning 12
principles 250
printing, introduction of 145
prison 275, 302, 305, 308, 311, 313
Private Life of Galileo 220
Proclus 40
prodigies 135, 140
prognosticate 102, 189
prognostication 16, 52, 61, 109, 111, 143, 149, 184, 187, 304
progress 134, 328, 358
Progress of Chemical Philosophy 238
projection 291, 298, 306, 349
Properties and Effect of Light and Heat 347
prophecies 119
Prometheus 12
Prutenic Tables 169, 175, 180, 183, 198
Ptolemy, Claudius 10, 19, 40ff, 79, 90, 163, 167, 169, 175, 178, 180, 185, 204, 210, 246, 280, 330, 352
puffer 307
putrefaction 255
Pythagoras 15, 21
Pythagorean theory 66, 214
Pythagoreans 40, 79

Q

quadrants 134, 167, 178, 182
Quadripartitem 10, 48ff, 164
qualities of astrologer 113
qualities, four 118, 153, 245, 328
quantitative procedures 319, 355
Querengo, Antonia 217
quintaessentia 339

R

Rabbi 290
Ramus, Pierre 178, 213
Rasis, Rhasis, Rhazis or Rhases 89, 246, 273, 281, 292, 320, 324
reason 355, 356
receipts 272
Recorde, Robert 197, 210
Read, John 267, 273
reflection 119
refraction 119, 163
Regiomontanus (Johann Muller) 97, 130, 167, 169
Reinhold, Erasmus 169, 172
rejuvenation 287, 305
Relation Betwixt Flame and Air 347
Religion of Babylonia and Assyria 7
remedies, mineral and vegetable 333
respiration 352
retrogressions 24, 26, 36
revelation 202

revolution 28, 202ff, 216
revolutionary ardor 330
Rey, John 348, 350
Rhodes 21, 292, 295
Rheticus, Georg Joachim 176ff, 200
Rinuccini 230
Ripley, George 291
Robbins, F. E. 48
Robert of Chester 82
Robert Grosseteste 91
Robert Holkot 103
Robinson, J. H. 135
Rochefort, Chancellor 106
Roeslin, Helisaeus 131
Roger of Hereford 83
Roman Astrologer as Historical Source 78
Rome 4, 17, 121, 177, 219ff, 241, 280, 282, 286
Rosen, Edward 35
Ross, W. D. 123
rotation 202ff
Rothman, Christopher 172, 174
rubification 255
Rudolph II 133, 169, 271, 275, 302, 304
Rudolphine Tables 185
Ruland, Martin 338
Rutzke, Martin 304

S

Sabbath 11
Sacrobosco 91, 151, 167, 196
Sages 264
Saggiatore, Il 224
Sala, Angelus 339, 340
Salamis 65
salt, diseases 334
  from sea water 293
Saracens 323
Sarpi, Fra Paolo 221
Sarah 267
Sarton, George 90
Saturn 7, 11, 18, 26, 108, 112, 178, 181, 186, 212, 217, 255, 270
Savonarola, Jerome 158
Savonarola, Michael 97
scale of ascending purity of substances 317
Scaliger 350
sceptics 354
  of alchemy 307
scepticism 92, 118, 135
Scheele, Carl Wilhelm 347
Schoner, Andreas 171
Schoner, Johann 170, 171, 177
Schreckenfuchs, Erasmus Oswald 197
Schweitzer, Siebald 304
Scot, Michael 90, 167, 273

380 INDEX

Scriptures 75, 78, 87, 199, 213, 216, 220, 258, 271, 277
Scultetus 133
Scythians 59
Seatown 306
seasons 57
secret formula 299
Secret of Liquor Alkahest 274
Secret Tradition in Alchemy 280
Secrets of Alchemy, The 272
Seleucus 32
Sendigovius, Michael 259, 271, 304, 309ff
Seneca 68, 71, 125
Serapion 245
Servitus, Michael 152
Sethon, Seton or Sethonius, Alexander 274, 306ff
Sextus, Empiricus 72
Sextus ab Heminga 166
Shapley, Harlow 203
Short History of Astronomy 179, 229
Short History of Chemistry 241
Siebenfreund 315
Sigismond, King of Poland 311
signatures, of plants 156
signs 89, 93, 99, 112, 139, 144, 160, 186
Simon de Phares 105, 151
Simon Magus 73
Simplicius 24, 29
Sinaragdine Table 267
Sirius 5
Sixtus V 151, 155, 156
Sizzi, Francesco 218
smelting 239
Smith, D. E. 168
Smith, J. A. 123
Social Factors in Medical Progress 339
Socrates 79
Solomon, King 260
solstices 10, 11, 61
Song of Songs 260
Sophic Hydrolith, The 263
sophic mercury 250, 268
sulphur 250, 265
sophists 354
Sophocles 204
sorcerer 188, 296
sorcery 302
Source Book in Astronomy 203, 226
Source Book in Greek Science 44
Soviets 228
Spagyric Art 332
Spain 246, 279, 285, 290
speciousness of some reasoning 352
Speculative Arithmetic and Geometry 151
Speculative Music 109

Speculum Astrologiae 196
Speculum Astrologium 148
Sphere of Sacrobosco 151, 167
sphere, treatise on 171
spheres 24ff, 122, 123, 152, 203, 209, 215, 217
spiritualism 303
Spinoza 239
spontaneous generation 75, 158
Squire, Thomas Herbert 292
Stahl, George Ernst 345
Stanhufius, Michael 196
Star of Bethlehem 144, 168
stars and transmutation 253
stations 26, 36
Steinbeck 5
Stephanus 241, 243
Stephen, King of Poland 305
Stern, J. B. 339
Sternglaube und Sterndeutung 64
Stillman, J. M. 241, 245
Stimson, Dorothy 198
stoic 65
stoicism 15
Stone of the Philosophers 275, 305
Story of Early Chemistry 241, 245
Strabo 32
Strauss, H. A. 183
Strauss-Kloebe, S. 183
Study of Chinese Alchemy 248
sublimation 250
sublunar 49, 185
succubi 85, 99
Sudhoff, Karl 331
Suidas 196
Sulla 79
sulphurous diseases 334
sulphur principle 250
  philosophic 345
Sultan Magdal Doulet 281
Sultan Seifeddoulet 280
Sum of Perfection 280, 324
Summa Philosophiae 92
sun 39, 40, 115, 137, 145, 165, 181, 195, 202ff, 215, 270
sun-dials 61, 171
sunspots 217, 224
superior planet 36
superstition 91, 107, 135, 138, 145, 146, 186, 190, 238
Sylvius, de le Boe 342
symbolic language 256
  drawings 259
symbolism 277
sympathy 64
Synesius 241, 242, 280
synodic period 25, 200
Syntaxis 40ff

INDEX 381

syphilis 149, 339
Syria 18, 245
Syriac 246
syzygy 61

T

table of eclipses 168
  of sines 168, 169
tables, astronomical 153, 171
Tachenius, Otto 350
Tacitus 65
Taliafero, R. Catesby 46
Tannsletter, George 168, 170
Taoism 247
Tartatus 336, 342
Taylor, A. E. 210
Taylor, F. S. 242, 243
Teatrum Chemicum Brittanicum 238
telescope 161, 213, 217
terms 58
Tertullian 74
Testament, Old 16, 194
  New 16, 194
Tetrabiblos, 10, 48ff, 90, 164, 172, 180
Thales 162
The Thirteenth, Greatest of Centuries 84
Thebes 60
Thebit ben Corat 148
Theodoricus, Sebastian 196
Theodosius, Emperor 245
theologians 102
theological influence on alchemy 315
theology 193
Theophrastus 14, 23, 240, 246
theory 202
thermometer, air 217
Theosebeia 242
theriac 337
Thermopylae 65, 71
Thomas Aquinas 92, 94, 136, 210, 254, 273, 283, 329
Thomas of Cantimpré 86
Thomas of Strassburg 97
Thorndike, Lynn 64, 66, 70, 73, 81ff, 170, 195
Thorpe, T. E. 345
Thoth 16
Three Copernican Treatises 177, 202
Thurneysser 338, 340
Tiberius 16
tides 181, 237
tincture, universal 263, 292
Timaeus 28, 210, 244, 277
time as factor in progress 319
Titus 290
Toledan Tables 169
Toulouse 299

Traglodytica 60
transformations 85
translators 82
transmutation 158, 243, 252ff, 281, 282, 289, 303, 328, 331
Treatise on Nature 310
trepidation 179, 196
Treves 295
Treviso 292
triangles 58
trigonometry 7, 39, 169, 210
triplicity 58
Trismegistus 204, 266
Trithemius 111, 295ff, 322
tropic of cancer 58
  of capricorn 58
True Causes of the Calamities of Our Times 147
Tschirnhaus, Count of 313
Tunis 286
Turba Philosophorum 300
Turks 174, 178
Turquet de Mayerne 340
twelve keys 270
Twelve Treatises 310
twins 70, 75
Tyler, G. E. 121

U

Ubangi 186
Ugo de Castello 103
uniform circular motion 43, 45
uniformity of curvature 45
University of Basel 323
  of Cambridge 192, 302
  of Fribourg 306
  of Halle 345
  of Louvain 199, 302
  of Mainz 345
  of Paris 210, 284
Uraniborg 182
Urban VIII 151, 157
urine 168, 274, 293, 342
van Helmont, Johann Baptist 339, 340
  his ingenious experiment 341
  his theory 341

V

Vanity of Judiciary Astrology 159
Varro 65
Venice 241, 296
Venus 7, 18, 26, 34, 56, 87, 135, 173, 174, 181, 186, 201, 217, 220, 255, 270
vernal equinox 183
Vesalius 3, 172, 336, 338
Villain 99, 111
Villanova, Arnold 273, 283, 300
Vincent of Beauvais 86

Voltaire 136
von Keltemberg 315
von Krohnemann 315
von Meyer, Ernst 256
von Neus, Louis 315
von Schonberg, Cardinal Nicholas 176, 200
von Suchten, Alexander 274
voyages of explorers 164

W

Waite, A. E. 240, 258, 273, 280, 324
Wales 303
Walsh, J. J. 84
wandering apostles of alchemy 306ff
Warsaw 311
watches of day 13
water-clocks 72
Watzelrode, Lucas 175
weather prediction 106, 160, 168
Wedel, T. O. 122
week 11
Week, The 11
Wei-Po-Yang 247
Weigel, Erhard 136
Werner, Johann 170, 178
White, J. W. 346
Widmanstad, John Albert 176
William of Auvergne 84
William of Conches 82
William, Count of Holland 283
Wilson, W. J. 241, 247, 315

witchcraft 85, 100, 147, 273
witch-mania 154
witches 158, 178
Witekind, Herman 198
Witelo 170
Wolf, Hieronymus 153
womb of the earth 265
Works of Geber 247
Writings of the Faithful Brothers 247
Wu, Lu-Chiang 248

X

Xerxes 139

Y

Yin and Yang 247

Z

Zachaire, Denis 296
Zanthosis 255
zenith 11, 12
Zeno of Citium 126
Zeno, Emperor 245
Ziglerin, Marie 315
Zinner, E. 168
zodiac 8, 10, 24, 57ff, 88, 127, 144, 161, 185
zodiacal signs 57ff
zoology vii
Zosims 242, 280
Zulu 189
Zwinger, Jacob 307

DATE DUE

WITHDRAWN
from
Funderburg Library